SYSTEMS
ELECTRONICS
A COURSE FOR GCSE

G. W. PILLINER

Assistant Secretary to the Associated Examining Board

D. A. SNASHALL

Teacher in charge of Electronics and Physics
Babington Community College, Leicester

Acknowledgements

The authors and publishers wish to acknowledge the following photograph sources: BBC Hulton Picture Library, p. 1; British Olivetti Ltd, p. 1; British Telecom, p. 164; The Electricity Council, p. 192; Chris Fairclough, p. 6; Mullard Ltd, p. 14; National Westminster Bank PLC, p. 189; Zefa Picture Library, p. 162. All the remaining photographs were taken by Barry Poultney.

The authors and publishers wish to thank the following who has kindly given permission for the use of copyright material:

Collins Publishers for extracts from COLLINS NEW CONCISE ENGLISH DICTIONARY

Every effort has been made to trace all the copyright holders but if any have been inadvertently overlooked, the publishers will be pleased to make the necessary arrangements at the first opportunity.

The authors wish to thank the many friends and colleagues who have willingly given advice and encouragement throughout the preparation of this book.

First published in 1987

Published by
MACMILLAN EDUCATION LTD
Houndmills, Basingstoke, Hampshire RG21 2XS
and London
Companies and representatives
throughout the world

Designed and typeset by Oxprint Ltd, Oxford
Cartoons drawn by Peter Lawrence

Printed in Hong Kong

British Library Cataloguing in Publication Data
Pilliner, G. W.
Systems electronics
1. Electronic systems
I. Title   II. Snashall, D. A.
621.38'1   TK7869
ISBN 0-333-40927-2

CONTENTS

Using this book   iv

CHUNK ONE
Systems

Chapter 1   What are systems?   1
Chapter 2   Some electronic systems   8
Chapter 3   Making systems work   14
Reference Section A: Systems; Transducers   20

CHUNK TWO
Signal processing

Chapter 4   Decision-making with electronic circuits   31
Chapter 5   Amplifiers   39
Chapter 6   Generating pulses and signals   44
Reference Section B: Voltage and current; Symbols; Logic gates;
          Amplifiers; Signal generators   51

CHUNK THREE
Components inside
building blocks

Chapter 7   Resistors   61
Chapter 8   Diodes   69
Chapter 9   Capacitors and inductors   76
Chapter 10   Transistors and integrated circuits   82
Reference Section C: Resistors; Diodes; Capacitors; Inductors;
          Transistors; Integrated circuits; Operational amplifiers   91

CHUNK FOUR
Building block circuits

Chapter 11   Transistor circuits   107
Chapter 12   Operational amplifiers   112
Chapter 13   Power supplies   118
Reference Section D: Transistor circuits; Operational amplifier
          circuits; Power supplies   124

CHUNK FIVE
Handling information

Chapter 14   Sequential logic   137
Chapter 15   Information by electronics   144
Chapter 16   Information storage   150
Reference Section E: Electronic counting; Information processing;
          Memory   154

CHUNK SIX
Communications

Chapter 17   Wires and fibres   159
Chapter 18   Radio   168
Reference Section F: Communication systems; Radio and television   180

CHUNK SEVEN
Computing and control

Chapter 19   Controlling the world with a computer   189
Chapter 20   Inside a computer   196
Reference Section G: Computing; Computer systems   209

CHUNK EIGHT
Measurement

Chapter 21   Making measurements   213

APPENDIX
ANSWERS

Teaching electronics through the systems approach   222
Answers to questions   229
Solutions to exercises   232

INDEX   233

USING THIS BOOK

This is an unusual book in a number of ways.

In the first place it is about real electronics. Most of the time a practising electronics engineer is interested in making systems do useful things. He or she does not need to know what is going on inside the various bits and pieces, but just what each part of the system will do. This book uses a 'systems' approach to electronics.

Secondly, it is not arranged in the same way as an ordinary textbook with chapter after chapter of dry facts to be mastered. The facts **are** all there, but the book is arranged so that you can enjoy reading the chapters, and then find the facts and ideas that have to be learned collected together for you to study, perhaps at a later time.

The book has been arranged in a way that will help you all the way through your course in electronics. You will need to use it in different ways. You will want to find out what electronics is all about. There will come a time when you have to learn some basic facts and ideas. When you are making electronic systems yourself, you may need information about how to deal with some of the parts. At the end of your course you will, perhaps, be taking an examination.

This book is divided into several 'chunks'. Each chunk deals with one part of the subject. The first chunk deals with systems; the third chunk deals with components; the seventh chunk deals with computers; and so on.

Each chunk has several chapters and a reference section. The chapters are designed to explain to you the important ideas that you have to understand. The reference section at the end has all the facts, information, and things which are to do with that chunk and which you have to know or learn.

When you first start work on a chunk, read the chapters. Each one is about a single topic. Once you have understood the chapters, you will find that the reference section has the information you need in note form. However, if you do not understand something in the reference section, you should look back at the chapters again.

To help you test yourself there are questions included in the text. They are marked in the margin like this: $\boxed{34}$. The answers to these questions are usually somewhere in the chapter you are reading or in an earlier chapter, but there is also a brief summary of the answers at the back of the book.

Some of the items in the reference section involve formulae and calculations. In each of these cases, there is at least one example of how to use the formulae, and two or three exercises for you to try. The answers to the exercises are also at the back of the book.

Electronics is a practical subject to do with making real systems that do useful tasks. Most of the practical work you will do is in 'Practical Systems Electronics' which is published as a companion to this book. However, there are sections in some of the chapters in this book describing practical work. For these sections it is intended that your teacher will make arrangements for you to try the various systems for yourself in the workshop or the laboratory. You may well find it better to read the chapter before you try out the practical work and then read the chapter again after you have seen what happens in practice.

This book has been written with the GCSE examination in mind, but it is intended as more than just a textbook for passing examinations. The GCSE examination is about finding out what you know, understand, and can do. The reference sections include what you **must** know, the chapters are designed to help you understand the subject, and the companion book 'Practical Systems Electronics' is the starting point for you to 'do' some electronics.

We hope that you enjoy using this book. We have tried to make the chapters interesting to read, and sometimes we have added things which are not on examination syllabuses, so that you can see what real electronics is all about. If you enjoy reading the book, don't stop when you reach the end of a chapter because it is all you have been told to read. Read on, skipping the reference sections when you come to them. You can go back to the reference sections later and learn what has to be learned.

1 WHAT ARE SYSTEMS?

Imagine life without any electronic machines!

That means no television or radio; no tape recorders or record players. You would take log tables or a slide rule to class instead of your pocket calculator. There would be no credit cards for shopping and no packets through your letter box personally addressed to you and offering you the latest bargains with your own free gift. All bills and accounts would be typed or written by hand; shop purchases would be rung up on a mechanical cash register.

These are only a few of the things in our everyday life that would be missing if there were no electronic machines. In industry, in commerce, in government and in transport, however, electronic machines play an even larger part. Almost every aspect of our life has been changed as a result of computers, radio, television, automatic control systems and automatic machines. Electronics has been the means by which we can do so many things that were only dreams fifty years ago.

Fig. 1.1 In the period between 1900 and 1930 there was a steady increase in the use of mechanical machines in the home. All of these machines have now been replaced by electrical or electronic equipment.

Before the electronics age began (in about 1900) mechanical machines were well advanced. For people with enough money there were clocks and telephones, carpet sweepers and wind-up gramophones. These were the things for the home that had come from earlier major changes in the way of life. However, as with electronics, the main effect of mechanical machines was felt in industry. The Industrial Revolution, as we now call it, gave people larger machines that were able to do heavier work and to do it more quickly. Steam engines and electric motors were used to drive the looms, forges, pumps and cranes of the factories. These machines were able to do the work that man could not easily do using his own muscles.

Today's electronic machines assist our brains in much the same way as mechanical machines assist our muscles. A man with a tractor can plough and cultivate much more land than a man with a spade. A man with a computer can sort and sift information much more quickly and reliably than an army of filing clerks in an office.

Machines are most useful to us when we have a task that must be done over and over again. For such a task, whether it is a thinking task (e.g. recording information for use at a later time) or a doing task (e.g. doing the washing-up), we always think out a sensible way of tackling it. For recording information we would probably organise the information in alphabetical order with an index, and we would expect to have a pen and paper. For doing the washing-up we could organise the dishes so that the glasses were done first and the pans at the end, and we would expect to have hot water and detergent available. We use a set pattern, that is, we use a *system*. The word 'system' is used frequently in electronics, but it is not a word that is special to electronics.

The importance of the systems idea is that if we want a machine to do a task for us then we must build into that machine the system **we** would use to do that task. It is obvious that a washing-up machine must not spray the water until the door is closed! Also it must add the detergent at the beginning of the process. The machine will only do these things if we design it to do them in the right order. This means that we have to understand first our own method of doing the task, our own *system*. A machine which aids us in thinking tasks rather than in doing tasks must also follow a suitable system, but it is often harder to decide how you think than to decide how you do something. (If you do not believe this try to work out all the mental steps involved in finding a piece of information from a text book!)

Understanding systems is, therefore, very important if you want to use electronics for any useful purpose. However, there is no need to be frightened of what, to you, may be a new way of looking at things. You will find that looking at tasks as systems usually makes them easier to understand. This is because it helps you understand which parts of the process are really important and it relates to the way your brain works.

Again, a simple domestic example will show you how thinking about tasks in terms of systems is very simple. Suppose that you did not know the meaning of the word 'domestic' when you read the last sentence. Your first thought may be to get a dictionary off the shelf and look up the word. As you turn through the pages you look *first* for D . . , then dO . . , then doM . , and so on until you find the word 'domestic' (see fig. 1.2). The dictionary is an efficient system you have learnt to use. You do not need to go through the words one by one. In fact, you do not need to bother with any other words at all. You have no need to know who found the words to go into the dictionary or how many there are. It does not matter who explained the meanings of the words or how they are sorted into order and printed. Once you know the simple rules for its arrangement you can use it to find the meaning of any word that you do not know. In exactly the same way you do not need to know how a computer works in order to use one. You only need to know what it will do and the rules of using it, and it will produce the answers you want. You need to understand the system, not the complexities inside the system.

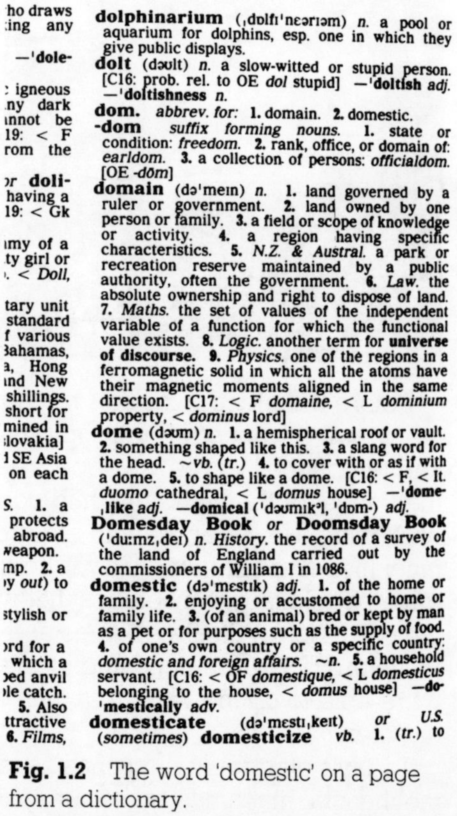

Using systems ideas

Surprisingly, perhaps, you can use this approach in designing a computer, or any other system. Computers will be considered later, but as an example of this approach let us think again about the washing-up machine

> A system is an organised process for carrying out a task in a reliable and successful way.

dolphinarium (ˌdɒlfɪˈnɛərɪəm) *n.* a pool or aquarium for dolphins, esp. one in which they give public displays.

dolt (dəʊlt) *n.* a slow-witted or stupid person. [C16: prob. rel. to OE *dol* stupid] —**'doltish** *adj.* —**'doltishness** *n.*

dom. *abbrev. for:* 1. domain. 2. domestic.

-dom *suffix forming nouns.* 1. state or condition: *freedom.* 2. rank, office, or domain of: *earldom.* 3. a collection of persons: *officialdom.* [OE *-dōm*]

domain (dəˈmeɪn) *n.* 1. land governed by a ruler or government. 2. land owned by one person or family. 3. a field or scope of knowledge or activity. 4. *N.Z. & Austral.* a region having specific characteristics. 5. *N.Z. & Austral.* a park or recreation reserve maintained by a public authority, often the government. 6. *Law.* the absolute ownership and right to dispose of land. 7. *Maths.* the set of values of the independent variable of a function for which the functional value exists. 8. *Logic.* another term for **universe of discourse.** 9. *Physics.* one of the regions in a ferromagnetic solid in which all the atoms have their magnetic moments aligned in the same direction. [C17: < F *domaine,* < L *dominium* property, < *dominus* lord]

dome (dəʊm) *n.* 1. a hemispherical roof or vault. 2. something shaped like this. 3. a slang word for the head. ~*vb.* (*tr.*) 4. to cover with or as if with a dome. 5. to shape like a dome. [C16: < F, < It. *duomo* cathedral, < L *domus* house] —**'dome-like** *adj.* —**domical** ('dəʊmɪk²l, 'dɒm-) *adj.*

Domesday Book *or* **Doomsday Book** ('duːmzˌdeɪ) *n. History.* the record of a survey of the land of England carried out by the commissioners of William I in 1086.

domestic (dəˈmɛstɪk) *adj.* 1. of the home or family. 2. enjoying or accustomed to home or family life. 3. (of an animal) bred or kept by man as a pet or for purposes such as the supply of food. 4. of one's own country or a specific country: *domestic and foreign affairs.* ~*n.* 5. a household servant. [C16: < OF *domestique,* < L *domesticus* belonging to the house, < *domus* house] —**do-'mestically** *adv.*

domesticate (dəˈmɛstɪˌkeɪt) *or U.S.* (*sometimes*) **domesticize** *vb.* 1. (*tr.*) to

Fig. 1.2 The word 'domestic' on a page from a dictionary.

mentioned earlier. The first thing we have to consider is its exact purpose: it is a machine which stores, cleans and dries glasses, pots and pans, crockery and cutlery. To do this it carries out a series of instructions called a *program*. Assuming the machine is loaded, the start of the program is:

    the door is closed;
    the start switch is operated;
    the water is turned on;
    the detergent is added . . . .

To describe the program we do not need to know, for example, how each part works. To turn on the water it is not necessary to know how water valves work. Even if you were constructing this machine, you would obtain a suitable water valve from a supplier, connect it up properly, and it would do the rest.

Thinking in terms of systems is a logical way of thinking about machines. It is a way of thinking about machines which is more concerned with what the machine can do than with how it does it. For example, many people who watch motor-racing would love to look inside the engines to see what is different about them and why they produce such speeds. However, the driver is only interested in getting the best out of his car, and he is the one who gets the results. The modern racing car is such a complex system that few will understand the intricacies of it and even fewer will be able to judge whether it could be better designed. The driver does not have to be able to do either of these things. He only has to know how to use the system he is driving to get the best out of it.

Both the washing-up machine and the racing car show us something else about systems. With the racing car, although the driver may only be interested in getting maximum speed, the mechanics will have to look after the braking system, the fuel system, the electrical system, and so on. The manuals will probably describe the ignition system (which produces the high voltage for the sparking plugs) and the lighting system, which are both parts of the electrical system.

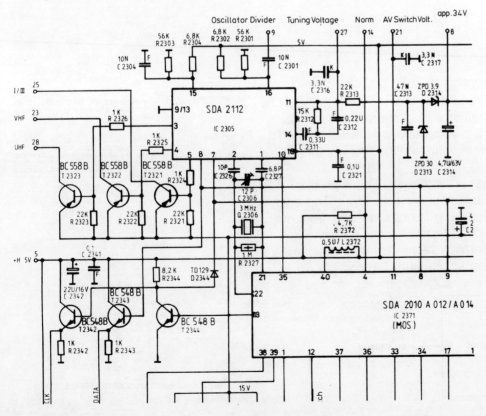

Fig. 1.3 This is part of the circuit of a colour television. You do not have to understand all this to be able to watch TV!

The word 'system' was used so many times in the last paragraph that perhaps you are thinking that everything is a system. Earlier in this chapter a system was defined as 'an organised process for carrying out a task in a reliable and successful way'. It is clear that all these systems in the racing car do carry out tasks in an organised way and so really are systems. But one system can be part of another system. Systems can be considered at various levels. We sometimes describe a system which is a part of another, larger system, as a *sub-system*. In this book we shall sometimes call the sub-systems *building blocks* because they are the blocks of electrical circuits that are joined together to make complete systems.

A system can have sub-systems within it and it can be a part of a larger system.

Think about the washing-up machine again. The water valve is a system. It controls the flow of water (that is its purpose) and it does so on instructions from the machine's program (it operates in an organized way). We do not normally call a water valve a 'water-flow control system' but that is what it is. It is also a sub-system of the washing-up machine. The whole washing-up machine is a system, but it is also a sub-system of the kitchen (which is the food-processing system in the home), and the kitchen is in turn a sub-system of your home.

Systems ideas are a way of thinking about all kinds of things, and that is why they are important. Electronics is a way of making better or more efficient systems, so that systems ideas help in understanding electronics and electronics helps in understanding more about systems.

> "Great fleas have little fleas upon their backs to bite 'em,
> And little fleas have lesser fleas, and so *ad infinitum*."
>
> *Augustus de Morgan*

SUMMARY 1A

A system is an organised process for carrying out a task reliably and successfully.

In order to use a system you need to know what to do to make it work but you do not need to know how it works.

Understanding systems is important for designing and operating machines, and allows people without special skills or knowledge to use very complex machines.

Mechanical systems (including those powered by electric motors) usually increase human muscle power. Electronic systems are concerned with increasing the power of the human brain and human senses.

A system can have sub-systems within it and can be a part of a larger system.

The parts of a system

What are the essential parts of a system?

A system carries out a program (specified function) to produce a useful result. A system is of no use if it does not give the intended result – the *output*. A sausage machine is useless if it does not produce sausages! To get the output there has to be something going into the system; this is called the *input*.

There is also something going on inside the system. This is an *operation* or *process*, which takes the input and transfers it to the output. This part of the system is called the *processor*. What the processor does to the input to get the output is called its *transfer function*. In fact a system always has several inputs, but more of that later. Perhaps the easiest way of picturing a complete system is to use a simple diagram (see fig. 1.4).

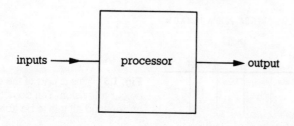

inputs ⟶ processor ⟶ output

Fig. 1.4 Diagram showing the form of a simple system.

In order to use a system the **only** information we need is: the nature of the inputs; what the system will do for us (its transfer function); and what the output will be.

Nearly every home in Britain has one very complex electronic system – a television set. To be able to watch pictures on the television set you do not need to know about the line flywheel synchronisation circuits or the demodulation of the intercarrier sound signal (look back at fig. 1.3). You go to a shop, buy a television set, plug it into the mains supply, connect the aerial, turn the set on, and set the volume and station controls to suit yourself. The supply, the aerial and the control adjustments are the various inputs. Buying the set was your choice of a suitable processor. The picture and the sound are the outputs.

It is obvious that there is more than one input to a television set. In fact, there are three types of input. The television needs power from the mains, a radio signal from the aerial, and control information from the switches that the viewer operates.

All systems have three types of input. Every system needs a *power input* to enable it to carry out its task, an input on which to operate (called a *signal input*), and *control inputs* to tell it what to do.

The idea of a machine that will keep going for ever with no supply of energy (or power) in any form has been the dream of inventors for a long time, but no serious engineer accepts that 'perpetual motion' is even a possibility. To do work requires a supply of energy. This is a basic law of nature to which there is no exception. Some electronic equipment, such as digital watches and calculators, use only very tiny batteries which may last for years. These batteries are still a source of energy, a *power supply*. (Power is really the rate at which energy is supplied, so that 'energy supply' would be a better name. However, power supply is the term in common use.)

There are some devices which appear to need no power supply at all, such as some measuring devices. In every case some energy is supplied from somewhere, often from the object being measured. For example, the heat needed to operate a thermometer comes from the hot object whose temperature is being measured. Sometimes the energy comes from the person using the device. When you use a ruler it is you that supplies the energy to move the ruler into the correct position to measure the length of something! This last example will show you that sometimes you have to think very carefully where the energy is coming from, but there is **always** a power input to a system.

Every system has some form of control. Very occasionally the only control is a program of operations inside the system, but usually there is at least one definite signal which starts the system operating. Electronic systems will normally have a number of controls because it is easy to build into the circuit switches and other components that may be required.

For example, a cassette tape recorder might have five or six function switches (for 'record', 'play', 'rewind', and so on), a volume control (possibly with an on-off switch built into it) and a tone control. These are the manual controls which the operator can use. There will also be some automatic controls within the machine, such as arrangements for keeping the performance of the recorder steady as the battery voltage varies or as the temperature inside the case rises.

Even the simplest of electrical devices, for which we would not usually use the word system, normally have a single control input. For example, the switch on a torch or on a car's windscreen wiper is a means of controlling a system, a means by which we can tell it to carry out its function. It should now be clear that the diagram of a system in fig. 1.4 was too simple. Three kinds of input have to be considered, as fig. 1.5 shows. This represents the general form of all systems.

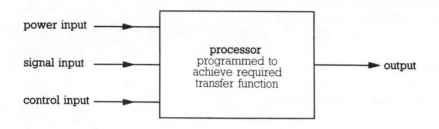

Fig. 1.5 Diagram showing the general form of all systems.

Try to fit the machines you have at home and in the laboratory to this
[2] systems pattern. The electric cooker, refrigerator, electronic calculator, and your domestic heating system are all worth thinking about. Think, too, about the electric door-bell, which is an example of a system with a program but no control input. (What is the purpose of the button the visitor
[3] at the door has to press?) To fit these machines to the general pattern, it helps to find answers to the following key questions:

- what is the machine intended to do? (what is its function?)
- what is the program of the machine? (what is the sequence of events in the machine?)
- from where does the machine get its energy?
- what is the functional input to the machine? (what has to be fed into it in order to produce an output?)
- how is the machine controlled?
- how many of the controls are automatic?

Fig. 1.6 Perhaps you should describe this as a juvenile containment and indoctrination system!

In thinking about simple systems and devices at home you may enjoy playing another 'game' at the same time, this time to do with the name of the device. Most systems are named by what they are designed to do. Try to work out what ordinary domestic machines would be called if they were ☐4 renamed with their system name. For example, a hair-dryer becomes a 'human hair moisture-level reduction system' and a deep-freeze a 'low temperature food preservation system'.

How would you describe the box full of water with a lever or a chain, ☐5 mounted behind the lavatory – and what is its function anyway?

The ideas you get from thinking about some of the mechanical and electrical devices around your home are very important in the understanding of electronics. You can make full use of the things at home without knowing about systems, but by understanding systems you will be able to design, build and use complex and powerful electronic equipment.

SUMMARY 1B

All systems have a specific function.

All systems have signal inputs, control inputs and a power supply.

---

2 SOME ELECTRONIC SYSTEMS

In the last chapter you met the idea that systems could be part of larger systems and also be made from smaller systems. This idea will become important as we look at some electronic systems. As in the last chapter, the place to start is with electronic equipment that you have used at home. Think about a simple radio receiver.

A radio receiver is a system. Its signal input is the radio waves from the transmitter. Its output is the sounds being broadcast by the radio transmitting station. It uses energy from a battery or the mains supply. There may be several controls you can operate, but there will certainly be a tuning control, a volume control and an on/off switch.

If we now ask what the radio receiver has to do, it is easy to see that there are several steps in the process of converting the message carried by the radio waves into sounds that you can hear. The receiver must have a means of picking up the radio waves and of selecting the transmission coming from the station you want to hear. The electric currents produced in the aerial of the radio are very small, so the receiver must have something to *amplify* the electric currents obtained. It must have an arrangement to obtain the required speech or music from the radio waves (in electrical form). It also needs a device to produce sounds from these electric currents.

Each *stage* in the receiver is a system in its own right. These smaller systems are the *building blocks* of the complete radio receiver. Each stage is usually known by a specific name. The blocks or stages in the radio receiver are the *aerial*, *tuner*, *amplifier*, *demodulator* and *loudspeaker*. Usually the output of the demodulator would be too small to drive a loudspeaker and a second amplifier block would be used. Fig. 2.1 is a diagram showing the various blocks that make up a simple radio receiver.

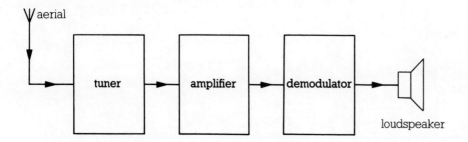

Fig. 2.1 A block diagram of a simple radio receiver. Where does the energy come from for the aerial and for the loudspeaker?

To make a working radio all that is necessary, in principle, is to obtain the appropriate blocks and connect them together. The blocks have to be suitable for connecting to one another, and unless each is to have its own power supply they must all work from the same supply (i.e. the same voltage).

It is not necessary to know anything about the inside circuit of any of the blocks in order to connect them together. Indeed, each of these blocks can have several possible internal arrangements and yet still operate as the same system.

Normally we do not buy a radio receiver as a selection of blocks or units that have to be connected together. Radio receivers are produced in enormous quantities and unless something special is wanted the cheapest way of getting a good radio is to buy a complete set from a shop. If you look inside a radio you find it hard to believe that it is made up from separate blocks. However, if you look at the electrical circuit it is possible to identify each block, and that is the easiest way to understand what seems to be a very complicated circuit.

Not all electronic equipment is made in vast quantities. If some form of electronic control is to be installed, the system used will depend on what is to be controlled. It is not likely that a complete system can be purchased cheaply. In this case the system is often constructed from the necessary blocks.

An electronic timer

Suppose that you wanted to construct an electronic timer, perhaps for timing athletic events to the nearest hundredth of a second. Equipment to do this can be purchased as a complete unit but would be fairly expensive. What would the separate blocks in this system be?

The system must have something to start the timing at the beginning of the race and something to stop the timing as the winner crosses the finishing line. There must also be something to indicate the time in hundredths of a second. The total time involved could be several minutes so the indicator will have to display numbers giving tenths of seconds, seconds up to fifty-nine, and tens and units of minutes. Lastly there must be an actual timing mechanism. Fig. 2.2 is a block diagram showing the various blocks in this system.

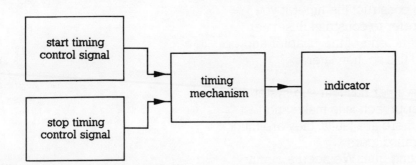

Fig. 2.2 A block diagram of an interval timer. Could this also be the block diagram of a clockwork stop-watch? If so, which part of the watch matches each block? ⟨7⟩

As in the case of the radio, each of these blocks has a simple name. The parts of the system which detect when the race has started or finished and which give an electrical signal that the rest of the system can use are called *input transducers*. (The word *sensor* is sometimes used.) The electrical timing mechanism produces an electrical pulse every hundredth of a second and so is called a *pulse generator* (or sometimes an *oscillator*). These pulses have to be counted by a *counter* and the number counted is transferred to the display. The display is also a transducer, but this time it is an *output* transducer.

There are transducers at both the input and the output. Every electrical system has an input transducer and an output transducer. A transducer is any device which converts non-electrical information into electrical form or electrical information into non-electrical form.

The one remaining part of the timing system is the part that allows the counter to count timing pulses only while the race is in progress. This part has to let through the pulses while the race is being run and then

> A transducer is a device which converts information from one form into another, one of those forms being electrical.

stop the pulses at the end of the race. Such a block is called a *gate*.

An ordinary switch is a gate. However, gates can also have several inputs and can be designed to let a signal through (or, more correctly, we should say "give an output") only if there is a correct combination of inputs.

In this timing system there would need to be two gates coupled together. One gate would be the block that turns on as the race starts and turns off at the end of the race. This is just like an ordinary switch, but is an electronic switch which is operated electrically rather than by a lever or a button. This block is called a *latch*.

The latch cannot start and stop the pulses from the pulse generator itself. This is the job of the second gate. In the second gate there will only be pulses at the output if there are both pulses at the input and a signal from the latch. For obvious reasons this kind of gate is called an AND gate. The latch is a special use of a block called a *bistable*.

SUMMARY 2A

A transducer is any device which converts non-electrical information into electrical form or electrical information into a non-electrical form.

An electronic system has transducers at both the input and the output.

Each block in a system has a name that describes what the block does (how the block processes the signal).

A pulse generator produces electrical pulses, a counter counts electrical pulses and a gate is an electrically-operated switch.

Putting together an electronic timer

The rest of this chapter explains, in more detail, the way in which the race-timer operates. It also tells you how to construct the timer if you have the necessary equipment. You may prefer to construct this timer later on. In this case turn to the summary at the end of this chapter and go on to chapter 3. You can then come back to this section later.

Looking back to fig. 2.2 you will see that the timer has four sub-systems. Wherever there are sub-systems the best approach is to make and test each sub-system separately. In that way, if there are faults, they are much easier to find. We can start with the input transducers.

The race starts with the sound of the starting gun. We need a circuit block that switches on when the gun sound is received. We also need a block that will keep the switch 'on' when it has been turned on. For testing purposes, when you make the timer, you will also need an indicator to show whether or not the sub-system is working. Fig. 2.3 shows the arrangement of blocks; fig. 2.4 on the next page is a photograph of a practical arrangement of boards built up from fig. 2.3. The *comparator* compares the input from the sound sensing unit with a control signal and, if the sound sensing unit is giving the larger of the two signals, the comparator gives an output signal to the next block.

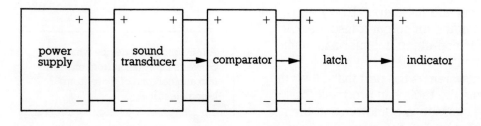

Fig. 2.3 Block diagram of a sound-operated switch. The control on the comparator is set so that the indicator comes on when there is a loud sound. The reset button on the latch turns the switch off again.

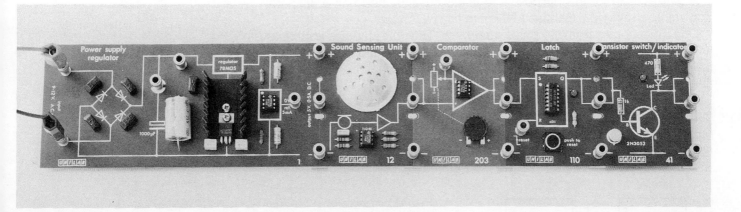

The second sub-system we need is a means of detecting when the winner crosses the finishing line. A common way of doing this is to use a light beam shining across the finishing line onto a light sensing transducer. This transducer is connected to a block which switches on when the light beam is interrupted. When you make this sub-system you should include an indicator so that the system can be tested to see if it is working. This sub-system is shown in fig. 2.5.

Fig. 2.4 Circuit boards used to form the sound-operated switch shown in fig. 2.3. It is easy to set up such a system by connecting together ready-made circuit boards. Each board has a single function corresponding to the block diagram.

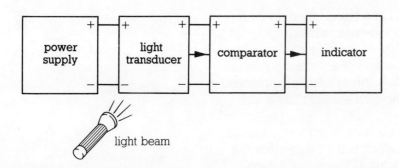

Fig. 2.5 The block diagram of a light-operated switch. The indicator should be on until the light beam is broken. If the indicator goes on when the beam is broken add an inverter to the system. Why is there [8] no latch in this system?

The third sub-system is the timing section. To demonstrate the principle it is suggested that you time only in seconds, not hundredths of a second. More sensitive timing can be achieved quite easily but needs more apparatus. The block diagram is shown in fig. 2.6.

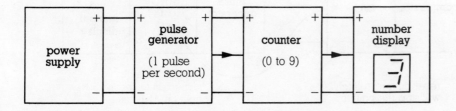

Fig. 2.6 The timing sub-system of an electronic timer. The counter and display will indicate seconds up to 10 s. Why do you [9] not need an indicator to test this system?

To use the timer you need a means of turning the timing sub-system on and off. You might think that all you have to do is to turn the power supply on and off. Although this would work it would give inaccurate timing for the first interval of a second, because the pulse generator would need a fraction of a second in which to start working.

An ordinary switch could be used, but such a switch produces extra pulses, which the counter would count. In any case, we need a switch that will work automatically rather than one which has to be operated by hand.

A gate is used for this purpose and in this case we need an AND gate. You will see in fig. 2.7 that the AND gate has two inputs.

One input comes from the pulse generator. The other input is connected (for the purpose of testing this part of the system) to either the positive or the negative of the power supply. Fig. 2.7 shows a switch being used for that purpose.

When the second input is connected to the positive, the counter receives pulses, but when it is connected to the negative the AND gate will not let pulses through. Chapter 4 deals with gates in more detail, but you do not need to know all about gates to use a gate in this system.

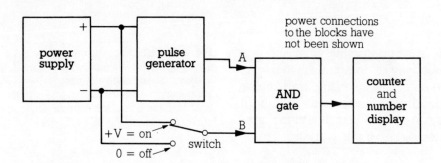

Fig. 2.7 Controlling the counter with an AND gate. If input B is connected to the positive of the power supply the gate allows pulses from the generator to go to the counter, but if input B is connected to the zero line (by pressing the switch) then pulses cannot reach the counter.

If you have assembled all three sub-systems and tested them to make sure that they all work, you can now join them together to make the complete timer. You do not need any extra blocks. You should use only one power supply for all three sub-systems, instead of a separate power supply for each one, but do make sure that each sub-system is connected to the power supply. You do not need the indicators either. They were only used to test the sub-systems.

The AND gate is the block where the sound sensor is connected to the timer. When you tested the sound-operated switch you arranged for the indicator to switch on when there was a loud sound. The signal which operates that indicator will also operate the AND gate, working in the same way as the switch shown in fig. 2.7. Fig. 2.8 shows the arrangement.

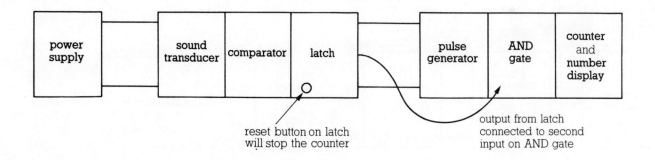

The purpose of the latch is to keep a positive voltage at the output of the sound-detecting sub-system once the loud sound (the starting gun) has been detected. The positive voltage will enable the counter to keep on counting.

Part of the latch circuit is a reset which turns off the latch when it has been latched on. The reset works by connecting a signal at the reset input of the latch. The signal can be obtained in one of two ways, depending on the design of the circuit. In some circuits the reset has to be connected to

Fig. 2.8 The sound sensing unit linked into the electronic timer. The timer should start operating when a loud sound is detected and continue timing until the reset button on the latch is pressed.

the positive of the supply, and in others it has to be connected to the negative of the power supply.

This resetting signal can be supplied in one of two ways. One way is to have a button which, when pressed, connects the reset input to the correct side of the power supply. The other way is to connect the reset input to some other block that can give a correct signal at its output. The light detector sub-system will provide this signal.

During testing you arranged that when the light beam was broken the indicator lit up, showing that there was a positive signal at the output. If the indicator is removed and the rest of the sub-system is connected to the reset of the latch then, when the winning athlete breaks through the light beam at the end of the race, the latch will be reset and the counter will not receive any more pulses to count.

This assumes a positive reset signal latch; if the latch you have needs a negative signal, an inverter must be connected between the light detector and the reset connection. Fig. 2.9 shows this final arrangement.

Fig. 2.9 The complete timer system.

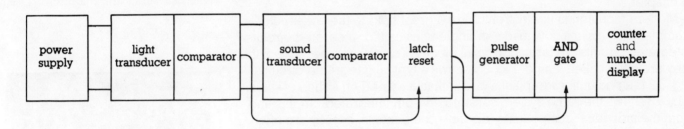

If several counter blocks are available you can connect them together to make the system count to 100 (two blocks) or 1000 (three blocks). What else would you have to do to make the system time in hundredths of a second? What do you notice about the numbers in the display itself if you connect two or more counters together?

SUMMARY 2B

When a system is assembled each sub-system is checked to see that it is working before the sub-systems are joined together.

A comparator is a block which compares two inputs and switches the output on when the desired input is larger.

A latch keeps an electronic switch turned on (or off) until the latch is reset.

A latch is one use of a bistable circuit block.

A gate is a block whose output is controlled by the combination of inputs it receives.

A counter is a block that counts electrical pulses.

3 MAKING SYSTEMS WORK

Anyone who has done much electronics will probably tell you that the greatest problem is not making electronic systems, but making the systems work. Using a systems approach to electronics makes this far less of a problem. This chapter is about the methods you can use to find faults and to check whether systems work as they should.

One reason why those who make electronic circuits have problems in getting their circuits to work is that they have tried to make complicated circuits with each block or sub-system having many separate components.

If you can locate the blocks it is often possible to check each sub-system by itself. You then connect the sub-systems together to complete the system. This was the way in which the building of the timer was described in chapter 2.

Modern techniques in electronics are a great help to the constructor. Complex circuits are now made as single units called integrated circuits. Integrated circuits are formed in small pieces of silicon and because of this they are often called 'chips'. Fig. 3.1 shows a typical integrated circuit. Fig. 3.2 is a photomicrograph of a circuit manufactured on a slice of silicon. Fig. 3.3 shows the same system constructed from integrated circuits and from the individual components (discrete components, as they are often called) used before the days of integrated circuits.

It might seem odd that using complicated devices is easier than using simple components. The reason is that you do not need to know what is inside these chips. All you need to know is the inputs to the chip, its function and its output. We have already used the term signal to describe the information going into and coming out of sub-systems. Finding out what is happening in a system is a matter of tracing these signals.

Testing circuit blocks

Testing the single blocks that make up a system is a good way of starting to learn the basic principles of testing in electronics. Suppose you have an OR gate and need to know whether it is working as it should. (You will learn more about OR gates in chapter 4 but all you need to know to test it is what it is meant to do.)

An OR gate has two signal inputs (some have more than two). The function of an OR gate is that if either of its two inputs (or both of them) is connected to a positive signal or the positive of the power supply then the output will be a positive signal. If both inputs are connected to the negative of the power supply, then the output will switch off and there will be no signal.

To test such a gate you will need a power supply to supply power to the board, and connecting wires to connect the signal inputs to the appropriate point. You will need something to show you what is happening at the output; the output tester could be an indicator lamp, or it could be a voltmeter.

Fig. 3.4 shows the arrangement using an indicator, and fig. 3.5 shows the results you might expect when you try the various ways of connecting the inputs. Fig. 3.6 shows how a voltmeter would be used for testing an OR gate.

Fig. 3.1 A typical integrated circuit. The silicon chip is inside the plastic block and is about 3 mm square. This block is 19 mm long.

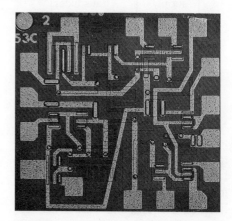
Fig. 3.2 A photomicrograph of the circuit on a silicon chip (magnified 20 times).

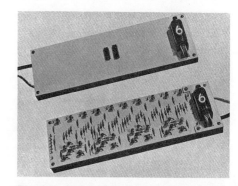
Fig. 3.3 Before the days of integrated circuits electronic circuits were made out of separate components. The circuits of the two counter units are the same, but the top one uses two integrated circuits instead of separate components.

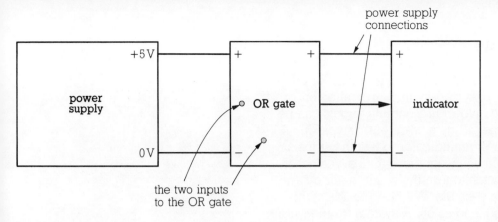

the two inputs
to the OR gate

power supply
connections

Fig. 3.4 Testing an OR gate. The indicator lights when the output of the gate is switched on. Fig. 3.5 shows the results that you would expect to get.

supply terminal, it will measure the voltage difference between these two points. If the output of the board is 'on', the voltmeter will show about 5 volts and if the output is 'off', then the voltmeter will show zero volts (or a very small reading).

Fig. 3.4 shows the arrangement using an indicator, and fig. 3.5 shows the results you might expect when you try the various ways of connecting the inputs. Fig. 3.6 shows how a voltmeter would be used for testing an OR gate.

Testing signals with a voltmeter

The voltmeter must be suitable for the voltages in the circuit. The power supply gives 5 volts, so that with this OR gate the meter must be able to measure up to at least 5 volts. A meter that will measure up to 10 volts would normally be used in this case. We say that the 'full scale deflection' (FSD) of the meter is 10 volts.

The scale on the meter would have the main divisions labelled, probably 0, 1, 2, 3, etc, or 0, 2, 4, 6, etc, up to 10. When the meter is indicating 5 volts the pointer will swing to the '5' division on the scale. Some voltmeters are *digital* meters, which means that instead of having a pointer and a scale they show the measurement directly as figures on a display panel.

A to +, B to −, light on

A to +, B to +, light on

A to −, B to +, light on

A to −, B to −, light off

Fig. 3.5 The results that you would expect from testing an OR gate. Can you draw similar diagrams for the results for an AND gate with two inputs tested in the
[12] same way?

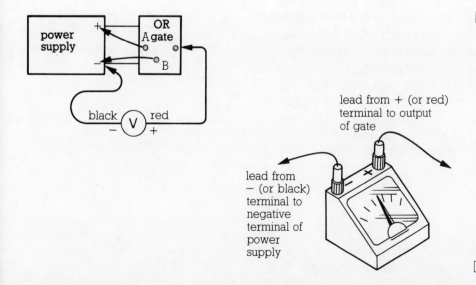

black   red
− (V) +

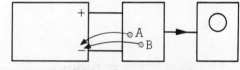

lead from + (or red) terminal to output of gate

lead from − (or black) terminal to negative terminal of power supply

Fig. 3.6 Using a voltmeter to test the output of a block. The leads of the voltmeter must be connected the right way round. What would happen if you connected the leads the wrong way round with the black lead instead of the red one
[13] going to the output of the gate?

Digital and analogue outputs

The output of the OR gate described on page 15 was either on or off, either 5 volts or zero. There are a lot of systems which are either 'on' or 'off' in this way. Such systems are said to give *digital* outputs. Inputs can be digital too, and the inputs used on the OR gate were of this type. In all these cases you can use a voltmeter or an indicator to test the signals.

There are lots of systems for which you want more than a 'yes/no' or 'on/off' effect. A radio with only a switch to turn the sound on or off and with no volume control would not be sensible. We need to adjust the sound level to suit the room, or mood, and so on. A system for measuring temperature is not much good if the only signal it gives is 'hot' or 'cold'. To measure temperature we want an output that changes in step with the changing temperature. Systems which behave in this way are called *analogue* systems.

For testing analogue systems you must use a voltmeter (or other kind of analogue measuring device). The indicator unit will not do because it cannot tell you whether the signal is changing as it should. The light-sensitive transducer is a good example of a block with an analogue output. To test it you would set up the transducer with a power supply and a voltmeter as shown in fig. 3.7.

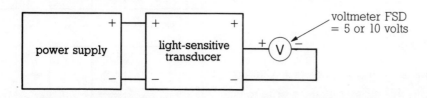

Fig. 3.7 Testing a block that gives an analogue output.

The light sensitive component on the block is the **l**ight-**d**ependent **r**esistor (LDR), which has a round transparent cover over a grid of gold-coloured lines. To increase the light falling on the LDR you can use a torch; to decrease the light falling on it use your hand to shade or cover it. If you vary the light intensity in this way and observe the meter at the same time, you should see the signal vary as the light intensity varies.

The light transducer board will also have a control to adjust the size of the output for any particular light level. This is used to make the circuit work as required, both under strong illumination and when there is very little light. If you were testing a light transducer block in the laboratory you would need to test both that the output changes as the light intensity changes and also that varying the control does in fact affect the output.

If you construct your own circuit boards it is essential to test each one separately before connecting it into the complete system. However, once each board has been checked to see that it is working, there is no real need to test each board each time you use it, unless a fault appears in the system. When a complete system does not work, and when – but only when – an incorrect signal is found, the blocks giving and receiving that signal should be removed and tested. The next section will show how you can test these signals.

Testing a complete system

To explain how you can test a complete system, this section uses one specific system as an example. It is a system for a driver to be able to open the garage door from inside the car. The arrangement of blocks is shown in fig. 3.8. It can be assembled in the laboratory if you have suitable equipment.

The system works like this. The driver has a magnet. As he drives up to his garage he stops and puts the magnet near the reed switch. The reed switch closes, and the system operates the solenoid. The solenoid unlocks the door, which then swings open.

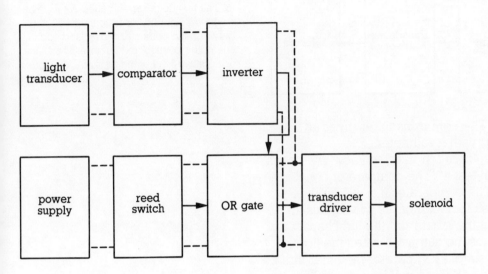

Fig. 3.8 A simple system for enabling a garage door to open.

If the driver is in the garage and wants to drive his car out of the garage, he turns on the headlights. The light-sensitive transducer then makes the solenoid unlock the door in the same way. The driver has to close the door manually. (Can you devise a way of making the door
14 close automatically?)

To start testing any system check that you know what each block in the system does. You need to decide whether it is digital, or analogue, or partly digital and partly analogue.

If the system does not work the first thing to check is the power supply to each block. The voltmeter is used for this. (An indicator needs a power supply and if the power supply is not working properly the indicator will give false results.) When checking, the negative (or black) terminal of the meter must be connected to the negative side of the power supply, and the positive (or red) terminal of the meter must be connected to the positive side of the power supply.
15 The output of the power supply board itself is tested first. (Why?) The power supply connections of each board are then tested in turn, starting with the board nearest to the power supply board (the reed switch board in fig. 3.8). In every case the meter should show the full 5 volts of the power supply (or whatever voltage the power supply should be giving). Fig. 3.9 shows part of the method for doing this.

Once you know that all parts of the system have a power supply, the signals from one block to the next are tested. The signal is tested with a voltmeter if it is an analogue signal, but an indicator can be used if the signal is digital. The signals are tested in two ways. You need to test that the correct signal (quite often that means 'no signal') is given when the circuit is not operated. Secondly, you need to test that when the system is operated, the correct **change** in signal is obtained.

Fig. 3.10 on the next page shows the points in the garage system

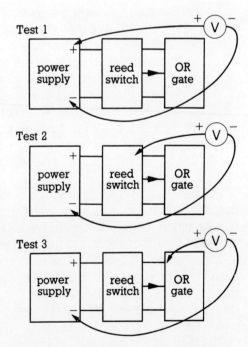

Fig. 3.9 What will you find if you test the power supply to each board using the method shown here, assuming that there is
16 no fault? If there is a fault, what results
17 might you get? What possible fault in the power supplies will not be found by
18 testing in this way?

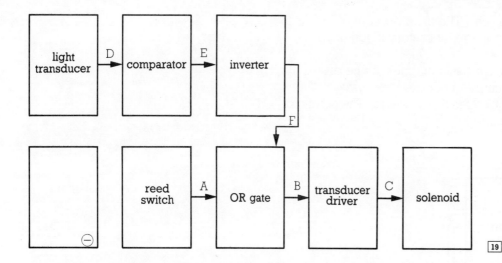

Fig. 3.10 The system shown in fig. 3.8 redrawn with only the signal lines marked in. The test points are labelled A to F. The voltmeter or indicator is connected between the point marked '−' and each one of the points A to F, in turn. The black or negative lead of the tester is connected to '−'. Which block gives an analogue [19] output?

where tests are made on the signals. The light transducer gives an analogue output so that must be tested with a voltmeter.

What does the comparator do in fig. 3.8? (You need to know what each block does in a system before you can test it.) The comparator converts analogue signals into digital signals. The comparator has two inputs, although fig. 3.10 shows only one. This block compares two signals. In fig. 3.10 it switches the output on when the input from the light sensor is the larger input of the two, and switches the output off when the light sensor gives the smaller input. In this simple comparator the other input is a control input. On the comparator block there will be a control which adjusts the second input to any signal value between 0 and 5 volts (the power supply voltage). How would you test that the control input was [20] working correctly?

To test the signals the negative lead of the voltmeter is connected to the negative terminal of the power supply. The positive lead is applied to each signal connection in turn. These are labelled A, B, C, D, E and F in fig. 3.10. These signal connections are the output of one block and the input [21] to the next. Can you work out what to expect when each point is tested?

Work through the system, from input to output, testing each point in turn. It is important to keep a record of each test as you do it, so that if you have to check back later you do not have to do the tests again. The best way to do this is to make a large copy of the block diagram (such as fig. 3.10) and for each point on the diagram write down the results as you get them.

For the garage door system you would start at point A. If there is no magnet near the reed switch there should be no signal. A should show 0 volts until a magnet is brought near, and then change to 5 volts when the reed switch responds to the magnet.

The next board is the OR gate, so now you test point B. If A is at 5 volts then you would get 5 volts at B. However, if A is at 0 volts the output depends on F. This is because the OR gate will give a 5 volt output if either A or F is at 5 volts. So, if F is at 5 volts, B will also be at 5 volts, even if A is at 0 volts.

The board following the OR gate is a transducer driver. The purpose of this is to give enough power to work the solenoid. The next test point is C.

You may be surprised to find that when its input to the driver is 5 volts, its output is 0 volts. You may be even more surprised to find that the solenoid operates when it gets a signal of 0 volts. There is an important idea to understand here. The solenoid is the *load* for this system. It is connected between the signal line and the **positive** of the power supply.

Test procedure:
- Before doing any tests find out what each block is meant to do.
- First test the power supplies to every block.
- Then test each block in turn, starting at the input.

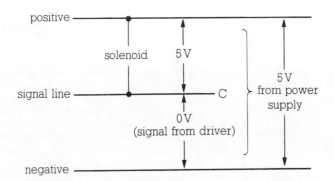

Fig. 3.11 How a solenoid can get 5 V when the signal input is 0 V. What would be the voltage between C and the positive power supply rail if the voltage between C and the negative rail is 2 V?

You have measured the voltage difference between C and the **negative** of the power supply. There is 5 volts between the positive and negative of the power supply. If there is 0 volts between C and the negative, there must be 5 volts between C and the positive. This is shown in fig. 3.11.

The next point to be tested in the garage door system is point D. It is an analogue signal. Varying light intensity will change the signal. The signal can also be adjusted by varying the control on the transducer board. The control should be adjusted to give a signal of about 1 volt in normal lighting. To test the board, shine a light on the transducer (this should cause the signal at D to increase) and then cover the transducer with your hand (the signal should go down to below 1 volt).

If the transducer is working properly then the next tests are made at the output of the block connected to the transducer. For the garage door system that is point E on the comparator.

The comparator is a block which has a control input, a signal input and a digital output. In this case the output is either high or low. High is about 4 volts (nearly the 5 volt power supply). Low is about 1 volt (i.e. not much more than 0). The change from high to low is sudden. The output is never at a voltage between 1 volt and 4 volts.

To check a block like this you need to see first what happens as the control is adjusted, and then what happens as the other input changes (by varying the light on the transducer). You need to work out what the outputs will be, by drawing up a table like table 3.1.

The control input must be set so that the system is working as intended. In the garage door system, the output at D is 4 volts when the headlight shines on the transducer, and 1 volt when it does not. We need the comparator to change from line 2 in the table to line 3 in the table. If this is what is happening then the comparator is working properly.

The test methods described in the last few paragraphs are for a particular system, but the ideas can be applied in a similar way to **any** system.

Final advice

For all testing and fault-finding, work **methodically**.

Table 3.1   Outputs at point E in fig. 3.10

	Light transducer	Input C	Control input	Output at D
1	not illuminated	low	lower than C	4 V
2		low	higher than C	1 V
3	illuminated	high	lower than C	4 V
4		high	higher than C	1 V

Test each block with and without an input.

If there is more than one input, test the effect on the block of every combination of inputs, changing one input at a time.

SUMMARY 3

Testing and fault-finding depends on checking the input and output signals for each block.

Signals can be analogue or digital. Digital signals can be tested with an indicator. Both digital and analogue signals can be tested with a voltmeter.

When using a voltmeter, the full-scale deflection of the meter must be more than the maximum signal being tested.

Before testing, find out what each block is meant to do.

Decide whether signals at each output are digital or analogue.

Check that each block is receiving its power supply.

Test each block in turn working from the input of the system to the output of the system.

Each block must be tested in two ways — firstly in its unoperated state, and secondly when it is operated.

If there is an adjustment or control, start with the control set at the middle of its range. Check that the control is producing the effect it is intended to produce and then adjust the control if necessary for correct operation.

If there are several inputs to a block, check each input separately, keeping the others unoperated. Then test again with the other inputs operated.

A REFERENCE SECTION

A1 — Systems

A1.1 — Structure of a system

All systems have:

- a specific function or purpose;
- a source of energy (a power supply);
- some form of processor;
- some form of control;
- an input of information (signals) or materials; and
- a defined output.

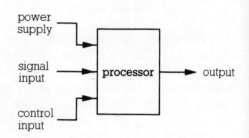

Fig. A.1   General block diagram of a system.

Fig. A.1 is a generalised diagram for all systems.

Electronic systems are concerned with the processing of information. The output of an electronic system may be either information or mechanical action.

Some systems use a special form of control known as *feedback*. Feedback is when a signal is obtained from the output of a system and fed back as a control signal to the inputs of the system.

The signal input and the output of an electronic system require transducers. A transducer is any type of device that converts information from one form into another.

A1.2 — Analogue and digital signals

Electronic signals are obtained by varying the voltage difference, the current or the frequency.

Signals may be in two forms.

(1) If the voltage, current or frequency always change in step with the quantity they represent, the signals are called analogue signals.
(2) If the information is coded in some way (such as turning it into a binary number code), the signals are called digital.

Analogue signals can vary in any manner; digital signals change in steps.

A1.3 — Electronic processing

Electronic processing can involve switching, amplifying, pulse or signal production, signal modification and memory (see Chunk Two).

Complex systems are combinations of basic processing blocks.

The next section lists all the common electronic processing blocks and their functions.

A1.4 — Common electronic processing blocks

(i) Switching blocks

Voltage sensitive switches:

(a) Voltage comparator — Compares two input voltages and gives a digital output state (1 or 0) depending on which input is larger.   A comparator has two inputs.

(b) Signal sensitive switch — Switches an output between digital states when input voltage is significantly larger than 0 volts.

Logic gates:

(a) AND	Output is logic 1 if all inputs are logic 1; otherwise output is logic 0.	AND gates have two or more inputs.
(b) OR	Output is logic 1 if any input is logic 1; otherwise output is logic 0.	OR gates have two or more inputs.
(c) NOT	Output is logical inverse of input.	
(d) NAND	Equivalent to AND followed by NOT.	NAND gates have two or more inputs.
(e) NOR	Equivalent to OR followed by NOT.	NOR gates have two or more inputs.
(f) Exclusive OR (EOR)	Output is logic 1 if one input is logic 1, but is logic 0 if both inputs are either logic 1 or logic 0.	EOR gates usually have two inputs but can have more.
Latch (bistable)	The logic state at the output goes to logic 1 when the input is at logic 1. The output is held until a reset signal is received.	A latch has a signal input and a reset. For other types of bistable see chapters 14 and 19, and reference sections E and G.
Schmitt trigger	The output changes from logic 0 to logic 1 when the input reaches a chosen level; the output stays at logic 1 when the signal falls, until it reaches a second (lower) chosen level, when the output changes back to logic 0.	A Schmitt trigger has one signal input and a control input.
Counter	Output corresponds to the number of pulses received at the input.	A counter has one signal input, a reset, and one output for each stage in the counter.

(ii) Amplifying blocks

Non-inverting amplifier	Output signal is the same waveshape as the input signal but is changed in magnitude (voltage).	
Inverting amplifier	Output signal is the same waveshape as the input signal but is inverted and changed in magnitude (voltage).	
Analogue summer	Output voltage difference is equal to the algebraic sum of the two input voltages.	A summer has two or more inputs.
Difference amplifier	Output voltage difference is an amplification of the voltage difference between the two inputs.	A difference amplifier has two inputs.
Power amplifier (driver)	Power available at output is larger than power at the input.	

(iii) Pulse and signal generators

Ramp generator (integrator)	Output voltage is a linearly-increasing voltage for the length of time that there is a voltage difference at the input.	
Continuous pulse producer (astable)	Output signal is a continuous square wave (i.e. a continuous train of pulses).	Also known as a pulse generator.
Triggered pulse producer (monostable)	Output signal lasts for a fixed period after a trigger signal is received.	
Oscillator	Any pulse producer could be called an oscillator, but an oscillator is usually a block that produces an alternating voltage with a sine waveform.	

(iv) Signal modifying blocks

Interfacing device (matching device)	A block used between two other blocks to enable them to be connected together.	Examples include transistor drivers, code converters.
Filter	A block that will allow some signals through more easily than others.	A radio tuner is a filter.
Modulator	A block that adds signal information to a carrier (usually a high-frequency alternating voltage).	
Demodulator	A block that extracts signal information from a modulated carrier.	

A1.5 — Connecting blocks together

Complete systems can be assembled by connecting separate blocks together, even if the blocks were originally parts of different systems, provided that the following points are checked.

Each block must have a power supply. If they are all connected to the same power supply, then they must all be designed to operate from the voltage difference given by that power supply.

If there is a common rail for the power supply and signals, then all the blocks must be negative earthed (i.e. the negative of the power supply must be connected to the common rail) or all the blocks must be positive earthed.

The output signal of each block must be a suitable signal for the input of the next block. For example, if the output of one block is digital pulses of, say, 5 volts peak, the next block must be able to accept digital pulses of 5 volts peak. If the output signal does not match the input to the next block, an interfacing block must be used between the two blocks.

The power required at the input of a block must not be more than that which the previous block can provide. If the source resistance of the output is greater than the input resistance of the receiving block, then it is likely that an interface will be required.

Maximum *power* is transferred from one block to the next if the source resistance is the same value as the input resistance to the next block. To get maximum *signal* from one block to the next, the input resistance must be as high as possible.

The power required by the various blocks must not be more than that which the power supply can provide.

Where high frequencies are involved, the connecting leads themselves are important and can cause severe loss of signals.

A1.6 — Fault-finding procedures

1. Remember that if the system worked properly before the fault occurred then there is only one basic fault (but if the system has never worked then there may be any number of faults in it!).
2. Always work logically. Use this list to guide you.
3. Look for obvious clues before starting detailed testing (e.g. blown fuses, broken wires, overheated or burnt out components, physical damage).
4. Has the power supply been switched on?
5. Find out what each section of the system is intended to do before attempting any testing or fault-finding.
6. Check that each part of the system has a power supply. Use a voltmeter to test this. (Remember that on/off switches can be faulty.)
7. If the power supply has failed, look for a reason before reconnecting the power.

8. Try to find which block in the system is faulty. Do this by working through the system stage by stage, from the input to the output, testing the signal between each pair of blocks. For d.c. signals use a voltmeter. For a.c. signals use an oscilloscope.

9. Keep a careful record of what you do and of the measurements you make. This will save you having to repeat tests at a later stage because you have forgotten the results of the first tests.

10. If you have to test later stages in a system without using the signal from the input, use a signal generator that gives the right kind of signal for the point you are testing.

11. Do not replace individual components one by one in the hope of clearing a fault. Besides this being time consuming and illogical, you may introduce a second fault into the system.

12. Avoid the temptation to "try this and see if it works". A gambler does not make a good electronics engineer and may not live long enough to become one!

13. If voltage-difference measurements do not indicate the fault it is sometimes possible to find a fault by measuring the current going to a particular block. You may need to find out or work out what the current should be before making the test.

14. If a block has been found to be faulty, disconnect it from the system and test it on its own (if possible), using a signal generator and an oscilloscope or voltmeter.

15. If a substitute block is available (and known to be free of faults!), it is often better to connect the new block in place of the suspect one and to test the whole system, rather than trying to find the fault within the suspect block.

16. If simple tests do not reveal the fault, obtain published circuit and system diagrams and any other relevant information before proceeding. For manufactured equipment, this information usually includes test voltages for the system when it is working correctly.

A2 — Transducers

A2.1 — The nature of transducers

A transducer is any device that converts information from one form to another. In electronics, one of these forms is electrical.

Transducers are used to produce an input signal to an electronic system. This kind of transducer is called an input transducer. The output of the transducer is electrical and the input to the transducer may be light, temperature, magnetism, touch, sound, or any other means of conveying energy to the transducer.

Transducers are also used at the output of an electronic system. This kind of transducer is called an output transducer. The signal from the electronic system goes to the transducer and the transducer converts this signal into light, or sound, or motion, or some other form of energy.

Every electronic system has at least one input transducer and at least one output transducer.

Input transducers are of two kinds. Some generate a voltage, like a battery. These are called *active* transducers. Other input transducers only affect the way in which electric currents flow in the electronic circuit. These are called *passive* transducers. Some people call passive transducers *sensors*.

Output transducers are also of two kinds, but in a different way. Output transducers may be used either to give information (e.g. a number display), or to produce some form of action (e.g. an electric motor). Transducers which give action are sometimes called *actuators*.

Transducers have the same functions for an electronic system as the five senses and the muscles of the human body do for our brain. The senses are input transducers and the muscles are output transducers.

A2.2 — Types of input transducer

Inputs to electronic systems are often signals using light, temperature, sound, or mechanical movement.

The most common of these is mechanical movement. A keyboard (such as that on a home computer), or a switch or push button, converts the movements of our fingers into electrical signals.

The transducer that changes sound into electrical signals is called a *microphone*. There are many kinds of microphones but they are all transducers for converting sound to electrical inputs.

The simplest device that responds to temperature change is called a *thermistor*. This name is really a shortened form of *thermo*-sensitive resi*stor*. A *thermocouple* is also an input transducer which detects temperature change. A thermistor is a passive device whereas a thermocouple is an active device.

The popular name for a device that responds to light is a photocell. There are several types of photocell. The simplest photodetector is a device known as a *light-dependent resistor*, usually called an LDR for short. *Photodiodes* and *phototransistors* are also input transducers that are sensitive to light.

The *magneto-dependent resistor* (MDR) and the *Hall probe* are two types of transducer that are sensitive to magnetism.

A2.3 — Types of output transducer

Most output transducers in electronic systems produce light or sound or movement. Light and sound are used to convey information. Movement can be obtained by the direct use of electric motors, but the power available from electronic systems is often not enough to produce the required action directly. Frequently the output transducer is a *relay*. A relay is a switch operated by a small electric current. A relay can be used to switch on powerful motors, heaters, etc. that cannot be powered by the electronic system itself.

There are many types of light producer. In addition to ordinary lamps (such as you would use in an electric torch), there are *light emitting diodes* (LEDs), the screen of a television or a computer display unit, various kinds of number displays, and lasers.

Sound is produced by a *loudspeaker*. There are several types of loudspeaker but they all have the same function. A telephone earpiece is a small loudspeaker.

In addition to electric motors and relays, various types of *solenoids* (electromagnets) can be used as transducers in electronic systems.

A2.4 — Switches

A switch is basically two metal contacts which are made to touch one another when the switch is operated, so completing the circuit and allowing an electric current to flow. The bell-push on your front door is an example of this simple type of switch. Most switches are a little more complicated than that, but the basic idea is always the same.

The switches for the lights in a house have to be latched in position by means of a spring mechanism, and the latch keeps the switch in its last position until it is operated again.

The buttons on the keyboard of a calculator or computer are also switches. In this case the switches must release as soon as the pressure is taken off the key. Keyboard switches are not latched.

A switch does not have to be limited to one set of contacts, or to only 'on' and 'off' positions. There are many possibilities.

The circuit can be on **until** the switch is pressed. This type of switch is known as a *press-to-break switch* because the circuit is disconnected or broken when the switch is operated.

There can be fixed contacts which touch the movable contact in both its positions. This type of switch is called a *change-over* or *two-way switch*.

A latched switch can have more than two positions, and some switches that are operated by rotating a knob have as many as twenty-four positions (or 'ways'). Some switches operate two, three, or even more sets of contacts using the same knob or lever. A switch with three sets of contacts would be called a 'three-pole' switch. Fig. A.2 shows the circuit symbols and names of some typical switches.

Switches do not have to be operated by human fingers or mechanical forces. Electromagnets can also be used, and a switch operated by an electromagnet is called a *relay*. A *reed switch* is another type of switch operated by magnets or electromagnets.

Normal switches can cause peculiar problems with electronic systems. For example, if simple push-to-make switches were used on a calculator one push on the button might enter the same number in the calculator several times over. The switch contacts 'bounce' when first closed, instead of touching cleanly. Each bounce is an input to the electronic system. Many systems have special electronic 'de-bounce' circuits to overcome this problem.

An alternative way of avoiding contact bounce is to use 'touch' switches. In these switches the electronic circuit reacts directly to the presence of the finger without any contacts to close.

A2.5 — Microphones

A microphone has to convert movements of the air (which is what sound waves are) into changes in electric voltage. There are several ways of doing this. Four types of microphone are commonly available: moving coil ('dynamic'); crystal (piezoelectric); capacitor ('electret'); and carbon microphones.

Moving coil microphones are used for high-quality sound recording. The output is small (a few thousandths of a volt). Moving coil microphones are active transducers. Their source resistance is low.

The crystal microphone is also an active transducer. Crystal microphones are smaller and lighter than moving coil microphones, are more directional and give a larger output. Source resistance is high. They are often used in public-address (PA) systems.

Capacitor microphones are very small but need a power supply. Often a signal amplifier and battery are built into the microphone case. 'Tie-clip' microphones and microphones used in cheap tape recorders are of this type. The source resistance of a circuit using such microphones has to be very high.

Carbon microphones are normally used in telephones. They behave like variable resistors (see reference section B) and need a power supply. Unlike the other types of microphone they are usually used to produce a varying current as the signal, instead of a varying voltage. They are suitable only for speech, not for music. They are used in telephones because they do not have to be used with an amplifier. They have a low resistance.

Loudspeakers will work quite well as microphones, and are often used in this way in intercom systems.

A2.6 — The light-dependent resistor

Fig. A.3 is a photograph of a typical light-dependent resistor (LDR). The LDR consists of a track of cadmium sulphide on a transparent plastic material. Wires are connected to the ends of the track.

In the dark very little electric current will flow through the cadmium sulphide, but when light shines on it electrons are released inside the cadmium sulphide and a very much larger electric current can flow. Its resistance to electricity has decreased.

To convert a change in the current in the LDR to a voltage signal, the LDR must be part of a circuit arrangement known as a voltage divider. Details of this are given in chapter 7.

Fig. A.4 is a typical characteristic for a light-dependent resistor.

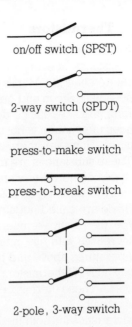

Fig. A.2 Circuit symbols for some typical types of switch.

on/off switch (SPST)

2-way switch (SPDT)

press-to-make switch

press-to-break switch

2-pole, 3-way switch

Fig. A.3 A light dependent resistor.

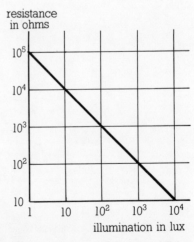

resistance in ohms

illumination in lux

Fig. A.4 A characteristic for an LDR.

A2.7 — Thermistors

An LDR and a thermistor are similar in many ways.

The resistance of every substance changes by a small amount as the temperature changes. Metals have higher resistance at higher temperatures. For substances like silicon and germanium (the semiconductors used for making transistors), their resistance decreases as the temperature rises. For these substances the change is not usually large enough for them to be useful as transducers. However, there are certain substances for which the change is very large. These substances are used for making thermistors.

Two types of thermistors are manufactured.

The more common type has a resistance which decreases as the temperature rises. These are called negative-temperature-coefficient (NTC) thermistors. The other type, the positive-temperature-coefficient (PTC) thermistor, has a resistance which increases with rise in temperature within a certain temperature range. For temperatures above and below that range these thermistors behave in the same way as NTC thermistors. PTC thermistors are not usually used as transducers. These thermistors are intended as devices for protecting some kinds of circuit.

Characteristics for both the NTC and PTC type of thermistor are shown in fig. A.5.

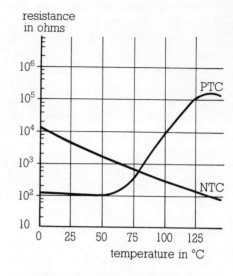

Fig. A.5 The characteristics of a typical NTC thermistor and a typical PTC thermistor.

A2.8 — Transducer characteristics

The normal way of stating how a transducer behaves is to obtain (either from the manufacturer or by a series of measurements made in the laboratory) a graph relating the input to the electrical output. Fig. A.4 is a characteristic of this type for a light-dependent resistor. Fig. A.5 shows the characteristics for the two types of thermistor. These characteristics can be used to work out how to connect the transducer to the rest of the system. There are further details on the use of this information in chapters 5 and 7.

Example of the use of a transducer characteristic

Some NTC thermistors are to be used in a system to control the temperature of a greenhouse. To design the circuit you need to find the resistance of the thermistor at 30°C from fig. A.6.

To do this you find 30°C on the horizontal axis of the graph. Now trace the vertical line for this temperature up the graph until it crosses the graph line (1). Then trace the horizontal line from this point to the resistance axis (2), and read off the resistance from the scale (3). For the graph in fig. A.6 the resistance is 4000 Ω or 4 kΩ.

(You can find out how this information is used in chapter 7.)

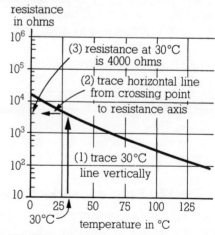

Fig. A.6 How to obtain data from a transducer characteristic.

Exercise 1 Using the characteristics of fig. A.5, find the resistance of the NTC thermistor and the PTC thermistor at 50°C.

Exercise 2 Using fig. A.5, find the temperature at which the resistance of the NTC thermistor is 1000 Ω.

Exercise 3 Using fig. A.4, find the resistance of the LDR when the light intensity is 100 lux.

A2.9 — Mechanical outputs

Electronic systems can be made to produce movement in several ways. For a small single movement such as the opening or closing of a lock, a *solenoid* can be used. A solenoid is one form of electromagnet.

An electromagnet is a coil of wire with a large number of turns in the coil (see fig. A.7). When an electric current flows through the coil it becomes a magnet and will attract any iron or steel object in the vicinity. The effect is larger if there is also some iron inside the coil. The greatest problem is getting a force large enough to carry out the intended task.

Solenoids are used in most remote-controlled locks. Many drinks machines and similar coin-in-a-slot systems also use solenoids. Most cars use solenoids to operate the starting motor and in some the solenoid also engages the gear between the starter and the engine.

Solenoids often need large electric currents, and often it is not possible to drive the solenoid directly from an electronic circuit. In these cases a relay might be used to turn on the power supply for the solenoid. A relay is a solenoid-operated device itself, but it only needs a solenoid that is strong enough to close the switch contacts (see reference section A2.12 on the next page).

More complex motion is obtained by using electric motors. The motor can drive wheels, or gears, or pulleys and so produce whatever kind of motion is needed. There are many kinds of electric motor. All electric motors depend on electromagnetism. For details of how they work and of the various kinds of motors that are available you should refer to textbooks on physics and engineering. Most motors require more power than can be obtained from an electronic system, so that in many cases motors are switched on and off using a relay.

A2.10 — Stepper motors

The *stepper motor* is a type of motor that can be controlled by a computer. A stepper motor has several sets of coils acting as electromagnets, but they are not all connected directly to the same power source. The computer can switch on the power to any of the sets of coils, as required. Each set of coils can make the armature (the moving part of the motor) rotate a certain amount, say 15°. The computer can switch the power to the first set of coils and make the armature turn 15°. It can then switch the power to the second set of coils to turn the armature another 15° and then switch the power to the third set for the next 15° If the first set of coils are now switched on again the rotation continues, and by switching between the three sets of coils in this way the motor can be made to turn continuously. The computer can make the motor turn rapidly or slowly, forwards or backwards, exactly the number of times required, all under precise control.

A2.11 — Loudspeakers

Most loudspeakers depend on electromagnetism. Fig. A.8 shows the construction of a typical loudspeaker.

Referring to fig. A.8, the cone (1) will make the air move and so generate sound waves. The cone is normally made of paper to be as light as possible. The outside edge (2) of the cone is fixed to the frame (3) of the loudspeaker. The cone is formed into one or more ribs (4) near the edge so that it will move freely. The middle of the cone is attached to a tube (5) on which is wound a coil (6). Connections to the coil are made by thin flexible wires (7). When a current flows through the coil it becomes an electromagnet and is attracted or repelled by the magnetic field produced by the magnet (8). The magnet is designed so that there is only a small gap (9) in which the coil can move. The smaller the gap, the stronger the magnetic field and the stronger the forces on the coil.

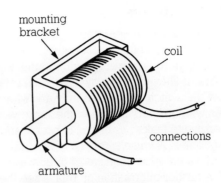

Fig. A.7 A simple solenoid.

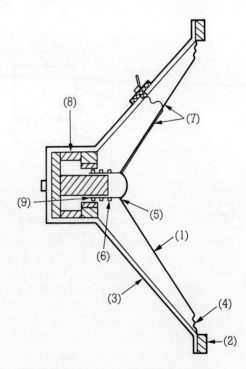

Fig. A.8 The construction of a loudspeaker. The numbers refer to the parts described in the paragraph to the left of the diagram.

A2.12 — Relays

A relay is a switch operated by the action of an electromagnet. Fig. A.9 shows the construction of a typical relay.

When there is current flowing in the coil, the relay is said to be *energised*. Diagrams showing the way in which a relay is connected in a circuit always show the switch contacts as they are when the relay is *de-energised*.

As with ordinary switches, there are various kinds of switch actions including 'energise to make', 'energise to break' and change-over. There can be from one to six poles. A *uniselector* is a type of relay that has more than two ways, and standard uniselectors have 11 or 25 ways.

For further information on relays see the next two sections, chapter 9, and section C4.4 in reference section C.

A2.13 — Latching a relay

Relays can be made to latch on in the energised position by electrical means. One set of switch contacts on the relay can be used to connect the power supply directly to the coil once the relay has been energised by the system driving it. This arrangement (or some other form of latch) would normally be used in an alarm system so that the alarm would keep on sounding until someone came to turn it off. Fig. A.10 shows the basic arrangement and the method of resetting the latch.

A2.14 — Using a relay as a reversing switch

It is sometimes necessary to be able to reverse an electric motor so that, for example, it will close a door as well as open it. To do this the current in the motor must be reversed, and that is often difficult to achieve with electronic circuits. A relay can be used as a reversing switch in these cases. Fig. A.11 shows the basic circuit arrangement. The circuit has been drawn twice so that you can trace the path of the electric current in each of the two positions.

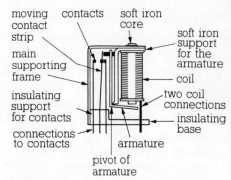

Fig. A.9   The construction of a relay.

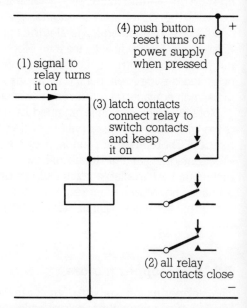

Fig. A.10   Using a relay as an electrically latched switch.

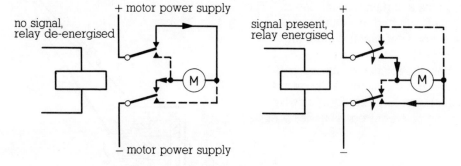

no signal, relay de-energised

signal present, relay energised

Fig. A.11   Using a relay as a reversing switch. The circuit has been drawn twice with solid lines showing where current is flowing, and dotted lines showing other parts of the circuit. The left-hand diagram traces the path of the current to the load when the relay is de-energised, and the right-hand diagram traces the current when the relay is energised.

A2.15 — Light-emitting diodes

Most indicator lamps on modern electronic equipment are light-emitting diodes (LEDs). The most common LEDs give red light, but yellow and green LEDs are also made. Fig. A.12 shows a typical LED.

The light-emitting diode is made from gallium arsenide or a similar material. Because it is a diode, current can only flow through the diode in one direction, and the red light is produced as a result of this current. LEDs are not the same as normal light bulbs. The main differences are as follows:

- LEDs are more efficient (this means that they convert a larger proportion of the electrical power which they consume into light);
- LEDs give only a low-power light;
- LEDs give light only if connected the correct way round. If connected backwards no current flows, and no light is given out;

Fig. A.12   Typical LEDs.

Fig. A.13 The layout of the segments in a seven-segment display.

- to prevent the forward current being too large, LEDs are always connected in series with a resistor;
- even though LEDs do not light when connected the wrong way round, voltage differences in excess of about five volts will destroy the diode.

When using a LED it is important to find which way round it should be connected **before** doing anything to it. The lead that has to be connected towards the positive supply is called the *anode*. The lead connected towards the negative is called the *cathode*. Sometimes the only way in which you can tell which lead is which is by looking at the length of the leads. More often part of the lower rim of the diode has been removed to make a 'flat', and this flat section is usually next to the cathode lead. You can see the flat clearly in the photograph (fig. A.12). It is always wise to check manufacturer's data for the details you need, but if that is not possible you can connect the diode, in series with a 1000 Ω resistor, to a 3 V battery and find out which way round the diode must be connected to get it to light.

A2.16 — Seven-segment displays

For number displays, an integrated unit with seven LEDs is used. The LEDs are formed into long thin strips and are arranged into a seven-segment display as shown in fig. A.13.

The integrated unit usually has eight pins. One end of each diode is connected to a separate pin. The other ends of all the diodes are connected together and connected to the eighth pin. If the cathodes of all seven segments are connected together the unit is called a common-cathode display, but if all the anodes have been connected together instead (when the device was made) it is called a common-anode display. You cannot tell the difference between the two when you look at each display but it makes a lot of difference which one is which when you connect the display into its circuit.

Each bar in the display can be lit separately. By lighting the correct bars each of the decimal numbers from 0 to 9 and the digits A, B, C, D, E, and F of the hexadecimal (hex) system can all be displayed. Fig. A.14 shows all these numbers. Some other letters can be obtained (e.g. G, H, J, L, P, U), but more complicated displays with more LEDs are used when letters, as well as numbers, are needed.

A2.17 — Display screens

The screen on a television or oscilloscope or computer monitor is also an electronic light output transducer. The screen is the front of a *cathode ray tube*. A beam of electrons is produced inside the tube, and light is produced whenever electrons strike the coating on the inside of the screen.

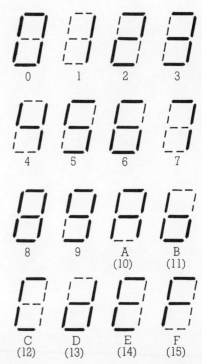

Fig. A.14 Decimal and hex numerals as displayed on a seven-segment display. Dotted lines represent the bars which are not illuminated. The decimal values of the hex numerals are shown in brackets.

4 DECISION-MAKING WITH ELECTRONIC CIRCUITS

The human brain is basically a decision maker. Many electronic systems are designed to help our mental processes, so they must be expected to make decisions too. However, although electronic systems can operate much faster and with much more information than the human brain, they can not match the range of decision-making that the brain can achieve. Although in science fiction there are computers or robots that are better than any human being, this is only fiction and, unless man stops thinking, it will always be so.

Decisions are of two kinds. Many decisions are automatic and logical. You blink automatically when something comes towards your face. You take a raincoat with you when the weather is wet. When riding a bicycle, you swerve or brake if someone runs in front of you. If you buy chocolate for 15p, you give the assistant the 20p coin in your pocket, not the 10p coin. You turn off the television when you go out, unless someone else is watching it.

Human beings can change their minds. You could leave your coat at home, or you can give the shop assistant the 10p coin and wait to be asked for more money. Both are illogical, but you can **decide** to be illogical.

Electronic systems can **only** be logical. To make them do seemingly illogical things you have to program them logically to be illogical, which is not easy! Electronic systems can make decisions, but the only decisions they can make are the logical decisions they have been constructed to make.

To understand decision-making you need first to understand the basic logic steps involved. This turns out to be very simple. Any logical process is a series of steps, but each step is only one of three possibilities. These are:

the NOT decision

"if you go out with John then I will not go out with you"

the AND decision

"if mum comes home and it has not gone dark I will call round"

and the OR decision

"if mum or dad come home I will be able to come round".

Any more complex set of conditions or actions can be broken down into these three steps:

"I will call round if mum *or* dad come home before it is dark *and* you have *not* gone out with John".

There is one other important part of human decision-making, and that is *memory*. Most human actions have to be remembered or learned. Even simple things have to be learned. For example, we all know that liquid will not stay in a cup if it is tipped over, but a small child does not hold a cup properly without being trained to do so. Training is the process of putting a series of instructions (called a *program*) into a memory, in this case the child's brain memory. More instructions can then be added as to when to use the program learned.

If you do not believe that picking up a cup is a long set of instructions, ask a friend to pretend to be an unthinking robot, and try to explain to your friend how to pick up a cup. The robot will cope with only one instruction

Humans can *decide* to be illogical.

and one movement at a time. It will keep on doing any action until it is told to stop. Your first instruction to the robot might be "move your hand in the direction of the cup", and your third instruction might be "straighten your fingers". What was the second instruction? Can you complete the set of instructions?

Electronic blocks with transfer functions that are the same as the three basic logic processes can be built. Blocks with the function of memory can also be made. This chapter deals only with electronic logic; memory will be considered in chapter 16.

Electronic circuits which carry out logic functions are called gates. You have already met systems using simple gates in chapters 2 and 3. Electronic circuits can only 'make decisions' about the electrical voltage signals they receive. Logic gates operate on digital input signals. This means that the input signal can be only one of two possibilities: either there is a voltage present or there is not. To work reliably in practice the signal voltage must be within fairly close limits, even though in theory the gates would work on any voltage.

When the voltage is present we say the input is 'logic 1' (you could think of this as the electronic 'yes'). When the voltage is not there we say the input is logic 0 (electronic 'no'). In the examples in previous chapters, logic 1 has been 5 volts and logic 0 has been 0 volts (see fig. 4.1). These are the most common voltages used in the logic systems, but it is possible to design a system using any voltage as logic 1.

The electronic gates used for decision-making only understand logic 1 and logic 0. The output can also only be logic 1 or logic 0. If electronics is to be used for making decisions, the logic functions of 'and', 'or' and 'not' have to be thought of in terms of logic 0 and logic 1.

Logic 1 means that the condition is met, and logic 0 means that it is not. The 'and' decision considered earlier was: 'if mum comes home and it is not dark, then I will call round'. There are two inputs to the system. Mum being at home is one input to the system, and it not being dark is the other:

"if mum is at home" the condition is met, and we call it logic 1 (yes);
"if mum is out" the condition is not met, which is logic 0 (no).

Similarly:

"if it is light" is logic 1;
"if it is dark" is logic 0.

The same method is used for the output:

"I can come round" is logic 1;
"I can not come round" is logic 0.

In terms of logic, the 'and' function can now be described as "the output from the system is logic 1 only if both inputs are logic 1".

This all seems very lengthy to explain. There is a type of mathematical shorthand that helps us keep logic explanations short. It uses symbols borrowed from Boolean algebra and is shown in table 4.1.

The electronic decision-making gates are given names describing the decision they make. These names are always written in capital letters. The gate that takes an 'and' decision is called an AND gate. The other basic decision gates are OR and NOT.

In practice other decision gates are also used. For example, a combination of the 'and' decision with the 'not' decision to give 'not and' is treated as a basic logic gate. It is called the NAND gate. An example of NAND (Not AND) is:

"if mum **and** dad are at home I will **not** come out with you"

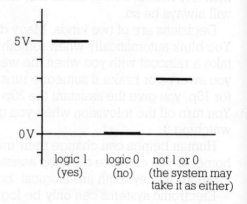

Fig. 4.1 Digital logic signals for a 5 V system. In most manufactured logic blocks the system will take any voltage from about 3.5 V to 5 V as logic 1, but it will not work properly if the signal is between 0.2 V and 3.5 V.

Table 4.1 Logic symbols used in Boolean algebra.

logic statement	written as
A and B	A . B
A or B	A + B
not A	$\overline{A}$
A or B, and C	(A + B).C
A, or B and C	A + (B.C)
A is logic 1	A = 1

The logic says "if no one is at home, or just mum, or just dad, then I will be able to come out". The NAND logic gate is the easiest and cheapest electronic logic circuit to make. For this reason, and others, the NAND gate is the gate used most frequently in real systems.

Similarly we can make another gate by mixing the 'or' decision with a 'not' decision. This gives us a NOR gate. An example of a 'nor' decision is:

"if mum **or** dad come home I will **not** be able to come out"
which means:

"if neither mum nor dad come home I will be able to come out"

How is this different from a 'nand' decision?

Another decision-making gate often used in electronics is the 'exclusive or' gate. It is often called an EOR gate. The 'exclusive or' decision is a combination of 'and', 'or' and 'not' decisions. An example will explain the 'exclusive or' decision:

"if mum **or** dad come home then I can come round, but **not** if both mum **and** dad come home"

Obviously you have to hope that mum and dad will never do the same thing!

Electronic logic systems usually use a number of gates, so that some way of drawing such systems is needed. In this book we will use the symbols shown in fig 4.2. They are a simplified form of the standard series of symbols known as BS3939. The symbols in fig. 4.2 are shown with just two inputs, but logic gates can have three or more inputs. The NOT gate is sometimes called an inverter and can **only** have one input.

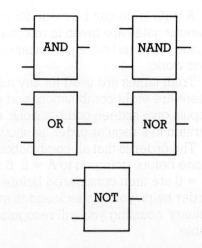

Fig. 4.2   The simplified BS3939 logic gate symbols. Other logic symbols are shown in the reference section (page 55).

SUMMARY 4A

The basic logic decisions are 'and', 'or' and 'not'.

All logical processes can be split down into a series of basic logic function steps.

Electronic logic gates can be made for each basic decision. The gates are called AND, OR and NOT.

NAND is AND followed by NOT, giving the NOT AND function.

NOR is OR followed by NOT, giving the NOT OR function.

Truth tables

Each logic function has been described in words, and its electronic equivalent gate has been given a symbol. To describe fully the function of an electronic logic gate we have to consider every possible combination of the inputs to the gate.

In a two-input logic system there are **only** four possible combinations of the inputs. To make it simple, we call one input 'A' and the other 'B'.

What are the four combinations for an 'and' decision? Remembering that an AND gate only gives an output if both its inputs are logic 1 ('yes' decisions), we get:

both inputs logic 0; output logic 0
input A logic 0 and input B logic 1; output logic 0
input A logic 1 and input B logic 0; output logic 0
both inputs logic 1; output logic 1

This is clumsy because it uses so many words. It is easier to make a table for this information and just fill in 1s and 0s. Every possible combinaton of inputs is included in the table. Such a table is called a *truth table*. You can think of it as describing the whole truth about the way in which the gate operates. Fig 4.3 shows a truth table for an AND gate with two inputs.

Input		Output
A	B	Z
0	0	0
0	1	0
1	0	0
1	1	1

Fig. 4.3   The truth table for a two input AND gate.

A truth table can be made for every type of logic gate. Truth tables for various gates are given in reference section B. Truth tables can also be made to tell us how a particular combination of decision-making gates will work.

Truth tables are used for any number of input signals. With three inputs there are eight combinations and eight lines in the truth table. Four inputs give sixteen combinations, and so on. The columns are always written in a regular order, as shown for the four-input OR gate in fig. 4.4.

The order is that all combinations with A = 0, B = 0, C = 0 should be done before going on to A = 0, B = 0, C = 1. All combinations of A = 0, B = 0 are then considered before A = 0, B = 1, and so on. This regular order helps you to check and to avoid mistakes. If you have done some 'binary' counting you will recognise the order of the 1s and 0s in the truth table.

A	B	C	D	Z
0	0	0	0	0
0	0	0	1	1
0	0	1	0	1
0	0	1	1	1
0	1	0	0	1
0	1	0	1	1
0	1	1	0	1
0	1	1	1	1
1	0	0	0	1
1	0	0	1	1
1	0	1	0	1
1	0	1	1	1
1	1	0	0	1
1	1	0	1	1
1	1	1	0	1
1	1	1	1	1

Fig. 4.4 The truth table for a four-input OR gate. An OR gate gives logic 1 if any input is logic 1. The output is 0 only when all four inputs are 0 (the first line in the table).

Using truth tables to solve a problem

How might a truth table help in a real situation? As an example, suppose boxes on a conveyer have to be checked to make sure that they are not filled too full or not filled enough. The checking point has three detectors using beams of high-frequency sound.

A gives a logic 1 when the box is correctly positioned.
B remains at logic 1 unless the box is too full.
C gives a logic 1 signal whenever a box is not properly filled.

The box is rejected when the system gives a logic 1 output.
Fig 4.5 is the truth table for this.

Line number	A Is the box in position?	B Is the box too full?	C Is the box not filled?	Z Should the box be rejected?	
1	0	0	0	0	⎫ box not in
2	0	0	1	0	⎬ position
3	0	1	0	0	⎭
4	0	1	1	0	
5	1	0	0	1	box too full
6	1	0	1	0	fault in system
7	1	1	0	0	accept box
8	1	1	1	1	box empty

Fig. 4.5 The truth table for the checking system. Why would the combination of inputs in line 6 indicate the system must be faulty?

The right-hand column of fig 4.5 indicates what decision the logic system must make. Looking at the truth table it is easy to see that line 8 is an AND combination. It is also easy to see that the box must be rejected if we get either line 5 OR line 8.

What logic decision will give line 5? The truth table indicates that line 5 is:

A at logic 1, B at logic 0 and C at logic 0

Remembering that B can only be at either logic 1 or logic 0, this could be written as:

A at logic 1, and not B at logic 1, and not C at logic 1 either.

Writing the sentence that way round gives the clue. To get 'not B' we must have the opposite of B. We need the opposite of C too. To get the opposite of B we need to pass the signal through a NOT gate. The opposite of B is often written as $\bar{B}$.

With B and C signals passed through NOT gates then when a faulty box is checked we get the output $A = 1$, $\bar{B} = 1$, $\bar{C} = 1$. An AND gate is needed, as shown in fig. 4.6.

This combination of NOT and AND gates gives us logic 1 for line 5 which is what was required. Any other combination of inputs will not give all logic 1s at the input to the AND gate, so the output will be logic 0. To make the logic system complete we have to combine the output from this logic circuit with the logic circuit that identifies line 8. In 'mixing' the two we want a signal out if one or the other gives a reject signal. This calls for an OR gate. The complete logic system would therefore be as shown in fig. 4.7. You should study this diagram and then work through this explanation again if you are not sure how the answers were obtained.

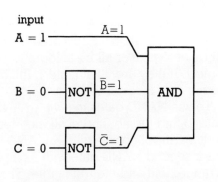

Fig. 4.6 The logic gates needed to identify line 5 of the truth table.

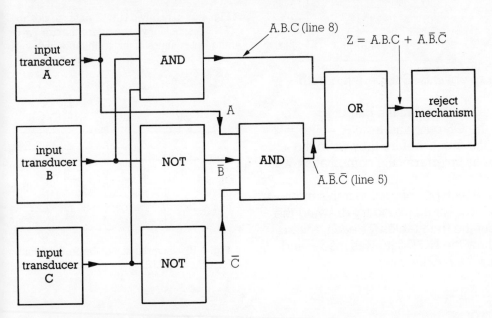

Fig. 4.7 The logic diagram for the conveyer control system. If you have the equipment construct this system and check that it works. Use a solenoid for the reject mechanism and light sensor blocks (or switches) for the inputs A, B and C.

Use of NAND gates

In the early days of electronic logic, large numbers of components had to be used to deal with practical problems, and electronics engineers took great care to ensure that the minimum number of gates was used. Each gate used a different circuit and a complete system would be a combination of the three different types of gate. When the technology of producing complex integrated circuits had been worked out, the cost was not governed by the number of components such as resistors and transistors but by the number of chips used and the number of gates you could get on one chip. In fact the problem now is not the number of gates you can put on the chip but the number of connections needed. The simplest and cheapest gate to make is the NAND gate.

NAND gates have one other advantage compared with AND and OR gates. Two NAND gates can be connected together to make an AND gate. Three NAND gates can be connected to make an OR gate and four can be connected to make a NOR gate. NAND gates can be used as inverters too. The result is that the whole of a logic system can be built using only NAND gates. As most chips have several NAND gates on them, it becomes very cheap indeed to use one type of gate for everything.

The whole conversion process depends on using a NAND as an inverter (NOT gate). A NAND gate gives logic 0 output when all its inputs are logic 1. If all the inputs are connected together, then they will either **all** be at logic 0 or **all** be at logic 1. If they are all at logic 0, the output is logic 1. If they are all at logic 1, the output is logic 0. The NAND gate has become an inverter (see fig. 4.8).

To use NAND gates to give an AND function we can use one NAND gate to find the not-and of all the inputs; then we need to find the inverse of that. This of course gives an AND. To invert the output to the NAND we use a second NAND gate with its inputs tied together. Fig. 4.9 shows the arrangement and the truth table. The truth table also shows what is happening at the various stages.

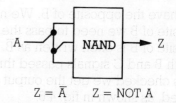

$$Z = \bar{A} \qquad Z = NOT\ A$$

Fig. 4.8 A three-input NAND gate connected as an inverter. A three-input NOR gate could also be connected as an inverter. How?

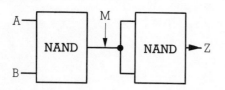

A	B	M	Z
0	0	1	0
0	1	1	0
1	0	1	0
1	1	0	1

Fig. 4.9 Using two NAND gates to get an AND function. If you compare the first two and last columns of this truth table with fig. 4.3 you will see that they are the same.

Getting an OR function is not quite so obvious. Compare the truth tables for OR and NAND in fig. 4.10.

Both tables in fig. 4.10 have three 1s and one 0 in the output line. The output 0 comes from A = 0, B = 0 in the OR gate and from A = 1, B = 1 in the NAND gate. Thus, if we invert the inputs **before** they go to the NAND gate (using other NAND gates as inverters), the combination will work as an OR gate. The arrangement is shown in fig. 4.11.

NOR gates can also be used to make all types of gate, but this method is not as common as using all NANDS. You might like to try drawing the block diagrams and then checking out the truth tables for each system you try. If you get stuck, think about how the NOT gate was made, and then try working on the OR and finally the NAND gates.

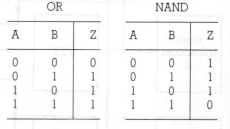

OR			NAND		
A	B	Z	A	B	Z
0	0	0	0	0	1
0	1	1	0	1	1
1	0	1	1	0	1
1	1	1	1	1	0

Fig. 4.10 Comparison of the truth tables for OR and NAND.

Combining logic gates

Logic systems which use a combination of these gates and nothing else are known as *combinational logic systems*. Any logic system can be made using only NAND gates. The method of designing a system uses a truth table in the same way as the 'reject box' example. To see the way the whole design idea works it is easiest to use an example. The following example is about the problems of controlling an air-conditioning unit.

The problem. In many large buildings there is an air-conditioning unit. The unit will heat the air if the temperature is too low, cool the air if it is too hot, and reduce the humidity (the water vapour carried by the air) if that gets too high. Transducers will detect these three conditions and signal the unit to switch on the cooler or heater. Humidity depends on temperature, so to reduce the humidity you can heat the air to a higher temperature. By cooling the air first and then heating it again, the humidity can be reduced without changing the temperature of the air in the building.

There are three inputs to this system. These are from:

A – the transducer giving logic 1 when the temperature is too high;
B – the transducer giving logic 1 when the temperature is too low; and
C – the transducer giving logic 1 when the humidity is too high.

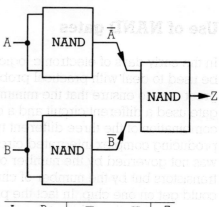

A	B	$\bar{A}$	$\bar{B}$	Z
0	0	1	1	0
0	1	1	0	1
1	0	0	1	1
1	1	0	0	1

Fig. 4.11 Obtaining the OR function using NAND gates. You should work out for yourself how to make a NOR gate from NAND gates.

There are two outputs to this system. These are from:

Y − logic 1 to switch on the heater; and

Z − logic 1 to switch on the cooler.

Working out the logic system. Having defined the signal inputs and the outputs of the system, the truth table can be made. This truth table is shown in fig. 4.12.

Line number	A too hot	B too cold	C humid	Y heater	Z cooler
1	0	0	0	0	0
2	0	0	1	1	1
3	0	1	0	1	0
4	0	1	1	1	0
5	1	0	0	0	1
6	1	0	1	0	1
7	1	1	0	−	−
8	1	1	1	−	−

Fig. 4.12 The truth table for an air-conditioning system. Look at lines 2, 7 and 8, and make sure that you understand why the outputs given in the table are correct.

The truth table indicates that there are three conditions for which the heater is on. These are lines 2, 3 and 4. The logic for line 2 is:

A = 0, B = 0, C = 1

We now convert this to all logic 1 states so that an AND gate can be used:

NOT A = 1, NOT B = 1, C = 1

For practical reasons the combination of NAND gates equivalent to an AND gate is used, so the input for line 2 becomes as shown in fig. 4.13. The logic for line 3 is worked out in exactly the same way. This is shown in fig. 4.14. You should work out the diagram for line 4 yourself.

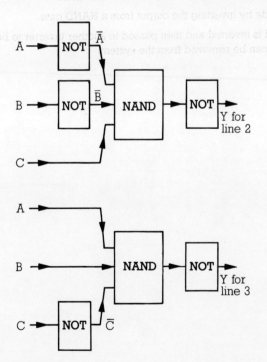

Fig. 4.13 The logic system corresponding to line 2 of the truth table in fig. 4.12.

Fig. 4.14 The logic system for line 3 of the truth table in fig. 4.12.

Putting the system together. The heater needs to come on if any of the three logic decisions we have worked out happens. This needs an OR gate. An OR gate is also made from NANDs (see fig. 4.11 on the previous page).

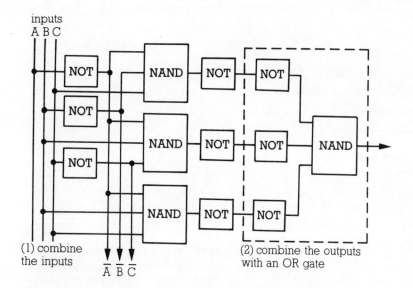

(1) combine the inputs

(2) combine the outputs with an OR gate

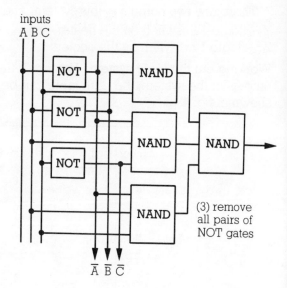

(3) remove all pairs of NOT gates

Fig. 4.15 The final steps in designing the heater logic as efficiently as possible.

Simplifying the logic system for the heater. The full system is shown in fig. 4.15. The left-hand diagram is the full system as we have worked it out so far. The right-hand diagram is the final form that would be used. We have 'lost' six NOT gates because one NOT gate followed by another NOT gate has no overall effect on the signal.

You should try designing the cooler logic circuit yourself. A summary of the steps that we have gone through is in reference section B3.8.

SUMMARY 4B

A truth table is a list of all possible input signals and what the output would be for each possible combination.

All logic functions can be made from NAND gates.

An inverter is made when all NAND inputs are connected together.

An OR is made by inverting each input to a NAND gate.

An AND is made by inverting the output from a NAND gate.

Where a signal is inverted and then passed to another inverter to be inverted again, both inverters can be removed from the system.

5 AMPLIFIERS

In chapter 1 it was stated that all systems have signal inputs. These signals must be large enough for the system to recognise, just as writing must be large enough to read and a warning bell must be loud enough to hear.

Many signals come from switches or keyboards. In these cases it is easy to make sure that the signals are large enough for the system to know they are there. However, input signals may come from transducers such as a microphone or an LDR, or from another electronic system. Often these signals are not large enough to make the system respond. In these cases the input signal has to be made larger. It has to be *amplified*.

Amplifiers do not have to be electronic. The three small bones in the middle part of your ear act as a very good amplifier. They make the small movements produced by the incoming sound into movements large enough to make the ear produce nerve impulses for the brain to understand. In this book, though, we only consider electronic amplifiers.

An amplifier usually receives a small signal at its input and produces a much larger version of that signal at its output. Most of the amplifiers described in this book amplify voltage differences and are called *voltage amplifiers*. It is equally easy to amplify the signal current or the power, and sometimes amplifiers are used for such purposes. Occasionally amplifiers are even used for making signals smaller.

It is a law of nature that you do not get something for nothing (in other words, energy cannot be created). Amplifiers cannot disobey this rule. Electronic amplifiers need a power supply and the extra power at the output comes from that power supply. This is true for any amplifier, whether it is used as a power amplifier or only used to amplify voltage differences.

Apart from understanding this rule you do not need to know how amplifiers work before you use them, which is good because how they work is not always simple to understand. Nowadays, most amplifiers are in the form of integrated circuits ('chips'), so there is no way you can find out what is inside them anyway.

If some writing is too small to read it needs to be enlarged. However, the degree of enlargement is important. The writing might still be too small to read if you made it twice as big, but if it was to be made ten times larger the words might not fit on the page. If you make it a million times larger it will be so big that you will not see enough of each letter to know that it is writing! In the same way the amount of amplification is important. In electronics the amount of amplification is called the *gain* of the amplifier. Electronic amplifiers with a gain of a million (i.e. where the output signal is a million times bigger than the input signal) can easily be made. Sometimes we need such a large gain. However, just as with the writing, it is important to get the right gain for the particular system. This is easy to achieve for electronic amplifiers.

... BACK A BIT - IT'S TOO SMALL

ELECTRONICS FOR GCSE

... NO! THAT'S TOO FAR

SUMMARY 5A

An amplifier is a system building block which receives an input signal and produces an amplified version of that signal at its output.

The extra power for the output signal comes from the power supply.

The number of times bigger that the output is compared with the input is called the gain of the amplifier.

Electronic amplifiers can amplify voltage, or current, or both.

Amplifiers in practice

Using a practical example will make these ideas clearer. If you have access to the components you can easily try out the ideas for yourself. This practical example uses a transducer which responds to magnetism. It is called a *Hall probe*.

The Hall probe has four connections. A steady current is passed through the probe. If the probe is near a magnet, and therefore in its magnetic field, then there will be a voltage difference between the other two connections. This voltage difference depends on how strong the magnetic field is. Even with a powerful magnet the voltage difference is less than a volt. It can be measured using a sensitive meter but it is not enough to do anything useful, like lighting an indicator lamp. Fig. 5.1 gives practical details for connecting the probe to a meter.

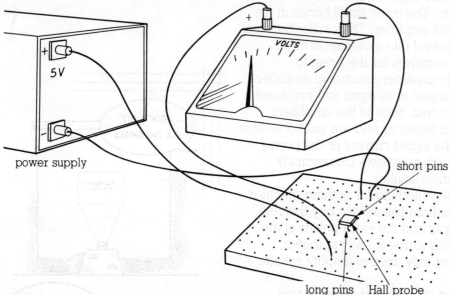

power supply

VOLTS

short pins

long pins   Hall probe

Fig. 5.1 Simple experimental work with a Hall probe. Moving the magnet about near the probe will show you how the signal from the probe varies. If the meter needle deflects backwards, turn the magnet round the other way. The component in the lead to the power [31] supply is a resistor. What is its purpose?

To operate a system using the signals from the Hall probe you need an amplifier. The output terminals of the probe can be directly connected to the input terminals of a voltage amplifier. The most convenient kind of voltage amplifier is known as an *operational amplifier*. The operational amplifier or *op-amp* itself is made as an integrated circuit. To use the op-amp as a block in an electronic system it must have a power supply and other components (resistors) to complete the circuit. The most common type of op-amp is known as a '741'. This number is the manufacturer's type number for the chip.

Op-amps will amplify both positive and negative voltage signals, but to do this they need two power supplies. They can be used in a number of ways (not just as amplifiers), and have two input connections rather than one. These are known as the inverting input and the non-inverting input. When the inverting input is used the output is not only amplified but inverted (compared with the input) as well.

The idea of inverting came in the last chapter when NOT gates were used. Inverting is not exactly the same in digital systems as it is in analogue systems. In digital systems (such as those using logic blocks) inverting means changing logic 1 into logic 0 or logic 0 into logic 1. In analogue systems, where you have varying signals, inverting means making the same signal voltage negative instead of positive or positive instead of negative. Fig. 5.2 at the top of the next page illustrates this.

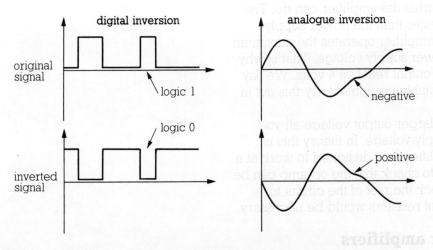

digital inversion

original
signal

logic 1

logic 0

inverted
signal

analogue inversion

negative

positive

Fig. 5.2 This diagram shows what is meant by digital inversion and analogue inversion.

When an op-amp is used in an amplifier block, the gain of the block can be set by the choice of the resistors that are connected to the op-amp. The way in which this works and the values of resistor you have to choose are described in chapter 12. All you need to know at this stage is how to use the amplifier block.

What gain would you need with the Hall probe? The maximum input signal from the probe is about 0.5 volts. Many electronic systems use 5 volt power supplies. The gain therefore needs to be 10, because 5 is ten times greater than 0.5. The arrangement is shown in fig. 5.3. Voltmeters connected at the input and output of the amplifier block would allow you to see what the block is doing. Also you would find that as the input voltage changes the output voltage changes in the same way, but with voltages ten times greater. Because this happens, the amplifier is said to be *linear*.

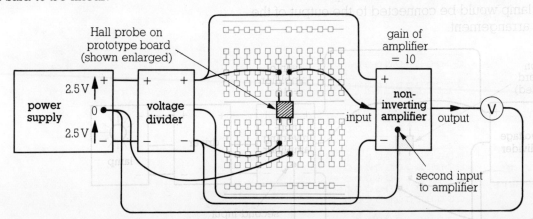

Hall probe on
prototype board
(shown enlarged)

gain of
amplifier
= 10

power
supply

2.5 V +
0
2.5 V −

voltage
divider

+   +

−   −

+
non-
inverting
amplifier
−

input

output

V

second input
to amplifier

Fig. 5.3 The practical arrangement for connecting the Hall probe to a non-inverting amplifier block. The probe is mounted on prototype board (shown enlarged in this diagram). The amplifier needs three connections to the power supply so that it can amplify positive and negative signals (see chapter 10). As the Earth behaves as a weak magnet, the voltmeter may not read exactly zero when there is no magnet nearby.

What would happen if you increased the gain of the amplifier to 20? Would you get 10 volts out when the magnet was so close that the probe gave its full 0.5 volts at the input?

For low input voltages the amplifier behaves in the same way as before but gives outputs twice as large as when the gain was 10. An input of 0.1 volts gives an output of 2 volts; an input of 0.15 volts gives an output of 3 volts; and 0.2 volts gives 4 volts. When the input voltage is 0.3 volts the output is still 4 volts! It will not increase it any more, even though the input is increased. (You may even have noticed this effect with a gain of 10 if you tried out the arrangement in the laboratory.)

Although the gain is 20 and the maximum input is 0.5 volts you cannot get the expected output of 10 volts. We have already come across the principle that the extra power the amplifer provides comes from the power supply. The power supply limits what the amplifier can do. The output of the amplifier can never be greater than the power supply voltage. In fact, because of the way the amplifier operates the maximum voltage is at least a volt less than the power supply voltage. That is why the amplifier stops amplifying when the output reaches 4 volts. We say the amplifier is *saturated*. If you have suitable equipment, try this out in the laboratory.

You may well think that if you need a larger output voltage all you need to do is to increase the power supply voltage. In theory this is completely correct, but in practice amplifiers are designed to work at a specific voltage. It would be necessary to check that the op-amp can be used at higher voltages, and then to check the rest of the circuit to see whether any changes in the values of resistors would be necessary.

Transducer drivers and power amplifiers

Could a lamp or a relay be connected to the output of the amplifier to make the system do something useful? The answer for the system in fig. 5.3 on the previous page is no. Although a total of 4 volts is available, if you connect a 3.5 volt lamp it would not light because there is not enough **power** to light it. If you connect the lamp, together with a voltmeter, to the output you will see that the output is no longer 4 volts but a fraction of 1 volt. Indeed, while most op-amps will stand this sort of treatment many other amplifiers would be damaged if required to give more power than they are capable of supplying. Op-amps are voltage amplifiers and are not designed to give a large amount of power. To light the lamp we need to amplify the available power as well as the voltage.

Power amplifiers are easily obtainable. They are often described as *drivers*. A driver block would be connected to the output of the voltage amplifier and the lamp would be connected to the output of the driver. Fig. 5.4 shows this arrangement.

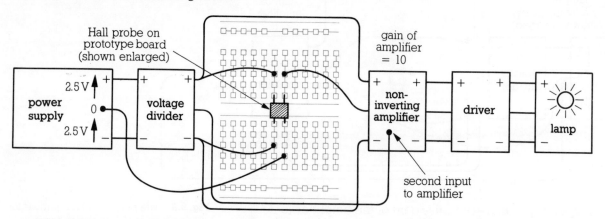

Fig. 5.4 The practical arrangement for adding a driver block to the Hall probe system so that it can drive a lamp or other device needing a significant amount of power.

What do we really mean when we say that an output transducer needs power? When an output transducer is connected to a system, it operates when it receives a voltage signal. That voltage difference makes an electric *current* flow. You can regard the voltage as the electrical driving force and the current as the stream of electrical particles being driven round the circuit. Those electrical particles are called *electrons*. It seems sensible to assume that the greater the driving force is, the more energy the electrons will have to do things. Similarly, if there are more electrons, more work gets done. Electric power would seem, therefore, to depend on both the energy and the number of the electrons, that is, on the voltage and on the current. This is indeed correct. There is more about current and voltage in reference section B.

A voltage amplifier increases the size of the signal but cannot supply a large current. This is all right if the signal is going to another block in the system, or to an indicator or number display. However, if the signal is going to an output transducer that has to produce a lot of energy (such as a large lamp or a loudspeaker) then the amplifier has to provide a large current as well as the amplified voltage signal.

A loudspeaker is a good example of an output device. What interests us is the power coming out of the loudspeaker. Where does this power come from?

The power must come from the electrical power supply to the loudspeaker. Thus, we have to be interested in the voltage and current supplied to the loudspeaker. This gives us a means of knowing what is happening, because voltage and current are easy to measure. All that is needed then is to know how the output power is linked to the voltage and current. That link is as follows:

power available from a loudspeaker	is equal to or less than	electrical power supplied to loudspeaker	which equals	voltage difference across loudspeaker	×	current flowing through loudspeaker

This same relationship applies to any device.

The power amplifier is a block that ensures that the amplified voltage multiplied by the amplified current gives enough power to drive the output transducer. Quite often the power amplifier does not amplify the signal voltage at all, but only amplifies the available current.

Power is measured in watts. If you measure the voltage difference in volts and the current in amps, and then multiply them together to find the power, the answer you get will be in watts.

If you use a 3.5 volt lamp which needs a current of 0.4 amps to light it, then the electrical power it receives is (3.5 × 0.4) which equals 1.4 watts. A transducer driver could supply this. Simple transducer drivers can supply up to 10 or 15 watts, but special power amplifiers are needed for powers up to about 200 watts. If you need more power than that, it cannot come directly from a power amplifier. This is why you cannot drive heaters and large motors directly from an electronic system. You have to use a relay or a thyristor to switch on the high-power circuits.

There is more information on amplifiers in chapter 11 and more information on electrical power in chapter 13. There have already been several references to resistors in this chapter and in earlier chapters. Before we can find out any more about amplifiers we need to know a lot more about resistors and electrical resistance, both of which are discussed in chapter 7.

$$\underset{\text{(in volts)}}{\textit{voltage difference}} \times \underset{\text{(in amps)}}{\textit{current}} = \underset{\text{(in watts)}}{\textit{power}}$$

The equation linking power, voltage difference and current. Power is abbreviated to P, voltage difference to V and current to I to give $V \times I = P$

SUMMARY 5B

An op-amp is a practical integrated circuit voltage amplifier.

The voltage output from an amplifier cannot exceed the voltage supply.

The power from an amplifier cannot exceed the power available from the power source.

Power depends on both voltage difference and current and is measured in watts.

The power of a device is worked out by:
power = voltage difference across device × current through device.

A power amplifier is often called a driver.

6 GENERATING PULSES AND SIGNALS

We are now going to think about two very special types of input and processing devices. These are circuits that generate electronic pulses and electronic waveshapes. They are very different from input transducers (which change a type of energy into an electronic signal) because generators only need electricity to make them work. They are a very important family because they are at the heart of radio systems, music synthesisers and all circuits that involve timing. Timing is much more important than just watches and clocks; most digital circuits contain a timer. For example, it is the timer at the heart of a computer that controls all the other circuits in that computer.

There are many differences between pulses and signals, the main one being that *pulses* are digital whilst the output from a signal generator is usually analogue. The circuits that generate pulses and signals are similar because they both work by feedback. The idea of feedback is explained later in this chapter. However, before we get into complicated electronics we really need to think about the function of different types of pulse and signal generators.

Pulse generators

A pulse generator does just what it suggests: it generates a pulse. A pulse is one steady voltage immediately followed by another steady voltage. The voltage then returns to the first value. This means that a pulse is digital, and we call the higher voltage logic 1 and the lower voltage logic 0. The pulse starts when it changes from logic 0 to logic 1 and finishes when it changes from logic 1 to logic 0 (see fig. 6.1).

There are two basic types of pulse generator. One type gives just one pulse and the second type gives a series of pulses. The important features of both types of pulse generator are the length of time the pulse lasts and the way in which the pulse is started. Pulse generators are given lots of different names depending on exactly what it is they do. A family name often used for pulse generators is *multivibrators*.

Triggered pulse producer

In a triggered pulse producer an electronic signal called a *trigger* makes the pulse start. This means that the triggered pulse producer is a processing block with an input and an output. The input is a trigger and the output is a single pulse.

A trigger in electronics is a change that, as it occurs, makes a sub-system do something. It is rather like a starting flag in a motor rally. When the starter drops the flag (i.e. the flag changes its position) the race starts, and it keeps going until it is finished, even if the flag is rolled up and put away! In a digital electronics system there are of course only two changes that can take place to make a trigger. The trigger can change from level 0 to level 1, or change from level 1 to level 0. The change from 0 to 1 is called a *positive-going edge* and the change from 1 to 0 is called a *negative-going edge*. Triggers are often represented on diagrams by the symbols shown in fig. 6.2.

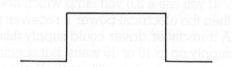

Fig. 6.1 This shows one complete pulse.

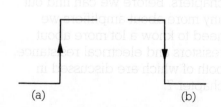

(a)   (b)

Fig. 6.2 The symbols used to represent triggers. A trigger signal is a changing voltage. Some triggered pulse producers look for a positive-going edge trigger (a) while others look for a negative-going edge trigger (b). Data about particular triggered pulse producers usually shows one of these symbols.

In many practical situations the input to the trigger of a triggered pulse producer is not digital. In these cases the circuit to be triggered waits until a particular voltage value is reached. This is called the *threshold voltage*. Most trigger inputs can identify a rising voltage or a falling voltage. In the diagram (fig. 6.3) we have a trigger that identifies a rising voltage and has a threshold of 2.3 volts. The moment the voltage rises above 2.3 volts the circuit triggers and the pulse will start.

The trigger activates the start of the pulse, and some time later the pulse stops. The length of time the pulse lasts is controlled by the circuit of the triggered pulse producer. This control circuit will always have a capacitor and a resistor in it. The length of time the pulse lasts depends on the values of the resistor and the capacitor, but each kind of pulse producer has its own formula linking the time period with these values. One very common pulse producer uses a '555' integrated circuit. The data and formula for this circuit are given in reference section B.

In chapter 2 we met an electronic block very similar to a triggered pulse producer. It was called a latch. The latch has a digital output and is activated by a trigger signal. One difference is that once the latch output has started it stays on until a 'reset' signal changes the output signal. How is this different from a triggered pulse producer?

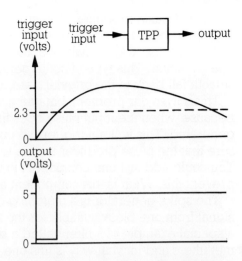

Fig. 6.3 An input signal and the output that comes from it when a triggered pulse producer is used with its trigger set at 2.3 V (positive going). The end of the output pulse is not shown. Can you redraw the diagram for a threshold of 1 V?

Using triggered pulse producers in practice

Most triggered pulse producers (known as TPPs) do have an input labelled 'reset' in addition to their trigger input, capacitor and resistor. To explain what the 'reset' on a TPP does, let us go back to the idea of a motor car race. If there is an accident we want to be able to stop the race. This is done by marshalls at one point on the track waving down the cars that are still racing. When the accident has been cleared away the race must be re-started. This would be done by the dropping of the starter's flag. The reset signal is like the marshall's flag. It will stop a pulse that has already started. The only way to start another pulse is for the triggered pulse producer to receive another trigger signal at the trigger input.

In the 555 timer referred to earlier, the reset input is usually at logic 1 and has to be at logic 0 to stop the output pulse. No pulse can then start until the reset is returned to logic 1 and held at logic 1. When the reset is at logic 0 it also stops the triggered pulse producer from starting any new pulse. If we want the triggered pulse producer to automatically reset, then we just connect the reset pin to logic 1. This means that a new pulse could start any time after the old pulse has stopped.

Another practical point is what happens to the trigger signal once it has done its job of starting the pulse. If a change from logic 0 to logic 1 triggers a pulse producer, then the trigger may have to return to logic 0 before the pulse stops.

One example of where this is a problem is in simple alarm circuits. For example, many computer printers have a 'paper-end' alarm. This sounds for a few seconds when the paper first runs out and then stops sounding. The circuit is triggered by a microswitch which senses that the paper has run out. However, the microswitch stays in its paper-out state until more paper is put in, but the alarm has to stop after a few seconds.

If the microswitch is the trigger to the triggered pulse producer, then the alarm will keep sounding until more paper is put in. This is because the switch has not returned to its 'normal' paper-in state. To overcome this problem we put a *spike generator* between the microswitch and the

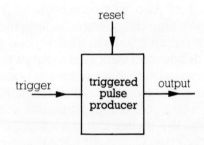

Fig. 6.4 The full block diagram of a triggered pulse producer.

triggered pulse producer. The 'spike' produced by the generator is like a very short pulse.

The simplest way to make a spike generator is to use one resistor and one capacitor. This type of spike generator gives a sharp rise and then a smooth fall back to the original state. This is shown in fig. 6.5.

This solves our problem, but can give rise to a new problem. This is because, when the input pulse does finally stop, a negative spike is generated. This will not trigger the pulse producer, but you must make sure that the pulse producer is able to take a negative voltage at its input. You could add just one component to the output of the spike generator to prevent this. What is this component and how would you connect it?

The spike generator is a *matching device*. This means that it makes the signal from one block suitable for the next block. The spike generator is a special example of a filter called a *differentiator*. Where else have you met filters and in what way is this one the same?

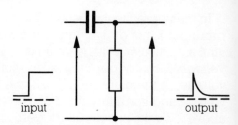

Fig. 6.5 The spike generator circuit, its input signal and the spike it produces. The value of the capacitor and resistor affect the sharpness of the spike.

Some uses of triggered pulse producers

Triggered pulse producers are used in many ways. One common use is as a time delay circuit. Can you think of any ways in which a time delay might be useful? Make a list of them and explain them. Here are two to help you on your way.

An exit and entry circuit on a burglar alarm. Many burglar alarms sense when a door opens. The control box for the alarm is inside the house and the first thing that you do after setting the alarm is to open a door to get out of the house. This would trigger the alarm. A time delay is often fitted to give you about a minute to get out before the alarm is turned on. Also, when you come back to the house, you may have a minute's time delay, from the time the door is opened, to turn off the alarm before it sounds, thinking that you are a burglar!

A debounced switch on a computer keyboard. Whenever a mechanical switch is pressed, it bounces. This means that it can send two or three electronic pulses very quickly one after another. When you switch on lights in your house this does not matter because the pulses are all over in a thousandth of a second (one millisecond), before the light has come on. Computer circuits can pick up these very fast pulses, so that if you pressed, say, the letter F, then the screen might show FFF. To overcome this, triggered pulse producers are used. The keys trigger the pulse producers. The outputs from the pulse producers go to the computer circuits. The first time the switch closes, as the key is pressed, the triggered pulse producer starts a pulse. This pulse lasts about 10 milliseconds and then the pulse producer is automatically reset. As the switch contacts bounce, the other pulses produced do not affect the triggered pulse producer, because once the pulse has started the changes at the trigger are ignored. This does not affect the function of the computer keyboard, because no one can type so fast that they hit the same key twice in one hundredth of a second!

Continuous pulse producers

Using a triggered pulse producer, you get only one pulse. This is like going to a Formula One car race and just seeing the start. It is much more interesting if the cars come round and round, so that you keep on seeing them. Each time they come in to view it is like a fresh start around the track. If you know the circuit where the race is taking place you may be able to position yourself so that the cars are in sight for more time than they are out of sight.

In electronics it is the job of the *continuous pulse producer* to be like the motor racing circuit and make the pulses (cars) come round and round again. Each pulse it produces needs to be like a fresh start.

The output from a continuous pulse producer is one pulse, followed by a gap followed by another pulse, another gap, and so on. Continuous pulse producers are given many different names: timers, pulse generators and astable multivibrators are among the most common.

Continuous pulse producers are no more than a clever development of the triggered pulse producer. Let us consider the block diagram (fig. 6.6).

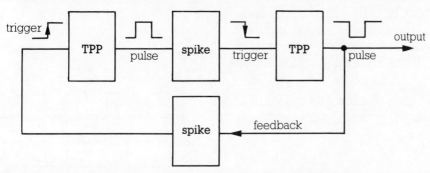

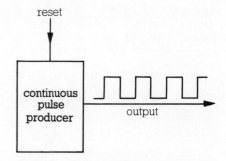

Fig. 6.6 The block diagram for two triggered pulse producers joined together. Why is it necessary to have the [38] spike generators? In how many ways is the second TPP the opposite of the first [39] TPP?

A trigger signal at the input to the first triggered pulse producer starts a positive pulse. When this stops, the second triggered pulse producer starts. This is a negative pulse producer. When this stops it starts the first one again, and the whole thing keeps going. This assumes that the two different types of triggered pulse producers are available. Can you draw the block diagram of the system if the second triggered pulse producer is the same as the first? You will need two inverters!

This is an example of feedback. This is an idea that we met with amplifiers; it is a process whereby signals from the output affect the input. In this case the output re-triggers the input so that the whole process keeps going. The output from this system is a regular pulse and its block diagram is drawn as shown in fig. 6.7.

A continuous pulse producer (known as a CPP) does not need any trigger, because it starts itself. It is, therefore, an input unit. We now have two timing periods to control. There is the 'pulse on' time (called the *mark-time*) and the 'pulse off' time (called the *space-time*).

We can control the time of the mark and the time of the space using resistors and capacitors. As with the triggered pulse producer, there are many ways of doing this, two of which are shown in reference section B.

The output of a continuous pulse producer is one pulse after another, and this is rather like a chain where one link is joined to the next. The output from a continuous pulse producer is usually called a 'pulse chain' or 'pulse train', each pulse being like a carriage of a train (see fig. 6.8).

Some pulse generator circuits have a 'reset' control with which we can control whether the circuit is producing pulses or not. This is exactly the same as the reset on the triggered pulse producer, and it stops the individual pulses. However, if we use the reset we have made an input for the continuous pulse producer and so made it into a processing device.

Fig. 6.7 The continuous pulse producer and its output waveform. The pulse producer may have an input labelled 'reset' which can be used to stop the pulse. Apart from this the CPP has no inputs (except power!).

Describing continuous pulse chains

If you spend a whole afternoon at a motor rally then you will see several different races. Trying to describe the events to a friend who was not

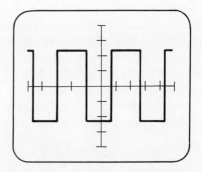

Fig. 6.8 The output from a continuous pulse producer shown on an oscilloscope. One control on the oscilloscope is marked 'trigger level'. Why does this make sure [40] that the trace always starts at the same [41] time? What is meant by 'trigger level'?

there might not be easy. For example you might want to describe the length of time between each lap, or how many cars went by in one go. The ideas are similar to those we need to describe a pulse chain from a continuous pulse producer. The terms that are often used to describe pulse chains are terms to do with the various times involved. They are: *frequency, period, mark-time, space-time* and *mark-space ratio*.

Of less importance is the amplitude of the pulse chain, which is really only a statement of the voltage of logic 1. Let us now consider these terms one at a time to see how they describe a continuous pulse chain.

Period. The period is simply the length of time taken for one complete pulse. A complete pulse in a continuous pulse chain is the mark **and** the space. If we know the length of time the mark lasts (the *mark-time*) and we know the length of time the space lasts (the *space-time*) we find the period by adding the two together. The period of a wave is measured in seconds (s). We often deal with very short times and use the millisecond (ms) and microsecond (μs).

Frequency. The frequency is simply the number of complete pulses in a second. The frequency is measured in *hertz* (Hz) (the old name of which was 'cycles per second'). Period and frequency are related by the formula:

$$period = \frac{1}{frequency}$$

The frequency of pulses can change over a very wide range. Slow pulses at one per second (1 Hz) may be used for controlling the 'bleep' on an electronic alarm clock. The pulses that control a computer are generated at several million pulses a second, that is, several megahertz (MHz). Pulses of this frequency are often made by a crystal that is squeezed and not by integrated circuits with resistors and capacitors.

When we have pulses going at this sort of speed it is impossible to measure their period on a stopwatch! We have to use an oscilloscope, which is a very useful instrument on which we can measure frequencies and observe waveshapes. The trace on the screen of the oscilloscope is like a graph. The *x*-axis (horizontal) is a measure of time. The *y*-axis (vertical) is a measure of the voltage difference. When the oscilloscope receives a signal it starts tracing out the voltage for a time period which you can select in advance. This time period can be anything from several seconds to millionths of a second. This is why the oscilloscope is such a useful instrument.

Mark-space ratio. This is fairly easy! The mark-space ratio tells us how much longer the mark-time is than the space-time. If the mark-time is twice as long as the space-time then the mark-space ratio is 2. Other mark-space ratios can be calculated using the formula:

$$mark\text{-}space\ ratio = \frac{mark\text{-}time}{space\ time}$$

Some pulse generators have a fixed mark-space ratio of 1 and others always have a ratio greater than 1 (see fig. 6.9).

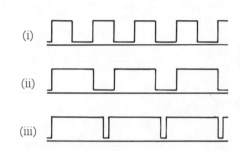

(i)

(ii)

(iii)

Fig. 6.9 Mark-space ratios of 1, 2 and 10. How would you turn pulse chain (iii) into a short-mark pulse chain? What would be its mark-space ratio? 42

SUMMARY 6A

Pulse generators are digital devices.

A trigger is a change in digital state that starts a function.

Triggered pulse producers generate one pulse whose length can be controlled by resistors and capacitors.

A reset signal will stop a pulse and make the triggered pulse producer wait for another trigger before starting another pulse.

A spike generator makes a trigger edge into a short pulse.

A triggered pulse producer is a processing device.

A continuous pulse producer gives a continuous pulse chain.

The logic 1 part of the waveform is called a mark and the logic 0 part is called a space.

The important features of a pulse chain are the frequency and mark—space ratio.

Signal generators

A microphone is a device that turns sound waves into electrical signals. In a way it is a 'signal generator', but we are now much more concerned with a way of generating signals entirely by electronic means. One reason for this is that we can then imitate or *synthesise* the noise coming from a microphone. The pulse generators we have already studied generate square-wave or digital waveforms, but if we look at the electrical signal pattern from a microphone we see it is far from digital. To look at a microphone signal pattern we again use an oscilloscope because it can show the fast changes in electrical signals. Ordinary speech is a jumble and seems to have no regular pattern. Someone whistling into a microphone does show a regular pattern (see fig. 6.10). If you have the equipment try this yourself.

The whistling pattern is an analogue one. The signal can take any value. If we could manage to make, electronically, an identical wave then we would have imitated someone whistling. The circuit that makes this shape (and many others) is called a signal generator. School and college laboratories often have a piece of equipment called a signal generator which can produce different waveshapes, including digital pulses. If you have a chance to look at this and use it with an oscilloscope it would be very worthwhile.

There are many different waveshapes but only one waveshape is particlarly important. It is the waveshape produced when musical instruments make pure notes, when radio waves are transmitted and even by the mains electricity delivered to your home. It is called a *sine wave* or a *sinusoidal* waveshape. One way of making a sinusoidal signal generator is shown in reference section B. It probably will not surprise you to know that sine-wave signal generators make use of feedback. The speed at which the output changes its voltage affects the input, which then affects the output, and so on. The waveshape is also controlled, like the continuous pulse producer, by resistors and capacitors. The sine wave is different from a pulse because its shape is always fixed (see fig. 6.11).

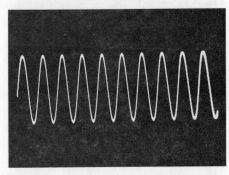

Fig. 6.10 Oscilloscope traces of (*above*) a speech pattern and (*below*) a whistle. Note the regular shape of the whistle trace. Regular shapes are much easier to synthesise than irregular ones.

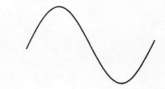

Fig. 6.11 A pure sine-wave shape.

Describing signal generators

The sine-wave signals from signal generators are measured in some of the same ways as pulses from the continuous pulse generator. Firstly there is the *frequency* of the wave. Obviously there is a period to the wave as well, but the period can no longer be described as the mark-time plus the space-time. Instead of mark and space we have the idea of one *wave*. One wave is described as 'from one point on the wave to the identical point on the next wave'. The period is the time for one wave and the frequency is the number of complete waves in one second.

The range of values of useful frequencies generated is vast. They range from a low audible note of about 25 hertz (for example, the boom from a drum) up to UHF (ultra high frequency) radio waves carrying television signals at thousands of millions of waves every second (gigahertz or GHz).

Whereas for pulse chains the size of the pulses is set by the voltage for logic 1, the voltage of a sine-wave signal is changing all the time. We describe the size of a sine wave as its *amplitude*. The amplitude is in fact the maximum positive (or negative) voltage the sine wave reaches.

The amplitude is not always the most useful thing to measure, and measurements of the size of sine-wave signals are made in three ways.

1. **The peak-to-peak voltage**. This is simply the voltage difference between the maximum positive voltage and maximum negative voltage on the wave.

2. **The peak voltage.** For the sine wave this is half the peak-to-peak voltage. Another way of looking at it is to call the line that goes through the centre of the wave 0 V. The peak voltage is then the maximum voltage above or below the 0 V. The amplitude of the wave is the same as the peak voltage.

3. **The root-mean-square voltage (r.m.s. voltage)** This is a clever way of finding the average amount of equal d.c. voltage a wave gives. We do not need to go into the complicated mathematics of how to work this out. You merely need to know that, for a sine-wave, the r.m.s. voltage is 0.7 of the peak voltage (see fig. 6.12).

Once generated, the size of a wave can be changed by an amplifier (see chapter 5). A music synthesiser uses lots of sine wave generators, each made to produce a different frequency. The frequencies for a keyboard synthesiser are the same as those for the strings of a piano. The amplitude (or volume) of each of the signal generators can be altered by amplifiers. The weird noises you can get from a synthesiser are all these separate signals mixed together by summing amplifiers. (To find out about summing amplifiers see reference section D.)

Phase

The *phase* of one wave compared with that of another sometimes needs to be known to describe the wave completely. Phase is only important if we want a way of describing two waves, one compared with the other. The two waves must be of the same frequency. If you look at fig. 6.13 then you will see that the second wave starts one quarter of a complete wave after the first wave. We say that it is 'out of phase'. When we describe waves being out of phase we usually talk about a *phase angle*. Again the reasons for this are linked with complicated mathematics which we do not need to worry about. All we have to remember is that one complete wave is 360°. If the second wave is one quarter of a wave after the first, then we say that it is 90° out of phase (90° is one quarter of 360°). Two waves that are half a wave out are 180° out of phase. This is sometimes called 'anti-phase'.

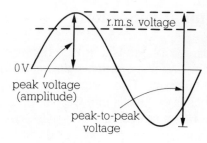

Fig. 6.12 The important parameters of a sine wave. The dotted line across the top part of the diagram is the r.m.s. voltage of the wave. If the peak voltage is 10 V on this wave, what are the peak-to-peak and [43] r.m.s. values?

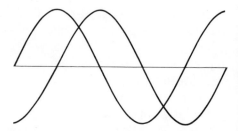

Fig. 6.13 These two waves are 90° out of phase. Try drawing waves 180° out of [44] phase. By how much is the output from an inverting amplifier out of phase compared [45] with the input? (See chapter 10.)

SUMMARY 6B

Signal generators make analogue signals by feedback.

The sine waveshape is the most important of the waves made by a signal generator.

To describe a sine waveshape you have to describe its amplitude and frequency.

There are three ways of measuring the magnitude of a wave: peak-to-peak, peak (or amplitude) and r.m.s.

When comparing two sine waves from two signal generators you have to describe the phase between the two waveshapes.

B REFERENCE SECTION

B1 — Voltage and Current

B1.1 — Electrons and ions

Electrical effects are due to the movement of charged particles. These particles are usually electrons, which carry a negative electrical charge.

The removal of an electron from a particle (e.g. an atom) leaves the particle with a positive electrical charge. This charged particle is called a positive ion. Adding an electron to a neutral particle gives it a negative charge and it becomes a negative ion. The movement of ions has a chemical effect as well as an electrical effect.

B1.2 — Electric current

A movement of electrons or ions is called an *electric current*. An electric current is always described as going from a point where there is an excess of positive charges (e.g. the positive terminal of a battery) to a point where there is an excess of negative charges (the negative terminal). This is called *conventional current*. The movement of electrons (*electron current*) is in the opposite direction to that of the conventional current.

Electric current is measured in amperes (usually abbreviated to amps or A). A current of 1 amp is the current when 1.6×10^{19} electrons pass by every second. The total charge on 1.6×10^{19} electrons is called 1 coulomb of electric charge.

In electronic circuits 1 amp is a large current; smaller units, the milliamp (mA) and the microamp (μA), are often used. Current is measured by an *ammeter*.

To get a continuous electric current there must be a complete circuit, around which the current can go, and an energy source. The energy source is normally a battery or a generator. A power pack is not a direct energy source; it matches your needs in the laboratory with the mains power supply coming from the generators at the power station.

> **Common units for currents**
> 1 mA = 1/1000 A
> 1 μA = 1/1 000 000 A = 1/1000 mA

B1.3 — Conductors

Materials which allow electric currents within them are called conductors. All metals are conductors. All substances that contain water will also conduct electricity because water contains ions.

Metals are not all equally good as conductors. Silver is the best conductor, followed by copper and aluminium. Metal alloys ('mixtures' of metals) are much poorer conductors than the pure metals from which they are made. One form of carbon (graphite) is a conductor of electricity, even though it is not a metal.

B1.4 — Semiconductors

Certain materials conduct electricity better because of the impurities that are present. The most important of these materials are silicon and germanium. Such materials are called semiconductors. Modern electronics depends on the properties of semiconductors.

B1.5 — Insulators

Materials which do not conduct electricity easily are called insulators. In general, non metals, liquids other than water, and all gases are insulators. No insulator is absolutely perfect. The best insulators are plastics such as p.v.c., nylon, polythene and polycarbonate.

Properties of conductors, semiconductors and insulators depend on the temperature at which they are being used. Glass, for example, is normally an insulator yet it can conduct electricity at very high temperatures.

B1.6 — Resistance

Even the best conductors offer some resistance to the movement of electrons. The energy source must supply enough energy to the electrons to overcome this resistance. If the electric current is also causing work to be done, for example, by driving an electric motor, then the energy source must provide the energy for this as well. There is a lot more about resistance in chapter 7 and reference section C.

B1.7 — Voltage difference and energy

When electrons pass through an energy source (e.g. a battery) they are given energy. The voltage difference of the source is a measure of the amount of energy that is given to the electrons.

Voltage difference is measured in volts. A voltage difference of 1 volt is obtained when a total of 1 coulomb of electric charge receives 1 joule of energy from the energy source.

When an electric charge is moving it is an electric current. We can, therefore, find the energy transferred to the current by the energy source. The energy transferred to the electric current is given by the formula:

$$E = V \times I \times t$$

In this formula:
E is the energy transferred,
V is the voltage difference across the source,
I is the current through the source, and
t is the time for which the current is passed.
If V is in volts, I is in amps and t is in seconds, then E is in joules.

Voltage differences also occur where energy is transferred from the current to some other form of energy. In a heater this is to thermal energy, and in a motor it is to magnetic and then to rotational energy. The energy transferred from the current is calculated using exactly the same equation as for the energy given to the current. There is always a voltage difference across the component from which energy is transferred. This voltage difference represents the amount of energy transferred for each coulomb of charge passing through.

Voltage difference is measured on a voltmeter.

Voltage difference is sometimes called 'potential difference' (p.d.) or just 'voltage'. Electro-motive force (e.m.f.) is sometimes used for the voltage difference of a source.

Example of the energy formula

A small light bulb, when working, has a voltage difference of 3 V between its terminals. The current through it is measured on an ammeter as 0.5 A. Calculate the energy transferred by the current in 2 mins.

Work out the time in seconds.
   $t = 2$ (minutes) $\times$ 60 = 120 s

Using $E = VIt$:
   energy = $3 \times 0.5 \times 120 = 180$ J

Exercise 4 — A car battery with a voltage difference of 12 V supplies 200 A to the starter motor of a car. If the car takes 5 s to start, how much energy has been supplied by the battery?

Exercise 5 — A bicycle front lamp is run by two 1.5 V batteries. The bulb, when working, has a current of 0.3 A through it. How much energy is changed to light and heat if the bulb is on for the whole of a 1 h journey?

B1.8 — Power

In electronics the number of joules being transferred every second is often more important than the total energy transferred. This rate of transferring energy is called the *power* of the system. Power is measured in watts. Power is worked out using the formula:

power transferred = current × voltage difference
that is, $P = IV$
where, if I is the current measured in amps and V is the voltage difference measured in volts, then P is the power measured in watts.

There is more about power and how to use this equation in chapter 5.

> Exercise 6 — Calculate the power of the car starter motor and the bicycle light bulb in exercises 4 and 5.

B1.9 — Currents in circuits

There will be no current if there is no energy (voltage) source. Even if there is an energy (voltage) source there will be no current unless there is a complete circuit.

Current (conventional current) goes from positive to negative in a circuit. It is forced from negative back to positive inside a voltage source.

The current in any part of a circuit is governed by the voltage difference across that part of the circuit and the resistance of that part of the circuit (see chapter 7).

Current is usually shown on a diagram by an arrow in the direction of conventional current flow (see fig. B.1).

B1.10 — Parallel circuits and currents at junctions

If there is more than one path that the current can take then the current will divide between the different paths. Where there are two or more paths they are called parallel circuits. If only one part of the circuit provides two paths then the parts connected in this way are said to be *in parallel*. The total of all the currents into any junction must be equal to the total of all the currents out of the junction. (This is one of Kirchhoff's laws.)

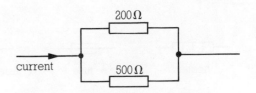

Fig. B.1   Parallel paths in a circuit. The current will flow in both these parallel paths. More current will flow in the top path because it has a lower resistance.

B1.11 — Voltage differences in circuits

A voltage difference can exist between two points in a circuit. To speak about 'a voltage at a point' has no meaning. However, in electronics it is usual to regard one part of the circuit as being at zero volts and measure all voltage differences from this point. We then talk about the voltage at a certain point without stating that this is the voltage difference between this point and the zero point. The negative terminal of the power supply is usually taken as the zero point.

The connections to this zero point are often called the *common*, *common line* or *ground*. If the circuit is connected to earth then this zero line may be called *earth*. If the circuit is built on a metal chassis or in a metal box then the chassis or box is usually connected to, and often becomes, the zero line.

Voltage differences on diagrams are usually shown by an arrow between the two points where there is a voltage difference. By tradition, the 'blunt' end or back of the arrow is usually at zero volts. Where zero volts is not important (for example, considering the voltage difference across a component) the blunt end of the arrow is at the lower energy (voltage) end (see fig B.2).

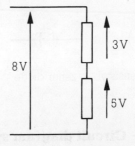

Fig. B.2   The symbols used for voltage difference. The arrows show which end of each component is at a higher voltage. The numbers are examples to show Kirchhoff's law.

B1.12 — Series circuits; adding voltage differences round circuits

In a complete circuit the voltage difference generated by the voltage source must always equal the voltage difference across the rest of the circuit. Where current passes through various parts of a circuit that are connected one after the other, the parts of the circuit are described as being *in series*. The total voltage difference across several parts of a circuit connected in series equals the sum of the voltage differences across each of the parts. (This is the second of Kirchhoff's laws.)

B2 – Symbols

B2.1 – Symbols for electronic circuit diagrams

The symbols for various components given below are those accepted for the British Standard (BS3939). In some cases other symbols are still in common use, and these are given below as 'old symbols'.

Circuit diagrams are normally drawn with connections at 90° to one another, and are usually drawn with the supply voltage line at the top of the diagram and the zero volts line at the bottom.

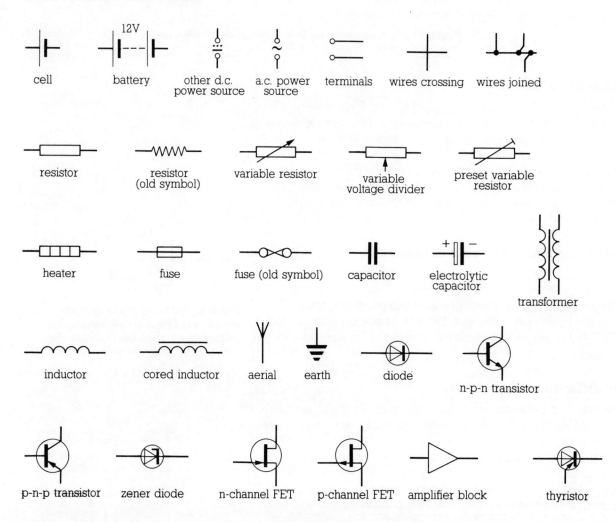

cell   battery   other d.c. power source   a.c. power source   terminals   wires crossing   wires joined

resistor   resistor (old symbol)   variable resistor   variable voltage divider   preset variable resistor

heater   fuse   fuse (old symbol)   capacitor   electrolytic capacitor   transformer

inductor   cored inductor   aerial   earth   diode   n-p-n transistor

p-n-p transistor   zener diode   n-channel FET   p-channel FET   amplifier block   thyristor

B2.2 – Circuit diagram symbols for switches and relays

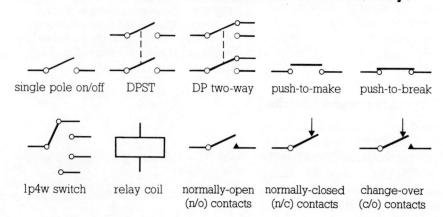

single pole on/off   DPST   DP two-way   push-to-make   push-to-break

1p4w switch   relay coil   normally-open (n/o) contacts   normally-closed (n/c) contacts   change-over (c/o) contacts

B2.3 — Circuit diagram symbols for transducers

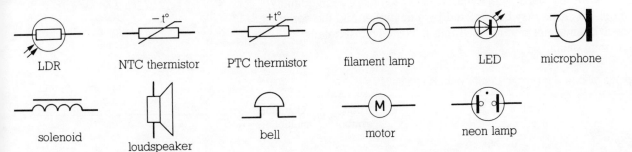

LDR   NTC thermistor   PTC thermistor   filament lamp   LED   microphone

solenoid   loudspeaker   bell   motor   neon lamp

B2.4 — Circuit diagram symbols for test instruments

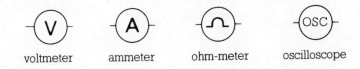

voltmeter   ammeter   ohm-meter   oscilloscope

B2.5 — Symbols for logic circuits

This book uses the 'simplified BS3939' symbols for logic circuits. Other common symbols include Mil-spec and the standard BS3939 symbols. Logic circuits never show any power connections.

Most other digital circuit blocks are shown as squares or rectangles with a label or symbols printed inside. Bistables are shown by a dotted line across the middle of the rectangle, as shown below.

Table B.1 Logic symbols

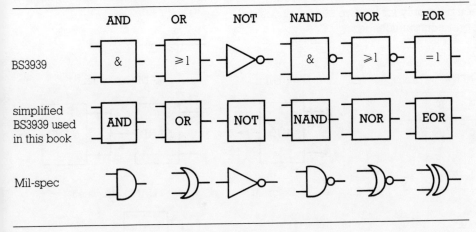

	AND	OR	NOT	NAND	NOR	EOR
BS3939	&	≥1	▷∘	&	≥1	=1
simplified BS3939 used in this book	AND	OR	NOT	NAND	NOR	EOR
Mil-spec						

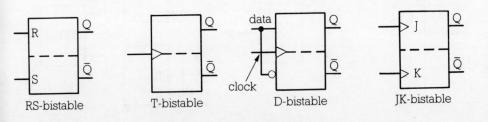

RS-bistable   T-bistable   D-bistable   JK-bistable

Note: for bistables inputs are always on the left. The Q output is from the top half; the 'set' input goes to the top half (a logic 1 at the 'set' input gives Q = logic 1).

B2.6 — Letter symbols for quantities

In equations standard letters are used for quantities. Table B.2 gives a list of electronic quantities, the standard letter symbol used, the unit of each quantity, and the unit symbol. Each unit may be prefixed by a multiplier and the common multipliers for each quantity are also listed. Table B.3 gives more details concerning these multipliers.

Table B.2   Common electrical quantities, their symbols and units

Quantity	Symbol	Unit	Unit symbol	Common multipliers
Current	I	ampere	A	m,μ
Voltage difference	V	volt	V	k,m
Resistance	R	ohm	Ω	k,M
Capacitance	C	farad	F	μ,n,p
Inductance	L	henry	H	m,μ
Power	P	watt	W	k,M,G
Energy	E	joule	J	k,M
Time	t	second	s	m,μ
Period	T	second	s	m,μ
Frequency	f	hertz	Hz	k,M,G

Table B.3   The meaning of multipliers

Multiplier	Prefix	Symbol
$\times 10^{-12}$	pico	p
$\times 10^{-9}$	nano	n
$\times 10^{-6}$	micro	μ
$\times 10^{-3}$	milli	m
$\times 10^{3}$	kilo	k
$\times 10^{6}$	mega	M
$\times 10^{9}$	giga	G

B3 — Logic gates

B3.1 — Digital signals

Digital signals are voltage signals. The value of the voltage is usually one of two values. These values are called logic 1 for the higher value and logic 0 for the lower value. A common value of logic 1 is 5 V and of logic 0 is 0 V. Many practical systems will interpret any voltage above a fixed value (e.g. 2.3 V) as being logic 1 and anything below this value is logic 0.

Digital signal processors are called *logic gates*. The output from any digital device will be only logic 1 or logic 0.

The term digital is sometimes used for circuits that have only a few different outputs. The term digital in this book has been used **only** for the two-state devices. Other devices are described as having 'discrete output voltages'.

B3.2 — AND gates

The AND gate gives a logic 1 output **only** if all its inputs are at logic 1; otherwise the output is logic 0.

(The details to the right are for a two-input AND gate.)

Truth table

A	B	Z
0	0	0
0	1	0
1	0	0
1	1	1

Diagram

NAND equivalent

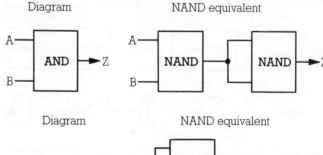

B3.3 — OR gates

The OR gate gives a logic 1 output if **any** of its inputs are at logic 1; otherwise the output is logic 0.

(The details to the right are for a two-input OR gate.)

Truth table

A	B	Z
0	0	0
0	1	1
1	0	1
1	1	1

Diagram

NAND equivalent

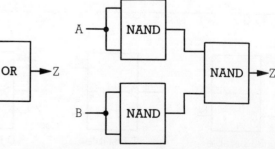

B3.4 — NOT gates

The NOT gate gives a logic 1 output when its input is logic 0 and a logic 0 output when its input is logic 1.

The NOT gate is frequently called an inverter.

Truth table

A	Z
0	1
1	0

Diagram

NAND equivalent

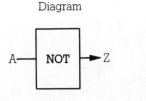
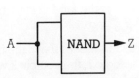

B3.5 — NAND gates

The NAND gate gives a logic 0 output **only** if all its inputs are at logic 1; otherwise it gives logic 1.

(The details to the right are for a two-input NAND gate.)

Truth table

A	B	Z
0	0	1
0	1	1
1	0	1
1	1	0

Diagram

B3.6 — NOR gates

The NOR gate gives a logic 0 output if **any** of its inputs are logic 1; otherwise it gives logic 1.

(The details to the right are for a two-input NOR gate.)

Truth table

A	B	Z
0	0	1
0	1	0
1	0	0
1	1	0

Diagram

NAND equivalent

B3.7 — Exclusive OR gates (EOR)

The Exclusive OR gate gives an output of logic 1 if **only one** of its inputs is logic 1; otherwise it gives logic 0.

(The details to the right are for a two-input EOR gate.)

Truth table

A	B	Z
0	0	0
0	1	1
1	0	1
1	1	0

Diagram

NAND equivalent

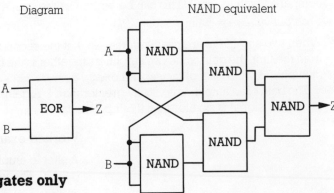

B3.8 — Steps in converting a logic system to NAND gates only

To make a logic system using NAND gates the steps are as follows.

1. Draw up a truth table for the system.
2. Find which lines of the table give the required output.
3. For one of these lines, invert inputs as required and feed the inputs to a NAND gate.
4. Invert the output of the NAND gate.
5. Repeat the last two steps for all the other lines giving the required output.
6. Combine all these lines using an OR gate.
7. Connect all the points requiring the same input to a single input point.
8. Remove all instances where one inverter follows another inverter.

B3.9 — Boolean algebra symbols

Boolean algebra is the mathematics of logic. It is a useful tool for advanced work in digital electronics, but the symbols used are also a useful shorthand for writing down logic statements for simple systems.

The symbols are as follows:

AND is (.), so that 'A and B' is written A.B
OR is (+), so that 'C or D' is written C+D
NOT is shown by a bar over the letter, so that 'not E' is written $\bar{E}$.

The NAND and NOR functions are shown like this:

NAND is written $\overline{A.B}$ NOR is written $\overline{C+D}$

An example of the kind of statement that might be used is:

$A.B + \overline{A}.\overline{B} = Z$

In words this means that if the inputs A and B are both at logic 1 or if A and B are both not at logic 1, then output Z will be at logic 1. (In other words, Z will be at logic 1 if A and B are the same, but not if they are different.) This is the opposite of an Exclusive OR function, and is sometimes called a coincidence gate.

B4 — Amplifiers

B4.1 — Analogue signals

An analogue signal is a signal whose magnitude varies in the same way as the information it represents. Typical examples of analogue signals are the signals produced by a microphone or an LDR.

The magnitude of an analogue signal can be changed by an amplifier. The waveshape of the output from an amplifier is normally the same as the waveshape of the input to the amplifier. Amplifiers are therefore called *analogue devices*.

B4.2 — Gain

The gain of an amplifier is the number of times larger the output of an amplifier is compared with its input. This can be written as the gain equation:

output voltage = gain × input voltage

When two amplifiers are used together so that the second amplifies the signal from the first, the gain of the two amplifiers together is the gain of the first amplifier multiplied by the gain of the second one.

The gain of an amplifier is usually greater than 1. A gain of less than 1 means that the output signal is smaller than the input signal.

Worked examples on the gain equation

A simple amplifier consists of a pre-amplifier of gain 100 and a main amplifier of gain 20. The input signal to the pre-amplifier is 5 mV. What is the gain of the whole system, and what is the voltage of the output signal?

Because there are two amplifiers, the overall gain has to be found first. To find the overall gain, multiply the gains of the two sections.

> overall gain = gain of pre-amp × gain of main amp
> = 100 × 20
> = 2000

(Note that there are no units for gain.)

This value can now be used in the gain equation.

> *output voltage = gain × input voltage*
> = 2000 × 0.005
> = 10 V

Exercise 7 — A signal generator feeds an input of 0.2 V to an amplifier with a gain of 15. What will be the output from the amplifier?

Exercise 8 — A television set uses two identical amplifiers to amplify the vision signal. If each amplifier has a gain of 40, what is the gain of the two amplifiers together?

Exercise 9 — A telephone booster must produce an output signal of 12 V. If the input signal to the booster is 300 mV, what gain must the amplifier have?

B4.3 — Signal inversion

Most amplifiers invert the signal that they amplify. This means that a waveshape appears to be turned upside down by the amplifier, as well as being made larger. For most applications this does not matter because, although the wave is inverted, its shape is still the same. This is called analogue inversion and is not the same as the function of a digital inverter.

When an amplifier inverts a signal, the gain has a minus value. For example, a gain of -2 makes the signal twice the size and also turns it upside down.

B4.4 — Power amplification

An amplifier can amplify voltage, or current, or both. An amplifier used for driving a transducer will be required to provide enough current, and therefore enough power, to make the driver work (see reference section B1.8). An amplifier for a purpose like this is called a power amplifier or driver. The power gain is high, but the voltage gain may be small.

A power amplifier will consume some power itself. This means that it is likely to get hot. In most power amplifiers some of the components will need to be kept cool. Cooling fins known as a *heatsink* are sometimes used.

Electronic power amplifiers giving more than 20 W output are not in common use in simple electronics. If there is a need to switch high power this is usually done by relays or thyristors rather than by integrated circuits or transistors.

B5 — Signal generators

B5.1 — Frequency

When a signal generator produces a regular alternating voltage the number of complete waves per second is called the frequency of the wave. The unit for the measurement of frequency is the hertz (Hz). Other units that are commonly used for measuring frequency are the kilohertz (kHz), megahertz (MHz) and gigahertz (GHz).

The time taken for one complete wave (cycle) is called the period of the wave. Period is measured in seconds. The formula linking frequency and period is:

$$frequency = \frac{1}{period}$$

1 kHz	= 1000 Hz	
1 MHz	= 1000 kHz	= 1 000 000 Hz
1 GHz	= 1000 MHz	= 1 000 000 kHz
		= 1 000 000 000 Hz

Example of the use of the relationship between frequency and period

A waveshape shown on an oscilloscope has four complete cycles (waves) displayed. The time for these four waves is found to be 20 ms. What is the period and what is the frequency of this wave?

To find the period, find the time for one wave. If four waves take 20 ms the period is 5 ms.

To find the frequency use the value for the period and the formula (remember that the time is in milliseconds and must be changed to seconds before it is used in the formula):

$$frequency = \frac{1}{period} = \frac{1}{5 \times 10^{-3}} = \frac{1}{0.005} = 200 \text{ Hz}$$

Exercise 10 — It takes 200 μs for the spot on an oscilloscope screen to go from one side to the other. The trace shows eight complete square waves. Find the period and the frequency of this square wave.

Exercise 11 — What is the period of a 200 kHz radio wave?

B5.2 — Square waves

Square waves are a series of pulses with a waveshape like the one in fig. B.3. Digital systems use square waves. The square wave switches between two voltage levels. The voltage levels can have any value but digital systems usually use 0 V and 5 V or −5 V and +5 V. The amplitude of the square wave is the difference between the two levels.

The time for which the square wave is at its higher level is called the mark-time and the time for which it is at the lower level is called the space-time. If these are equal then the mark-space ratio is 1. Sometimes a mark-space ratio other than 1 is used.

When square waves are used to carry information they are usually not a regular shape. The different mark-times and space-times are the features of the waves that carry the information. Each unit of information carried by the square wave is called a baud (see fig. B.4). A mark or a space can be one or more bauds. The *baud rate* is the maximum number of bits of information that a square wave can carry, and that is twice the maximum frequency of the square wave.

B5.3 — Pulse (square-wave) generators

Pulse generators are of two types, triggered and continuous. Triggered pulse producers are used where a time delay is required, and continuous pulse producers are used where a chain of pulses is needed.

Fig. B.3 The waveshape of a square wave.

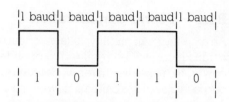

Fig. B.4 The information wave for the binary number 10110, showing the meaning of the term 'baud'.

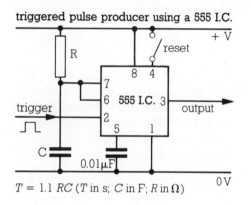

triggered pulse producer using a 555 I.C.

$T = 1.1\,RC$ (T in s; C in F; R in Ω)

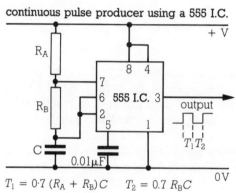

continuous pulse producer using a 555 I.C.

$T_1 = 0.7\,(R_A + R_B)C$ $T_2 = 0.7\,R_B C$

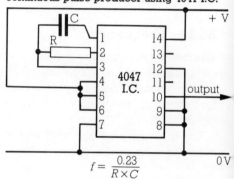

continuous pulse producer using 4047 I.C.

$f = \dfrac{0.23}{R \times C}$

Fig. B.5 (Above) Three simple circuits for pulse producers. The left-hand circuit is a triggered pulse producer. The other two circuits produce continuous chains of pulses.

Three simple practical circuits for pulse producers are shown in fig. B.5. With each diagram is a formula which can be used to find the values of the components for a chosen period of frequency; R is the value of a resistor in ohms (Ω), C is the value of a capacitor in *farads* (F), and T is the period in seconds. Remember that 1 farad is 1 000 000 microfarads (μF).

B5.4 — Sine waves

For analogue systems the basic waveshape is a sine wave. This shape is shown in fig. 6.11. (It is called a sine wave because its shape is the same as the shape of the graph you get when you plot the sine of an angle against the value of the angle.) Any waveshape can be made (synthesised) by mixing various sine waves.

A sine wave is described by its frequency and its amplitude. The amplitude is always changing, so that the amplitude of a sine wave is stated in terms of either the peak voltage (or current), the r.m.s. voltage, or the peak-to-peak voltage. See reference section D3.12 for details.

There are many circuits that will produce sine waves. Fig. B.6 shows one simple, common circuit. In this circuit the frequency depends on the resistors and capacitors used. Most other sine-wave generators use inductors and capacitors to set the frequency of the circuit.

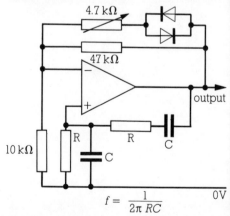

$f = \dfrac{1}{2\pi\,RC}$

Fig. B.6 A simple sine-wave generator using an op-amp. The frequency of the output from this circuit can be found using the formula shown.

7 RESISTORS

All the chapters so far have been about systems and the blocks that are joined to make systems. One look at the working parts of any electronic system will tell you that the blocks are made from a variety of parts connected together. We use the word *components* for the parts that are connected together to make a block or an electrical circuit. Fig. 7.1 is a photograph of a typical circuit board. There are various kinds of components on it. The rectangular blocks with connecting pins along two sides are integrated circuits (usually known as ICs or 'chips'). Resistors are often used in large numbers and usually have coloured bands painted on them. Transistors can be identified by the three wires or pins which they have. All components come in many shapes and sizes, so you cannot always be sure what a component is from its shape or size.

What are resistors used for? In fact they have many uses. They can be used to limit the electric current flowing in a circuit. They can act as voltage dividers. They can be used with some transducers to produce a voltage signal from that transducer. They can control the gain of amplifiers.

What do resistors 'resist'? In simple terms they resist the flow of electricity, but that is not the whole of the story. Before going on to the rest of the story we must know a little more about electric currents.

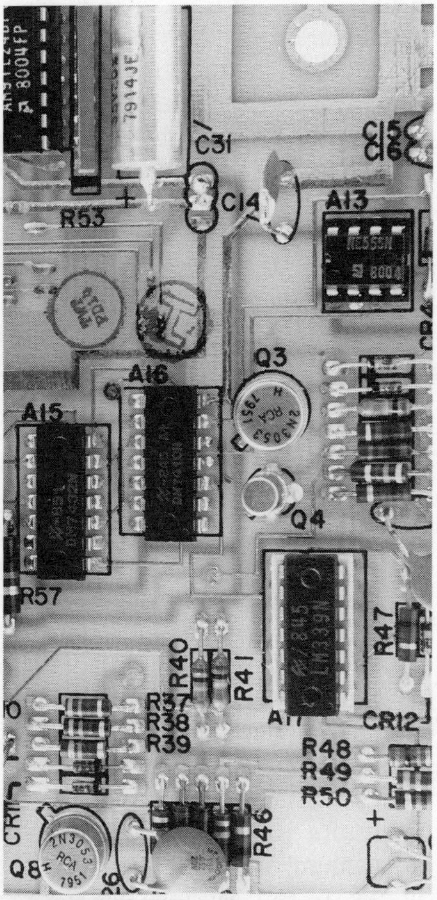

Electric current

Electricity is due to electrons. An electron is one of the particles that make up the atoms of all substances. What we call electricity is the range of effects when these electrons are released from atoms, or when they move from one place to another, or are stored in any way. Whenever something electrical happens, electrons are moving. A flow of electrons is called an *electric current*.

Electric current is measured in amps. A very large number of electrons are on the move when the current is 1 amp. A total of 1.6×10^{19} electrons will pass every point in a circuit every second when there is a current of 1 amp in that circuit. Although this is such a large number, most electric currents we use are often about 1 amp. For example, most light bulbs carry between 0.1 amp and 1 amp, most electronic equipment requires a current of between 1 milliamp (1/1000 or 10^{-3} amps) and 1 amp, and most domestic equipment, such as heaters, vacuum cleaners, refrigerators and dishwashers, takes currents of up to 13 amps. For electronics, where currents are usually less than 1 amp, it is often more convenient to measure the currents in milliamps (10^{-3} amps) or microamps (10^{-6} amps). (See reference section B1, page 51.)

Conductors and insulators

There can only be an electric current in certain types of materials. The ordinary connecting wires in most electrical equipment are made of copper, although there is often a coating of tin on the surface to make soldering easier. Copper is an *electrical conductor*. All metals are

Fig. 7.1 Part of a typical circuit board with several integrated circuits (chips) and resistors. Most components are either resistors or integrated circuits but there are other types of component used as well.

conductors, but electricity will not flow equally easily in every metal. The best conductor is silver, but copper is nearly as good and is normally used in electronics. (Why not use silver?) Overhead cables used for the mains electrical supply are usually made of aluminium, with a strand of steel for extra strength. Although the aluminium conductor needs to be larger than a copper conductor would be, the lower density (mass of unit volume) and lower cost of aluminium compared with copper, are the main reasons for its choice.

Substances that do not allow electricity to flow through them are called *insulators*. In fact no substance is absolutely perfect as an insulator, and some insulators are better than others, but for most purposes the differences can be ignored. Most non-metallic solids and all gases are insulators. The best insulators are plastics such as polythene, p.v.c. and polycarbonate. Although carbon is a non-metal, the common form of it (known to the chemist as graphite but in fact the main constituent of substances such as charcoal) is a conductor.

Pure water conducts electricity to a small extent, and when substances are dissolved in water, the conductivity of it is usually increased, often by a very large amount. It is because of this that electricity can flow through the human body and give an electric shock. The process of conduction in water is not due to electrons alone and chemical changes occur as the electric current passes, often causing corrosion of metals in contact with the water or solution. Solutions that behave in this way are called electrolytes. It is a very good general rule to protect all electrical equipment from water or dampness at all times, and never to handle electrical equipment with moist hands.

There is one group of materials that behave in yet another way to the flow of electricity through them and these are known as *semiconductors*. They are non-metals which are basically insulators, but they become conductors when there are impurities present or when the temperature rises enough to free some electrons within the material. Silicon is the most important of these because it is the basic material from which most transistors and integrated circuits are made, but there are others such as germanium, and gallium arsenide, the substance in many light-emitting diodes (LEDs). Modern electronics depends on the special properties of these materials and the way in which those properties can be varied using different impurities.

Table 7.1 lists the common conductors, semiconductors and insulators used in electronics.

Table 7.1 Common conductors, semi-conductors and insulators

Conductors	
copper	silver
tin	brass
solder	gold
carbon	aluminium
iron (and steel)	

Semiconductors	
silicon	gallium arsenide
germanium	cadmium sulphide

Insulators	
p.v.c	polythene
polycarbonate	polystyrene
nylon	paxolin
bakelite	mica
resin-bonded glass-fibre	

SUMMARY 7A

An electric current is a movement of electrons.

Electric current is measured in amps; one thousandth of an amp is called a milliamp; one millionth of an amp is called a microamp.

Conductors are materials that will allow an electric current to pass. Metals are conductors.

Insulators are substances that an electric current will not pass through. Most non-metallic substances are insulators.

Silicon, germanium and gallium arsenide are semiconductors.

Resistance

An electric current passes through a piece of ordinary copper wire freely. Only a very small quantity of electric power is required to make the current pass. Wires made of other materials behave in the same way, but very fine wires, wires made from mixtures of metals (alloys), and other materials which conduct electricity, all require much more electrical power to drive a current through them. We say that they have *resistance*. Electrical energy is used. The energy used changes from an electrical form into heat.

A *resistor* is any device which is put in an electrical circuit because it has a resistance to electric current.

What controls the amount of resistance a resistor has? If a resistor is made of a metal alloy wire, then the longer the wire, the greater the resistance (because there is more of it for the current to be forced through). The thinner the wire is, the greater its resistance becomes, too, because there is less material for the current to 'squeeze' through. In fact the resistance depends on the area of the cross-section of the wire. If you have two wires of the same length but the diameter of one is half the diameter of the other, the thinner wire has **four times** the resistance of the thicker one.

Resistors used in electronics are rarely made of wire. Tin oxide or carbon are commonly used, and by mixing these substances with other materials, larger or smaller resistances can be obtained. The resistors used in an electronic assembly often all look the same size, but they are manufactured with a very wide range of resistances. The value of the resistance is marked on the outside, usually by means of a code using coloured bands.

Effect of resistance on current and voltage difference

In earlier chapters we used the idea of voltage difference in two ways. We used it as a quantity to measure signals, and also as a measure of what drives a current through a loudspeaker or other transducer. The energy converted by an electric current is directly related to voltage difference.

If a resistor uses up electrical energy, it is worth asking how the voltage difference across any particular resistor affects the current being driven through it. There is a simple rule, and the next few paragraphs describe how you could investigate this rule in the laboratory. The rule itself is printed on the next page.

For the investigation there are two sets of instructions, one to follow if you intend to use batteries and the other to follow if you intend to use a mains-operated power unit. The panel on the right shows you what you will need and fig. 7.2 shows you how to connect the parts together.

In this investigation, the milliammeter is used to measure the electric current. It is called a milliammeter because it measures current in milliamps. The circuit is first connected using the lowest supply voltage (1.5 volts or 5 volts). Read the meter to find the current through the resistor. Write down the voltage difference given by the supply, and the current. Now connect the next higher voltage difference and repeat the procedure; repeat again for the other voltage difference(s).

When you look at the voltage differences and currents that you have written down you should find that doubling the voltage difference (from 1.5 volts to 3 volts, or 5 volts to 10 volts) doubles the current, that trebling the voltage difference trebles the current, and so on. Because there is just one component – the resistor – in the circuit, the voltage difference given by the supply is the same as the voltage difference across the resistor. Thus we can say that the current is *proportional* to the voltage difference across the resistor. If you used a resistor with a different resistance, the current that you would measure in the investigation would

---

Investigation of the effect of resistance on current and voltage

Using batteries as the power supply

You will need:

- 3 or 4 batteries type U2 or U11 which you can connect to give 1.5 V (one battery); 3 V (two batteries); 4.5 V (three batteries) and 6 V (four batteries).
- a milliammeter with 10 mA FSD.
- a resistor with coloured bands as follows:

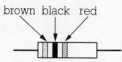

brown black red

- connecting wires.

Using a mains low-voltage power unit

You will need:

- a power unit which can give 5 V, 10 V, and 15 V.
- a milliammeter with 10 mA FSD.
- a resistor with coloured bands as follows:

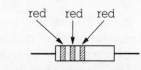

red red red

- connecting wires.

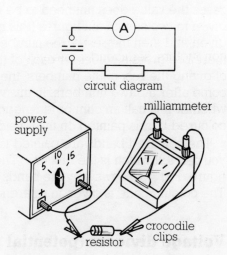

Fig. 7.2 How to connect the components to investigate the rule for voltage, current and resistance. The drawing at the top is the circuit diagram for the circuit shown in pictorial form below it.

not be the same, but the rule would still apply. We use this fact to measure resistance. The unit for measuring resistance is called the *ohm*. This gives us:

the resistance of the resistor (in **ohms**)	=	voltage difference across resistor (in **volts**)	÷	current through resistor (in **amps**)

The rule that current is proportional to voltage difference is an important rule in electronics and is known as *Ohm's law*. The unit of resistance has, as you can see, been named after the person who discovered this law. The rule applies to all metals, provided that the temperature of the metal does not change.

The formula printed above is called the *resistance equation*. It is used when we need to find the value of a resistor, but the value of a resistor is not something that keeps on changing. We usually need to use the formula to find the current when the resistor is connected with a particular voltage difference or to find the voltage difference across the resistor if we know the current through it. The formula can be arranged so that you can use it in this way. Using V for voltage difference, I for current and R for resistance, the three versions are:

$$R = \frac{V}{I} \text{ (as above)} \quad V = I \times R \quad I = \frac{V}{R}$$

You can use the 'triangle trick' shown in fig. 7.3 to remember these formulae.

Fig. 7.3 The triangle trick. Cover up the symbol for the quantity you need to find and the other two will be as they are in the formula. You can remember that V comes at the ∧ of the triangle.

Resistors

Resistors in electronics may have resistances of any value between less than one ohm and tens of millions of ohms. Where the resistance is thousands of ohms the value is usually quoted as so many *kilohms* (kΩ), and where it is millions of ohms the value is usually given in *megohms* (MΩ).

The value of each resistor is marked on the outside by the manufacturer. Usually a colours code is used to mark the value. In most cases the value does not need to be extremely precise, and normally it is given to two significant figures (this means that the first two figures are given and then the rest of the number is written as zeros). The code therefore gives a colour for each of the first two figures, and then, instead of giving the rest of the numbers, the code indicates how many zeros come after the two numbers. In this way the value of any resistor, whether it is half an ohm or ten megohms, can be given using three coloured bands painted on the outside of the resistor.

The coloured bands are painted towards one end of the resistor so that you can tell which is the first one. The band nearest the end is the first figure. Fig. 7.4 shows how the bands are usually arranged on a resistor. The colours code is given in reference section C1.7, page 92.

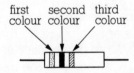

Fig. 7.4 The position of the colour bands on a resistor.

Voltage dividers (potential dividers)

In electronics, we often use two resistors connected across a voltage source to work as a *voltage divider*, or a *potential divider*, as it is also known. Fig. 7.5 shows a simple voltage divider using only two resistors. The resistors are connected *in series* (that means, one after the other) across a 6 volt battery. The problem is to find the voltage difference between the negative rail and the point X where the two resistors join. (Many people would just say 'the voltage at X'. Remember! That means the voltage difference between X and the negative rail. The negative rail is taken as being 0 volts.)

In simple systems it is fairly easy to calculate the voltage difference of a voltage divider. To do this we need to know the total resistance of the two resistors in series. That is easy! To find the total resistance of two (or more) resistors in series their separate values are added together. In fig. 7.5, the two resistors are 1500 ohms and 2200 ohms, so the total resistance is 3700 ohms. This rule can be written as a formula. If the separate resistances are R_1, R_2, R_3, etc, then the total resistance of these connected in series (R_t) is given by:

$$R_t = R_1 + R_2 + R_3 + \ldots$$

The output (signal) voltage in fig. 7.5 is the same fraction of the input voltage as the 1500 ohm signal resistor is of the total resistance. This can be written as a formula as shown below. The formula is sometimes called the voltage divider formula:

$$\frac{\text{signal voltage } (V_{\text{out}})}{\text{supply voltage } (V_{\text{in}})} = \frac{\text{signal resistance}}{\text{total resistance across supply}} = \frac{R_2}{R_1 + R_2}$$

It is often useful to rearrange this formula:

$$V_{\text{out}} = V_{\text{in}} \times \frac{R_2}{R_1 + R_2}$$

Whilst these formulae may be the easiest way of working out currents or voltages in simple cases with a single resistor or two simple values in a voltage divider, there are other ways of working out the effect of resistors in a circuit which you may find easier to use, at least in some cases. One depends on graphs.

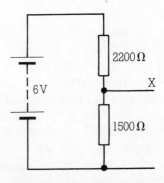

Fig. 7.5 A simple voltage divider. What is the voltage at X?
47

SUMMARY 7B

Semiconductors are substances in which there are conduction electrons as the result of impurities or temperature.

Resistance is a measure of the energy required to drive an electric current through a conductor.

Ohm's law states that the current through a particular resistor is proportional to the voltage difference across the resistor (providing the temperature does not change).

Resistance is measured in ohms. The resistance value in ohms equals the voltage difference in volts divided by the current in amps.

Resistance values are usually marked on resistors using a colours code.

For resistors in series the total resistance is the sum of the resistances of each separate resistor ($R_t = R_1 + R_2 + R_3 + \ldots$).

For a voltage divider the output voltage is given by:

$$\text{output voltage} = \frac{\text{signal resistance}}{\text{total resistance}} \times \text{input voltage}$$

Graphical methods of dealing with resistance

You can start to understand the graphical methods of dealing with resistance by thinking about the results of the investigation of the rule for resistors described earlier in this chapter. If you had plotted your results as a graph you would have got a straight-line graph as shown in fig. 7.6. The straight line is sometimes called a *resistance line*. The graph line in fig. 7.6 is the resistance line for the 1000 ohm resistor. Would the resistance line for the 2000 ohm resistor have a steeper or shallower slope?

48

Let us now apply this idea to the voltage divider shown in fig. 7.4. The graphical method will give us another way of finding the voltage at X.

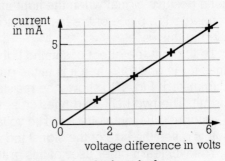

Fig. 7.6 A graph of results from measuring the current through a 1000 Ω resistor (brown, black, red) at various voltages, as in the investigation shown in fig. 7.3.

The first step is to draw graph axes as shown in fig. 7.7. The graph shows two vertical axes, one drawn at zero voltage and the other drawn at the 6 volt supply voltage.

The resistance line for the 1500 ohm resistor is drawn in the normal way, starting from the zero volts axis (one end of this resistor is connected to the zero volts rail).

We do not need to find the points for the resistance line by experiment. We know the line will be straight, and we can use the formula to calculate one point on the line.

Choose easy numbers:

if the current $I = 1$ milliamp (1/1000 amp),

then, using the formula $V = IR$, we can work out that

$V = 1/1000 \times 1500 = 1.5$ volts.

Plot this point on the graph.

Using a ruler draw a straight line through your point and the 0, 0 point. We already know that when there is no voltage there is no current, so we have enough information to draw the graph for the 1500 ohm resistor.

The second step is to do the same for the other resistor.

This time we work **backwards** from the 6 volt axis, because the 2200 ohm resistor is the load resistor connected to the 6 volt rail.

Using the formula again in the same way as before (choosing easy numbers!) we find that for a current of 1 milliamp there is a voltage difference across the resistor of 2.2 volts.

Working backwards from the 6 volt axis we draw the *load line* for this resistor.

It is sometimes helpful, when you start using this method, to write down the voltage differences from the 6 volt axis underneath the original figures, as has been done in fig. 7.8. With practice you will soon find that you can manage without doing this.

Fig. 7.8 shows the complete graph. The point at which the load line and the resistance line cross corresponds to the voltage at X.

You may wonder why the resistance line and load line give you the voltage in this way. All the current in the 2200 ohm resistor must flow through the 1500 ohm resistor as well (nothing else is connected at X). Where the two lines cross, the current in the two resistors is the same. Thus the crossing point tells you **both** the current in the two resistors **and** the voltage where they join.

This kind of voltage divider is used to obtain a signal from transducers such as LDRs and thermistors. The LDR is connected in series with a normal resistor to form a voltage divider. If the LDR is in the dark its resistance is high, but if light shines on the LDR its resistance is low. To get a positive signal when the light intensity increases the LDR must be connected in place of the load resistor. Fig. 7.9 shows the voltage divider used in this case.

To find out the effect of shining light on the LDR we draw two load lines for it: one for when it is in the dark and the other for when it is illuminated. Fig. 7.10 shows the resistance and the load lines for this circuit. The two LDR load lines cross the resistance line for the 1500 ohm resistor at different voltages. The voltage difference between these two points gives the size of the signal the LDR will give.

You will learn other uses of this graphical method for finding out what is happening in an electronic circuit in the chapter on transistor circuits (chapter 11).

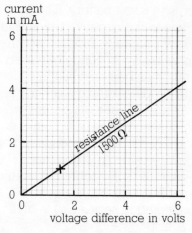

Fig. 7.7 The first stage in finding the voltage at the point X in fig. 7.5. The resistance line for the 1500 Ω resistor has been drawn.

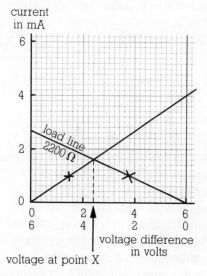

Fig. 7.8 The completed load line diagram for the voltage divider drawn in fig. 7.5. The voltage where the resistance line crosses the load line gives the voltage at X.

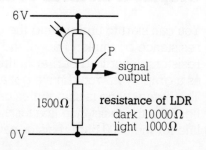

Fig. 7.9 Using a potential divider to obtain a signal from an LDR.

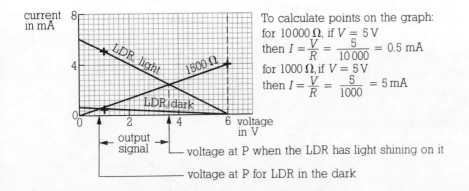

To calculate points on the graph:
for $10\,000\,\Omega$, if $V = 5\,V$
then $I = \dfrac{V}{R} = \dfrac{5}{10\,000} = 0.5\,mA$
for $1000\,\Omega$, if $V = 5\,V$
then $I = \dfrac{V}{R} = \dfrac{5}{1000} = 5\,mA$

Fig. 7.10 The load lines and calculations of the signal for a circuit in which a potential divider is used to obtain a signal from an LDR.

Connecting a load to a voltage divider

So far we have assumed that nothing is connected to X in fig. 7.5 or to P in fig. 7.9. In practice there will be a component connected there, because we want the signal that is produced to do something useful. Most of the components that we might connect there will behave like resistors. This means that we can work out what happens by thinking about the effect that connecting another resistor might have. Fig. 7.11 shows the basic idea.

How will the 3300 ohm resistor shown in fig. 7.11 affect the voltage divider? The current through the 2200 ohm resistor has two possible paths when it gets to X. It could go through the 1500 ohm resistor or it could go through the 3300 ohm resistor. In fact, the current will divide, and some will go each way. More will go through the 1500 ohm resistor than the 3300 ohm resistor, because 1500 ohms is the lower resistance. However, because there is a second path for some of the current, the total resistance of the bottom half of the voltage divider will be less than 1500 ohms. Resistors connected in this way are said to be *in parallel*. (Will the result of this be to make the voltage at X lower or higher than before, or will it be unchanged?)

What happens at X is an example of a very important principle. If you measure the current in the 1500 ohm resistor and the current in the 3300 ohm resistor, and add them together, the sum will be the same current as in the 2200 ohm resistor. Whenever there is a junction in a circuit, the sum of all the currents flowing into that junction is **always** equal to the sum of all the currents flowing away from the junction. This is called Kirchhoff's current law, but it is more important to remember the idea than to remember its name.

One way to work out what is happening in the circuit shown in fig. 7.11 is to work out the effective resistance of the two resistors in parallel; in other words, work out the value of a single resistor that could be put in place of both the 1500 ohm resistor and the 3300 ohm resistor without affecting the voltage at X. The next section is about the formula for working out the effective resistance of two resistors in parallel.

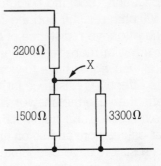

Fig. 7.11 A resistor has been connected to point X in fig. 7.5 to represent the circuit that uses the signal from the potential divider. The resistor could have any value, but to explain what happens a value of 3300 Ω has been chosen.

Whenever there is a junction in a circuit, the sum of all the currents flowing into that junction is ALWAYS equal to the sum of all the currents flowing away from the junction.

The effective resistance of resistors in parallel

We have already seen that if a number of resistors are connected in series, the total resistance is found by adding together the resistances of all the individual resistors. But how can we calculate the resistance in circuits like those in fig. 7.11 where there are resistors in parallel?

Where two resistors are in parallel the effective resistance of the pair is less than the resistance of either resistor. This is because there are two paths for the electric current to flow through, making it easier for the current to pass. With more than two resistors in parallel the effective resistance is less than the smallest individual resistor.

The formula for working out the effective resistance (R_{eff}) of two resistors (with resistances R_1 and R_2) in parallel is as follows:

$$\boxed{\begin{array}{c} \text{effective} \\ \text{resistance} \end{array}} = \frac{\text{product of the two resistors (i.e. values multiplied)}}{\text{sum of the two resistors (i.e. values added)}}$$

which is the same as:

$$R_{eff} = \frac{R_1 \times R_2}{R_1 + R_2} \quad \left(\frac{\text{product}}{\text{sum}} \right)$$

You can remember which way up the formula is written by remembering that the answer is (nearly always) greater than 1. Multiplying two numbers gives a larger value than adding them so the top term is the multiplication. (Looking back at fig. 7.11, the two resistors in parallel are the 1500 ohm resistor and the 3300 ohm resistor. Use the formula to check that the effective resistance of these two resistors is 1030 ohms.)

For three or more resistors in parallel, you would have to work out the effective resistance for two of them, then use the answer with the next resistor and do a second, similar calculation, and so on until all the resistors have been taken into account. Examples of this kind of calculation and further information about dealing with resistors in series and in parallel are given in reference sections C1.10, C1.11 and C1.12.

SUMMARY 7C

A resistance line is the graph of current against voltage difference for a resistor.

In a voltage divider, the load is the resistor or other component that produces the output. It is most often connected between the positive supply rail and the junction where the signal output is connected.

A load line is a graph of the current through the load against the signal output voltage.

The output voltage of a voltage divider is found by plotting the load line and resistance line and finding the point where they cross.

A voltage divider is used to get a signal from an LDR or a thermistor.

When resistors are in parallel the total current is the sum of the currents in each resistor.

At any junction in a circuit the sum of all the currents flowing into the junction must equal the sum of all the currents flowing out of the junction.

When two resistors are connected in parallel the effective resistance of the combination is equal to:

$$\frac{R_1 \times R_2}{R_1 + R_2} \quad \left(\frac{\text{product}}{\text{sum}} \right)$$

8 DIODES

What makes a signal go from the output of one block to the input of the next one, but not backwards from the input to the previous output? In many cases it is the fact that the power supply for the signal is part of the block that produces the signal. However, sometimes we have to include a component which will only allow the signal to go one way. This component is called a *diode*.

A diode is a component that will allow an electric current to pass through it in one direction but will not allow an electric current through it in the opposite direction. Fig. 8.1 illustrates this using diagrams of a simple experiment you could use to show the effect. This arrangement is a good way of testing a diode, so long as the lamp only takes a small current.

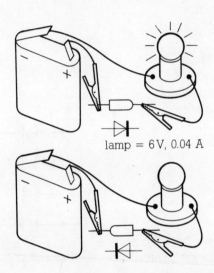

lamp = 6 V, 0.04 A

Fig. 8.1 Testing a diode using a lamp and battery. The lamp will light with the diode connected one way round but it will not light if the diode is connected the other way round. If the lamp does not light whichever way the diode is connected, 51 what **four** faults are possible?

Diodes are used in many ways in electronic circuits. They are used for steering currents in the right way (such as making the current go to an input but not back from the input to the output of the previous block). They are used to protect circuits from unwanted currents, and to prevent power supplies being connected the wrong way round. They can be used as *demodulators* for obtaining the wanted signals from radio waves. Diodes are used in large numbers to convert a.c. power supplies into d.c. power supplies. This is an important use because the mains supply is a.c. and almost all electronic circuits need d.c.. There are also special diodes that give out light, called *light-emitting diodes*, or *LEDs* for short.

Fig. 8.2 shows a selection of common diodes. All these diodes must be connected the right way round. The case of the diode is therefore made so that it is easy to identify which way the diode should be connected. One end may be rounded, or have coloured spots or rings painted on it. For larger diodes, one of the connections is the metal case of the diode. To find out which connection is which you have either to do a simple test on the diode before you use it or to look up the information in data tables. Two diodes may **look** the same but may conduct electricity in opposite directions.

If you test the diode you can use the technique shown in fig. 8.1. You could also use an ohm-meter, in which case the meter will indicate a low

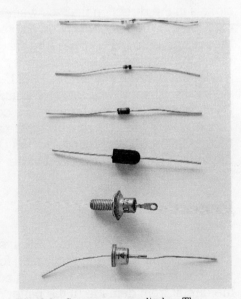

Fig. 8.2 Some common diodes. The larger diodes are used for converting a.c. into d.c, where large currents are used. The small diodes are used for steering or demodulating signals.

resistance when the diode is tested one way round and a very high resistance when it is tested the other way round. However, you may not be able to work out which way round to connect a diode in its circuit by testing it with an ohmmeter. This is because, in some multimeters, the red terminal is negative and the black terminal is positive when it is switched to the ohms ranges.

The symbol used for a diode in a circuit diagram has to show you the way in which the current can pass. Fig. 8.3 shows the symbol. You will notice that it looks like an arrow drawn on the circuit line. This 'arrow' tells you the direction in which the current will pass. (Electrons move through the diode in the opposite direction. If you do not know why this is turn to reference section B1.2 to find out.)

The side of the diode where the current enters is known as the *anode*. The side of the diode where the current leaves is called the *cathode* (sometimes spelt kathode). If you remember the saying 'let Ann in but put the cat out' it will help you to remember that current passes **out** of the diode at the **cat**hode.

The one-way property of a diode comes from the semiconductor that is used to make it. You learnt in the last chapter that semiconductors conduct electricity because of the effect that small amounts of impurity present in the semiconductor have.

There are two kinds of impurity that can affect semiconductors. These are known as p-type impurities and n-type impurities. If a piece of a semiconductor, such as silicon, is made with part of the silicon having p-type impurity and the rest having n-type impurity, then current will pass across the junction between the two layers one way but not the other. The anode of the diode is the p-type side of the junction in the diode, and the cathode is the n-type side of the junction.

Steering diodes

At the start of this chapter, diodes were introduced as devices that stop a signal going the wrong way. This is one example of using a diode to steer signals in the direction that you want them to go. There are lots of other examples of diodes being used as *steering diodes*. For example, these diodes can be used to make sure that you can not connect a battery to electronic equipment the wrong way round. Four diodes are used, as shown in fig. 8.4. If you connect the battery one way round, diode D1 steers the current to the positive connection of the equipment and diode D4 steers current from the negative connection back to the battery. Diode D2 prevents current going the wrong way. If you connect the battery the other way round, diodes D2 and D3 steer the current and diode D4 blocks the unwanted route.

Protection diodes

Diodes can be used to protect circuits or components in a number of ways. For example, instead of using four diodes to steer current, whichever way round the battery is connected, it is cheaper to protect the circuit from damage (if the battery is connected the wrong way) by using one diode that will stop current flowing in the wrong direction. Fig. 8.5 shows a diode used in this way.

It is quite common to use diodes to protect expensive meters, but this uses another property of diodes as well. Although diodes conduct very

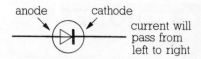

Fig. 8.3 The circuit symbol for a diode. The arrow shows the direction of current in the diode. The circle is not always drawn.

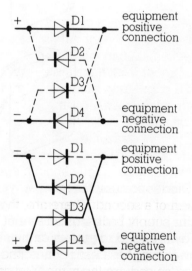

Fig. 8.4 Diodes arranged to steer current to the correct terminals of a piece of equipment regardless of which way round the battery is connected.

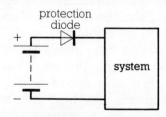

Fig. 8.5 A protection diode in the power-supply lead to a system. If the battery is connected the wrong way round, no current can flow because of this diode.

well in the forward direction, there is a voltage difference across the diode when the current is flowing. In a resistor, the voltage difference depends on the current, but diodes do not obey Ohm's law and you cannot apply the resistance equation to them. The voltage difference across a diode is hardly affected by the current at all. It depends on what the diode is made of. For a silicon diode, the voltage difference is about 0.7 volts whether the diode is large or small, or whether the current is a few milliamps or several amps.

Most meters only need a voltage difference of about 0.1 volt to get full scale deflection. Meters are not usually harmed by 0.7 volts, even though the meter needle goes right to the end of the scale. Larger voltages will spoil the meter. As there must be 0.7 volts to get current through a diode, connecting a diode in parallel with the meter will have no effect so long as the meter is used correctly. If the voltage difference exceeds 0.7 volts the diode conducts and so protects the meter. A second diode can be connected in parallel the other way round and this will protect the meter from being connected the wrong way round. Fig. 8.6 shows the arrangement.

Another use of protection diodes is with relays. Details of this type of arrangement are included in the section on relays in chapter 9.

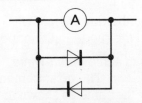

Fig. 8.6 Protecting a meter from voltages and currents beyond the normal range of the meter. Can you explain how this circuit protects the meter from too much current, as well as from too large a voltage?
[52]

Converting a.c. to d.c.

The mains electricity supply is an *alternating current* supply. It is often called the mains a.c. supply. Alternating current is electric current which passes round the circuit first in one direction, then in the reverse direction, then in the first direction again, and so on. However, electronic equipment must have a d.c. (*direct current*) supply. It is easy to turn a.c. into d.c. by using diodes. When diodes are used for this purpose they are often called *rectifiers*, and the process of turning a.c. into d.c. is called *rectification*.

If you measure the voltage of the mains supply over a period you find that, although it is called a 240 volt supply, the actual voltage varies as shown in fig. 8.7. You cannot measure this with an ordinary voltmeter because one complete wave, or *cycle* as it is called, takes only one fiftieth of a second. There are, therefore, fifty cycles each second and the mains supply is described as a *50 hertz* a.c. supply.

Rectifying a.c. represents the same problem as protecting a system from damage if a battery is connected the wrong way round, and the circuits used are the same. You can either use one diode and stop negative voltages reaching the system, or you can use four diodes and steer both the positive half of the cycles and the negative half of the cycles the same way through the system. When you use only one diode the method is called *half-wave rectification*. This is because only the positive half of the wave gets through. This is illustrated in fig. 8.8.

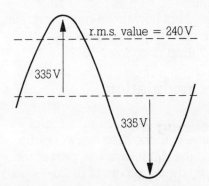

Fig. 8.7 The waveform of the mains supply. Although this is called a 240 V 50 Hz supply, the maximum voltage difference is about 335 V.

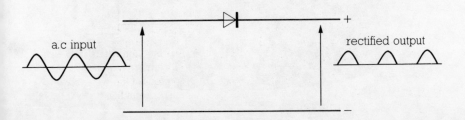

Fig. 8.8 Half-wave rectification of a.c. What would happen if the diode were the other way round (current flowing from right to left in the circuit diagram)?
[53]

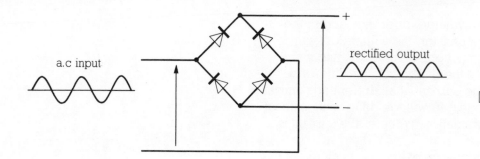

a.c input

rectified output

Fig. 8.9 A bridge rectifier arrangement giving full-wave rectification. Can you show that this arrangement is exactly the same as the arrangement shown in 54 fig. 8.4?

Fig. 8.10 A crystal set from 1923. The crystal and cat's whisker can be seen on the top of the set.

The alternative is to use four diodes to achieve *full-wave rectification*. The arrangement is exactly the same as shown in fig. 8.4, except that an a.c. supply replaces the battery. This arrangement is often called a *bridge rectifier*, and is usually drawn as shown in fig. 8.9.

To get a d.c. supply suitable for electronic equipment you have to smooth out the variations in voltage as well as rectify the a.c. Details of how these diode circuits are used in power units are included in chapter 13.

Demodulation

The start of modern electronics came with the discovery of radio, and the diode was one part of the early development of radio (although it was not called a diode in those days). In order to listen to a radio programme you have to use some means of extracting the sound information from the radio waves. This process is called *demodulation* (in the early days of radio it was known as 'detection'). How it was discovered that a fine wire held on the surface of crystals of certain minerals would demodulate radio waves has long been forgotten (fig. 8.10) but that arrangement of a crystal and a fine wire (called a 'cat's whisker') is a crude diode.

Fig. 8.10 shows a typical crystal set (actual size) from the early days of radio. It needed an aerial, an earth connection, and earphones. It was tuned by moving the slider on the coil.

Modern radio circuits use semiconductor diodes made from silicon or germanium, but the principle is much the same. Chapters 16 and 17 explain demodulation in more detail.

Choosing the right diode

When a diode is used for rectifying a.c, the current through the diode can be large. Diodes used for demodulation only have to deal with very small currents. Rectifying diodes will therefore produce much more heating when they are in use than those used for demodulation. When choosing a diode remember that it has to be capable of carrying the maximum current that might be present in the circuit.

When a diode has to carry several amps (or more), the heating may be such that the inside of the diode gets very hot. If the temperature gets too high the diode will be damaged. To prevent this, high-current diodes are made with metal cases that can be bolted firmly to another piece of metal. The metal acts as a *heat sink*. Because metals are good conductors of heat, heat is carried away from the diode itself, and because the heat sink has a large surface area it can lose heat to the surrounding air in large quantities.

A diode has not only to carry the forward current but has also to stop any reverse current. When the diode is used to prevent a reverse current it is acting as an insulator. Different diodes vary in the way in which they can behave as an insulator.

The voltage difference across a diode in the forward direction is only 0.7 volts. However, the voltage difference across the diode in the reverse direction, when the diode is not conducting, is the full voltage of the supply, or even more. If the diode is being used together with a d.c. smoother to rectify the mains, there can be as much as 700 volts across the diode, even though it is connected to the 240 volt mains supply.

The insulation of the diode must be able to withstand this voltage difference when the voltage is in the reverse direction. The insulating property of the diode is quoted as the *peak inverse voltage* (PIV) rating. This PIV rating is the absolute maximum voltage the diode can withstand in the reverse direction, and this rating must never be exceeded.

The characteristics of a diode can be represented by a graph. The graph must show both the forward and the reverse behaviour of the diode. Fig. 8.11 is a typical diode characteristic. Note that the graph scales are not the same to the left and to the right of the zero, nor are they the same upwards and downwards.

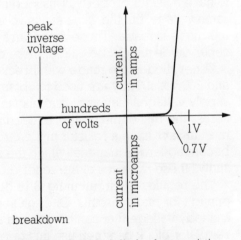

Fig. 8.11 A typical diode characteristic curve. Note that the four axes have difference scales.

Light-emitting diodes

Most diodes are made of silicon. Other semiconductors can also be used. A few of these semiconductors emit light when electricity passes through the diode. A substance called gallium arsenide is used for making light-emitting diodes, and these diodes can be used for indicator lamps and seven-segment displays (see reference sections A2.15 and A2.16).

Light-emitting diodes (LEDs) can easily be damaged if they are not used correctly. They will be damaged if the current is too large, but they will also be damaged when they are not conducting if the reverse voltage difference is too large. Most LEDs will only withstand a reverse voltage difference of about 5 volts, so the circuit has to be arranged so that there is never more than 5 volts across the diode. Alternatively, the diode can be protected by putting it in series with a normal diode. To prevent too much current, there must be a resistor in series with the diode too. Fig. 8.12 shows the two possible arrangements for protecting an LED.

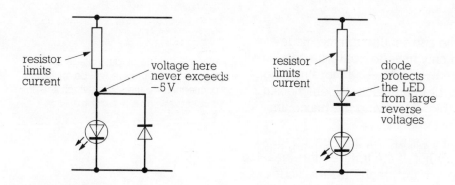

Fig. 8.12 An LED must always be protected from currents which are too large, and from reverse voltages of more than 5 V. The left-hand arrangement is used where large reverse voltages cannot occur . Where these are possible, the right-hand arrangement is used.

Zener diodes

For a normal diode, if you exceed the peak inverse voltage (PIV) rating, the diode will be destroyed. Once the insulation of the diode junction has broken down there is nothing to prevent the current and the diode just burns out. It is possible to make diodes that can withstand quite a lot of heating when the diode breaks down, and these diodes have been found to have a useful property. This kind of diode always breaks down at the same voltage, but the value of this voltage will depend on the way in which the diode is made. These diodes are called *zener diodes*. (Some types of zener diode should be called, more correctly, *avalanche diodes*.)

Zener diodes are made with breakdown voltages between 2.7 volts and 200 volts. They are used to obtain steady voltages in circuits where supply voltages may vary, and also to prevent the voltage difference across the rest of the system exceeding a chosen value. Zener diodes must always have a resistor in the circuit; this will prevent the current becoming larger than that which the zener diode can withstand. Fig. 8.13 shows these two uses of the zener diode.

The regulating circuit in fig. 8.13 does not keep the d.c. voltage steady enough for many circuits. One solution is to use a zener diode to produce a steady voltage that can be used as a *reference voltage*. A *voltage regulator* block can then use this reference voltage in a circuit which can compare that voltage with the input voltage from the power supply, and produce the steady voltage that is required.

Regulated power supplies all use this kind of system. Although it sounds much more complicated than the zener diode used alone, the

varying d.c. input voltage

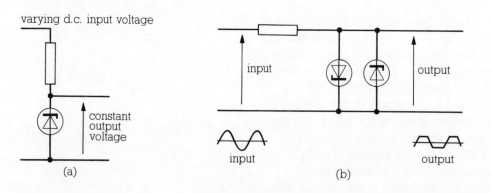

Fig. 8.13 Two typical uses of the zener diode. In the left-hand circuit the diode is acting as a voltage regulator, so that the output voltage is unaffected by variations in the power supply voltage. In the right-hand circuit the diodes prevent the voltage at the output exceeding the required value. (Note the symbol for the zener diode.)

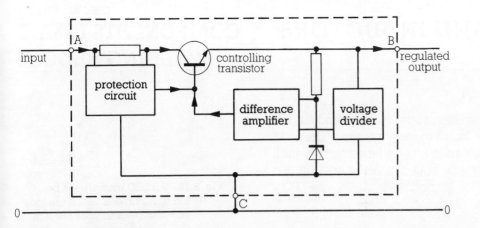

input

A

controlling transistor

protection circuit

difference amplifier

voltage divider

B regulated output

0

C

0

Fig. 8.14 The block diagram of a complete voltage regulator. All of this system is contained within a single chip, so that when you use a regulator all you have to do is make three connections (marked A, B, and C on the block diagram). If the output voltage is adjustable then there will be an extra connection for the signal which sets the output to the desired voltage.

whole regulator can be made as an integrated circuit on a single chip. Fig. 8.14 is a block diagram of a complete voltage regulator. (Voltage regulators are sometimes called *stabilisers*.)

When you buy regulators there are two types from which to choose. Some are designed to give one specific voltage, such as 5 volts or 12 volts. The other type has a variable control which enables the regulator to be set to any voltage you might want.

There is one other thing to be considered when choosing a regulator. They must be able to carry the current required without overheating. Like diodes, regulators designed to carry large currents are usually fixed to heat sinks.

SUMMARY 8

A diode is a component which can carry a current in one direction only.

Diodes are used for steering signals, protecting components, demodulating radio signals, and rectifying a.c.

LEDs are diodes which emit light when a current passes through them.

The current enters a diode at the anode and leaves the diode at the cathode.

When a silicon diode is conducting there is a voltage difference of approximately 0.7 volts across it.

Half-wave rectification is the conversion of a.c. to d.c, which uses only one half of the a.c. cycle.

Full-wave rectification involves steering both halves of the a.c. cycle to give a d.c. output. A bridge circuit of four diodes is usually used.

Diodes have two critical ratings: the maximum current they can carry and the peak inverse voltage they are able to withstand.

A zener diode is a diode designed to give a constant voltage difference for reference or protection purposes.

A voltage regulator is a chip designed to have the same function as a zener diode but to give a much more constant output voltage.

9 CAPACITORS AND INDUCTORS

Resistors are part of every electronic system, together with transistors or integrated circuits (chips). Diodes are found in most systems. There are two other main groups of components, capacitors and inductors, which are also important in many kinds of system. This chapter is about these two types of component.

Capacitors

Capacitors come in all sorts of shapes and sizes. The photograph (fig. 9.1) shows a few typical capacitors. Fig. 9.2 shows the circuit symbols used for capacitors.

A common type of capacitor consists of two strips of thin metal foil and two strips of thin plastic rolled up so that the two pieces of metal never touch (see fig. 9.3). All capacitors are made of two metal 'plates' insulated from one another in some way. As electricity does not flow through plastic or any other insulator, what do capacitors do?

Capacitors store electricity. The metal plates soak up electrons. But, unlike paper soaking up water, a plate will only soak up electrons (which are, remember, negative) if the other plate in the capacitor is positive. The electrons are attracted into the capacitor by the positive plate but the insulator stops the electrons getting to the positive plate.

Where a very large capacity to store electricity is needed, *electrolytic capacitors* are used. In these capacitors the insulator is a very thin layer formed on the surface of the metal by a chemical reaction caused by the electricity. The chemical reaction only occurs on the positive plate. To be able to use this kind of capacitor one plate must be positive all the time, so that this type of capacitor has to be connected the correct way round. One of the connections on an electrolytic capacitor is usually labelled with a plus (+) or a minus (−) sign, but if it is not, then it is safe to assume that the outer metal casing of the capacitor is the negative connection.

The capacity of practical capacitors for storing electricity is measured in *microfarads*. Details are included in reference section C3.

This property of a capacitor to store electricity is used, for example, in smoothing the direct current obtained when alternating current has been rectified using diodes. (Why does the d.c. need smoothing? Refer back to the last chapter if you do not know.)

Wherever a voltage difference needs to be kept steady, a capacitor may be used. They are used to prevent stray pulses from outside interfering with the pulses in a computer. Whenever motors, powerful heaters or fluorescent lights are turned on, there is a change in the mains voltage for a fraction of a second. To remove this interference a capacitor is used. The interference pulse is cancelled out by electricity flowing in to or out of the capacitor.

Capacitors used for d.c. blocking

Capacitors have a more surprising use with alternating currents. Although electricity cannot get through the insulator, capacitors behave

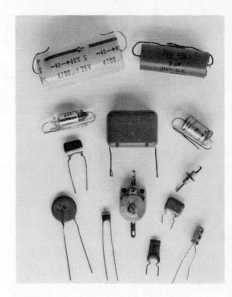

Fig. 9.1 Some of the different types of capacitors used in modern electronic equipment.

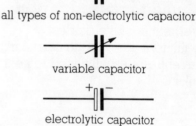

all types of non-electrolytic capacitor

variable capacitor

electrolytic capacitor

Fig. 9.2 The circuit symbols used for various types of capacitor. Although capacitors are made in a number of different ways only electrolytic capacitors have a different symbol.

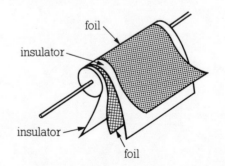

Fig. 9.3 A capacitor consists of two metal 'plates', separated by an insulator. Many capacitors are manufactured by rolling up two strips of metal foil separated by two strips of thin plastic. One connecting wire is connected to each piece of foil.

as though a.c. can get through. The higher the frequency of the a.c, the more does it seem that a.c. goes through. The way in which it works is to do with the physics of electric charges and metal plates close to one another. All you need to know is that capacitors behave as though a.c. passes through them. This property of a capacitor is called *reactance*. It can be used to separate alternating currents from direct currents and to send them different ways. Here are two simple uses of this idea.

In a standard telephone there are four different sub-systems. These are for: (i) dialling; (ii) talking; (iii) listening; and (iv) ringing the bell when a call comes in.

Dialling, talking and listening use d.c. supply, but the bell uses a.c. The a.c. signal is sent along the same two wires as the d.c. supply. Inside the telephone the bell is connected to the two wires through a capacitor (and also through a switch which stops the bell ringing when you pick up the phone). Fig. 9.4 shows the circuit.

The second example is found in hi-fi systems. In most hi-fi amplifiers the output to the loudspeaker is taken from the common line and from the junction between two transistor power amplifiers connected in series. This junction is, on average, at half the power-supply voltage (typically a voltage difference of 20 volts between this point and the common line). The loudspeaker would therefore have a large d.c. current through it, short-circuiting one of the two amplifiers (and not doing the loudspeaker much good either!). A capacitor blocks the d.c. but allows the a.c. signals for the loudspeaker to pass. This capacitor would be a large electrolytic capacitor and must be connected the correct way round. Fig. 9.5 shows the basic circuit.

Capacitors used for timing

Most electrical timing circuits use capacitors. Capacitors behave as electron storage tanks. If the tank fills slowly, it takes a long time. If it fills quickly the time needed to fill the tank is less. Resistors control the flow of electrons. If the current charging a capacitor flows to it through a high resistance the capacitor will take a long time to charge up. If the resistance is low the capacitor charges more quickly.

You can easily test this idea if you have the necessary laboratory equipment. Fig. 9.6 shows the basic timer system. The capacitor is charged by a current from the power supply through the timing resistor. The voltage difference across the capacitor is used as one signal to a comparator. The indicator shows when the comparator output changes over.

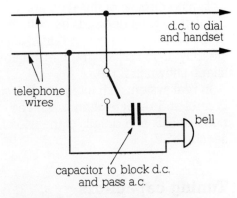

Fig. 9.4 The basic circuit used to separate the a.c. for the bell from the d.c. needed for the other circuits inside a telephone. (When you speak into the microphone you produce alternating current signals. Why do these travel along the telephone wires, instead of being short-circuited through the bell and 56 capacitor?)

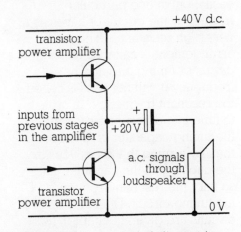

Fig. 9.5 Using an electrolytic capacitor to prevent d.c. flowing through the loudspeaker of a hi-fi amplifier. What would happen if this capacitor were connected the other way round (with + on 57 the right)?

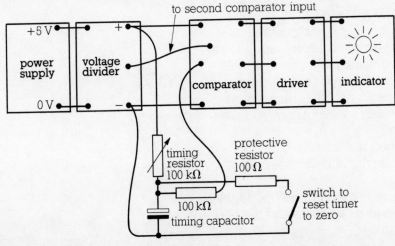

Fig. 9.6 A simple timing circuit using a capacitor. To investigate this circuit you should start with both the timing resistor and the comparator control set at the middle of their range. Close switch S and then open it again. If the timing capacitor is 100 μF, it should take about 5 s after switch S is opened before the indicator changes over. You can then check the effects of varying the timing resistor, adjusting the comparator control, and using 47 μF or 220 μF capacitors instead of the 100 μF capacitor.

Timing circuits of this type are usually called *RC circuits*. The time delay they give depends on both the value of the capacitor and the value of the resistor. The voltage difference across the capacitor does not rise steadily. If you plot a graph of voltage difference against time it has the shape shown in fig. 9.7.

In real systems, an integrated circuit containing the comparator, control and reset is often used. The commonest type has the type number 555, and details of the use of this chip are given in reference section B5.3.

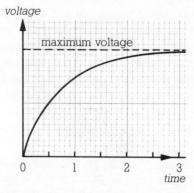

Fig. 9.7 The timing curve for an RC timer. The number of milliseconds it takes for the voltage difference to reach two thirds of the maximum value is equal to the resistance of R (in kΩ) multiplied by the capacitance (in μF). It takes twice this time for the voltage difference to reach 90 per cent of the full voltage difference given by the power supply.

Tuning capacitors

There is one other way in which capacitors can be used. When you turn the knob or dial on a radio to find a particular station, that knob or dial is usually operating a variable capacitor. The capacitor is used in a circuit with an inductor. (Inductors are described in the next section of this chapter.) When the radio signals collected by the aerial reach the circuits of the radio they are alternating currents which alternate at very high frequencies. The capacitor and inductor will pass most frequencies easily, but at one particular frequency the circuit behaves as a very high resistance. This arrangement is called a *resonant circuit* or tuning circuit. The frequency it will not pass is called the resonant frequency. In order to tune into different radio stations the tuning capacitor is made so that, by turning the knob, you vary the capacity of the capacitor and so vary the resonant frequency of the tuning circuit. Details of tuning circuits are given in chapter 18.

> **SUMMARY 9A**
>
> Capacitors store electric charge. The quantity of charge stored depends on the capacity and the voltage difference.
>
> Capacity is measured in farads but the capacity of practical capacitors is measured in microfarads (sometimes nanofarads or picofarads).
>
> Direct current (d.c.) will not flow in a capacitor, but a.c. 'passes' through a capacitor.
>
> Capacitors are either electrolytic or non-electrolytic. Electrolytic capacitors must be connected the correct way round. Electrolytic capacitors are used where a large capacitance is required.
>
> Capacitors are used for smoothing, for suppressing interference, for blocking d.c. and for separating d.c. from a.c.
>
> Timing circuits use capacitors with resistors.
>
> Tuning circuits are circuits that are resonant at one frequency and use a capacitor together with an inductor.

Inductors

An inductor is a coil of insulated wire. In high-value inductors the coil is fitted on an iron frame called a core. Nowadays a substance called ferrite is often used instead of iron. Ferrite is a hard black magnetic material.

You have already met some uses of inductors. The tuner in a radio uses an inductor, together with a capacitor. You might not have realised that some transducers (for example, the loudspeaker) are inductors too. Can you think of any other examples of inductors?

The special property of an inductor is called *inductance*. Inductance is measured in *henries*. Inductors with iron or ferrite cores typically have inductances in the range 0.1 to 1 henry.

Inductors used for tuners and other applications with radio frequencies do not normally need to have inductances as large as these and they are usually coils of wire with no iron or ferrite core.

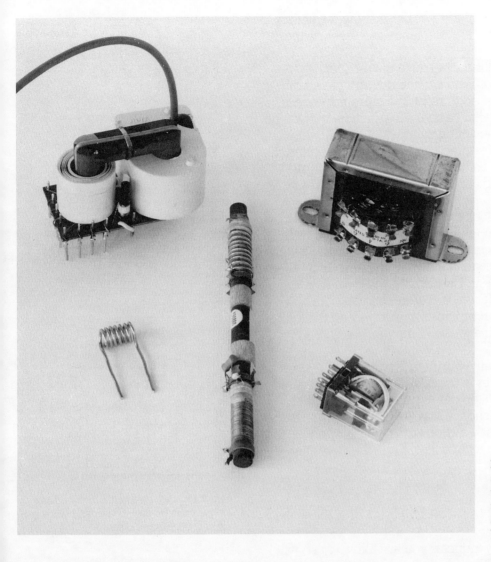

Fig. 9.8 Some typical inductors. They are: (*top left*) a high-voltage transformer used in televisions; (*top right*) a mains transformer; (*centre*) a ferrite rod radio aerial; (*bottom left*) a tuning coil from a VHF radio; and (*bottom right*) a relay.

Fig. 9.8 shows some typical inductors found in electronic equipment. Fig. 9.9 gives the symbols used for some types of inductor.

Whereas resistors and capacitors are made and sold in a large range of standard values, inductors are often specially designed for a particular circuit. Inductors are much more costly to make than resistors and capacitors, or even integrated circuits. Inductors are not used as frequently as other components.

The next two sections deal with two common uses of inductors and also explain how they operate. The chapter on power supplies (chapter 13) gives some of the basic properties of transformers, which are also a type of inductor.

Blocking a.c. using inductors

In the earlier part of this chapter we found that a capacitor blocks d.c. but because of its reactance it 'passes' a.c. Inductors also have a reactance for a.c, but they behave in a different way.

As an inductor is only a piece of coiled-up wire, it will pass d.c. easily. However, its reactance makes an inductor act like a resistor for a.c. This

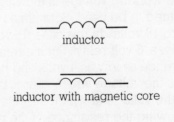

inductor

inductor with magnetic core

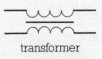

transformer

Fig. 9.9 The symbols used for inductors in circuit diagrams.

reactance depends on the frequency of the a.c. For d.c. the frequency is zero, so that the reactance is zero, but the reactance increases as the frequency increases.

A real coil of wire has some resistance, because the perfect resistance-less wire cannot be made! With a.c. the coil will have both resistance and reactance. You will need to refer to a more advanced book for details of how to work out what happens in practice, but you do need to know one more word which is often used when talking about inductors. The combined effect of resistance and reactance is called the *impedance* of the inductor. It might be helpful to remember that 'an inductor **impedes** the flow of electric current because the wire **resists** it and the coil **reacts** to it'.

One important place where the blocking effect of an inductor for a.c. is used is in preventing signals passing to or from electronic equipment along the mains wiring. Almost all signals are of a higher frequency than the 50 hertz of the mains supply, so a small inductor will have little effect on the supply current to the equipment. However, it will have a much greater effect on high frequencies. It can, therefore, be used (for example) to stop signals inside one computer travelling along the mains wiring and interfering with signals in another computer being used nearby (see fig. 9.10).

The same idea is used, in a different way, in hi-fi systems with several loudspeakers. Often, one loudspeaker is used for high frequencies and another one for low frequencies. To stop the high-frequency signals passing through the low-frequency loudspeaker (the 'woofer') an inductor is connected in series with it, whilst the high-frequency loudspeaker (the 'tweeter') is connected in series with a capacitor. Fig. 9.11 shows the circuit used.

Relays

In simple electronic circuits, the only inductor you are likely to use will be in a relay. A relay is a switch which is made to operate by an electromagnet (see reference section A2.12). The electromagnet is a coil of wire wound on a soft iron bar and is, of course, an inductor.

Relays are used as output transducers in electronic systems where you need to switch on and off devices that use high voltage or high power. When you choose a relay there are five things you need to think about: (i) size; (ii) resistance; (iii) the voltage it is expected to work on; (iv) the number and arrangement of the switch contacts; (v) the maximum current the contacts can carry safely (without sparking or overheating).

The working voltage is the voltage difference with which the relay is designed to be used. Sometimes the manufacturer quotes a range, such as '6 to 15 volts'. In this case, 15 volts is a maximum. Other relays are sold as, say, a '6 volt relay'. Such a relay will probably work on a voltage difference as low as 4 volts and be safe to use up to 9 volts. With all relays the voltage which causes the relay to switch on is always higher than the voltage at which the relay will switch off ('release').

Knowing the resistance of the relay will let you work out the current it will take when it is used with d.c. It is important to do this so that you can be sure that the output from your system gives enough power to work the relay. You must not forget that the relay is an inductor, so that if it is being used with a.c. the current will be less than you calculate (why?). This will also happen if you use a d.c. supply from the mains, if that supply has not been smoothed.

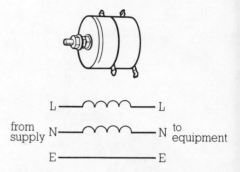

Fig. 9.10 A typical suppressor choke and the way in which it is connected in the mains supply circuit. This choke is rated at 1 mH per section, maximum current 0.5 A. Why is this current stated? What will happen if the current is more than 0.5 A?

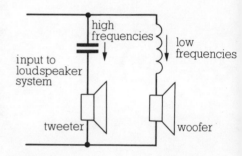

Fig. 9.11 Separating the high and low frequencies for the tweeter and woofer in a hi-fi loudspeaker system.

Relays only work slowly. It takes about 100 milliseconds for a relay to switch over. That is not very long, but compared with the pulse rates in many electronic circuits it is a very long time. Many computers have circuits which switch in as little as one hundredth of a microsecond (10 picoseconds). Compared with this the relay is ten million times slower!

When relays are used in electronic circuits there is one precaution that must **always** be taken. The cost of forgetting this can be a lot of transistors or integrated circuits to replace. When the current in the coil is switched off, the magnetic field produced by the coil disappears very quickly. When this happens, a large voltage is produced for a fraction of a second. This effect is known as *self-induction*.

The effect can be used (not in a relay) to produce the high voltages needed to operate the picture tube in a television, but high voltages will destroy transistors and chips.

The self-induced voltage is always of opposite sign to the power supply voltage, so that it is easy to protect the rest of the circuit. A diode is connected in parallel with the relay so that the high voltage is shorted out. The diode does not affect the power supply or the way in which the relay works. Fig. 9.12 shows how this is done. A relay should never be used in an electronic circuit working on d.c. unless a protection diode is used.

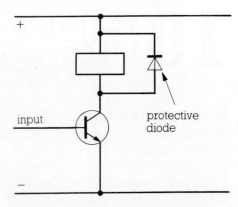

Fig. 9.12 Using a diode to protect an electronic system from high voltage pulses generated by a relay when it switches off.

SUMMARY 9B

Inductors are coils of wire; the coils are sometimes wound on iron or ferrite cores to increase their inductance.

Inductance is measured in henries.

Inductors have a higher impedance to a.c. than d.c. The reactance of an inductor increases as the frequency of the a.c. increases.

Relays must always have a protection diode in parallel with them when used in electronic circuits working on d.c.

10 TRANSISTORS AND INTEGRATED CIRCUITS

In the last three chapters you have learned about four of the main kinds of components used in electronic circuits. Transistors are yet another kind of component, but they are different from the others in several important ways. Unlike the other components, transistors have three connections instead of two. Transistors must have their own power supply, whereas if a signal is passed through a resistor it will behave as a resistor without needing any special power supply. Thirdly, the signal at the output of a transistor can be an amplified version of the input signal. (When a signal goes through a resistor, capacitor, inductor or diode the output is not amplified.)

Because of these differences transistors are sometimes called *active components* and resistors and other such components are called *passive components*. Transistors are not the only kind of active components. Part of this chapter is about integrated circuits, and these are active components too. An active device has to have its own power supply in order to work as it is intended. Passive devices do not need their own power supply.

Transistors

The transistor is perhaps the most important component of modern electronics. For many years, electronic systems used a lot of separate transistors. They could be seen on circuit boards like resistors and capacitors. Now, however, transistors are incorporated into the design of integrated circuits. Single transistors are only used in places where an integrated circuit has not been made that will do the job or where a transistor will do the job better.

Even though transistors are not often used as separate components in new circuits, it is still useful to know something about the way they are used in complete systems. There are two reasons for this. Knowing something about transistors will give you some idea about what an integrated circuit really is. Secondly, although the transistor is no longer being used by circuit designers, there is a lot of equipment with circuits that contain transistors, so you will need to recognise and use them.

Like the other components, transistors come in a range of shapes and sizes. They can usually be recognised because they have three connecting leads (but some other components have three connections, too). Fig. 10.1 is a photograph of some common types of transistor.

Not only do transistors come in different shapes and sizes, but there are different kinds of transistor too. The two main types of transistor are known as *bipolar transistors* and *field-effect transistors*. Most bipolar transistors are *n-p-n* transistors. 'n-p-n' refers to the way in which the transistor has been made and the direction of the electric currents in the transistor. Bipolar p-n-p transistors are also made. The direction of the currents in a p-n-p transistor is opposite to the direction of the currents in an n-p-n transistor.

The physics of transistors is complex, and beyond the scope of this book. We shall be concerned only with how transistors behave and, in chapter 11, with how they are used. For this purpose we shall deal only with n-p-n bipolar transistors.

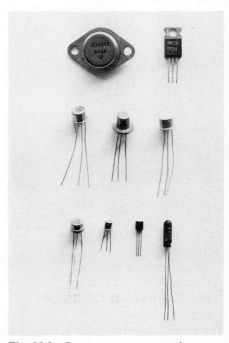
Fig. 10.1 Some common types of transistor.

The bipolar transistor has three connections. With resistors, capacitors and inductors it does not matter which way round you connect them. With diodes, the current only goes one way so you have to connect the diode the right way round. The transistor is like the diode, and there is only one way in which it may be connected. With three connections there are **five** ways you could connect it incorrectly, so it is important to be careful!

The three connections are known as the *emitter*, the *base*, and the *collector*. In normal circuits the input is connected to the emitter and the base. The output is connected to the emitter and the collector. The power supply to the transistor forms part of the output circuit. Because the emitter is part of both the input circuit and the output circuit, this arrangement is known as the *common emitter configuration*.

The symbols for n-p-n and p-n-p bipolar transistors are shown in fig. 10.2. The arrow shows which connection is the emitter, and also shows which way the current flows through the transistor. In a p-n-p transistor the emitter is 'p' and the base is 'n', so that current flows from emitter to base and the arrow points from the emitter to the base. An n-p-n transistor is the other way round.

Although a large number of different types of n-p-n transistor are manufactured, you only need two or three types of transistor for almost all the circuits you are likely to meet. These types vary in the power they can handle, the maximum voltage differences that can be applied to them, the case and construction of the transistor, and a characteristic which specifies how the output current depends on the input current. This characteristic is known as h_{FE}. Later in this chapter h_{FE} is considered in more detail.

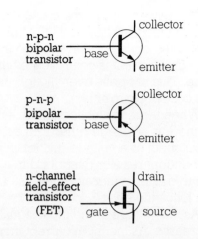

Fig. 10.2 Transistor symbols. The circle is sometimes not drawn. What would be [61] the symbol for a p-channel FET?

SUMMARY 10A

Transistors are active components; resistors, capacitors, inductors and diodes are passive components.

Active components need their own power supply in order to operate, and they use this power supply to produce an output which is larger than or in some other way different from the input.

Passive components cannot amplify the signal applied to them.

Integrated circuits are active devices (components).

Transistors can be of the bipolar type or the field-effect type.

Bipolar transistors can be either p-n-p or n-p-n. The difference is the direction of the currents in the transistor.

Bipolar transistors have three connections: the emitter, base and collector.

In normal use the input is connected to the emitter and base and the output is connected to the emitter and collector. This is known as the common emitter configuration.

Transistors in circuits

Transistors can be used in two types of circuit. They can be used in amplifier blocks, or they can be used in circuits that operate as switches, such as in gates. The same transistors can be used either way. The different transfer functions depend on the circuit in which the transistor is connected, and the values of the resistors in that circuit.

A typical transistor circuit is shown in fig. 10.3. The input signal causes a current to flow round the circuit formed by the base and emitter of the transistor. R_1 is used to ensure that the current does not exceed the value that the source can safely give or that which the base can safely accept. R_2 is used to control the behaviour of the circuit by providing extra current through the base emitter junction of the transistor. We say that the transistor has to be *biassed*, and R_2 is the *biassing resistor*. There are other ways of getting bias, but this method is the simplest. Some switching circuits do not need a biassing resistor.

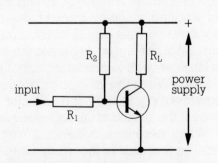

Fig. 10.3 A basic transistor circuit. R_1 limits the input current; R_2 is the biassing resistor; R_L is the load resistor.

The power supply will cause a current through the load resistor R_L and through the transistor from the collector to the emitter. This current is called the *collector current*. The transistor has the property that the collector current is controlled by the current from the input through the base. This happens even though the base current is much smaller than the collector current.

When there is a collector current, this current passes through R_L and so there is a voltage difference across R_L. The transistor and the load resistor act as a voltage divider in just the same way as with the light-dependent resistor described in chapter 7. The voltage difference across the transistor is therefore less than the power supply voltage. This has the following effect.

As the voltage of the input signal increases, the input current increases. As the input current increases, the collector current increases. As the collector current increases, the voltage difference across R_L increases. As the voltage difference across R_L increases, the voltage difference across the transistor decreases. The voltage across the transistor is the output signal. Thus, as the input signal increases, the output signal decreases. The circuit inverts the signal, and thus behaves as an inverter.

It is easy to find out how the collector current of the transistor is affected by its input current at the base. Fig. 10.4 shows an experimental circuit you can use if you have the necessary equipment. When you carry out this investigation you will find that the collector current is always in proportion to the base current, but is between 30 and 600 times greater than the base current. Fig. 10.5 shows a set of results obtained with a type BC108 transistor.

How much greater the collector current is than the base current depends on the type of resistor you use. This is the factor h_{FE} mentioned earlier. We talk about the 'H, F, E' of the transistor, and manufacturers quote a value for h_{FE} in the specifications for their transistors. The term h_{FE} is defined by this equation:

$$\frac{\text{collector-emitter current}}{\text{base-emitter current}} = \frac{I_{CE}}{I_{BE}} = h_{FE}$$

The h is not a quantity like current or voltage difference. You will have to turn to an advanced book about electronics if you want to know why this strange quantity is used. However, like so many things in electronics, you can use this quantity (or *parameter*, to give it its correct name) without needing to know all the theory on which it is based. For example, you should have been able to work out that the value of h_{FE} for the transistor used to produce the graph in fig. 10.5 was 200.

A transistor can do nothing by itself. It is only a useful component if it is part of a circuit with resistors and a power supply. Although h_{FE} is useful for working out how a circuit behaves, the way the circuit operates depends on what else is in that circuit. In a real circuit the collector current is not always h_{FE} times the base current. Unless the input voltage is large enough to produce current in the base there will be no collector current. When the voltage difference across the load resistor equals the power-supply voltage, the collector current cannot become any larger, even if the base current increases further.

When there is no collector current the transistor is said to be *turned off*. The junctions of the transistor each behave like a diode. To get current through a diode or through the base-emitter junction of the transistor, there has to be a voltage difference across the junction of about 0.7 volts (assuming the transistor is made of silicon, which almost all

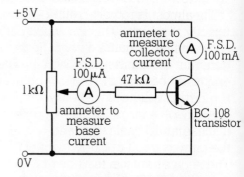

Fig. 10.4 The circuit arrangement that can be used to find how the collector current of an n-p-n transistor depends on its base current. What changes would you have to make if the transistor were a p-n-p [62] type?

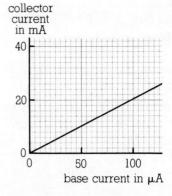

Fig. 10.5 The variation of collector current as the base current is varied, for a type BC108 transistor. What is the gradient [63] (slope) of the line on this graph? Not all BC108 transistors will give the same gradient, even though they are sold as the [64] same type of transistor. Why?

are). If the input voltage is less than 0.7 volts the transistor will be turned off. If the input signal is more than 0.7 volts, current will flow in the input circuit and cause a collector current.

When the circuit current has reached a maximum the transistor is said to be *saturated*. The voltage difference between collector and emitter is about 0.2 volts. The current in the collector circuit has become so large that the voltage across the load resistor is, apart from the 0.2 volts across the transistor, the whole of the power supply voltage.

It is this behaviour of the transistor that allows transistor circuits to be used in two ways. If we design a circuit so that the transistor is always either turned off or saturated, then the circuit behaves as a switch, and the output is either 'high' (5 volts or whatever the power supply voltage is) or 'low' (almost zero volts). (Why almost zero volts, rather than exactly zero volts?)

On the other hand, if we make sure that the transistor is always working between the two limits, the circuit will behave as an amplifier.

Chapter 11 deals in detail with these two circuit arrangements and shows how the resistor values are calculated.

SUMMARY 10B

Base current is the current into the base from the signal source.

Collector current is the current at the collector.

The transistor's power supply provides the collector current.

The base current controls the collector current.

Transistors can be used in amplifier circuits, switching circuits, and pulse or signal generators.

When there is no base current and no collector current, the transistor is turned off.

When the collector current cannot increase any further the transistor is saturated.

The current gain of the transistor (h_{FE}) = $\dfrac{\text{collector current}}{\text{base current}}$

Integrated circuits

Although the invention of the transistor was the start of the present era of electronics, transistors are now rarely used in new electronic design work. They are obsolete. Large numbers of transistors are still being made, but they are being used in systems that were designed some time ago. New equipment uses devices called *integrated circuits*. Integrated circuits are often called ICs, or chips, for short. These integrated circuits use transistors as part of their internal circuits, but the transistors are not separate. They are part of the complete device.

A transistor is made by specially treating a small wafer ('chip') of very pure silicon. In an integrated circuit the same idea is used to make a complete circuit with resistors, capacitors, diodes and all the connections, as well as a large number of transistors, all on one chip of silicon. Fig. 3.3 in chapter 3 shows a circuit made from individual components and the same circuit made as an integrated circuit, for comparison.

The first chips that were manufactured in large numbers were chips that carried out a single function in a system. Examples of these are the various logic gates, and complete amplifier blocks. Often, the logic gate chips have several separate gates made on one chip. Logic systems use lots of gates so that less space is needed if the same chip has, say, four AND gates on it. One type of amplifier, the *operational amplifier*, is particularly important, and the last part of this chapter is about this kind of integrated circuit.

Single function chips are very widely used and are very useful to the person wanting to design and build his or her own system. Manufacturers of electronic equipment have a different problem. They want to be able to make equipment as quickly, cheaply and reliably as possible. Once a chip has been designed, the manufacturer can mass-produce it and know that each one is the same. There is one item to test, instead of thousands of separate components which could be faulty or which could be assembled in the wrong way. There are now chips that have all the circuits for things like a calculator or major sections of a television set. In the electronics industry, 'very large scale integration' (VLSI) has become important. In some computers there are integrated circuits which include many tens of thousands of transistors and all the other components on a single chip.

A typical chip is a piece of extremely pure silicon about 3 millimetres square and about 0.2 millimetres thick. The circuit is 'drawn' on the chip by photographic methods, and then the circuit itself is built up by a series of special chemical processes.

One of the biggest problems the manufacturer has to solve is how to make connections to something so tiny. It would be impossible to connect ordinary wires to the chip. The chip is therefore mounted in a piece of black plastic and connections are made to pins along the edges of the plastic. This means that all chips look much the same, however complicated they may be inside.

A standard system has been used for almost all chips. They have connecting pins set at a standard distance apart along two sides, and a standard spacing between the two rows of pins. This arrangement is known as a *d.i.l. package*. The initials d.i.l. stand for *dual in line*. Many chips have fourteen pins, seven down each side, but any number of pins between four and sixty-four may be used for different types of IC.

Fig. 10.6 shows some typical chips of various kinds.

Fig. 10.6 Some typical integrated circuits, including operational amplifiers, logic gates, a memory chip and a microprocessor (about two-thirds actual size). Almost all integrated circuits are d.i.l. packages.

Operational amplifiers

In chapter 5 you learned that the most common kind of amplifier is an operational amplifier, or op-amp for short. What does 'operational' mean? What does an op-amp do? Before answering these questions let us find out a little more about these amplifiers.

Modern op-amps are amplifiers made as integrated circuits. The circuit on the chip is complex, often having twenty or thirty transistors built into it but, as with all electronic equipment, all you need to know for most purposes is what the inputs and outputs are, what power supply is required, and how to control it.

At the present time the most frequently used op-amp is known as a 741. This number is a manufacturer's type number, and has no special meaning. Like most chips, the op-amp is made in a standard d.i.l. package. The 741 has eight pins, four on each side. There are two 741s in fig. 10.6.

Although there are eight pins on a 741, in simple circuits only five of them have to be connected. Which five are used, and how they have to be connected, is information an electronics engineer would get from data sheets supplied by the manufacturer. Part of the data sheet for the 741 is shown in fig. 10.8 on the next page. You should not try to learn this sort of information because each type of chip is different and trying to remember will lead to costly mistakes.

If you study a data sheet you will find a diagram showing what the connections are. This has been redrawn in fig. 10.7. There is a hollow dot moulded into the case to show which pin is pin 1, and you then count down along one side and back up the other to find out which pin is which.

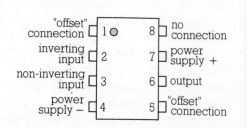

Fig. 10.7 The connections for a 741 op-amp. A hollow dot is moulded in the case next to pin 1.

Absolute maximum ratings over operating free-air temperature range (unless otherwise noted)

	μA741C	UNIT
Supply voltage V_{CC+} (see Note 1)	18	V
Supply voltage V_{CC-} (see Note 1)	−18	V
Differential input voltage (see Note 2)	±30	V
Input voltage any input (see Notes 1 and 3)	±15	V
Voltage between either offset null terminal (N1/N2) and V_{CC-}	±0.5	V
Duration of output short-circuit (see Note 4)	unlimited	
Continuous total power dissipation at (or below) 25°C free-air temperature	500	mW
Operating free-air temperature range	0 to 70	°C
Storage temperature range	−65 to 150	°C
Lead temperature 1.6 mm (1/16 inch) from case for 10 seconds	260	°C

NOTES: 1 All voltage values, unless otherwise noted, are with respect to the midpoint between V_{CC+} and V_{CC-}.
2 Differential voltages are at the noninverting input terminal with respect to the inverting input terminal.
3 The magnitude of the input voltage must never exceed the magnitude of the supply voltage or 15 volts, whichever is less.
4 The output may be shorted to ground or either power supply.

Electrical characteristics at specified free-air temperature. $V_{CC+} = 15$ V. $V_{CC-} = -15$ V

	Parameter	Test conditions[†]		μA741C Min	Typ	Max	Unit
V_{OM}	Maximum peak output voltage swing	$R_L = 10$ kΩ	25°C	±12	±14		V
		$R_L \geq 10$ kΩ	Full range	±12			
		$R_L = 2$ kΩ	25°C	±10	±13		
		$R_L \geq 2$ kΩ	Full range	±10			
A_{VD}	Large signal differential voltage amplification	$R_L \geq 2$ kΩ	25°C	20	200		V/mV
		$V_O = \pm 10$ V	Full range	15			
r_i	Input resistance		25°C	0.3	2		MΩ
r_o	Output resistance	$V_O = 0$	25°C		75		Ω
C_i	Input capacitance		25°C		1.4		pF
I_{OS}	Short-circuit output current		25°C		±25	±40	mA
I_{CC}	Supply current	No load, $V_O = 0$	25°C		1.7	2.8	mA
			Full range			3.3	
P_D	Total power dissipation	No load, $V_O = 0$	25°C		50	85	mW
			Full range			100	

[†] All characteristics are measured under open-loop conditions with zero common-mode input voltage unless otherwise specified.

Fig. 10.8 Part of the data sheet for the Texas type μA741C operational amplifier.

You may have expected the connections to be labelled 'input', 'output', 'power supply' and so on. It is not quite as simple as that. There are two input connections, and two power supplies are needed. The reason for this is to do with the original purpose of operational amplifiers but it is also what makes op-amps such useful devices.

These amplifiers are called operational amplifiers because, among other things, they will amplify both positive and negative input signals. Operational amplifiers were used first of all for doing mathematical 'operations' by electronics. They formed a major part of a type of computer called an *analogue computer*. Analogue computers are not often used now, but operational amplifiers were found to have many other uses once they could be manufactured very cheaply as integrated circuits.

The two inputs are labelled *inv* (pin 2) and *non-inv* (pin 3). 'Inv' is short for *inverting* and 'non-inv' is short for *non-inverting*. The meaning of 'inverting' was described in chapter 5. When a signal is applied to the inverting input, the output signal is both amplified and inverted. If an input signal is applied to the non-inverting input, it is amplified but not inverted.

To invert signals the amplifier must be able to cope with both positive and negative signals because even if all the input signals were positive, they would (if applied to the inverting input) give negative-going output signals. To do this the amplifier has to have two power supplies, one with a positive voltage difference to the common line and the other with a negative voltage difference to the common line. Pin 7 is marked $+V_{CC}$ and this is the connecting pin for the positive power supply. Pin 4, marked $-V_{CC}$, is for the negative supply. You may notice that there is no pin for the common line. Because both inputs, both power supplies and the output are all connected between their particular pin and the common line, the op-amp itself does not need a connection to the common line. Some op-amp circuits use one power supply but divide that supply into the two supplies needed by the op-amp within the circuit itself.

In a circuit diagram, the op-amp is shown as a triangle, as shown in fig. 10.9. The inverting input is marked with a minus sign (−) inside the triangle, and is drawn at the top. The non-inverting input is marked with a plus sign (+), and is drawn below the other input. In most circuits power supply connections are not shown (everyone knows there must be a power supply so leaving out the lines on the diagram just helps to make the diagram clearer). In fig. 10.9 they have been shown as dotted lines.

How does the amplifier know which input to amplify? Both input pins have to be connected to something or the amplifier will not work at all. In fact you can connect two inputs to the amplifier at the same time. The amplifier always amplifies the **difference** between the two inputs (and so it can subtract when it is used to do mathematical operations). It is sometimes called a difference amplifier for that reason. When you want to use only one input, the other input has to be connected to the common line.

The gain of the 741 for d.c. signals is about 100 000. For practical purposes you would not need a gain anything like as large as this, but in any case you need to be able to control the gain of the system as required. The reason for this very high gain is to ensure that, in circuits where the gain is controlled, any variation between chips when they are manufactured will not affect the way the system works as a whole.

Controlling the gain of the op-amp

Although the gain of the op-amp may be very large, the amplifier system is the whole of the circuit, not just the chip. Fig. 10.10 shows the circuit of a simple inverting amplifier block. In this block, R_1 and R_2 control the gain of the system. Surprisingly, so long as the op-amp is there, it does not affect how much gain the *system* has when it is used in this way. R_{IN} is called the input resistor. The input signal is never connected directly to the input. There must always be a resistor in the input circuit. R_F is called the *feedback resistor*. But what is feedback?

Feedback

Feedback is used in almost all control systems. Think about cleaning your carpets with a vacuum cleaner. You can just push the cleaner over the carpet and pretend it is clean, but to do the job properly you watch the carpet around the cleaner as you work. You do this to see where the dirt is and then whether the cleaner has picked it up. This second piece of information tells you how the cleaner is doing its job. If the carpet still has bits on it you go back and clean that bit again. If you have to keep on going back, you realise that you are trying to do the job too quickly and

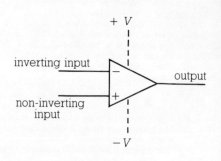

Fig. 10.9 The circuit symbol for an operational amplifier. In most cases the power supply connections are not shown.

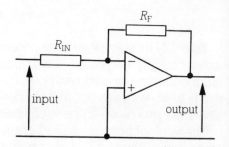

Fig. 10.10 A simple inverting amplifier system using an op-amp. R_{IN} is the input resistor, and R_F is the feedback resistor. In this circuit the non-inverting input has been connected directly to the common line.

you work more slowly. This is information on how the job is being done (the output) which is being fed to you so that you can control the machine. Fig. 10.11 shows this movement of information pictorially.

In this example of the cleaner a human being makes the decisions about what to do, but in an automatic system there has to be a block in the system (a 'processing' block) to compare what is happening with what is wanted, and to adjust the system to suit. Feedback is the process by which a signal from the output is fed back to the input of the system and compared with the input signal so that the system is adjusted as required.

In the op-amp shown in fig. 10.10, the feedback resistor is feeding signals from the output to the input. By choosing the values of the input resistor and the feedback resistor you can get any value of gain you want from the system. The op-amp gain formula for this is:

gain of amplifier system $= -\dfrac{value\ of\ feedback\ resistor}{value\ of\ input\ resistor}$

or

$$G = -\frac{R_F}{R_{IN}}$$

Fig. 10.12 shows an op-amp circuit with a gain of -20. The minus sign shows that the input is going to the inverting input so that the output is inverted. A gain of -20 has been achieved by making $R_{IN} = 10$ kilohm and $R_F = 200$ kilohm. The circuit would have also had a gain of -20 if R_{IN} had been 400 kilohm and R_F had been 8 megohm, or if any other pair of values which give a gain of -20 when you use the formula had been used.

In practice, the input resistor is usually between 1000 and 10 000 ohms. If the value is too high then the amplifier may be affected by stray interference, whereas if the value is too low the currents taken from the source of the input signal are larger than they need to be.

The last section in this chapter explains how the op-amp gain formula is obtained. Chapter 12 deals with the ways in which operational amplifiers can be used in blocks with various functions and uses.

Where the op-amp gain formula comes from

To see where the op-amp gain formula comes from, you have to think about what is happening at all the points in the circuit. Think about the amplifier itself, first of all.

The op-amp has a very high gain, of around 100 000. This means that if the output signal is 1 volt, the input signal which produces it is one hundred-thousandth of a volt (1/100 000 volt), which is very small indeed. The amplifier has, in fact, two inputs, and it amplifies the difference between the voltages at the inverting and non-inverting inputs. That means that the voltage difference between the two inputs is this very small amount. The difference is so small that we can assume that the voltage at the two inputs is always the same.

In fig. 10.13 the non-inverting input is connected to the common (zero volts) line, the line which is normally 'earthed'. This is a common way of using an op-amp. In this case, the other (inverting) input is also virtually at zero volts. We say the inverting input is at *virtual earth*.

Look at fig. 10.13. All the currents and voltages in the circuit are labelled and the next part of this section will use those symbols.

If the inverting input is at virtual earth, that means that we can assume it is at zero volts. If it is at zero volts we can work out the currents in R_{IN}

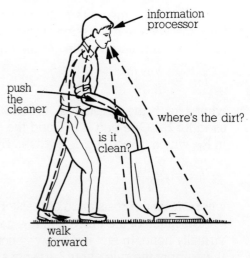

Fig. 10.11 The information cycle when you use a vacuum cleaner. What you see provides the feedback to you so that you can control what is happening.

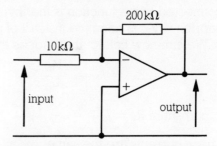

Fig. 10.12 An op-amp with suitable resistors to give the system a gain of -20. It is NOT possible to get a gain of $+20$ by connecting the resistors to the non-inverting input. The way in which to avoid the amplifier inverting the output is explained in chapter 12.

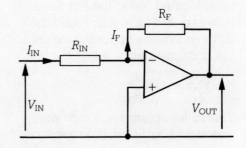

Fig. 10.13 The circuit of an inverting amplifier system with the various voltages and currents labelled to show the symbols used in the text.

and R_F. For R_{IN} the voltage at one end is V_{IN} and at the other end it is 0. Thus the voltage difference across R_{IN} is $(V_{IN} - 0) = 0$. Using the resistance formula we can get the current in R_{IN}, which is labelled I_{IN}:

$$I_{IN} = \frac{V_{IN}}{R_{IN}}$$

where R_{IN} is the resistance of resistor R_{IN}. The same argument can be used for R_F. One end is at 0 and the other end is at V_{OUT}, so the current in R_F, which is labelled I_F, is given by:

$$I_F = \frac{V_{OUT}}{R_F}$$

where R_F is the resistance of resistor R_F.

How much of the current in R_{IN} goes into the amplifier? The answer is virtually none. In fact it is a few nanoamps (1 nanoamp is 10^{-9} amps). So if we apply the rule about currents at a junction we must say that very nearly all the current flowing into the junction from V_{IN} must flow out of the junction to V_{OUT}. For current to flow from V_{IN}, V_{IN} would have to be a positive voltage. For current to flow from virtual zero to V_{OUT}, V_{OUT} must be *negative*. This should not be surprising – the amplifier input connected to the junction is the *inverting input*. (Can you say what must happen if V_{IN} is negative instead of positive?)

We can now collect these ideas together:

$$\text{current in } R_{IN} = I_{IN} = \frac{V_{IN}}{R_{IN}}$$

$$\text{current in } R_F = I_{OUT} = -\frac{V_{OUT}}{R_F} \qquad (\textbf{minus because current flows to } V_{OUT} \text{ from zero})$$

These currents are the same.
Because the currents in R_{IN} and R_F are the same, we can write:

$$-\frac{V_{OUT}}{R_F} = \frac{V_{IN}}{R_{IN}} \qquad \text{(call this equation A)}$$

"So what?", you may say! Remember what we are looking for. We wanted a formula for the *gain* of the system. The gain of the system is the number of times greater the output signal is when compared with the input signal. The gain of the system is therefore:

$$\frac{V_{OUT}}{V_{IN}}$$

Equation A can be rearranged to get both V_{OUT} and V_{IN} on one side. Moving V_{IN} to the left-hand side and also changing round the signs so that the minus sign is on the right, we get:

$$\frac{V_{OUT}}{V_{IN}} = -\frac{R_F}{R_{IN}}$$

This is the op-amp equation which was stated earlier in the chapter.

SUMMARY 10C

An integrated circuit is a complete circuit manufactured on a silicon chip.

The initials d.i.l. mean 'dual-in-line' and describe how the pins on an integrated circuit are arranged along both sides.

Operational amplifiers are a type of integrated circuit.

An operational amplifier is a linear voltage amplifier capable of amplifying both positive and negative signals.

Operational amplifiers need two power supplies: one positive and the other negative.

The gain of an op-amp is controlled by the use of feedback.

Feedback is the process by which a signal from the output of a system is fed back to the input of the system and compared with the input signal, so that the system can be adjusted as required.

When feedback is applied, the gain of the system is $-\dfrac{R_F}{R_{IN}}$ and does not depend on the gain of the op-amp.

C REFERENCE SECTION

C1 — Resistors

C1.1 — Uses of resistors

Resistors are the most common components in electronic circuits. They are used for many purposes, the most important being:

- two resistors used as a voltage divider;
- to limit the current flowing in a circuit;
- to act as a load for a voltage amplifier;
- to produce bias voltages, particularly for transistors;
- to reduce the voltage applied to a component or circuit block to the correct level;
- to set the gain of an operational amplifier.

C1.2 — Fixed and variable resistors

Most resistors are fixed resistors, manufactured with some particular value of resistance. Variable resistors are also manufactured.

Variable resistors are usually used as variable voltage dividers and are normally called potentiometers because of this. Most variable controls on electronic equipment are potentiometers.

Variable resistors used to control the current in a circuit are sometimes called rheostats. The origin of this strange word is from the Greek and means, literally, 'current constant'.

C1.3 — Non-linear resistors

Non-linear resistors are special kinds of resistor whose properties depend on some physical factor such as temperature, pressure, light intensity or magnetic field. Each type of non-linear resistor has a special name.

A *thermistor* is a resistor which is strongly affected by temperature.

A *light-dependent resistor* (LDR) is a resistor which is strongly affected by the level of illumination ('brightness').

A *pressure-sensitive resistor* is a resistor which is varied by the pressure applied to it.

A *magnetic-dependent resistor* (MDR) is strongly affected by putting it in a strong magnetic field. A Hall probe is a special type of MDR.

C1.4 — Resistance

Resistors have the property that when a current flows through them there is a voltage difference between the two ends of the resistor. This property is called resistance and is measured in ohms. If the current is one amp when the voltage difference across the resistor is one volt then the resistance is one ohm.

C1.5 — The resistance equation

Resistance, voltage and current are linked by the *resistance equation*. It can be written in three ways:

$$R = \frac{V}{I} \qquad I = \frac{V}{R} \qquad V = I \times R$$

These formulae are often called Ohm's law. They are related to Ohm's law but they are not the law discovered by Georg Simon Ohm.

Example of the use of the resistance equation

What resistor should you use to limit the current to a transistor to 5 mA when the voltage difference that will appear across the resistor is 15 V?

Use the formula in the form $R = V/I$ because it is the resistance that you are trying to find. Substitute the numbers in the formula. V is 15. Before putting the value for I in the formula it must be converted into amps (5 milliamps is 5×10^{-3} amps). This gives:

$$R = \frac{V}{I} = \frac{15}{5 \times 10^{-3}} = \frac{15 \times 10^3}{5} = 3000 \ \Omega$$

Exercise 12 – An LED operates with a voltage difference of 2 V and is to be used on a 5 V supply. What resistor would you use in series with the LED to drop the extra 3 V if the current for the LED is to be 15 mA?

Exercise 13 – The input resistor for a logic gate is 2000 Ω When there is a signal there is 5 V across the resistor. What current goes to the gate?

Exercise 14 – A suppressor is fitted into one lead of a mains supply to a computer. If the resistance of the suppressor is 2 Ω and the computer takes a current of 0.3 A, what is the voltage difference across the suppressor?

C1.6 – Manufactured resistors

Resistors are manufactured in a large range of values and sizes. In electronics, values from 1 Ω to 10 000 000 Ω are commonly used.

Large resistances are usually quoted in kilohms or megohms. One kilohm is 1000 ohms. Kilohm is usually abbreviated to kΩ, so that 22 000 ohms would be written as 22 kΩ. Sometimes it is written as 22 k; this is not a good way of writing down resistances but you need to recognise it if you see it.

In the same way, resistances of more than a million ohms are written in megohm (MΩ).

$$1\,000\,000 \ \Omega = 1000 \ k\Omega = 1 \ M\Omega \qquad 6\,800\,000 \ \Omega = 6800 \ k\Omega = 6.8 \ M\Omega$$

1 kΩ = 1000 Ω
1 MΩ = 1000 kΩ = 1 000 000 Ω

The size and shape of a resistor do not indicate its value. The manufacturer marks the value of the resistor using a colours code or a code of letters and numbers.

C1.7 – Resistance colours code

Standard resistors are marked with three or four colour bands. The bands are painted towards one end of the resistor so that it is easy to identify which is the first band in the code.

The bands have the following meanings:

band 1 (nearest the end of the resistor) – the first figure in the value;

band 2 – the second figure in the value;

band 3 – the number of noughts that follow those figures when the value is written down; and

band 4 – the manufacturing tolerance to which the resistor has been made. If there is no fourth band this tolerance is 20 per cent.

Table C.1 gives the values of the colours.

Some resistors have five bands. These are close-tolerance resistors. The first three bands give three figures. The fourth band gives the number of noughts.

Table C.1   The colours code for resistors

colour	first band	second band	third band	fourth band
black	not used	0	no noughts	not used
brown	1	1	0	1%
red	2	2	00	2%
orange	3	3	000	not used
yellow	4	4	0000	not used
green	5	5	00000	not used
blue	6	6	000000	not used
violet	7	7	not used	not used
grey	8	8	not used	not used
white	9	9	not used	not used
gold	not used	not used	multiply by 0.1	5%
silver	not used	not used	multiply by 0.01	10%

It is worth learning this code. In electronics it has to be used very frequently. You will notice that the colours (from red to violet) are in the same order as the colours of the rainbow.

C1.8 — Numbers code for resistors (BS1852)

The numbers code is used mainly for printing resistance values on circuit diagrams but it is also used occasionally for marking the resistors themselves. Table C.2 shows the codes used for different values. The position of the R, K, or M in the code shows where the decimal point should come in the value. There is sometimes another letter added after these codes to show the tolerance.

Code	Value	
1R0	1.0	
10R	10	
100R	100	
1K0	1000	(1 kΩ)
10K	10 000	(10 kΩ)
100K	100 000	(100 kΩ)
1M0	1 000 000	(1 MΩ)
10M	10 000 000	(10 MΩ)

Table C.2 Numbers code for resistors

C1.9 — Tolerance

When resistors of a particular value are manufactured, the manufacturing process results in some variation of actual values from the intended value. For most purposes this does not matter, providing the variation is not too great. The acceptable range in the value is called the tolerance.

For 330 Ω resistors manufactured with a 10% tolerance, the value of any one resistor might be anything between 330 − 33 Ω (297 Ω) and 330 + 33 Ω (363 Ω). If the value is less than 297 Ω or more than 363 Ω the resistor will not be accepted as a 330 Ω resistor. The value 330 Ω is known as the *nominal value* of the resistor.

Resistors can be readily purchased with manufacturing tolerances of 20%, 10%, 5% and 2%. The closer the tolerance, the more the resistor costs. Even lower tolerance resistors are available, but they are expensive and are only required for special purposes.

Because there is a tolerance on the value of resistors, manufacturers only produce resistors with certain nominal values known as *preferred values*. Table C.3 gives the preferred values for 5%, 10% and 20% tolerance resistors. These values are known as the E24, E12, and E6 ranges respectively. On the E6 range there are six values between 1 Ω and 10 Ω, six values between 10 Ω and 100 Ω, and so on, over the whole range of values. In the same way the E12 range has twelve values between 1 Ω and 10 Ω, and the E24 range has 24 values. Table C.3 shows the standard values in each of these ranges.

Table C.3 Preferred values for manufactured resistors

E24 range
10 11 12 13 15 16 18 20 22 24 27 30 33 36 39 43 47 51 56 62 68 75 82 91

E12 range
10 12 15 18 22 27 33 39 47 56 68 82

E6 range
10 15 22 33 47 68

Preferred values are chosen to avoid overlap in possible ranges of values. How this is done is shown in this example, based on resistors in the E12 range. These have a 10% tolerance.

Nominal value (ohms)	Actual value at the −10% tolerance limit	Actual value at the +10% tolerance limit
270	243	297
330	297	363
390	351	429
470	423	517
560	504	616

C1.10 — Resistors connected in series

If two or more resistors are connected in series the effective (total) resistance is larger than that of the largest resistor.

To find the effective resistance the resistance values of the individual resistors are added together. The formula is:

$$R_{\text{effective}} = R_1 + R_2 + R_3 + \ldots\ldots$$

where R_1, R_2, R_3, and so on, are the resistances of each of the resistors that are connected together.

Example of the use of the formula for resistors in series

What is the effective resistance of the three resistors shown below?

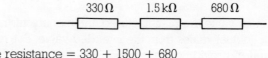

330 Ω   1.5 kΩ   680 Ω

effective resistance = 330 + 1500 + 680
$$= 2510\ \Omega$$
$$= 2.5\ k\Omega$$

(Note that the answer is given to two significant figures because the tolerance on the resistance values would normally be more than 1%. All resistor values are given to two significant figures, except in special cases.)

Exercise 15 – What is the effective resistance of four 200 Ω resistors connected in series?

Exercise 16 – What is the effective resistance of a 2.2 MΩ resistor and a 470 kΩ resistor connected in series?

Exercise 17 – Two resistors are connected in series. One has colour bands yellow, violet, red. The other has brown, green, orange bands. What is the effective resistance of the two resistors together?

C1.11 – Resistors in parallel

Where resistors are connected in parallel the effective resistance is less than that of the lowest value resistor in the arrangement.

There are two ways of calculating the effective resistance. The easier method takes much longer if there are more than two resistors.

Method 1

For any **two** resistors R_1 and R_2, in parallel, the formula is:

$$R_{\text{effective}} = \frac{R_1 \times R_2}{R_1 + R_2} \qquad \left(\frac{\text{product}}{\text{sum}}\right)$$

For three or more resistors in parallel, this formula is used for two of the resistors. These two are then imagined to be one resistor with the value calculated from the formula, and the formula is used again to find the effective resistance of this imaginary resistor connected in parallel with the third actual resistor. The process is repeated for the fourth resistor, if there is one, and so on.

Method 2

For any number of resistors R_1, R_2, R_3, etc, in parallel, the effective resistance is given by the formula:

$$\frac{1}{R_{\text{effective}}} = \frac{1}{R_1} + \frac{1}{R_2} + \frac{1}{R_3} + \ldots$$

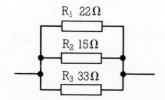

R₁ 22 Ω

R₂ 15 Ω

R₃ 33 Ω

Example of the use of the formulae for resistors in parallel

What is the resistance of the arrangement shown on the left?

Using method 1:

Work out R_1 and R_2 first. Call the effective resistance of R_1 and R_2 combined R_x.

$$R_x = \frac{22 \times 15}{22 + 15} = \frac{330}{37} = 8.918 \approx 8.9 \text{ (to 2 sig. figs.)}$$

Now work out R_x with R_3 to give the total resistance R_t:

$$R_t = \frac{8.9 \times 33}{8.9 + 33} = \frac{294}{41.9} = 7.01 \approx 7.0 \ \Omega$$

Using method 2:

$$\frac{1}{R_t} = \frac{1}{22} + \frac{1}{15} + \frac{1}{33}$$

Now change the fractions to decimals using a calculator or tables, and add them together:

$$\frac{1}{R_t} = 0.0455 + 0.0667 + 0.0302 = 0.1424$$

You **must** now remember to find the inverse (reciprocal) of this answer:

$$R_t = \frac{1}{0.1424} = 7.02 \approx 7.0 \ \Omega$$

Exercise 18 – Two 1.8 kΩ resistors are connected in parallel. What is the effective resistance of the two resistors together?

Exercise 19 – Find the effective resistance of a 100 Ω resistor in parallel with a 2 kΩ resistor.

Exercise 20 – Resistors of values 680 Ω, 1.2 kΩ and 1.5 kΩ are connected in parallel. What is the effective resistance of this combination?

C1.12 – Arrangements with resistors in both series and parallel

For complex arrangements of resistors both rules are used in turn.
 (i) Add the values of all resistors that are connected in series with nothing else connected to the junctions between them.
 (ii) Redraw the circuit with a single resistor replacing the groups of resistors you have dealt with. Its value is the value that you have calculated.
 (iii) Calculate the effective resistance of each combination of resistors in parallel.
 (iv) Redraw the circuit with a single resistor replacing the group of resistors you have now dealt with.
 (v) Repeat steps (i) to (iv) until you are left with a single resistor in your final redrawn circuit.

> Remember that for two resistors of the same value connected in parallel the effective resistance is half the resistance of one of the resistors. Thus, two resistors of value 68 kΩ in parallel have an effective resistance of 34 kΩ

C1.13 – Power ratings

Resistors are manufactured in a variety of physical sizes. Fig. C.1 shows four different sizes of 100 Ω resistor. When resistors are in use they convert electrical energy into heat and their temperature rises. Large-sized resistors can lose more heat to the surroundings (i.e. dissipate more heat) than small ones and can therefore convert energy at a higher rate. The rate of converting energy is called power. Resistors are given power ratings that specify the maximum power they can dissipate without overheating. The resistors shown in fig. C.1 are rated at 1/4 W, 1/2 W, 1 W and 2 W.

To find out which rating a resistor should be, the resistance equation and the power formula are used. The voltage across the resistor and the current through it are calculated, using known information about the circuit and the resistance equation. The power being dissipated is then found by multiplying the current by the voltage. The rating of the resistor must be larger than the power it is actually dissipating. An example of this calculation is given on the next page.

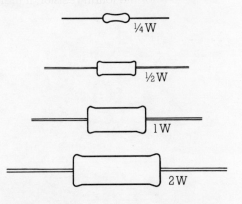

Fig. C.1 Four 100 Ω resistors of various power ratings.

Example of the calculation of the power rating of a resistor

What must the rating of a 100 Ω resistor be if it is to be used in a circuit with a voltage difference across it of 6 V?

(i) Calculate the current in the resistor. Use the resistance equation as follows:

$$I = \frac{V}{R} = \frac{6}{100} = 0.06 \text{ A}$$

(ii) Use the power formula to calculate the power dissipated by the resistor:

$$P = V \times I = 6 \times 0.06 = 0.36 \text{ W}$$

(iii) Choose the next **larger** rating of resistor. The value of 0.36 W calculated above is more than 1/4 W but less than 1/2 W. A resistor rated at 1/2 W would be chosen.

(Any 100 Ω resistor with a power rating of 1/2 W or more would be suitable, even one rated at 100 W, but resistors with bigger ratings are more expensive.)

Exercise 21 − A 200 Ω resistor is to be connected across a 12 V power supply. What power rating should be specified for this resistor?

C1.14 − Voltage dividers

A voltage divider has the arrangement shown in the top part of fig. C.2. The formula for the output voltage in a voltage divider is:

$$V_{OUT} = V_{IN} \times \frac{R_2}{R_1 \times R_2}$$

Often, when the output voltage is connected to some other section of the circuit, that circuit behaves like another resistor connected across R_2 in parallel (see the lower part of fig. C.2). The extra part of the circuit is an *external load* on the voltage divider. In this case the effective resistance of R_2 and the external load resistance R_x must be calculated first and then the answer to this calculation (which is the total 'load' for the voltage divider) is used in the voltage divider formula. **Note**: The word 'load' can be used in two different ways in these circuits, meaning either the external load or the total load.

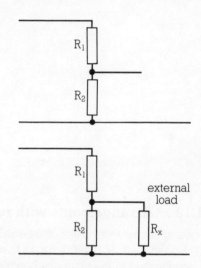

Fig. C.2 A voltage divider network (*above*) and the same circuit with an external load connected (*below*).

Example of the use of the voltage divider formula

A voltage divider using the bottom circuit shown in fig. C.2 is connected to an input of 15 V. If R_1 is 10 kΩ, R_2 is 2 kΩ, and R_x is 1 kΩ, what will be the voltage difference across R_x?

First you must find the effective resistance of R_2 and R_x together (we will call this R_L). Use the 'product over sum' formula. As long as you keep **all** the resistances in kilohms you do not need to change them into ohm values. Using the formula we get:

$$R_L = \frac{R_2 \times R_x}{R_2 + R_x} = \frac{2 \times 1}{2 + 1} = 0.67 \text{ k}\Omega$$

Now put the values into the voltage divider formula and calculate V_{OUT}. V_{OUT} is the voltage difference across both R_2 and R_x, because they are in parallel.

$$V_{OUT} = V_{IN} \times \frac{R_L}{R_1 + R_L} = 15 \times \frac{0.67}{10 + 0.67} = \frac{15 \times 0.67}{10.67} = 0.94 \text{ V}$$

Exercise 22 − A voltage divider is made up from a 22 kΩ resistor and a 33 kΩ resistor, and is connected across a 5 V supply. Calculate the voltage difference across the 22 kΩ resistor when a load of 56 kΩ is connected across it. Also calculate the voltage difference across this resistor when the load is disconnected.

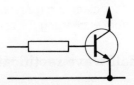

C1.15 — Current limiter

This is a simple application of the resistance equation. A resistor is connected in series in the line supplying the current. A typical example is the resistor used to limit the current as shown in fig. C.3.

In choosing a resistor for limiting current it is important to remember that the current must **never** exceed the limit set. The preferred value used must, therefore, always be greater than the answer you calculate, and you must remember to allow for the tolerance of the resistor you use.

Fig. C.3 A current-limiting resistor in the base circuit of a transistor.

Example of the calculation of a current-limiting resistance

If the supply voltage for the transistor in fig. C.3 is 5 V and the voltage between the base and the emitter is 0.7 V, what resistor must be used if the base current must not exceed 5 mA?

The first step is to find the maximum voltage difference across the resistance. In this case it is 4.3 V.

The resistance equation can now be used to calculate the resistance required:

$$R = \frac{V}{I} = \frac{4.3}{5 \times 10^{-3}} = 0.86 \times 10^3 = 860 \ \Omega$$

The next preferred value up the scale is now considered. This value is 1000 Ω If a 10% tolerance resistor is used, its value might be anything between 900 and 1100 Ω As 900 is larger than 860 this resistor would be all right. A 1000 Ω, 20% tolerance resistor would not be suitable, however. (Can you explain why?)

Exercise 23 — What resistor would you connect in series with an LED which operates at 2 V and takes 10 mA, if you want to connect the LED to a 12 V supply?

C1.16 — Voltage droppers

A resistor can be used as a voltage dropper. Suppose you need to run a 2.5 V 0.1 A lamp from a 12 V supply. A resistor can be connected in series with the lamp. The voltage difference across the resistor will be (12 − 2.5) = 9.5 V. The resistance value can be calculated using the resistance equation. (The calculation gives 95 Ω; a 100 Ω resistor would normally be used.)

This arrangement is only sensible where the current is constant. If it were used with, say, an electric motor, then the motor would not operate properly. When the motor starts to move its load, the current that it takes increases. The voltage dropper would therefore drop a larger voltage, so that the motor gets less power at a time when it needs more.

C1.17 — Other uses of resistors

The other uses of resistors are considered in the chapters on transistor circuits (chapter 11) and operational amplifiers (chapter 12).

C2 — Diodes

C2.1 — Uses of diodes

A diode conducts electricity in one direction only. Diodes are used for:

- steering signals and currents;
- rectifying a.c;
- protecting other components in a circuit;
- demodulating radio signals.

Light-emitting diodes are diodes which emit light as they conduct electricity. They are therefore used as indicators and for seven-segment displays.

Zener diodes are diodes designed so that they can break down in the reverse direction without damage. They are used for giving a steady (stabilised) voltage in a circuit and for clamping (preventing the voltage applied to the protected part of a circuit from exceeding the zener diode voltage).

C2.2 — Half-wave rectification

Fig. C.4 shows a half-wave rectifier circuit that will convert a.c. from the transformer into unsmoothed d.c. The a.c. waveform and the rectified waveform are also shown. This arrangement is called half-wave rectification because only one half of the waveform is used to produce d.c. The diode must be able to carry the maximum current required by the load, and to withstand the peak reverse voltage the transformer can provide. If the d.c. is smoothed, the diode must withstand twice the maximum reverse voltage. For a 12 V (r.m.s.) input from the transformer and smoothing the diode must withstand a reverse voltage difference of 35 V.

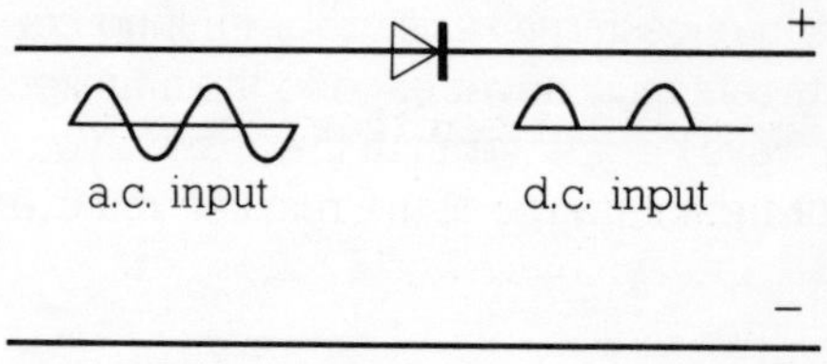

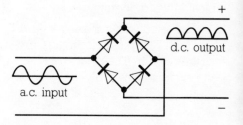

Fig. C.4 A half-wave rectifier circuit and the input and output waveforms.

C2.3 — Bridge rectification

Fig. C.5 shows a standard bridge rectifier arrangement, together with the waveforms in the circuit. This is one method for full-wave rectification. Each diode carries half the current required by the load (on average), but each diode must be able to withstand the full reverse voltage, as for half-wave rectification. The output voltage of a bridge rectifier is slightly lower than that for a half-wave rectifier, because the current passes through two diodes instead of one.

Fig. C.5 A bridge rectifier circuit and the input and output waveforms.

C2.4 — Diode characteristics

A diode is specified by stating:

 (i) the maximum forward current that it can carry; and

(ii) the peak inverse voltage that it can withstand.

When it is conducting, the voltage difference across a silicon diode is about 0.7 V. For a germanium diode the voltage difference is about 0.2 V. For gallium arsenide diodes used as LEDs the voltage difference is about 2 V.

C2.5 — Choosing diodes

Diodes are not sold in a series of standard values like resistors and capacitors, so that finding the right diode means referring to manufacturers' information to find the diode nearest to your needs. Diodes should not be used in series or in parallel to get higher voltage or current ratings. This is because no two diodes are absolutely identical and one of the two may still be in excess of its maximum ratings. In general, there is no problem using a high-voltage diode in a low-voltage circuit, and no problem using high-current diodes in circuits where the current is much less than the maximum that the diode can take.

When choosing diodes, remember that for use on the mains supply the peak inverse voltage rating must be at least 800 V, that for diodes carrying several amps or more a heat sink will be needed to dissipate the heat produced by the diode, and that for radio signals germanium diodes are usually used.

Exercises on selecting diodes

Exercise 24 — You have the following diodes in your spares box:

type 1N4001 — max current 1 A, peak inverse voltage 50 V
type 1N4004 — max current 1 A, peak inverse voltage 400 V
type 1N4007 — max current 1 A, peak inverse voltage 1000 V
type 1N5406 — max current 3 A, peak inverse voltage 600 V
type BY127 — max current 1.5 A, peak inverse voltage 1250 V
type 0A202 — max current 80 mA, peak inverse voltage 150 V.

 (i) Which of these diodes could be used for a battery charger using 2 A from a 12 V a.c. supply?

(ii) Which of these diodes could be used to give a current of 30 mA directly from the mains supply (240 V a.c.)?

(iii) Which diode would be the best diode to use in a logic circuit where it would be connected in series with a 1000 Ω resistor and used on a 5 V power supply?

C2.6 − Light-emitting diodes

Light-emitting diodes giving red, orange, yellow or green light (and also infrared) are available. Red LEDs give more light (are more efficient) than the other colours.

Most LEDs have ratings in the following ranges:

maximum current	20 − 50 mA
typical operating current	10 − 20 mA
maximum reverse voltage	5 V
typical forward operating voltage	2.0 − 2.4 V

LEDs are used with a series resistor. To calculate the value of the resistor, subtract the LED voltage from the supply voltage to find the voltage difference across the resistor. Then calculate the resistance using that voltage difference, and the current that the LED is to carry, in the resistance equation.

Example of the method of calculating series resistors for use with LEDs

Suppose an LED is to be used on an 8 V supply with a current of 15 mA.

(i) Find the forward voltage of the diode from tables. If you cannot find it, assume that it is 2.0 V. (Why assume the *lowest* likely value?)

68

(ii) Find the voltage across the resistor:
$$V_R = 8.0 - 2.0 = 6.0 \text{ V}$$

(iii) Use the resistance equation to find the value of the resistor:
$$R = \frac{V_R}{I} = \frac{6.0}{15 \times 10^{-3}} = 400 \ \Omega$$

(iv) Use the next preferred value that is above the value you have calculated: the nearest preferred value above 400 Ω is 470 Ω

Exercise 25 − Find a suitable value for the series resistance for an LED with a forward voltage of 2.2 V and working current of 10 mA, if it is to be connected to a 5 V power supply.

Exercise 26 − What resistor would you use with a 20 mA LED connected to an operational amplifier that can give an output signal of up to 13 V?

C2.7 − Zener diodes

Zener diodes are used to give a steady reference voltage and also in circuits where the voltage must not be higher than a specified amount. To give a reference voltage they are connected in series with a resistor, as shown in fig. C.6. When they are used to 'clamp' a voltage so that it does not go above the specified level, no resistor is used but there must be a resistor in the power-supply lead to prevent the zener diode burning out (see fig. C.7).

Zener diodes behave as normal diodes when you connect them so that current passes in the forward direction. They behave as zener diodes when they are connected so that the current is flowing in the reverse direction. Zener diodes may have to dissipate large amounts of power unless the current is small.

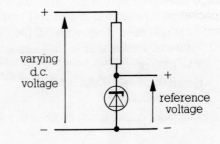

Fig. C.6 The use of a zener diode as a voltage reference.

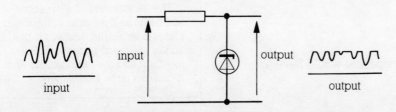

Fig. C.7 The use of a zener diode as a voltage clamp.

C3 — Capacitors

C3.1 — Uses of capacitors

Capacitors are used for the following purposes:

- storing electric charge;
- smoothing the d.c. output from a mains power supply;
- interference suppressors;
- keeping bias voltages steady (e.g. in transistor circuits);
- allowing a.c. signals through, but blocking d.c;
- separating high-frequency signals from low-frequency signals;
- with a resistor, for timing circuits;
- with a resistor, for integrating circuits;
- with an inductor, for tuning circuits and other resonant circuits.

C3.2 — Types of capacitor

There are two main types of capacitor — those in which an insulator is placed between the plates, and those for which the insulating layer is produced electrochemically. This second group of capacitors are called electrolytic capacitors. The differences between the two types are given in table C.4.

Non-electrolytic capacitors are made with any of the following materials as the insulator: polyester (cheapest), mica, ceramics, polystyrene, polycarbonate (most expensive). Variable capacitors have air or mica as the insulator.

Most electrolytic capacitors use aluminium as the plate metal, but high-quality electrolytic capacitors use tantalum.

Table C.4 Comparison of electrolytic and non-electrolytic capacitors

non-electrolytic capacitors	electrolytic capacitors
Capacities between 1 pF and 10 µF	Capacities between 1 µF and 0.1 F
Large physical size	Much smaller size than non-electrolytics of same capacity
High maximum working voltages	Low maximum working voltages
Can be connected either way round	Must be connected with + connection always positive
Can be used with a.c.	Cannot be used with a.c. unless there is a d.c. voltage too
d.c. resistance between plates over 100 MΩ	There is always a leakage current of a fraction of a milliamp
Very little change if not used	Current flows to reform electrochemical insulator each time capacitor is used
Can be made with close tolerance	Tolerance typically −20% to +50%
Large capacitances are expensive	Cheap to make
Can be made as variable capacitors	Only fixed values possible

C3.3 — Capacitance

Capacitors store electric charge. The quantity of charge stored depends on the voltage difference across the capacitor and the *capacitance* of the capacitor. Capacitance is measured in farads (F) but the capacity of most capacitors in electronic equipment is between 100 picofarads and 1000 microfarads. 1 picofarad is 10^{-12} farads; 1 nanofarad is 10^{-9} farads; 1 microfarad is 10^{-6} farads. Thus:

$$1 \text{ nF} = 1000 \text{ pF}$$
$$1 \text{ µF} = 1000 \text{ nF} = 1\,000\,000 \text{ pF}$$
$$1 \text{ F} = 1\,000\,000 \text{ µF}$$

The formula for capacitance is given in the panel on the right.

C3.4 — Typical values of capacitors used in electronic equipment

The following are typical values used for capacitors in standard circuits:

smoothing capacitors	$1000 - 10\,000$ µF
interference suppression	0.1 µF
bias voltage stabilisation	$10 - 100$ µF
blocking d.c.	$1 - 100$ µF
timing: for example, a 100 kΩ resistor and a 1 µF capacitor would have a period of 100 ms.	
tuning	500 pF

The capacitance formula

Electric charge is measured in *coulombs*. One coulomb is the charge moved when there is a current of 1 amp for 1 second. Capacitance is measured in farads. A capacitor of 1 farad capacitance would hold 1 coulomb if the voltage difference was 1 volt. The formula for capacitance is:

$$\text{capacitance (in \textbf{farads})} = \frac{\text{charge stored (in \textbf{coulombs})}}{\text{voltage difference (in \textbf{volts})}}$$

The capacitance of a capacitor will be large if the area of the metal plates is large, the insulator is thin and/or the metal plates are close together, and the insulator has what is called a large *permittivity*.

For an a.c. of 1 kHz a capacitor of 1 μF behaves as though it has a resistance of 160 Ω. At 100 kHz this reactance (as it is called) is a hundred times less (1.6 Ω). The larger the capacitance, the lower is the reactance.

C3.5 — Capacitors in series and in parallel

If capacitors are connected in *parallel* the total capacitance is the sum of the separate capacitances (like resistors in *series*).

For capacitors in *series*, use the 'product over sum' formula (like resistors in *parallel*).

C4 — Inductors

C4.1 — Uses of inductors

The following are common uses of inductors:

- transformers;
- relays;
- loudspeakers;
- microphones and pick-ups
  (such as those used for record players and tape-heads);
- solenoids and electric motors;
- blocking a.c. but allowing d.c. to pass;
- interference suppressors;
- with capacitors, in tuning circuits and resonant circuits.

C4.2 — Inductance

Inductors have the property of inductance. Inductance is measured in henries. The larger the inductance, the greater the effect the inductance has on alternating currents. For all inductors that effect increases as the frequency of the a.c. increases. Inductance is a result of the magnetism produced when there is an electric current.

C4.3 — Transformers

A transformer has two coils which are not connected together with wires but are close enough for the magnetism produced by one coil to affect the other coil. Usually the two coils are fitted on to an iron or ferrite core to get maximum effect. Fig. C.8 is a cut-away diagram of a typical transformer for the mains supply. The coil to which the power supply is connected is called the *primary* coil and the coil which gives the output from the transformer is called the *secondary* coil. Typically, the coils have between 5 and 10 turns for each volt of the supply voltage to the primary coil.

Fig. C.9 shows the circuit symbol for a transformer.

Transformers will operate only with alternating currents.

The alternating voltage difference across the secondary coil (the output) is related to the voltage difference across the primary coil by the formula given below:

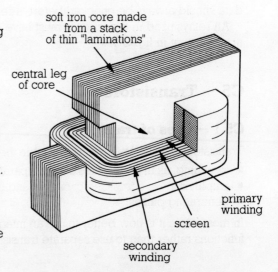

Fig. C.8 A cut-away diagram showing the construction of a mains transformer.

$$\frac{\text{alternating voltage difference}}{\text{alternating voltage difference}} = \frac{\text{number of turns in}}{\text{number of turns in}}$$
across secondary coil / across primary coil = secondary coil / primary coil

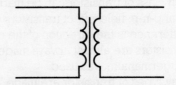

Fig. C.9 The circuit symbol for a transformer.

Example of the use of the transformer equation

Suppose you need a transformer that can be connected to the mains supply to give an output of 9 V. The mains supply is 240 V. How many turns would you put in each coil?

The primary would have between 5 and 10, say 8, turns for each volt of the supply. That means that the primary would have $8 \times 240 = 1920$ turns.

Putting these numbers into the transformer equation we get:

$$\frac{9}{240} = \frac{N_s}{1920} \qquad \text{where } N_s \text{ is the number of turns in the secondary}$$

$$N_s = 72 \text{ turns}$$

Exercise 27 − A mains transformer is to have 5 turns per volt and is to give an output of 12 V. How many turns will there be in the primary and secondary coils?

Exercise 28 − A monitor has to have 2000 V to operate the display tube. This is to be obtained from a 10 V alternating supply using a transformer. If the primary coil has 60 turns, how many turns will there be in the secondary?

Exercise 29 − A transformer has 80 turns in the primary and 200 turns in the secondary. What output will it give if it is connected to a 30 V alternating supply?

C4.4 − Relays

A relay is an electromagnetic switch that is used as an output transducer where it is needed to switch on high-power circuits (e.g. motors) or high-voltage circuits (e.g. mains). The coil must be chosen to suit the electronic equipment. Relays are specified by their coil resistance and their working voltage. A typical 6 V relay would operate between 4 and 9 V and have a resistance of 50 Ω. A 12 V relay would operate between 9 and 20 V and have a resistance of 200 Ω. Manufacturers' data should always be checked before a relay is chosen.

All relays used in d.c. circuits must have a protection diode, as shown by the arrangement in fig. C.10.

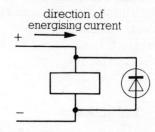

Fig. C.10 A relay with a protection diode connected.

C5 − Transistors

C5.1 − Uses of transistors

Transistors are used in circuits to enable them to carry out the following functions:
- switching, as in logic gates and comparators;
- amplifying;
- generating pulses.

In most cases it is now better to use an integrated circuit to carry out these functions rather than to use separate transistors.

C5.2 − Types of transistor

There are two main classes of transistor. The first class is bipolar transistors, which are current amplifiers (although they are often used in circuits which operate as voltage amplifiers). The second class is field-effect transistors, which are voltage amplifiers.

Each class of transistor can be made in two forms. Bipolar transistors can be n-p-n or p-n-p; field-effect transistors can be n-channel or p-channel. In each case the difference is the direction of the currents in the transistor.

Transistors are almost always made from silicon. When transistors were first made, germanium was used.

Many types of transistor are made, but three common types of bipolar transistor and one type of field-effect transistor will suit most purposes. Different manufacturers use different code numbers for the same types of transistor, and

Table C.5 Transistor equivalent types

2N3819			
BFW61,	MPF102		
BC108			
BC107,	BC109,	BC147, .	BC148,
BC149,	BC207,	BC208,	BC209,
BC237,	BC238,	BC239,	BC317,
BC318,	BC319,	BC347,	BC348,
BC349,	BC547,	BC548,	BC549,
BC171,	BC172,	BC173,	BC182,
BC183,	BC184,	BC382,	BC383,
BC384,	BC437,	BC438,	BC439,
BC414			
2N3053			
BFY51,	BFY52,	BFY53,	BFY50,
BFX84,	BFX85,	BFX86,	2N1613,
2N1711,	2N1893,	2N2102,	2N2270,
2N2405,			
2N3055			
BDY20			

different code numbers are used if the casing of the transistor is different. The four types are:

2N3819 – an n-channel FET
BC108 – a low-current, high-gain 'general purpose' n-p-n transistor
2N3053 – a medium-current, medium-gain n-p-n transistor.
2N3055 – a high-current, low-gain 'power' n-p-n transistor.

Table C.5 on the previous page gives the type numbers of transistors which are electrically the same or near equivalents. Manufacturers' data sheets should be consulted for more details. For almost all circuits using a BC108 transistor, any general-purpose transistor would be suitable. Some transistors are described as 'switching transistors'. Any transistor can be used in a switching circuit but these types are designed for high-speed digital circuits. They can usually be used as general-purpose transistors too.

C5.3 – Transistor symbols

Fig. C.11 shows the circuit symbols, the name of each part, and the currents and voltages around n-p-n and p-n-p transistors.

C5.4 – Current gain and h_{FE}

The bipolar transistor is basically a *current amplifier*. The collector current (from the power supply through the collector and emitter) is controlled by the base current (from the signal source through the base and emitter). The collector current is proportional to the base current. (This is not exactly true but you can ignore the small variation.) Thus:

$$\frac{collector\ current}{base\ current} = h_{FE}$$

The value of h_{FE} is constant for any particular transistor. The value lies between 10 and 1000, depending on the type of transistor. Even for one particular type the value can vary greatly. Type BC108 transistors are quoted as having h_{FE} values between 110 and 800.

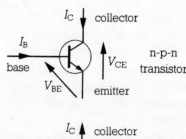
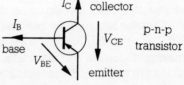

Fig. C.11 The symbols, currents and voltages for n-p-n and p-n-p types of transistors.

Example of the use of the h_{FE} equation

A transistor is needed to drive a relay. The relay needs not less than 120 mA to make it switch on. The signal source can only give a maximum of 3 mA. What is the minimum suitable value of h_{FE} for this transistor?

In this case the collector current must be at least 120 mA. The base current is not more than 3 mA. Use these two values in the formula:

$$\frac{120}{3} = h_{FE} = 40$$

It is wise to allow a little more than the minimum of 120 mA to operate the relay, so a value larger than 40 would be better.

Exercise 30 – The output current from a logic gate is 100 μA. This is connected to the base of a transistor and a 6 V, 0.04 A lamp is connected to the collector. The lamp lights brightly when the gate gives logic 1. Find the minimum value of h_{FE} that this transistor can have.

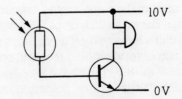

Fig. C.12 The circuit for Exercise 31.

Exercise 31 – Fig. C.12 shows an LDR connected to a transistor which operates a buzzer. If the value of h_{FE} for the transistor is 250 and the buzzer needs 50 mA to operate, what current must the LDR pass to make the buzzer sound?

C5.5 — Other bipolar transistor characteristics

In choosing a transistor, factors besides h_{FE} must be considered. These are:

- the maximum voltage difference between base and emitter;
- the maximum voltage difference between collector and emitter in either direction;
- the maximum power the transistor can dissipate and whether it needs a heat sink to assist this process;
- the maximum collector current;
- the maximum frequency at which the transistor can operate.

The maximum collector-emitter voltage may be as little as 20 V. Some transistors are designed for much higher voltages. Using a high voltage means the transistor has to dissipate more power, and it is the power dissipated that often limits the supply voltage.

Most transistors that 'blow' do so because there has been too large a reverse voltage difference between the base and the emitter when the transistor has been turned off. For some transistors −5 V can be enough.

The maximum current and maximum power can be found from data tables. If these values are exceeded, the transistor will rapidly overheat and be destroyed.

Almost all transistors will work up to frequencies of 1 MHz but, for radio or fast pulse switching, transistors with a high maximum operating frequency ('switching transistors') must be used.

C5.6 — Connections to transistors

Transistors are made with a wide range of arrangements for connections. Fig. C.13 shows the connections for BC108, 2N3053 and 2N3055. Manufacturers' data sheets should be checked before connecting a transistor into a circuit. Even two transistors which look the same may have different internal arrangements.

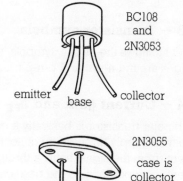

Fig. C.13   The pin connections for BC108, 2N3053, and 2N3055.

C6 — Integrated circuits

C6.1 — Types of integrated circuits

There is now a very large range of integrated circuits. It is not safe to assume that because two chips look the same they are the same type. There are those having standard functions (such as logic gates and amplifiers), those with special systems (such as microprocessors and complete radio receivers), and those which are just several transistors or resistors in a d.i.l. package for convenience. The type number should always be identified before a chip is used.

Integrated circuits are sometimes described as 'linear'. Linear ICs are amplifiers and other analogue devices. Switching circuits and logic gates are sometimes called 'digital' ICs.

Two manufacturing methods are commonly used for ICs. Most modern ICs are of a type known as CMOS (CMOS stands for **c**omplementary **m**etal **o**xide **s**emiconductor and is pronounced 'seemoss'). The other type is based on, and manufactured in the same way as, bipolar transistors. Logic ICs made by this method are known as TTL chips (TTL stands for 'transistor-transistor logic').

CMOS chips have several advantages compared with bipolar types. Power consumption is very low, and they will operate from a wide range of supply voltages (3 V to 18 V; TTLs have to operate on 5 V). CMOS chips can be sensitive to stray high-voltage pulses. Soldering irons and mains-powered measuring equipment should be properly earthed and this will avoid the main cause of problems. The other source of high-voltage pulses is static electricity from the human body and clothing. CMOS circuits should not be handled more than is necessary, and when they are handled, finger contact should be with the insulated parts of the chip or circuit only.

C6.2 — TTL logic

There is a very large series of TTL logic circuits available. The standard types are known as the '74 series' and they have type numbers such as 7401, 74221, 74LS33 and 74ALS05. Almost all of them are made as 14 or 16 pin d.i.l. packages. Most have several gates on one chip. For example, 7402 is a 'quad 2-input NOR', which means that the chip has four NOR gates on it, each with two inputs.

C6.3 — CMOS logic

Like TTL, there is a family of CMOS logic chips. They are known as the 4000B series, and have type numbers such as 4001B. Although 4001B is a quad 2-input NOR like TTL 7402, you cannot plug a 4000 series CMOS chip in a socket intended for a TTL chip. In general, a system is made to use all TTL or all CMOS (although you can now buy CMOS chips which can be used in circuits designed for 74 series TTL chips). Most CMOS ICs are in 16 pin d.i.l. packages.

C6.4 — Other common integrated circuits

There are three other common groups of integrated circuits that are fairly easy to use. These are:

operational amplifiers type 741 or similar (**note**: this is **not** a member of the '74 series') (refer to chapter 10);

timers type 555 or similar (refer to reference section B5);

voltage regulators in the 78 or 79 series (e.g. 78L05) which are used for stabilising power supplies (refer to chapter 13).

For all other integrated circuits, it is **essential** to have manufacturers' data before attempting to use them.

C6.5 — Connections to integrated circuits

Almost all ICs are packaged in standard d.i.l. packages. It is possible to solder these ICs directly into a circuit, but it is much better to use a holder into which the IC can be plugged. This avoids the possibility of damage during construction, and allows replacement. It is impossible to unsolder all 16 pins of a d.i.l. package at the same time if you need to remove the chip!

In data books, connection diagrams often number the pins and then give a list of connections to each pin. The package has a notch or a dot at one end to show that that is the end for pin 1. From the dot, pins are counted anti-clockwise down one side and back up the other (see fig. C.14) when looking at the **top** of the package. It is easy to plug a chip in the wrong way round, so check carefully when you make up a circuit or plug a chip in its holder.

When inserting an IC into its holder, take great care not to bend the pins.

If you use a chip with several gates on it, and do not need to use all the gates, the remaining pins may have to be connected to logic 0 or logic 1 to prevent connections inside the chip affecting the way in which the circuit works. You should always check manufacturers' data to find out what extra connections must be made.

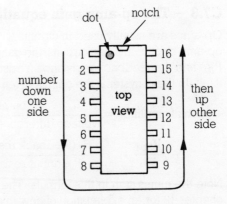

Fig. C.14 The numbering of the pins on an integrated circuit.

C7 — Operational amplifiers

C7.1 — Characteristics of operational amplifiers

Op-amps are voltage amplifiers that can amplify both positive and negative voltages.

The gain is very high (typically 100 000, which is shown in manufacturers' data as 100 dB. A gain of 10 000 = 80 dB; 1 000 000 = 120 dB).

There are two inputs, one of which is an inverting input and the other a non-inverting input. The amplifier amplifies the difference in voltage between these two inputs. Feedback is usually used with op-amps; feedback is connected to the inverting input.

Op-amps need two power supplies, one negative and the other positive. Typically, they operate on supply voltages between $-5/0/+5$ V and $-15/0/+15$ V.

The amplifier will 'saturate' when it reaches within 2 V of the power supply voltage. For an amplifier using a $-10/0/+10$ V supply, the maximum output is $+8$ V and the minimum output is -8 V (approximately).

The input resistance of the amplifier is very high (typically more than 1 MΩ), so that it takes very little current from the signal.

The output resistance of the amplifier is low (typically about 150 Ω), and most op-amps are protected from damage that might be caused by short circuits at the output.

C7.2 — The uses of op-amps

Operational amplifiers can be used for the following functions:
- voltage amplification with or without inverting the signal;
- finding the sum of two signals;
- finding the difference between two signals;
- as an integrating system;
- as a comparator which switches when a signal reaches a pre-determined level;
- as a pulse generator;
- as a generator of alternating voltages (a signal generator).

Most of these uses are described in detail in chapter 12.

C7.3 — The op-amp gain equation

Op-amps are usually used in circuits with feedback. Fig. C.15 shows the basic op-amp circuit. In these circuits, the gain depends on the input resistance (resistor R_{IN}) and the feedback resistance (resistor R_F), but not on the gain of the op-amp itself. In these systems the gain is given by the following formulae:

$$\text{gain of amplifier} = \frac{\text{output voltage } (V_{OUT})}{\text{voltage difference between the two inputs } (V_{IN})}$$

$$\frac{V_{OUT}}{V_{IN}} = -\frac{R_F \text{ (feedback resistance)}}{R_{IN} \text{ (input resistance)}}$$

Note the minus sign in this formula. The amplifier is an inverting amplifier. See chapter 12 for an explanation of how this formula is obtained.

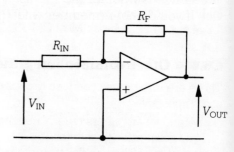

Fig. C.15 The basic op-amp circuit. In this circuit the non-inverting input is connected to the zero line but it may be connected differently in other circuits.

Example of the use of the op-amp formula

Suppose that, in fig. C.15, R_{IN} is 10 kΩ and you want the system to have a gain of -5. What value would R_F have to be?

$$\text{gain} = -\frac{R_F}{R_{IN}}$$

Filling in the numbers we get:

$$-5 = -\frac{R_F}{10\ 000}$$

$$R_F = 50\ 000\ \Omega$$

(nearest value in E12 range = 47 kΩ)

Exercise 32 — If R_F in fig. C.15 is 100 kΩ and R_{IN} is 3.3 kΩ, what is the gain of the system?

Exercise 33 — If the output voltage in fig. C.15 has to be 6 V when the input voltage is -2 V, suggest suitable values for R_{IN} and R_F.

11 TRANSISTOR CIRCUITS

A transistor cannot do anything by itself. It is only a useful device when it is connected in a circuit. This chapter, and the next two chapters, are not about complete systems but about the way in which certain components are used in circuits that can be useful building blocks in a system.

Transistors can be used in three ways: in switching blocks; in amplifying blocks; and in blocks which generate pulses. The main difference is whether the transistor can be turned off and saturated, or not. If you do not remember what these terms mean, turn to pages 84–85.

Using the transistor in a switching circuit

Suppose you need an inverter block but you do not have a circuit for it. You would have to design your own circuit. You have a BC108 transistor and you have to use a 5 volt supply because that is the power supply to the rest of the system. The input signal to the inverter may be less than 5 volts when it is a logic 1 signal so, to be sure the inverter will work, it must give a logic 0 output for any signal greater than 1.5 volts.

Table 11.1 Data for the BC108 transistor. (A complete manufacturer's data sheet for the BC108 transistor would also include graphs showing the performance details.)

Collector-emitter voltage (with $V_{BE} = 0$)	maximum	30 V
Collector-emitter voltage with base open-circuit	maximum	20 V
Emitter-base voltage (base negative, open collector)	maximum	5 V
Peak value of collector current	maximum	200 mA
Continuous collector current	maximum	100 mA
Total power dissipation (outside temperature < 25°C)	maximum	300 mW
h_{FE}	minimum	110
	typical	180–520
	maximum	800
Base-emitter voltage for forward bias with collector current = 10 mA	maximum	0.77 V
Collector-emitter voltage at saturation with collector current = 10 mA	maximum	0.25 V

These details are called the *specification* for the block. A specification is a statement of what the system is expected to do. What important point is missing from this specification?

To design the circuit you will need to know more about the transistor. You need to know h_{FE} for the BC108. You must be sure that this transistor can be used with a 5 volt supply without damaging the transistor. You must know the safe maximum current and power the transistor can withstand. All this information is available in the manufacturer's data. Table 11.1 shows some of the more important data for the BC108 transistor. You can see that h_{FE} will be between 110 and 800, that the maximum current is 100 milliamps, and that the maximum power is 360 milliwatts. All voltage differences specified in the sheet are at least 5 volts, so there is no problem in using a 5 volt power supply.

To understand how to use this transistor, start by thinking of the transistor as a system. There must be signal, control and power inputs, and an output. To get an output, the transistor must be used with a *load*, just like the LDR in chapter 7. Fig. 11.1 shows the systems diagram for a transistor circuit, drawn over the basic circuit for a transistor (see fig. 10.3, page 83). For a transistor, the control signal is called *bias*.

It is no use designing a circuit without finding out whether it can do the job that it is meant to do. The specification given at the top of this page did not describe the output of the system. The inverter we want to design will only be giving a voltage signal, so the output will not have to give very much current.

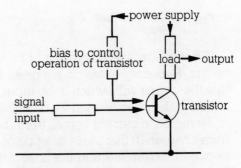

Fig. 11.1 The system diagram for a transistor circuit, drawn over the basic circuit for a transistor. Compare this system diagram with fig. 1.5 in chapter 1. Which part of this diagram is the processor part of the system?

When signals go from one block to the next, the current will be perhaps 1 milliamp. The total current in R_L needs to be 5 to 10 times more than the current needed by the output. This is so that the current used by the next block has little effect on the way this circuit operates. This tells us that the collector current for the transistor has to be about 10 milliamps. Can the transistor carry 10 milliamps? Looking at table 11.1 you can see that this is much less than the maximum current the transistor can carry, so we can go to the next step in designing the inverter circuit (fig. 11.2).

An inverter is a switching circuit. When a transistor acts as a switch it is either saturated, or turned off. This means that when this transistor is saturated, the collector current must be 10 milliamps. (What will be the collector current when the transistor is turned off?) This tells us what we need to know to start calculating the values of the resistors, voltage differences and currents in the circuit (fig. 11.3).

Start with the load resistor. When a transistor is saturated, the whole of the power-supply voltage is across the load, except for the 0.2 volts between the collector and the emitter of the transistor. So we know that the voltage difference across R_L must be 4.8 volts (5 volts − 0.2 volts), and we also know that the current in R_L must be about 10 milliamps. We can use the resistance equation to find the value for R_L; it is 480 ohms.

In practice we would have to use the nearest preferred value; that is 470 ohms. A resistor with 10% tolerance would be suitable. With 10% tolerance the value could be anywhere between 423 ohms (470 − 47) and 517 ohms (470 + 47), but that is close enough in practice. We said the collector current had to be *about* 10 milliamps.

The next thing to find is the base current (fig. 11.4). We use the value of h_{FE} to find that. In fact the data tables give a wide range of possible values for the BC108 transistor, so that you have to decide which value to use. It is important that the circuit will work, whatever the value of h_{FE}. We therefore always use the **lowest** value given for h_{FE}. If you use a high value then a transistor with a lower value of h_{FE} will need more current than you have provided at the base, but if you do your calculations with the lowest value of h_{FE} then any transistor of type BC108 will work because there is always enough, or more than enough, base current.

It would be very convenient if in electronics you could always get exact answers, but in real life it is not possible to make components with that kind of accuracy. This means that the art of working out values is to allow for all possibilities (rather like life itself!).

The lowest value for h_{FE} is 110 for the BC108 transistor. Using the h_{FE} formula to calculate the base current I_{BE}, we get:

$$h_{FE} = \frac{I_{CE}}{I_{BE}} \quad \text{so that} \quad I_{BE} = \frac{I_{CE}}{h_{FE}} = \frac{0.01}{110} = 0.00009 \text{ A} \approx 100 \text{ } \mu\text{A}$$

We can now find the values of R_1 and R_2. As this is a simple switching circuit, R_2 is easy − we do not need R_2 at all! For R_1, we must be sure that the circuit will switch if the input voltage is more than 1.5 volts, as stated in the specification for this inverter given on page 107 (fig. 11.5).

All the base current comes from the input source. You will remember from chapter 10 that there must be at least 0.7 volts voltage difference between the emitter and the base if there is to be any base current at all. This means that, if the source voltage is 1.5 volts, there will be 0.8 volts across R_1. (Can you state which law has been used to get this answer?)

The resistance equation can now be used to find the value of R_1:

$$R_1 = \frac{voltage\ difference}{base\ current} = \frac{0.8}{0.00009} = 8900 \text{ } \Omega$$

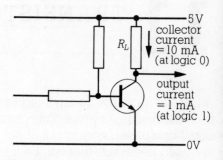

Fig. 11.2 The currents in the output of a switching circuit. The transistor must be able to carry them.

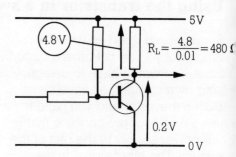

Fig. 11.3 Calculating the resistance of the load.

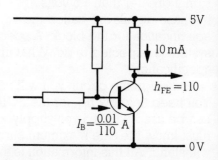

Fig. 11.4 Calculating the base current using the value of h_{FE}.

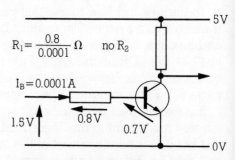

Fig. 11.5 Finding the values of the resistors in the input circuit.

As before, you would need to choose the nearest preferred value, but you have to be a little more careful this time. The current must not be *less* than 0.00009 amps, so the resistance cannot be more than 8900 ohms. The nearest preferred value in the E12 range is 8.2 kilohms. With a 10% tolerance this could be 9020 ohms in reality. To be absolutely certain that the resistance did not exceed 8.9 kΩ it might be better to go to the next lower resistor in the series. This would give R_1 as 6.8 kilohms.

All the component values have been worked out and the final circuit for the inverter can be drawn. This is shown in fig. 11.6. There are, however, two more questions. Is the power that the transistor has to take too great? What happens if the input voltage is less or more than 1.5 volts?

The power ratings in the inverter circuit are no problem. The maximum current in the transistor is 10 milliamps and the maximum voltage is 5 volts. Even if the whole of this were applied to the transistor (which it cannot be) the total power would only be 50 milliwatts, which is well inside the 360 milliwatts rating of the transistor. (In fact, the maximum power that the transistor has to dissipate is about 12.5 milliwatts. Can you explain why? This is a hard question to answer.)

The voltage problem is not quite as easy. There is no difficulty if the voltage is above 1.5 volts, because that will make the base current larger than the 0.00009 amps and the transistor will switch as it should. If the voltage is below 0.7 volts, there is no problem either, because the transistor will be turned off and the output will be 5 volts (logic 1). (Why?) However, between 0.7 volts and 1.5 volts we do not know whether the circuit would switch or not. Often that would not matter. If it were a real problem the solution would be to use either a lower value for R_1 or a higher value for R_L.

This section has described the way in which a switching circuit is designed using the simplest possible circuit. The basic ideas are no different when the circuit you are designing is a logic gate with several inputs. Fig. 11.7 shows a two-input NOR gate circuit and a two-input NAND gate circuit, based on the same ideas. You should make sure that you know why there are diodes in these circuits (see chapter 8); why the circuits will switch at 2.2 volts instead of 1.5 volts (the answer to this is also in chapter 8); how to make the NOR gate into an OR gate (see chapter 4); and why the NAND gate needs bias resistors (think about what happens when the input signal is logic 0).

The transistor used in amplifier circuits

To use the transistor as part of an amplifier system, it must be used in such a way that it does **not** turn off and it does **not** saturate.

In the last section, where the transistor was used as a switch in the inverter circuit, the transistor was turned off for input signals below 0.7 volts and was saturated for signals above 1.5 volts. However, what happens between those two voltages?

The way to find an answer to a question like that is to plot a *characteristic* for the system. A characteristic is a graph showing how any two voltages or currents in a system are related. We are interested in amplifier circuits for amplifying voltage signals, so the characteristic we are interested in is the relationship between the input signal voltage and the output signal voltage. This is called the *transfer characteristic* of the amplifier system.

To find out what the transfer characteristic looks like, all we need to do is to take a series of measurements of voltages and draw a graph of the

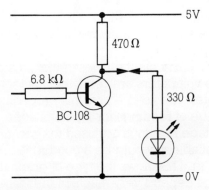

Fig. 11.6 The circuit for the inverter discussed in this chapter. This circuit will work if it is correctly assembled, and it can be tested using an LED and resistor, as shown.

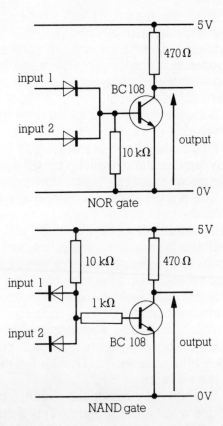

Fig. 11.7 The circuits of transistor NOR and NAND gates. The values of the components would be calculated in the same way as for the inverter. These circuits will work if assembled correctly.

results. Fig. 11.8 shows the circuit of the inverter with a voltage divider to give a variable input signal and voltmeters to measure the input and output voltages.

To carry out the investigation, the power supply is turned on and the two voltmeters are read; the voltage divider is then adjusted and the meters are read again; this procedure is continued until there is a good range of readings for input voltages, from zero to maximum. The voltage readings are used to draw the graph. If you have the equipment available, it would be a good idea to carry out the investigation yourself.

Fig. 11.9 shows the type of graph that you might get, but the graph does depend very much on the value of h_{FE} for the transistor you use, so that you would not necessarily get a graph exactly the same as the one shown here.

In the graph in fig. 11.9 you will see that for input voltages between 0.8 volts and 1.4 volts the output changes in step with the input. For a change of 0.6 volts at the input there is a change in the output voltage from 4.8 volts to 0.4 volts. Thus the output voltage change is about seven times the change in input voltage. The voltage gain of the circuit is about seven.

If you use transistors with a different h_{FE}, or change the values of the resistors, the gain of the circuit will change. However, the principle is the same. If you use a transistor in the range between cut-off and saturation ('bottoming'), the circuit will behave as an amplifier. In this case, for input signals varying between 0.8 volts and 1.4 volts, the circuit will amplify the *variation* in the input.

Suppose you wanted to amplify the output from a microphone which gives a peak voltage difference at its output terminals of 0.2 volts. As this is an a.c. signal, and is less than 0.7 volts anyway, the circuit will not give any amplification. It will be cut off all the time. Is there any way of using the circuit to amplify signals like this one?

The answer to this problem is to arrange that when there is no input from the microphone there is a steady input equivalent to 1.1 volts (1.1 volts is half way between 0.8 and 1.4 volts). The microphone voltage will then be added – and subtracted (remember that the microphone gives an a.c. signal) – to this steady voltage. Using this steady voltage is known as biassing the transistor. The bias resistor was not needed for the inverter, but biassing is always needed when a transistor is used in an amplifier circuit. Fig. 11.10 shows the basic circuit. The value of R_2 has been calculated for a transistor with $h_{FE} = 110$. There is no separate R_1 in this case because the resistance of the microphone does the same job. (See reference section D1.6 for the method of calculating the values of these resistors.)

In adding the bias to the circuit, a capacitor has had to be included in series with the microphone. This is an example of a capacitor used to block d.c., but pass a.c. Without the capacitor, the current in the bias resistor would pass through the microphone instead of passing through the transistor. The capacitor can be an electrolytic capacitor, because the bias will make sure that the positive plate is kept positive at all times.

Other bias arrangements

The bias arrangement in fig. 11.10 works, but there are a lot of problems with a circuit as simple as that. You might guess that one of them is that the resistor has to be chosen to suit the h_{FE} of the transistor, so that putting another BC108 in the same circuit could mean that R_2 had to be

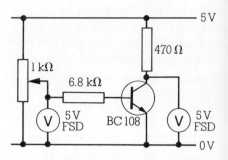

Fig. 11.8 The transistor inverter circuit described in the last section with a voltage divider used as an input source, and meters added, to enable the transfer characteristic of the circuit to be investigated.

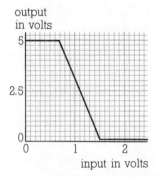

Fig. 11.9 The transfer characteristic of the circuit shown in fig. 11.8 when a transistor with $h_{FE} = 110$ is used. The graph only shows the source voltage from 0 to 2 V, because increasing the input voltage above 1.5 V makes no difference to the output of the circuit.

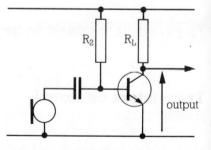

Fig. 11.10 The simplest transistor amplifier circuit. R_2 is the biassing resistor. Its value has to be chosen to ensure that, when there is no signal, the input is in the middle of its working range. The easiest way of checking this is to measure the output voltage at the collector with no input signal (apart from the bias). This voltage should be 2.5 V if the power supply is 5 V. What is the purpose of the capacitor in series with the microphone?

changed too. Most transistor amplifiers use a more complicated bias arrangement to solve this problem. The circuit is shown in fig. 11.11. Calculation of the values of the resistors is beyond the scope of this book and you should refer to a more advanced book on electronics for details of the design of these circuits.

Load lines for transistor circuits

In chapter 7 we used a graphical method of finding out what was happening when an LDR is used in a voltage divider. In the transistor circuits in this chapter, the transistor and its load resistor are working as a voltage divider in the same way. We can, therefore, use the same kind of graph to work out what is happening. The load line is drawn in exactly the same way as in chapter 7, but instead of the resistance lines we need a set of 'transistor lines'.

The correct name for these 'transistor lines' is *collector characteristics*. As for the LDR they are graphs of current against voltage and, as for the LDR there will be more than one. For the LDR it was increasing light that made its resistance line steeper; for the transistor it is the base current that controls the transistor collector current. Unlike the lines for the LDR, the collector characteristics are not straight lines. Fig. 11.12 shows a set of collector characteristics for a BC108 with $h_{FE} = 110$.

Fig. 11.12 also has a load line drawn on it (the dotted straight line on the graph). This is a load line for a 470 ohm resistor and it is drawn in the same way as for the LDR circuits in chapter 7. We can use this to find out how the collector voltage changes as the base current changes. Thus, as the base current changes from 40 μA to 80 μA, the output voltage in this case changes from 3.9 V to 1.9 V.

It can also be used to find the bias current needed when there is no input signal. The collector voltage should then be half-way between zero and the power-supply voltage. Point X on the load line is where the collector voltage is 3.0 volts; the base current there is about 58 μA, for a 470 ohm load.

The same load line shows what happens when the circuit acts as a switch. Points P and Q on the diagram are the logic 0 and logic 1 outputs as a switching circuit, when the load resistor is 470 ohms.

Transistors as signal generators

By using positive feedback rather than negative feedback (see chapter 10), any amplifying or switching device can be turned into a generator of pulses or alternating voltages. Operational amplifiers and logic gates are better for this than circuits using separate transistors (see chapter 6 and reference section B5).

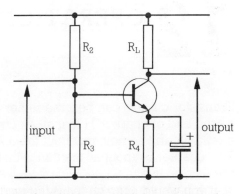

Fig. 11.11 A better way to bias a transistor for use as an amplifier. R_4 increases the voltage difference between the zero line and the emitter of the transistor above 0.7 V; the capacitor keeps that voltage steady.

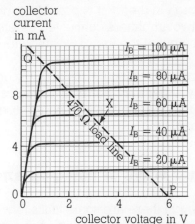

Fig. 11.12 Collector characteristics and a load line for a BC108 transistor. The load line is the dotted line. Each solid line corresponds to a different base current.

SUMMARY 11

The behaviour of a transistor circuit depends on the whole circuit, not just on the transistor.

Bias is a steady voltage or current supplied to the base of a transistor to make it operate in the required manner.

For designing or analysing a transistor circuit the starting point is the specification of the circuit.

When making calculations, start at the output. Determine load current, collector current, load resistor, transistor h_{FE}, base current, bias resistor (if needed), and finally input resistor, in that order.

In a transistor switching circuit the transistor is either turned off or saturated but never between the two states. For an amplifier it operates between the turn-off point and saturation.

When there is no input signal an amplifying circuit has the transistor biassed half-way between the turn-off point and saturation.

The collector characteristic of a transistor is a set of graphs showing how the collector current changes as the collector-emitter voltage varies, for various base currents. Adding a load line will show the behaviour of the circuit in which the transistor is being used.

12 OPERATIONAL AMPLIFIERS

Transistor circuits can become rather complicated, and you may have felt by the end of chapter 11 that all electronic circuits are difficult. You have already learnt something about the operational amplifier in chapter 10. This chapter is about all the things that an op-amp can do, and op-amps are easy to use.

The basic op-amp circuit is the *inverting amplifier*. This was discussed in chapter 10, but the diagram of the circuit is repeated here (fig. 12.1). If the op-amp is being used as a simple amplifier, this is the circuit that is normally used. You simply decide the gain you want and choose the resistors you need to get that gain.

In practice it is not sensible to try to get a gain of more than about 50, although in theory it is possible to do so. For higher gains it is better to use two amplifiers connected together so that the second one amplifies the output of the first. Two amplifiers, each with a gain of 20, will give a total gain of 400 in this way.

Ordinary op-amps are not very good for the high-frequency signals that you get in radio receivers so carefully-designed transistor circuits, or special op-amps, are used for these particular applications instead.

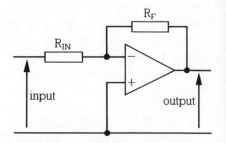

Fig. 12.1 The circuit for a standard inverting amplifier using an op-amp, as described in chapter 10. Power supply connections are not normally shown in circuit diagrams for op-amp circuits.

Other ways of using op-amps

Although there are some limits to what an op-amp can do, it is surprising how many electronic functions an op-amp can be made to do. Op-amps were originally designed to perform mathematical processes, so it is not surprising that op-amps can be made to add, subtract, multiply, divide, take logarithms, integrate and differentiate, and carry out much more complex mathematical processes too. Op-amps are not used any more to do these processes inside computers because digital computers can do the same job more accurately (but using much more complicated circuits). However, most of the processes are important for electronics as well as for analogue computing.

The next sections describe a few of the processes for which you can use op-amp circuits.

Most of the circuits are so simple that it would be easy to try them out in the laboratory if you have the necessary equipment. Prototype board is particularly suitable for these circuits.

Summers

This sort of summer is nothing to do with hot sunny days! A summer *adds* two input signals together. In hi-fi and in recording studios the block that does the same job is called a mixer.

A summer (or mixer) can be made very simply using an op-amp. All that is necessary is to add a second input to the inverting amplifier, and the system will do the rest. The circuit of this block is shown in fig. 12.2, and the design equation of this circuit is given in reference section D2.2 on page 126.

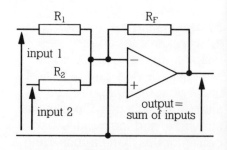

Fig. 12.2 The basic circuit of an op-amp summing block.

A non-inverting amplifier

It may not always be convenient to have the amplifier inverting the signals as well as amplifying them. In this case, a signal can be connected to the non-inverting input of the op-amp. However, the feedback resistor must go to the inverting input so that it can control the gain (the feedback is described as *negative feedback* to give the idea that it is opposite in sign to the input signal). Fig. 12.3 gives the circuit of a non-inverting amplifier block. (See also reference section D2.4.)

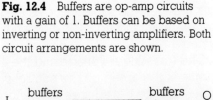

Fig. 12.3 The basic circuit of a non-inverting amplifier block.

Buffers

An op-amp may also be used to provide a gain of 1 (or -1 if the amplifier is an inverting amplifier). This may seem a bit useless, but in fact it is far from useless. Although the voltage amplification is 1, the current at the output is much more than the current at the input, so the amplifier is a power amplifier. Circuits used like this are called *buffers*. Fig. 12.4 shows the two ways of using an op-amp as a *unity gain buffer*.

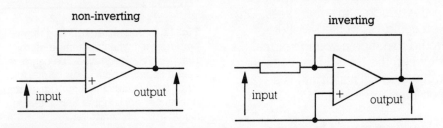

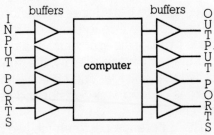

Fig. 12.4 Buffers are op-amp circuits with a gain of 1. Buffers can be based on inverting or non-inverting amplifiers. Both circuit arrangements are shown.

This does not explain what they are used for. Buffers are often used in signal lines to and from electronic equipment, particularly computers. The place where you feed signals into a computer is called an input port, and the output comes from the output ports. It is important that when you connect something to the computer you do not run any risk of upsetting the circuits inside the computer. The input and output ports of a computer are often connected to the computer circuits through buffers. The buffer protects the computer by making sure that whatever you connect to it will not upset the circuits inside. Fig. 12.5 shows the kind of arrangement used in a computer. There are plenty of other examples where a buffer is used in much the same way.

Fig. 12.5 A block diagram showing how buffers are used on the input and output ports of computers.

Difference amplifiers

When you are using a machine of any sort, you control it by deciding what it is meant to be doing and comparing that with what it is doing. You decide what difference there is between the two. That tells you what action to take. You have already met this idea in chapter 10. It is the basis of control by feedback.

If the control is achieved using electronics, blocks in the system must perform the functions described in the last paragraph. There will be a transducer on the machine, and some program or selector which tells the system what is meant to be happening. Each of these two signals will be a voltage. The electronics must find the difference between them. Using the two inputs on the op-amp is a simple but good way of doing this.

The circuit of the difference-finding block is shown in fig. 12.6. All four resistors are given the same value, which means that the gain of the

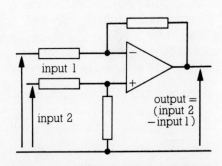

Fig. 12.6 The basic circuit of a difference amplifier. All resistors are the same value.

amplifier system is 1 (the signals are not amplified). It is used in this way so that it will give the true difference between the two inputs. A second amplifier block can be used to increase the output signal, if necessary.

When feedback signals are used in this way it is called negative feedback. Feedback always has to be negative feedback when it is used for control purposes. It is negative because it is subtracted from the input signal. You can have positive feedback too, but positive feedback is used in generating circuits and would not involve a difference amplifier.

Comparators

A difference amplifier finds the difference between two signals, but very often all we need to know is which one of two signals is the larger. A comparator does this, and op-amps make good comparators. Again, both inputs are used.

Suppose you need a warning device to tell you when, say, the level of radiation in a research laboratory is too high, or you need a control unit which turns off a heater when the desired temperature is reached. In each case you would use a transducer giving a voltage signal, and that signal would increase as the radiation or the temperature increases. On your control box would be a knob that you could set to the level or temperature you wanted. This control would produce a voltage signal. You now need a circuit which will detect when the transducer voltage has reached the same value as the control voltage. This circuit is a comparator, and fig. 12.7 shows how an op-amp circuit can be used for doing this.

The transducer voltage and the control voltage are fed to the two inputs of the op-amp. The control voltage normally goes to the inverting input and the transducer signal normally goes to the non-inverting input. (When you have read this section, try to work out what happens when these two signals are connected to the comparator the other way round.)

| 80 |

If the temperature is low, the control voltage will be greater than the transducer voltage. The op-amp amplifies the difference. In this case there is no feedback resistor and no connection from either input to the zero line.

The difference between the two input voltages could be a volt or two. The op-amp will try to amplify this voltage difference and give an output of thousands of volts, but it cannot do that, because the output voltage cannot be greater than the power supply voltage. The power supply might be $+15$ volts and -15 volts (remember that an op-amp has two power supplies). So the output goes to -15 volts (why *minus* 15 volts?).

| 81 |

We say the amplifier has *saturated*.

As the temperature rises, the voltage from the transducer rises. There comes a point where the transducer voltage and the control voltage are the same. With another microvolt or so the transducer voltage becomes greater than the control voltage. The voltage at the non-inverting ($+$) input to the op-amp is now larger, and because of this the output goes to (almost) $+15$ volts and saturates. In other words:

  if the $+$ input is at the higher voltage, the output is at positive saturation;
  if the $-$ input is at the higher voltage, the output is at negative saturation.

The circuit compares the two voltages and gives an output which states which of the two is the larger.

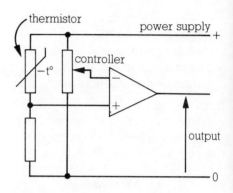

Fig. 12.7 A comparator used to give an output signal when the temperature reaches a desired level. The comparator output changes from a 'low' signal to a 'high' signal when the input signal from the transducer goes higher than the input signal from the controller.

Integrators and ramp generators

It will be clear by now that op-amps can do a lot more than just amplify. Some of the most interesting effects are where the output depends, not only on what the input is, but also on how long the input is there.

The component that gives timing is a capacitor. As you found out in chapter 9, the capacitor stores electric charge. As the amount of charge it stores increases, so does the voltage across its terminals. Fig. 12.8 shows a simple circuit you can use to show the effect, and the kind of result you can expect.

Capacitors can be used with op-amps, either in the inputs or instead of the feedback resistor. If the capacitor is connected in the feedback loop between the input and the output, as shown in fig. 12.9, the circuit behaves as an 'integrator'.

Integration is a process which is in Advanced Level Mathematics courses, but you do not need A-level maths to learn and understand the basic idea. Here is an example of how integration works.

If a car is being tested to find out how fast it gains speed (accelerates), you find how many seconds it takes to go from, say, standing still to sixty miles per hour. Suppose the speed *increases* by 5 miles per hour every second. After 1 second, the car is travelling at 5 miles per hour. After 2 seconds it is going at 10 miles per hour. After 3 seconds it is going at 15 miles per hour, and so on, so that (in theory, at least) it will take 12 seconds for the speed to reach 60 miles per hour. Suppose now that the driver does not drive the car as hard, and only gains 3 miles per hour every second after starting. In 12 seconds he will be going at 36 miles per hour. The output (his final speed) depends on both the input and on how long the input is there. We multiply the rate at which the car is gaining speed (the acceleration) by the time the car has been accelerating, and the answer is the final speed. Although we do not need any special mathematics to work this out, this is an example of integrating. We have 'integrated the acceleration over a period of time to find the final speed'.

The problem could be more difficult if the input was not constant. The driver might accelerate by 5 miles per hour every second for two seconds, then by 3 miles per hour every second for 3 seconds, and then by 1 mile per hour every second for 6 seconds. His speed will be 10 miles per hour after 2 seconds, 19 miles per hour after five seconds, and 25 miles per hour after 11 seconds. In this example the acceleration changed only three times, but the same process is possible, however many times the acceleration changes. Integration is the name of this process.

In the circuit shown in fig. 12.9, if a steady voltage is applied to V_{IN}, the output, V_{OUT}, goes down steadily from 0 volts until the op-amp is saturated at its limiting negative voltage. It goes down, rather than up, because the input is connected to the inverting input of the op-amp.

If the input voltage is disconnected, the output stays at the voltage it reached. Fig. 12.10 on the next page shows, by means of graphs, how the input and output depend on one another for various patterns of input voltage.

The value of the capacitor and resistor in fig. 12.9 have been chosen to make the voltage rise only **slowly**. The rise in output voltage in each second is called the *ramp rate*, because the graph of this voltage over a period of time looks just like a ramp. For this reason the integrator used with a steady input is usually called a *ramp generator*. The ramp rate depends on the values of both the capacitor and the resistor. If the input

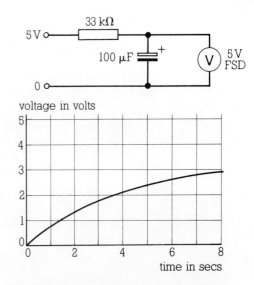

voltage in volts

Fig. 12.8 The charging of a capacitor and the voltage-time graph that you will get. Can you suggest two reasons why the final voltage on the meter is about 3 V, instead of 5 V, when the capacitor is fully charged?

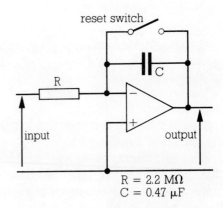

R = 2.2 MΩ
C = 0.47 μF

Fig. 12.9 The basic circuit of an op-amp integrator. The component values are suitable for experimental work in the laboratory.

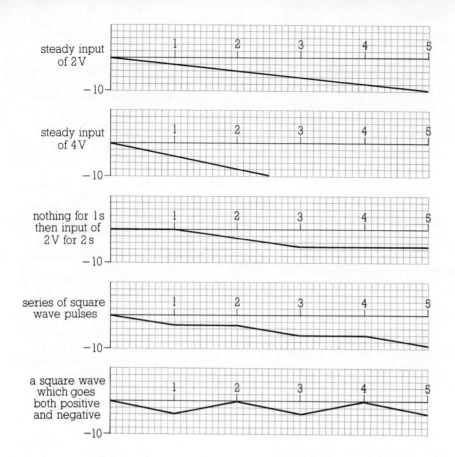

Fig. 12.10 The output obtained from the integrator circuit shown in fig. 12.9 for various inputs. The times are based on the component values given for R and C. If different values were used the effects would be the same, but the time scale would alter.

voltage is a steady 1 volt, the time it takes for the output to reach −1 volts (why minus?), measured in microseconds, is equal to the resistance (in ohms), multiplied by the capacitance (in microfarads). This time is known as the *time constant*:

time constant = $R \times C$

Note that if the time constant is in seconds, the capacitance must be measured in farads.

Real amplifiers, when used as integrators, do not always work as they should in theory. We have assumed that when the difference in the two input voltages is zero, the output is exactly zero. This may not be so. To allow for this, many op-amps have connections labelled 'offset null'. The tables of data show which connections these are.

The purpose of the offset null connections is to allow you to balance out any effect of this sort, using an extra circuit. The details of this will be found in more advanced books.

What are ramp circuits and integrators used for? They are found in digital voltmeters and many other measuring devices, televisions, synthesisers, and timers. In almost all cases they are used with other circuit blocks, such as pulse generators, summing amplifiers and comparators.

A television picture is not like a photograph, with all of the picture there all of the time, but is made up of a pattern of lines produced one after the other so fast that the eye can only see the whole picture. The pattern, called a *raster*, looks like fig. 12.11, except that in a real raster there are 625 lines altogether in a television picture.

The lines on the screen are produced by a beam of electrons scanning across the screen (from behind the glass screen). To deflect the beam of electrons from the left of the screen to the right, the system has to produce a steadily rising voltage. This voltage has to drop back to its

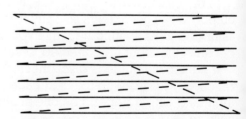

Fig. 12.11 The pattern of lines forming the picture on a television screen. The line varies in brightness to produce the picture. For colour there are three sets of lines: one red, one green, and the other blue. In British television , 625 lines are used.

starting value very quickly when the beam reaches the right-hand side of the screen, so that the next line can be scanned. The next line must be further down the picture than the previous one. A second ramp generator produces another steadily increasing voltage which moves the electron beam down the screen.

A digital voltmeter (often known as a DVM) also uses a ramp generator based on an integrator circuit. In a DVM the output from a ramp generator and the voltage to be measured are both fed to a comparator. When the ramp voltage becomes larger than the measured voltage the comparator switches. All the instrument has to do is to measure the time it took for this to happen. If the ramp rises at 1 volt every second, and the timer measures the number of seconds, then the time in seconds is equal to the measured voltage difference in volts. In practice the system will work faster than this, but the idea is the same. The block diagram of the system is shown in fig. 12.12. Many DVMs have more complicated systems but the principle is still the same.

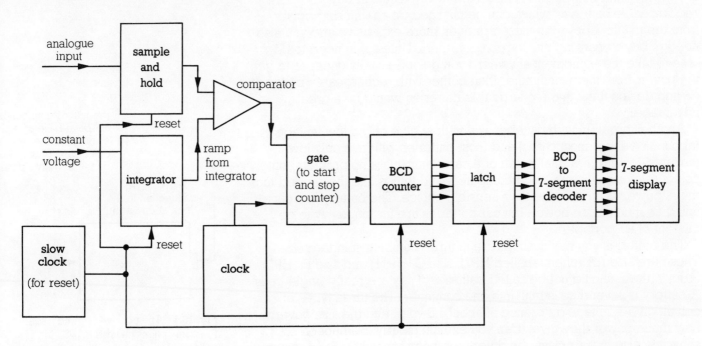

Fig. 12.12 The block diagram of a simple digital voltmeter. The latch holds the reading on the display so that you have time to read it.

The versatile op-amp

There are also yet other ways in which op-amps can be used, some of which are described in later chapters. Electronic systems consist of transducers, power supplies and a processing block. All processing blocks are either switches, amplifiers, or signal generators. Op-amps can be used in all three types of process. This makes them very important components in electronics.

SUMMARY 12

Circuits with op-amps can be used as inverting or non-inverting amplifiers, buffers, summers, difference amplifiers, comparators, integrators, and most other amplifying, switching or generating circuits.

The gain of an op-amp circuit used as an amplifier is controlled by feedback.

When feedback is used for controlling it is negative feedback.

An integrator (ramp generator) is an inverting amplifier with a capacitor in place of the feedback resistor.

The time constant of the integrator depends on the input resistor and the feedback capacitor.

13 POWER SUPPLIES

All electronic systems need an energy source – a power supply. Remember that you can never get something for nothing. We have used a power supply as a building block in every system. We must now find out a little more about the various kinds of power supply.

For electronics, the simplest power supply is a battery. A battery can fit inside the equipment, so that you can take it anywhere. You do not need a power point to plug it in. Most batteries are small and not very heavy. So why not use batteries all the time?

Batteries are a very expensive way of getting electricity. They produce electricity by chemical reactions inside the battery. When the chemicals are used up the battery has to be thrown away. You can buy *rechargeable* batteries, which can be charged up again using power from the mains supply, but these are even more expensive and you also need to buy a charging unit to recharge them. Unless you need to be able to take the equipment anywhere you go, it is usually cheaper to get the power from the mains rather than bother with rechargeable batteries.

84 (When do you think that rechargeable batteries *would* be a great advantage?)

Another problem with batteries is that they give only a low voltage (about 1.5 volts in most cases) and most batteries will give only low currents, too. For a digital watch or a calculator this is no problem, but colour televisions, hi-fi's, microcomputers and things like these need too much power to make batteries a sensible choice. The battery in a car will give much more power, but car batteries are far too heavy to be thought of as 'portable'!

The batteries you buy in shops are in three common standard sizes. These are size AA (often labelled HP7), size C (HP11) and size D (HP2). Strictly, these should not be called batteries. They are really single *cells*. A battery is several cells built into one container. The three types of cell all give a voltage difference of about 1.5 volts, and the size governs how much power they give. (Can you explain clearly, perhaps to

85 someone else in your class, the difference between voltage and power? If not, then refer back to chapter 5.)

To get larger voltage differences the cells are connected together in series to make a battery. For example, the type PP3 battery which gives 9 volts has a total of six cells connected together in series inside the battery.

When cells are connected together they have to be connected the right way round. Most batteries have the two connections marked + and –, but fig. 13.1 shows how you can decide which terminal is which on the three common types of cell if the + (positive terminal) and the – (negative terminal) are not marked.

To connect cells together in series, the + of one cell goes to the – of the next cell, and the + of that cell goes to the – of the third cell, and so on. Two 1.5 volt cells in series give 3 volts, three cells give 4.5 volts, four give 6 volts, and so on. Fig. 13.2 shows the symbols for a cell and for a battery, and the way in which cells are connected together. (What will

86 be the voltage difference for the group of cells shown connected
87 together in the diagram? How many cells are there in the 12 volt battery?
88 What has all this to do with Kirchhoff's law?)

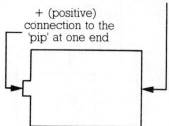

Fig. 13.1 The positive (+) and negative (–) connections on type AA, C, and D cells.

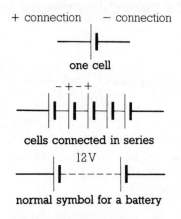

Fig. 13.2 The symbols and connections for cells and batteries. The longer line in the symbol is the + connection. Remember 'you need twice as much line to draw a plus sign (+) as a minus sign (–)'.

Internal resistance

If all the cells give 1.5 volts, why are they made in different sizes? One reason is that larger cells contain more chemicals and so give more electrical energy. (Why would it be **wrong** to use the word 'power', instead of 'energy', in the last sentence?)

There is something else that depends on the size of the battery. If you try to use type AA cells (the smallest size) on a cassette tape-recorder (which should use the big type D cells), the voltage will be right but the recorder will not work properly. The electrons moving round the circuit also go through the battery, collecting more energy as they do so. But, like the rest of the circuit, the inside of the cell resists the flow of electricity. So the electrons lose some of the energy they have gained even before they get out of the cell. This resistance is called the *internal resistance* or *source resistance* of the cell. Just as thicker wires have lower resistances, so large cells have a lower internal resistance than small cells. The internal resistance of the type D cell is about 0.5 ohms, but the internal resistance of the type AA cell is about 5 ohms.

How does this affect the tape-recorder? The motor of the recorder may need 0.3 amps to operate it. A type AA cell cannot give 0.3 amps because 1.5 volts would be needed to push 0.3 amps through the 5 ohms internal resistance, and the cell can only give 1.6 volts altogether at a maximum. This leaves a maximum of 0.1 volts for the recorder! (Work out the internal resistance of a 12 volt battery made up from eight type D cells, and explain why five type AA cells have a voltage difference of 7.5 volts and an internal resistance of 25 ohms.)

SUMMARY 13A

A cell is a single unit that turns chemical energy into electrical energy.

Most cells give about 1.5 volts.

A battery is a number of cells connected together in series, with + of one connected to − of the next, and so on.

Batteries are portable and convenient, but they are expensive, and they give only low power and low voltages.

All power supplies have an internal resistance. It is part of the total resistance of the circuit to which power is being supplied.

Mains supplies

It is much cheaper to get electricity from a dynamo or generator than from a battery. The larger the generator, the cheaper is the electricity produced.

Most of our electricity comes from the mains supply. The type of generator used for the mains supply is called an alternator. One alternator at a power station might produce 50 megawatts. To get some idea of how much this is, remember that most homes use a kilowatt or two on average and, with most things switched on, could use 20 kW at peak times.

The mains supply comes into our homes as a 240 volt alternating current (a.c.) supply. What is a.c.? As the central part of an alternator (called the armature) rotates, the alternator produces first a positive voltage, then a negative voltage, then a positive voltage again, and so on. This makes the current in the circuit flow first one way, then the other, as the voltage changes. The waveshapes of the alternating voltage and of the alternating currents produced by it are sinusoidal. (Can you sketch a sinusoidal wave? If not, refer back to fig. 6.11 in chapter 6.)

The frequency of any alternating voltage source is also an important quantity. The alternators which produce the mains supply of electricity are made to operate so that the *direction* of the current changes one hundred times every second and the *pattern* of changes repeats itself fifty times a second. We say there are fifty cycles of alternating current every second and that the frequency is thus 50 hertz. The a.c. in Britain is therefore a 50 hertz supply. Most countries have 50 hertz mains supplies although some, including USA, have 60 hertz supplies. (What is the period for a 50 hertz supply? What is the period for a 60 hertz supply?)

Almost all electronic equipment needs a power supply which gives direct current (d.c.) at a steady voltage. Direct current is current which always flows in the same direction. Batteries not only give d.c., but also provide an almost steady voltage.

If we need d.c. for electronics, why is the mains supply produced as a.c.? Apart from being cheaper to produce, a.c. supplies have a number of advantages. Cookers, electric fires, electric lights and most motors work perfectly well on a.c. supplies. Switches for a.c. are smaller and safer than for d.c. However, there is one much more important advantage, and it is as much an advantage for electronics as for anything else. You can use transformers for a.c. but not with d.c.

Transformers

What is a transformer? You have probably seen transformers at electricity sub-stations, but not all transformers are as big as that. A transformer can change the voltage of an a.c. supply. A transformer can be made so that you can feed one voltage into its input and get a different voltage, either larger or smaller than the one you started with, from the output. This means that if you need a 12 volt supply for some electronic equipment, you can get a transformer which can have its input connected to the 240 volt mains and give you 12 volts a.c. at its output.

The transformer has another advantage too. Although the input is connected to the mains, the link between the input and output is by magnetism, and the output is completely insulated from the mains supply.

A transformer is two coils of insulated wire placed side by side on a frame made of iron or other magnetisable material. The frame is called the *core*. The input is connected to one of the coils. The output is taken from the other coil. The core provides an efficient magnetic path round the two coils. The transfer of energy from one coil to the other is via the magnetism produced in the core. Because the effect depends on **changes** in the magnetism in the core, a transformer will only work with a.c. Fig. 13.3 shows the structure of a typical transformer. It also shows the circuit symbol for a transformer.

The voltage given by the output of a transformer depends on the number of turns of wire in each of the coils. The coil connected to the input is normally called the *primary coil* or the *primary winding*. For use on the 240 volt a.c. mains it might have 1200 turns of wire. The coil that gives the output is called the *secondary winding*. If that had 1200 turns too, the output would also be 240 volts a.c., but for a 12 volt a.c. output there would be only 60 turns in the secondary. In this example there are five turns for each volt.

In practice we do not normally make transformers. You would buy a transformer for the job it has to do. When buying transformers you have to make sure that the transformer will give the current needed by the system connected to it.

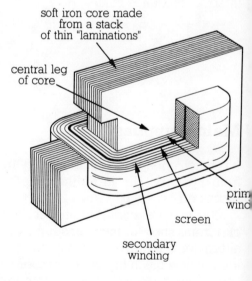

soft iron core made from a stack of thin "laminations"

central leg of core

prim wind

screen

secondary winding

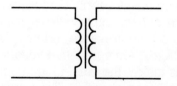

Fig. 13.3 The structure of a transformer, and its circuit symbol.

Using a transformer to get low voltages from the mains

When using a transformer, you have to make sure that it is properly connected to the mains. The transformer should be firmly fixed inside a closed **metal** case, so that the case will not melt or catch fire. The metal case, and the core of the transformer, must be connected to the earth conductor of a three-core cable. (Which colour is that? See reference section D3.5 if you do not know.) This earth connection is there so that if there is a fault, the user is not in danger if he or she touches the metal of the case or the inside fittings.

The primary coil should **not** be connected directly to the live and neutral leads. You must include a double-pole on/off switch. This is to make sure that when the system is turned off the transformer is completely isolated from the mains supply. A single pole switch will not do because, even when the switch is turned off, all the wiring is still connected directly to the mains. Fig. 13.4 shows how this is so.

In addition to the switch there should also be a fuse in the live lead, a neon lamp indicator to show when the unit is plugged into the mains, a proper clamp to hold the cable firmly, and a grommet (a rubber protective ring) to prevent damage to the cable where it passes through the metal case. Finally, a second fuse should be connected in the secondary circuit. Fig. 13.5 illustrates all these precautions diagrammatically.

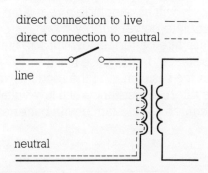

Fig. 13.4 If a single-pole switch is used to turn off the mains supply, the whole of the wiring is still connected to the mains when the switch is off. Many appliances only have single-pole switches. Such switches are in the **line** connection, never the neutral, but this is no guarantee of safety if the appliance is faulty. Always **unplug** mains equipment before working on it.

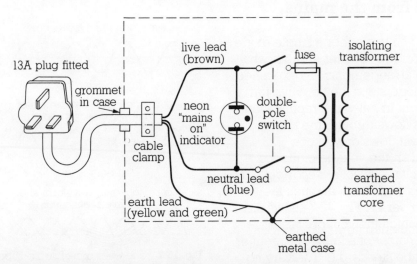

Fig. 13.5 The requirements for a properly-designed and safe mains unit. These precautions should apply to any mains-operated equipment, but **all** home-constructed equipment should use a transformer to isolate the equipment from the mains and so give better protection to the constructor **and** to others who may use the equipment afterwards.

Protection in mains supply systems

The mains supply system itself is designed so that there is automatic protection against major hazards. The possibility of electric shock is real and the standards of insulation have to be high. However, this is not the greatest risk. The risk of fire caused by electricity is much greater. You might think that fire would be the result of sparking at faulty contacts, and it is true that fires can start that way. The main cause of fire, however, is in wires and cables which carry too much current and become overheated. The heating process may take several hours but when the cables are hot enough to melt the insulation then a fire can start very quickly. Any wire or cable carrying 0.5 amp or more is a risk, and you should ensure that all such wires are of the correct size. It is important that you know and understand how the system should be operated. Details are included in reference sections D3.4 to D3.12.

Obtaining d.c. from the power supply

To convert the low-voltage a.c. output of the transformer into d.c. a *rectifier*, and some *smoothing* is required. For some purposes the d.c. has to be held at a very steady voltage, and in these cases the power supply will also include a *regulator*. Fig. 13.6 is a block diagram of the complete power supply.

Just like batteries, low-voltage units of this kind have internal resistance. In this case it is the resistance of the wiring in the transformer and the resistance of the rectifier which causes this. It is easier to keep the internal resistance of a low-voltage power supply low than it is to get low internal resistance with batteries.

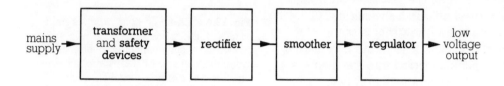

Fig. 13.6 The block diagram of a mains power supply unit. It is not always necessary to include a regulator. For further information on rectification see chapter 8 and reference section C2. For further information on regulators see reference section D3.13.

Smoothing d.c. supplies obtained from the mains

When you rectify the a.c. supply to get d.c., you use either a single diode as a half-wave rectifier, or four diodes as a bridge rectifier and get what is called a full-wave rectification. These two arrangements are explained in chapter 8. In half-wave rectification the diode stops the negative part of the alternating current from getting through. In full-wave rectification the diodes steer the current so that it always flows through the load in one direction only. This means that the current flows only in one direction, so it is direct current (d.c.). However, the voltage of the a.c. supply is changing all the time, so the d.c. voltage is not a *steady* voltage. It is a voltage which varies between zero and maximum, in much the same way as the input voltage to the rectifier varies. Fig. 13.7 shows the waveform of the a.c. supply and the way in which the voltage varies at the output of a half-wave rectifier and at the output of a full-wave rectifier.

For an electronic circuit, the voltage must be steady d.c. The varying voltage from the rectifier will not do, as the circuit will treat the variations as signals. To overcome this the output from the rectifier is *smoothed*.

In chapter 9 it was explained that a capacitor will store electricity and can therefore be used to smooth a varying voltage. The simplest way of smoothing the d.c. from a rectifier is to connect a capacitor across the positive and negative lines of the d.c. supply. The rectifier charges up the capacitor to the maximum voltage, and the capacitor will then supply current to the circuit until the next time the voltage is large enough to recharge the capacitor. Fig. 13.8 shows this arrangement.

As long as the capacitor is large enough (i.e. it has a large enough capacitance), this is fine. However, the voltage will not be exactly constant. As the capacitor supplies current the amount of electricity it is holding goes down, so the voltage difference across the capacitor goes down. Fig. 13.9 on the next page shows the way the output voltage changes when this type of smoothing is used.

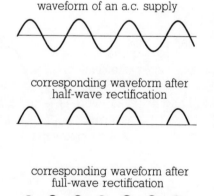

Fig. 13.7 The waveform of an a.c. supply and the corresponding waveforms of the outputs after half-wave and full-wave rectification. These waveforms represent the variation of voltage differences over a period of time.

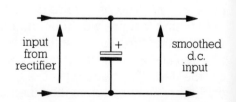

Fig. 13.8 The simplest form of smoothing circuit. A large-capacity electrolytic capacitor would be used. The output using this circuit is shown in fig. 13.9.

If the smoothed output from the rectifier is not smooth enough, and it is not convenient (or perhaps even possible) to get a larger capacitor, then a voltage regulator is used. This is an integrated circuit that keeps the output voltage constant, even though the input voltage may vary. Chapter 8 and reference section D3.13 include some information on regulators.

Voltages in a.c. circuits

How can we say that the voltage of an a.c. supply is 240 volts when the voltage is always changing?

When electricity was first used for lighting and heating, the generators produced d.c. When the electricity companies began to install new generators that gave a.c., they needed to be able to assure users that 240 volts on the a.c. system would give as much light and heat as 240 volts on the d.c. system. If you measure the voltage throughout a complete cycle of a.c. and record the results as a graph, it gives the graph shown in fig. 13.10. Clearly, if for some of the time the voltage is less than 240 volts, there must be other times during the cycle when the voltage is more than 240 volts so that the overall effect of the a.c. supply is the same as that of 240 volts d.c.

The value of 240 volts is called the *r.m.s. value* of the alternating voltage (r.m.s. is short for 'root mean square', but everyone talks about r.m.s. voltages). The maximum value of the alternating voltage is called the *peak value* of the voltage. These two voltages are related by the r.m.s. formula:

peak voltage = $\sqrt{2}$ × *r.m.s. voltage* ($\sqrt{2} \approx 1.4$)

Using this formula it is easy to show that the peak value for the 240 volt mains is 338 volts. This is no problem for cookers, heaters, lights or motors. However it does matter when you have to decide how thick the insulation for a 240 volt a.c. supply has to be.

It also makes a difference to the output voltage you get from d.c. power supplies. When the power supply has smoothing, the smoothing system takes the output voltage nearly up to the **peak** value of the a.c. that has been rectified. This means that a 12 volt a.c. output from the transformer will give more than 16 volts as the d.c. output, not 12 volts. It is important to allow for this when you are designing a power supply for a piece of equipment.

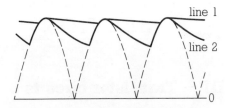

Fig. 13.9 The waveforms for the d.c. output of a rectifier with smoothing. Line 1 would be obtained with a large capacitor, and line 2 would be obtained with a capacitor that was not large enough. The dotted line is the full-wave rectified output you would get if the smoothing capacitor was disconnected. The size of the capacitor that you need to use depends on the current which the system is taking from the power supply. Can you sketch the graphs you would get with half-wave **96** rectification? Would you need a larger or a smaller capacitor if you used half-wave **97** rectification, instead of full-wave? Why?

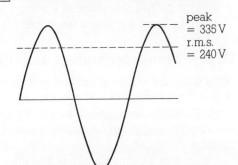

Fig. 13.10 The relationship between peak and r.m.s. voltages for the mains supply. These relationships apply for any supply giving a sinusoidal waveshape but not other a.c. supplies.

SUMMARY 13B

The mains supply in Britain is 240 volts, 50 hertz, a.c.

A transformer is a device for changing the voltage of a.c. supplies.

A transformer will isolate a low-voltage supply from the mains but it must be connected through a double-pole switch and fuse.

The voltage of an a.c. supply is quoted as the r.m.s. value. The peak value of a sinusoidal alternating voltage is $\sqrt{2}$ × r.m.s. value.

A low-voltage power unit comprises a transformer with switch, etc., a rectifier, a smoothing system, and (possibly) a regulator.

The output voltage of a low-voltage supply with smoothing depends on the peak voltage of the a.c.

D1 — Transistor circuits

D1.1 — Standard transistor circuits

The standard arrangement for a transistor is the common emitter circuit with the input connected to the base and emitter, and the output connected to the collector and emitter. The base usually has to be biassed. Fig. D.1 shows the arrangement used for direct bias and fig. D.2 shows the standard arrangement used for stabilised biassing.

D1.2 — Transistor switching circuits

For a transistor circuit to act as a switch, the transistor must be turned off when there is no signal at the base, and saturated when there is a signal present. The input signal or the biassing resistor (if used) must be such that this can be achieved. (Refer to chapter 11 for details.)

A transistor switching circuit is always an inverter. A logic 1 at the input produces a logic 0 signal at the output.

D1.3 — Transistor voltage amplifier circuits

For a transistor circuit to act as a voltage amplifier, the transistor must be biassed so that it always operates between the cut-off point and the saturation point. This depends on the resistances used in the circuit and the h_{FE} of the transistor. The stabilised biassing circuit is usually used for voltage amplifiers. (Refer to chapter 11 for details.)

A transistor amplifying circuit also inverts the input signal.

D1.4 — Power amplifiers using transistors

A transistor gives power amplification because the collector current is larger than the base current. To use a transistor as a power amplifier, the lamp, relay, or whatever requires power, is connected in place of the load resistor in the collector lead of the transistor. The maximum power available is limited by the supply voltage and by the maximum current the transistor can carry without being damaged.

If the power being produced by the transistor is large, the transistor is mounted on a heat sink to help dissipate the heating that is produced in the transistor itself.

A power amplifier used in this way does not invert the input signal: a logic 1 at the input will cause power to be fed to the load.

D1.5 — Characteristics of transistor voltage amplifiers

The most important characteristic of a voltage amplifier circuit is the transfer characteristic, which shows the relationship between input signal and output signal. A typical transfer characteristic is shown in fig. D.3.

D1.6 — Calculation of base currents and input voltages

The procedure for calculating base current is as follows.
  (i) Find the collector voltage. This is known because you usually know what the circuit is intended to do. If the circuit is an amplifier, then the output should be half the power-supply voltage when there is no signal. If the circuit is a

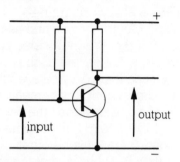

Fig. D.1 The transistor circuit using direct bias at the base of the transistor.

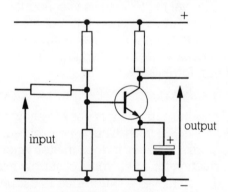

Fig. D.2 The transistor circuit using stabilised biassing at the base of the transistor.

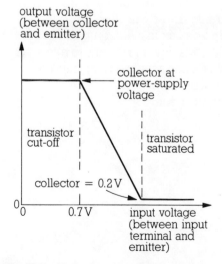

Fig. D.3 The voltage transfer characteristic for a transistor amplifying circuit.

switch, then when the transistor is saturated the collector voltage will be 0.2 V.

 (ii) Find the resistance of the load resistor used.
(iii) Calculate the voltage difference across the load resistor.
(iv) Use the resistance equation to find the collector current.
 (v) Look up the value of h_{FE} for the transistor.
(vi) Use the h_{FE} equation to calculate the base current.
(vii) Find the value of the bias resistor used.
(viii) Find the voltage across the bias resistor (= power-supply voltage − 0.7 V).
(ix) Calculate the bias current using the resistance equation.
 (x) Subtract bias current from total base current to find the input current.
(xi) Use resistance equation to find voltage difference across input resistor.
(xii) Add 0.7 V to find the actual input voltage.

If the base current is known but the collector current has to be calculated, this procedure is reversed.

Example of calculations involving transistor base and collector currents and resistor values

Find the resistor values for the input and bias resistors in the circuit shown in fig. D.1, if the circuit is to be used as an amplifier, the load resistor R_3 is 470 Ω, h_{FE} for the transistor is 110, and the power supply is 5 V.

Start by finding the collector current. Because this is to be an amplifier, you need to know what happens when the collector voltage is 2.5 V (half-way between zero and the power-supply voltage). If the voltage difference across the transistor is 2.5 V, the voltage difference across R_L is also 2.5 V. (If the voltage across the

[98] transistor were 2.4 V, what then would be the voltage across R_L?

Now use the resistance equation to find the collector current. (Why can we

[99] calculate the current in R_L and say it is the same as the collector current? Is there

[100] any case when this would not be correct?)

$$collector\ current = \frac{voltage\ difference}{load\ resistance} = \frac{2.5}{470} = 0.0053\ A = 5.3\ mA$$

The next stage is to find the base current. The h_{FE} equation links base current and collector current:

$$h_{FE} = \frac{collector\ current}{base\ current}$$

$$base\ current = \frac{0.0053}{110} = 48\ \mu A$$

Having found the base current we need to know the value of the bias resistor that will provide this current. The voltage difference across this resistor is 5 V minus the base-emitter voltage. The base-emitter voltage is 0.7 V. The voltage across the bias resistor is therefore 4.3 V. Use the resistance equation again:

$$bias\ resistance = \frac{voltage\ difference}{base\ current} = \frac{4.3}{0.000048} = 90\ k\Omega$$

The value 90 kΩ is not a preferred value. For an amplifier circuit we want the nearest preferred value to the calculated answer: 82 kΩ (in the E12 range) would be a good value to choose.

Note: There are several factors that have not been allowed for. This fairly simple way of finding the resistance value is good enough for most purposes, however.

There is another example of this type of calculation in chapter 11, on page 108.

Exercise 34 − A transistor amplifier has a load resistor of 1 kΩ and an input resistor of 47 kΩ The power supply is 6 V and h_{FE} is 150. If the output voltage is 3 V, find: (i) the collector current; (ii) the base current; and (iii) the input voltage, if there is no biassing resistor at all.

Exercise 35 − A transistor has h_{FE} = 200 and a load resistor of 2.2 kΩ If the circuit is operating from a 9 V power supply and the base current is 5 μA, find the collector current and the voltage at the collector.

Exercise 36 − The power supply to a transistor circuit is 5 V. The circuit is a switching circuit with a load resistor of 1.2 kΩ The h_{FE} for the transistor is 80. Find the minimum base current that will saturate the transistor.

Exercise 37 − The input current to a transistor with h_{FE} = 100 is 2 mA. The load resistor is 1.5 kΩ and the power supply is 10 V. What is the voltage at the collector?

D1.7 − The collector characteristic of a transistor

The collector characteristic of a transistor is a graph of collector current against collector voltage. The graph will show a series of curves for a range of base currents. Fig. D.4 shows a typical collector characteristic. The bold lines on the graph are the collector characteristic for a BC108 transistor with h_{FE} = 200.

D1.8 − Load lines

The performance of a transistor as a voltage amplifier can be determined using the collector characteristic. A load line is drawn for the load resistor (as for a simple voltage divider) with the load line starting from the power supply voltage point on the horizontal axis. Fig. D.4 shows a load line for a 100 Ω resistor with a 9 V power supply, drawn on the characteristic for a BC108 transistor.

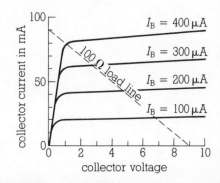

Fig. D.4 The collector characteristic for a BC108 transistor (bold lines) and a load line (dotted line) to show its behaviour in a circuit with a 100 Ω load and 9 V power supply.

D2 − Operational amplifier circuits

D2.1 − The inverting amplifier

When an op-amp is used as an inverting amplifier the input is connected to the *inv* or − input terminal through a resistor. The circuit is shown in fig. D.5. When this circuit is used, the gain of the circuit is given by the op-amp formula:

$$\text{gain} = -\frac{R_F}{R_{IN}}$$

For further details of the inverting amplifier and for the derivation of this formula see chapter 10; for examples of the use of this formula see reference section C7.3.

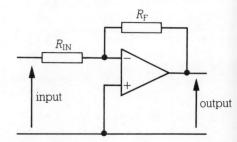

Fig. D.5 The basic circuit for an op-amp inverting amplifier.

D2.2 − Summers

The circuit of an op-amp summer is shown in fig. D.6. Using the symbols on the circuit diagram, the transfer characteristic of this system is given by the formula:

$$\text{output voltage} = V_{OUT} = -\left(\frac{R_F}{R_1} \times V_1 + \frac{R_F}{R_2} \times V_2 \right)$$

Typically, the value of R_1 would be between 1 kΩ and 10 kΩ. If R_1 and R_2 are equal in value, then:

$$V_{OUT} = -\frac{R_F}{R_1}(V_1 + V_2)$$

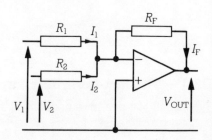

Fig. D.6 The basic circuit for an op-amp summing block.

Examples of the use of the summing amplifier formula

How would the summing amplifier in fig. D.6 behave if R_1, R_2, and R_F were all 5.6 kΩ?

If you substitute 5600 for each of the resistances in either formula, the formula comes out as:

$$V_{OUT} = V_1 + V_2$$

Suppose now that $R_1 = 1$ kΩ, $R_2 = 4$ kΩ, and $R_F = 10$ kΩ, how would the output voltage be related to the two inputs? Substituting these values in the first formula we get:

$$V_{OUT} = -\left(\frac{10\,000}{1000} \times V_1 + \frac{10\,000}{4000} \times V_2\right) = -(10\,V_1 + 2.5\,V_2)$$

If $V_1 = 0.5$ V and $V_2 = 0.8$ V, what would the output voltage be with these three different resistors?

$$V_{OUT} = -(10 \times 0.5 + 2.5 \times 0.8) = -(5 + 2) = -7\,V$$

Exercise 38 − In fig. D.6, if R_1, R_2, and R_F are all 15 kΩ, $V_1 = 2$ V and $V_2 = 3$ V, find the value of V_{OUT}.

Exercise 39 − In fig. D.6, if $R_1 = 1$ kΩ, $R_2 = 2$ kΩ, and $R_F = 3$ kΩ, find V_{OUT} when V_1 and V_2 are both 2 V.

D2.3 − Derivation of the summing amplifier formula

Referring to fig. D.6, because the + input of the amplifier is connected to the zero line, the voltage at the − input is virtually zero ('virtual earth'). Thus (using the resistance equation):

current I_1 in R$_1$ $= \dfrac{V_1 - 0}{R_1}$;   current I_2 in R$_2$ $= \dfrac{V_2 - 0}{R_2}$;   and

current I_F in R$_F$ $= \dfrac{0 - V_{OUT}}{R_F}$

$$I_1 + I_2 = I_F \qquad \text{(Kirchhoff's law)}$$

Substituting the right-hand side of the above three equations for each value of I in the Kirchhoff's law equation (and leaving out all the 0's), gives:

$$\frac{-V_{OUT}}{R_F} = \frac{V_1}{R_1} + \frac{V_2}{R_2}$$

$$-V_{OUT} = \frac{R_F}{R_1} \times V_1 + \frac{R_F}{R_2} \times V_2$$

D2.4 − The non-inverting amplifier

The circuit of a non-inverting amplifier using an op-amp is shown in fig. D.7. The transfer characteristic for this amplifier is given by the equation:

$$V_{OUT} = V_1 \times \left(\frac{R_F}{R_1} + 1\right)$$

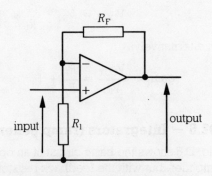

Fig. D.7 The basic circuit of a non-inverting amplifier block.

Example of the use of the formula for non-inverting operational amplifiers

A non-inverting amplifier with a gain of 10 is required. The circuit of fig. D.7 is to be used with resistor $R_1 = 33$ kΩ. What should be the value of R_F?

If the gain is 10, then $V_{OUT} = 10 \times V_{IN}$. Putting all these values in the equation, and then cancelling V_{IN} because it appears on both sides, we get:

$$10 = \frac{R_F}{33\,000} + 1$$

$$9 = \frac{R_F}{33\,000}$$

$$R_F = 9 \times 33\,000 = 297\,000 \ \Omega$$

The nearest preferred value is 270 kΩ, although in this case, because the required value is right at the edge of the tolerance range it would be better to use a 5% tolerance resistor of nominal value 300 kΩ, or to use a 270 kΩ resistor and a 27 kΩ resistor in series.

Exercise 40 – A non-inverting amplifier using the circuit of fig. D.7 is to have a gain of 4. If the feedback resistor is 4.7 kΩ, what should be the value of R_1?

Exercise 41 – In fig. D.7, if R_1 and R_F are both 10 kΩ, what will be the gain of the amplifier?

D2.5 – Derivation of the formula for the non-inverting amplifier

For an op-amp, the voltage at the + and − inputs are always virtually equal. The voltage at the non-inverting (+) input of the op-amp is V_{IN}. This means that the voltage at the inverting input (−) of the amplifier is also V_{IN}.

Op-amps take (almost) no current at their input terminals. This means that the current I_1 in R_1 is equal to current I_F in the feedback resistor R_F. Thus (using the resistance equation):

$$I_1 = \frac{V_{IN} - 0}{R_1} = I_F = \frac{V_{OUT} - V_{IN}}{R_F}$$

This gives:

$$\frac{V_{IN}}{R_1} = \frac{V_{OUT} - V_{IN}}{R_F}$$

$$V_{IN} \left(\frac{1}{R_1} + \frac{1}{R_F} \right) = \frac{V_{OUT}}{R_F}$$

$$V_{OUT} = V_{IN} \left(\frac{R_F}{R_1} + \frac{R_F}{R_F} \right)$$

And this leads to:

$$V_{OUT} = V_{IN} \left(\frac{R_F}{R_1} + 1 \right)$$

or, alternatively:

$$\text{gain} = \frac{V_{OUT}}{V_{IN}} = \frac{R_F}{R_1} + 1$$

D2.6 – Integrators (ramp generators)

Fig. D.8 shows the basic circuit of an op-amp integrator. It is like the inverting amplifier, but with the feedback resistor replaced by a capacitor.

The output voltage depends on *how long* the input has been applied, as shown by the equation given at the top of the next page:

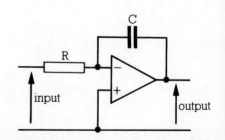

Fig. D.8 The basic circuit of an op-amp integrator. If R = 1 MΩ and C = 0.1 μF the time constant of the integrator is 0.1 s. For an input voltage of 0.3 V, the output will reach 0.3 V in 0.1 s, 0.6 V in 0.2 s, 0.9 V in 0.3 s, and so on.

output voltage at time t after process began	$=$	integral of V_{IN} over the period from start to time t	$\times$	$\dfrac{1}{R \times C}$

If the input voltage is steady, the output voltage falls at a steady rate. (Why does it fall rather than rise?). The output is called a 'ramp'. The ramp rate depends on the values of both the capacitor and the resistor. If the input voltage is a steady 1 V, the time it takes for the output to reach -1 V (why minus?), measured in μs, is equal to the resistance (in Ω) multiplied by the capacitance (in μF). This time is known as the *time constant*:

time constant $= R \times C$

Note that if the time constant is in seconds, the capacitance must be measured in farads.

D3 — Power supplies

D3.1 — Voltage sources in series

Whenever batteries or any other voltage sources are connected in series, the total voltage difference is the sum of the voltage differences produced by each of the voltage sources taken in order. Where it is intended to increase the total voltage by connecting several batteries or power supplies together, the positive terminal of the first source is connected to the negative of the second, the positive of the second is connected to the negative of the third, and so on.

Examples of calculations with voltage sources

Suppose the output voltage of a d.c. power supply is to be boosted by connecting a battery in series with it. The power supply gives 10 V and the battery is a 6 V battery. What will be the total output voltage?

The answer to this depends on which way round the battery is connected. If the $-$ terminal of the battery is connected to the $+$ terminal of the power supply, then there will be 16 V between the $-$ terminal of the power supply and the $+$ terminal of the battery. If the battery is connected so that the $+$ terminal goes to the $+$ terminal of the power supply, the output will be only 4 V. When it is difficult to work out the voltages, draw a circuit diagram and mark on the voltages as shown in fig. D.9. Work round the circuit to each source in turn. The direction of the voltage arrow will tell you whether to add or subtract the voltages.

Fig. D.9 The output voltage from connecting a battery and a d.c. power supply in series.

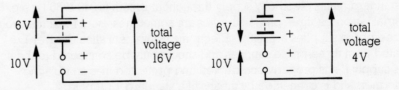

Exercise 42 — A tape recorder uses five 1.5 V batteries in series as its power supply. What total voltage should these batteries give? What voltage will they give if one of the batteries is fitted the wrong way round?

Exercise 43 — Three zener diodes were all connected the same way round in series. The zener diodes were rated at 3.3 V, 5.1 V, and 15 V. Zener diodes act like voltage sources. What was the total voltage difference across the three zener diodes?

D3.2 — Voltage sources in parallel

Voltage sources should never be connected in parallel. The only exception is if the two voltage sources have the same voltage difference. It is then permissible to connect the two positive terminals together and the two negative terminals together. This will not affect the voltage but it will reduce the source resistance of the source. It is not good practice, and in all cases it is better to replace these voltage sources with a single source with a lower source resistance.

D3.3 — Source resistance

Source resistance (or internal resistance, as it is often called) is the resistance the power source gives to the current in the circuit. Its effect is that when the source is giving current, the voltage measured across the output terminals is less than the source voltage. The source resistance can be found by using the following formula (this is a special use of the resistance equation):

$$\boxed{\begin{array}{c} \text{source} \\ \text{resistance} \end{array}} = \boxed{\frac{\text{source voltage} - \text{voltage measured at output ('lost volts')}}{\text{current supplied by the source}}}$$

Example of finding the source resistance ('internal resistance')

The voltage of a battery was found to be 9.6 V when measured with a good meter, but when the battery was used to run a radio the voltage it was giving was found to be only 8.4 V. If the radio takes a current of 0.25 A, what is the source resistance of the battery?

Using the source resistance formula, we get:

$$\text{source resistance} = \frac{9.6 - 8.4}{0.25} = \frac{1.2}{0.25} = 4.8 \ \Omega$$

Note that 1.2 is the value of the 'lost volts', i.e. the drop in voltage when the load is connected.

Exercise 44 — An electronic lock operates from a 6 V battery. The electronic circuits use very little current but the solenoid passes 0.5 A. The battery voltage drops to 4 V when the solenoid is switched on. What is the source resistance of the battery?

Exercise 45 — When an amplifier was tested it was found that the output was 3 V a.c, but when the loudspeaker was connected the output was only 1.5 V a.c. If the loudspeaker had a resistance of 8 Ω, find: (i) the a.c. current in the loudspeaker; and (ii) the source resistance of the amplifier. (Treat the a.c. currents and voltages as though they were d.c.)

D3.4 — Mains supplies

The standard mains electricity supply throughout Britain is 240 V 50 Hz a.c. For industrial purposes 'three phase' supplies are sometimes used. Maximum voltages on three-phase supplies are 440 V. Electronic equipment should never be operated from three-phase supplies and should only be connected to the normal mains supply if it is properly constructed and protected, has an isolating transformer, and is connected by means of a standard 13 A plug.

Other countries use different supply voltages. Much of Europe uses 220 V 50 Hz a.c; the USA uses 110 V 60 Hz a.c.

D3.5 — 13 amp plugs

Fig. D.10 shows the correct way to wire a typical 13 A plug. Whatever the design of the plug, there are three terminals labelled L, N, and E. The 'live' wire has **brown** insulation and goes to the L terminal. The 'neutral' wire (which is not necessarily neutral and could give a shock!) has **blue** insulation and goes to the

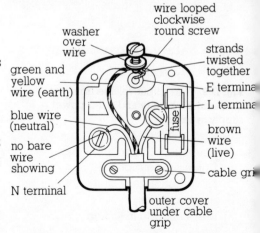

Fig. D.10 The wiring of a 13 amp mains plug.

N terminal. The 'earth' wire has **green and yellow striped** insulation and goes to the E terminal.

If a manufactured appliance has only two connecting wires, then they should be brown and blue, and should be connected to the L and N terminals. All equipment constructed at home must have an earth connection.

If the wires have insulation of colours other than these standard colours, do not connect the appliance. Other countries use different colour codes and the risk of accidental shock can be high.

The plug must be fitted with a fuse. The fuse should be either a 3 A or a 13 A fuse of type BS1362. For electronic equipment 3 amp fuses are usually used. The size of the fuse depends on the size of connecting cable between the plug and the equipment.

The outer cover of the cable must be firmly clamped by the cable clamp, and the three wires inside the plug must be cut to length so that they are neither stretched tight nor so loose that they have to be folded to fit.

D3.6 — Electric shock

When electricity passes through the human body it affects the nerves and the muscles, and it causes heating and burning. The result of these effects is known as an electric shock.

For currents below about 3 mA there is little effect apart from a tingling sensation.

Currents above about 5 mA affect muscles. If the supply is d.c, the affected muscles will be paralysed until the electricity is turned off. If the supply is a.c, then the muscles paralyse and release in step with the a.c. In either case, the heart muscles can stop operating, leading to death.

Currents above about 50 mA will cause serious skin and internal burning, even if the current does not pass near the heart muscles.

The voltage necessary to produce these currents depends on the resistance of the skin. If the skin is moist or wet, the danger of shock is much greater.

There is no danger from voltages below 25 V. Under most circumstances, a normal healthy person can withstand a shock from a supply giving up to about 100 V. People do survive shocks from supplies at much higher voltages, but the 240 V mains can, and does, kill.

The action to take in the case of an electric shock is as follows.

1. **TURN OFF THE SUPPLY** — there is no point getting a shock yourself.
2. Call for help.
3. If the victim has stopped breathing, start mouth-to-mouth resuscitation and keep it up until medical help arrives.
4. Treat the victim for shock, i.e. keep the victim warm; give no drugs or stimulants (even tea).
5. Make certain that the cause of the accident has been identified and that the fault is corrected before the supply is turned on again.

D3.7 — Safety precautions to avoid risk of electric shock

(i) Check visually all mains equipment every time before you use it. Look for damaged insulation, loose wires, broken fittings, etc.
(ii) Never work on electrical equipment with wet hands or in damp surroundings.
(iii) Always check circuits and earthing before connecting mains to new equipment for the first time.
(iv) **Unplug** the supply before making any adjustments or alterations.
(v) Never ignore any slight tingling sensation you might feel. It could be a slight electric shock.
(vi) Use tools with insulated handles.
(vii) Wear rubber-soled shoes and stand on a rubber or plastic mat.
(viii) If you need to work on equipment which is switched on, use one hand only and put the other hand in your pocket or behind your back.

(ix) Never use temporary connections to the mains.

(x) Make sure that all equipment is resting safely and firmly on the bench.

(xi) Remember that a capacitor may hold its charge after the supply has been disconnected.

(xii) If equipment is not working properly remember that the fault could be anywhere, including at the mains switch itself.

D3.8 — Electrical cables

All wires and cable must be able to carry the full current of the circuit continuously, without overheating. In most electronic equipment, thin wires can be used because the currents are very small. For any equipment using significant amounts of power, cable and wire ratings have to be calculated. The power equation is used to determine the current. The cable or wire with a rating higher than the maximum current of the circuit is then chosen.

Example of deciding the correct cable size

A computer workstation is to be connected to the mains supply. Each item of equipment is to be plugged into a distribution box which will be connected to a 13 A socket using a flexible cable. There are 3 A, 6 A, 10 A, and 13 A cables available.

The first thing to find out is how much power the various items in the workstation will require. The station is to have a computer requiring 80 W, a printer requiring 220 W, a monitor requiring 190 W, two desklights each needing 100 W, and a fan which requires 60 W.

We start by working out the total power required if everything is turned on:

$$\text{total power} = 80 + 220 + 190 + 100 + 100 + 60 = 750 \text{ W}$$

The mains voltage is 240 V. Using the power equation we can find the maximum current:

$$\text{current} = I = \frac{P}{V} = \frac{750}{240} = 3.125 \text{ A}$$

As this is more than 3 A, the 3 A cable will not do. Any of the other three could be used, so long as the fuse in the plug is rated at the same as or less than the rating of the cable. Thus, 6 A cable would be the cheapest choice if the plug had a 5 A fuse.

D3.9 — Fuses

Fuses protect cables and equipment from overheating (and catching fire) when they carry too much current (an 'overload'). The wire in the fuse is designed to melt and switch off the circuit before the other wires get too hot. Fuses are not intended to protect equipment from damage due to faults or to protect users from electric shocks (although they will do so if the fault produces a large overload).

Fuses are rated by the current which they can carry without overheating and the speed with which they 'blow'. You can buy fuses rated at currents between 20 mA and 30 A (current ratings that are even higher are used in the electricity supply).

There are two main kinds of fuse: rewirable fuses, where you fit a new wire if the fuse blows; and cartridge fuses which have the wire inside a glass or ceramic tube. When cartridge fuses blow you have to throw the cartridge away and fit a new one. Cartridge fuses may be fast blowing, normal, or slow blowing. Fuses fitted in 13 A plugs are type BS1363 cartridge fuses, and either 3 A or 13 A fuses are used.

A fuse will not blow if the current is less than **twice** the rated value, and even then it may take several minutes to blow. It will blow quickly if the current is four or more times the rated value. In other words, a 3 A fuse in a plug needs over 12 A to make it blow in a few milliseconds (see fig. D.11).

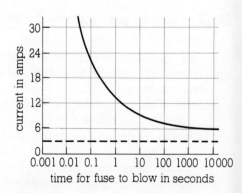

Fig. D.11 The graph showing the relationship between the current and the time it takes for a 3 A, BS1363 fuse to blow.

To decide the right size of fuse for new equipment, choose a rating which is higher than the normal current that the equipment takes. However, this rating **must** be lower than the rating of all connecting wires and cables. (If it is not, fit thicker cables.)

When the fuse blows:
(i) find out what fault caused the fuse to blow before fitting a new fuse; and
(ii) make sure that the new fuse is an exact replacement in current rating, size and type.

Always turn off equipment and, if it is mains powered, pull out the plug, before checking for faults or replacing a fuse. If a fuse blows, it might be the on/off switch that is faulty.

D3.10 — Circuit breakers

Circuit breakers are automatic switches. There are two types of circuit breakers. One type, often known as a *cut-out*, acts like a fuse when there is an overload, but it can be reset after it has blown. The other type, often known as a *trip*, is a safety device for protecting users from electric shock.

Good mains supply systems are fitted with both a trip and fuses. The trip is designed to operate when the current in the live lead is not the same as the current in the neutral lead (because there is a fault and some of the current is going to 'earth' — possibly through you!). This kind of trip is often called an *earth leakage circuit breaker*, but the correct name for it is a *residual current circuit breaker*.

D3.11 — Earthing

Earthing is a safety precaution used in the mains supply. It is also used as a means of avoiding unwanted interference in some electronic equipment.

Domestic mains wiring has three conductors. The live and neutral are the two wires necessary for the complete circuit. The third wire is known as the earth wire (more correctly, the 'earth continuity conductor'). The purpose of the earth wire is to provide a second return path for the electric current if a fault occurs, and to make sure that there is no voltage difference between the metal outside parts of equipment and the earth.

The earth acts as a conductor (it is wet!). At electricity sub-stations the neutral conductor is connected to the earth. The earth conductor in your house is also connected directly to the earth.

If the live conductor becomes faulty and touches metal parts of the equipment, a current will flow (because these are earthed). The earthed parts will not be at a dangerous voltage. The current will make a trip operate, or, if it is large enough it will blow the fuse. The supply will then be automatically disconnected from the circuit.

All mains-operated equipment should be built into a metal box and the box should be earthed. The core of the mains isolating transformer should also be earthed.

Some manufactured equipment is 'double insulated' and has no earth connection. The manufacturer provides a second layer of insulation, often a plastic case, so that if a fault occurs the metal parts still cannot be touched. This method is safe as long as the case is not opened or broken. It is not safe to double insulate equipment constructed at home because you, the constructor, will open the case. It is also not safe if there is a danger that the equipment will overheat and melt the case.

Electronic equipment is often put in an earthed metal case for another reason. Interference, in the form of radio waves (electromagnetic radiation) is caught by the earthed metal and does not reach the circuits inside. For the same reason connecting cables for hi-fi equipment often have an outer metal sheath which is earthed.

D3.12 — Peak and r.m.s. voltages

In a.c. supplies the voltage is not constant.

The *peak voltage* is the maximum voltage difference.

The *peak-to-peak voltage* is the total voltage difference between the positive peak voltage and the negative peak voltage.

The *r.m.s. voltage* is the equivalent d.c. voltage that would produce the same heating as the a.c. voltage during a complete cycle.

For a waveform such as the mains supply (called sinusoidal a.c.), the supply voltage is taken as the r.m.s. voltage. (The mains supply is 240 V r.m.s.) Peak voltage is $\sqrt{2}$ × r.m.s. voltage ($\sqrt{2} \approx 1.4$). Peak-to-peak voltage is twice the peak voltage. The peak voltage of the a.c. mains is 340 V and the peak-to-peak voltage is 680 V.

For a.c. supplies which are not sinusoidal (for example, square waves), the definitions are still correct but the arithmetical relationships are different.

Power supplies giving d.c. by rectification of a.c. will give the peak voltage if there is a smoothing circuit.

Insulation needs to be sufficient to withstand at least the peak-to-peak voltage so that it can be effective under the largest possible voltage difference that the circuit might produce.

In other cases the r.m.s. voltage is used.

Currents in a.c. circuits can also be quoted as r.m.s., or peak, or even peak-to-peak. When a current is quoted, assume it is an r.m.s. value, unless it is stated that it is a peak value.

Exercises on peak and r.m.s. voltages using the relationship that peak voltage is $\sqrt{2}$ times the r.m.s. voltage

Exercise 46 − What are the peak and peak-to-peak values of the voltage given by the 12 V secondary of a mains transformer?

Exercise 47 − A 20 V a.c. supply is rectified and smoothed. What d.c. voltage will be obtained?

Exercise 48 − Telephone cable has insulation rated at 225 V d.c. What is the maximum r.m.s. a.c. voltage that can be applied safely to it?

D3.13 — Voltage regulators

Modern voltage regulators are integrated circuits designed to give an unchanging d.c. output, even though the input voltage and the load current may vary.

A common type of regulator is the 78/79 series of devices. The 78 series is for positive power supplies, and the 79 series is for negative voltage power supplies.

Type 7805 is a typical example of one of these types of regulator. The output voltage is 5 V for currents from 0 to 1 A and supply voltages between 7 and 25 V. If the output is accidentally short-circuited, the device limits the current to 750 mA. The current is shown in fig. D.12. The two capacitors and the resistor are intended to ensure that the regulator works properly under all possible conditions.

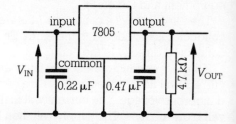

Fig. D.12 The circuit for the type 7805 voltage regulator. For other types, check the manufacturer's data sheet for details.

D3.14 — Protection for safety in mains-operated power supplies

Any power supply which is to be operated from the mains supply must include the following:

  (i) an isolating transformer;
 (ii) a double-pole switch in the mains input;
(iii) a fuse of the correct rating in the line conductor to the transformer;
 (iv) a metal case;
  (v) an earth connection to both the metal case and the core of the transformer;
 (vi) a neon mains indicator, connected on the supply side of the switch, which will light whenever the unit is connected to the mains;
(vii) a fuse of the correct rating in the output lead;

(viii) a mains cable of sufficient current rating for the fuse in the plug;

(ix) a proper cable grip to clamp the mains cable where it enters the case;

(x) a grommet (rubber protecting ring) fitted in the hole through which the cable enters the case;

(xi) a properly wired 13 A plug, fitted with the correct fuse (probably a 3 A fuse), on the mains cable;

(xii) all components, particularly the transformer, firmly mounted in the case;

(xiii) all mains wiring well separated from the rest of the circuit; and

(xiv) all mains connections adequately insulated to prevent accidental contact with the case or with you when the circuit is being tested.

These points are illustrated in the circuit and diagram shown in fig. D.13.

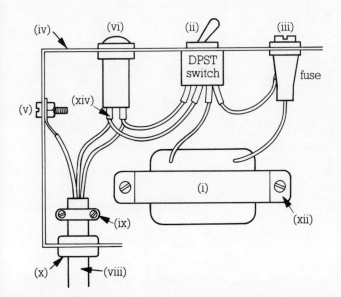

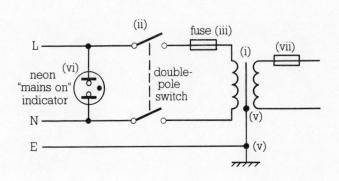

Fig. D.13 The correct way to construct a mains power supply.

D3.15 — Typical component values for low-voltage power supplies

Table D.1 gives some typical component ratings for power units based on the circuit shown in fig. D.14. If a half-wave rectifier is used instead of the bridge rectifier shown in fig. D.14, the capacitor value must be doubled and the output voltage will increase by about 0.7 V.

Table D.1 Typical component values for power supplies

Output voltage required	5	5	12	15	25
Maximum current required	100 mA	2 A	1 A	500 mA	1 A
Transformer secondary r.m.s. voltage required (V)	5	5	10	12	19.2
Minimum PIV rating of rectifier (V)	13	13	27	34	54
Smoothing capacitor value (μF) to smooth within 1 V	1000	20 000	10 000	5000	10 000
Capacitor working voltage (min)	10	10	16	25	40

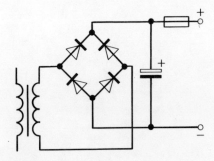

Fig. D.14 Standard circuit for the low-voltage side of a power unit.

14 SEQUENTIAL LOGIC

Many electronic systems are concerned with decision-making, and the circuits that have this function are called logic circuits. In chapter 4 you learnt about the basic circuits that carried out functions such as the AND decision and the OR decision. Logic systems can be made up using a number of these gates, and these are called combinational logic systems. Very often, we need not only to combine the various logic functions but also to arrange that they happen **one after another** in the right order. We need things to happen in a *sequence*. We need a system that can follow a process that is of the type "do this, **then** do that, **then** do the other". This kind of system is called a *sequential logic system*.

The magic trick performed by a sequential system is in remembering what it has just done, so that it can do the next step. The extra block that does this is a kind of electronic memory. In fact, such a block was used in one of the systems in an earlier chapter. A latch was used in chapter 2 to remember that the race had started and to keep the counter switched on until the race had finished. The counter could **then** be switched off.

The latch was not the only example of a block with memory in that race-timer system. The counter itself also uses sequential logic. Any method of counting or timing relies on remembering what the last number or the previous time was.

The basic unit of all sequential logic is called a *bistable*. There are lots of kinds of bistable in use, but they all have the same basic function. The output that a bistable gives depends on both the input signal and the previous signal that the bistable received.

In this chapter we shall find out about counters and systems for controlling a series of steps in a process. We shall also find out about some of the bistable blocks themselves. One of the main uses of bistables is in the memory and registers of computers. This is described in chapter 19.

> A bistable is a logic gate with an output which depends both on the input signal and on the previous signal the bistable received.

Counters

You may think that counting is easy! Saying "one, two, three" is easy, but counting a number of 'things' needs something more. Let us think about what it actually is that we count.

Ask a friend to make a pile of 2p coins on a table at the other side of the room. Can you count how many coins there are in the pile? You can guess how many there are but you cannot count them. Now go over and look closely at the pile. Without touching the pile you can now count how many there are. The difference is that you can see the edges of each of the coins and so find the gaps between the coins. If you cannot see the gaps, you cannot count. The same is true of all counting methods.

In digital electronics we count pulses. In a train of pulses the *mark* of each pulse is separated from the next by a *space*. The counter counts the marks of a pulse train. The circuit is triggered by the change from the space to the mark. This is often called the *rising edge* of the pulse. Without the spaces it would be impossible to count the marks. (Some circuits use the falling edge of the pulse — the change from the mark to the space — instead.)

Counting in electronics is not based on our ordinary numbers. We count in tens, but it is very difficult to design circuits that have ten different voltage levels. The easiest way of counting by electronics is to use normal digital electronics with just two logic levels. It might seem that with only logic 0 and logic 1 to work with you could never count beyond one. However, we can count beyond nine with ordinary decimal numbers, and in the same way we can count beyond one using *binary* numbers.

Binary counting

When we count in the normal way we use the ten numerals, 0, 1, 2, 3, . . . up to 9. What happens when you get to nine, the largest numeral? If you are writing down the numbers you start off another column called the 'tens' column and go back to 0 in the original column of numerals. The same thing happens when you come to the largest number using two columns (99); you start a 'hundreds' column.

In binary counting the only numerals are 0 and 1. The biggest numeral is 1. To count beyond 1 we start a second column to count twos. Thus 0, 1, 2, 3, become:

decimal	binary		
units	twos	ones (units)	
0		0	
1		1	
2	1	0	(1 two + no units)
3	1	1	(1 two + 1 unit)

Number 4 now becomes easy. We have got to 'biggest numbers allowed' in the 'ones' and 'twos' columns, so we add a 'fours' column:

decimal	binary		
units	fours	twos	units
4	1	0	0
5	1	0	1

The next column along is 'eights', then 'sixteens', and so on. Just as, with decimal numbers, each column is *ten* times the previous one, so in binary numbers the next column is *twice* the previous one. Two, four, eight are the *place values* of each column. (What are the next four binary place values after sixteen?)

Apart from having different place values and only two numerals, the counting process is exactly the same as in normal decimal counting. For example, the decimal number 325 means 3 hundreds, 2 tens and 5 units. Similarly the binary number 101000101 means one two-hundred-and-fifty-six, no one-hundred-and-twenty-eight, one sixty-four, no thirty-two, no sixteen, no eight, one four, no two and one unit. If you add 256 + 64 + 4 + 1, it comes to 325. The binary number 101000101 is the same as the decimal number 325. Table 14.1 lists some other binary numbers and their decimal equivalents. Reference sections E1.2 and E1.3 show the methods for changing from decimal to binary numbers, and from binary to decimal numbers.

Electronic counting systems

Suppose you needed to count the number of cars going into a car park

Table 14.1 Decimal and binary numbers

decimal	binary	decimal	binary
1	1	15	1111
2	10	16	10000
3	11	17	10001
4	100		
5	101	31	11111
6	110	32	100000
7	111	33	100001
8	1000		
9	1001	64	1000000
10	1010	100	1100100
11	1011	128	1000000
12	1100	256	100000000
13	1101	512	1000000000
14	1110	1000	1111101000

electronically. To keep it simple we will assume that the car park has only fifteen spaces.

Any electronic system has to have a signal input. For a counter the input has to be a series of pulses. Each time a car entered the park it could break a light beam and so produce one pulse for the electronic circuit. The counter would count the rising edge of each pulse.

What about the output? Fifteen is the binary number 1111. There are four places in this number. The figure in each place of a binary number is called a *bit*. The bit that represents the units (i.e. the bit with the smallest place value) is called the *least significant bit* (LSB) and the bit with the largest place value (the 'eights' bit in 1111) is called the *most significant bit* (MSB).

Because there are four bits in this number there will have to be four outputs, one for each bit. These are called *parallel outputs*, because we have to look at all four outputs at the same time to work out the value of the number.

What sort of blocks are used inside the counter? The basic block for this kind of system is the bistable. Bistables are used in all sequential logic systems. There are different kinds of bistables for various kinds of system. The bistable used in a counter is called a *triggered bistable* or *T-bistable*. (Some of the other kinds of bistable are mentioned later in this chapter.) There would be four T-bistables in our car-park counter, one for each bit in the binary number.

The counter works like this. When the first car comes in the pulse it produces goes to the first bistable. The output of that bistable changes from logic 0 to logic 1. After the car has crossed the light beam the pulse is finished, but a special feature of the bistable is that once it has been made to change its output to logic 1, the output **stays** at logic 1 until another pulse comes.

When the next car comes in, there is another pulse at the input. This pulse changes the first bistable back, to give a logic 0 output again. As there are now two cars in the park the counter has to be at the binary number 10. The first bistable must now pass a pulse to the second bistable. The input of the second bistable needs to change to logic 1 but the output from the first bistable has changed from logic 1 to logic 0. We need a block that gives a logic 1 output when the input goes to logic 0. In other words we need an inverter. If the output of the first bistable is inverted and fed to the input of the second bistable, the output of the second bistable will change to logic 1 and stay there until another logic 1 signal comes from the first bistable. Fig. 14.1 shows this arrangement, and also the effect of the first two pulses on the two bistables.

The third car to enter the car park will change the first bistable yet again. It will make the output a logic 1 output again. Now the outputs from both the first and the second bistable are at logic 1.

The fourth car changes the first bistable back to logic 0 once more. This change goes through the inverter and makes the second bistable change. It was at logic 1 after the second car so it now becomes logic 0. This output is inverted and passed to bistable three, which counts the fours. Fig. 14.2 shows the arrangement of the full counter for the car park which has four bistables altogether. The fourth bistable counts the 'eights'.

The counter block is therefore a series of bistables connected together through inverters. In a real bistable you do not need separate inverters. You can get two outputs from the bistable itself; a normal output and an inverted output. These are often labelled as Q and $\overline{Q}$ ('not Q') on diagrams. The 'not Q' output is the inverted output and is the one that is connected to the next bistable.

104
105
106
107

Using a light beam to count the cars is not a very good system in practice. Why? A mat in the road would be much better, but would give the wrong answer. Why? How could the problem be overcome? What else do you need if the counter is to show the number of cars that are in the car park at any time?

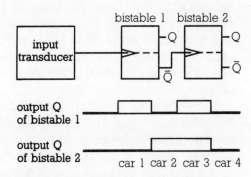

Fig. 14.1 The first two stages of the car-park counter. Note the symbol for a triggered bistable. The graphs below the diagram show what happens at the various points in the circuit as the first four cars enter the park.

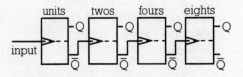

Fig. 14.2 The block diagram for a complete four-bit counter. Each bistable has two outputs. The output marked $\overline{Q}$ is the inverted output from the bistable, and is connected directly to the next bistable.

Timing systems

Timing systems work in exactly the same way as counting systems. The only difference is in the pulses that go to the input of the counter. For a timer the input is a continuous pulse train from a pulse generator. The pulse generator is designed to give regular pulses, perhaps one every thousandth of a second, exactly. Input pulses used in this way are often called *clock pulses*. Computer systems use clock pulses in this way to take the machine step-by-step through its program. However, if you need to use the timer as an electronic clock or stopwatch, there have to be extra circuit blocks to turn the binary numbers into decimal numbers for the display.

More about counters

What would happen to the car-park counter described earlier if a sixteenth car went through the light beam? If you have followed how the counter works you will realise that once the counter has reached 1111 the next pulse makes it go back to 0000. Most counters you can buy are four-bit counters made as integrated circuits. Does this mean that electronic counters can only count as far as 15? The answer is obviously no! The clever way to overcome this problem is to use the 'eights' output from one counter as the input to the next counter. The first bistable on the next chip then counts in sixteens. You can connect as many counters as you like, one after the other, in the same way. Connecting counters like this is called *cascading* the counters.

[108] Sometimes we need circuits that count to less than 15. If we need counters to count to three or seven (why not four or eight?), then we only use two or three bistables instead of all four of the bistables in a four-bit counter. However, suppose that we want to make the circuit that counts as we normally count, in tens. We would want the circuit to go back to 0 every time it reaches the 9-to-10 changeover. Most counter circuits have another input, a control input that will 'reset' all the bistables to 0. All we need to do is to connect a logic circuit to the output of the counter [110] which will give logic 1 when the counter has got to 1010 (why not 10? [111] why not 1001?) and then reset the counter. Fig. 14.3 shows how this is done.

There is nothing to stop us cascading a second counter to the output of a counter that has been made to count up to ten. If the two counters are identical then the first counter will count in units and the second one counts in tens. This type of counter is used for the 'binary coded decimal' (BCD) system described in the next chapter.

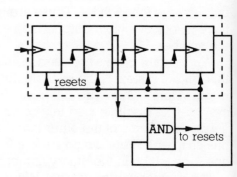

Fig. 14.3 A four-bit counter arranged to count in tens by using the reset input. Everything inside the dotted box would be part of the integrated circuit of a counter chip. What would you have to do to make the counter reset when it had [109] counted five pulses instead of ten?

SUMMARY 14A

A counter counts the number of pulses reaching it.

Electronic counting is based on binary numbers.

Binary numbers use only two numerals, 0 and 1. Each figure in a binary number is called a bit.

The place values of the figures in a binary number are units, twos, fours, eights and so on, multiplying by two each time.

The units in binary numbers are the least significant bits (LSB); the bit with the highest place value in a number is the most significant bit (MSB).

Counters use bistables. Each bistable represents one bit.

A timer is a counter clocked by regular pulses from a pulse generator.

Counters have parallel outputs. A four-bit counter has four output lines.

Counters can be cascaded together to count to larger numbers.

Most counters have a reset to make them go back to 0. The reset can be used, together with logic gates, to make a counter count up to any number.

Control systems

There are lots of examples of systems that operate by a number of steps one after the other in sequence. Common examples are traffic lights, controlled pedestrian crossings, railway level crossings, and so on. There are many more examples in industrial production. A machine might be required, say, to pick up a board, fit a component, fasten it in place and then replace the board in its rack. (There were other examples of sequential systems mentioned in chapter 1. What were they?)

There are several ways of making processes take place one after another. Often they are controlled by electromagnetic switches (*uniselectors*), but the use of counter systems is now an important method for controlling a sequential process. We will use a very simple example to show how such systems can work using bistable blocks.

Think about the automatic level crossings where a railway crosses a road. When a train is due, the signalman has to close the crossing and then signal the train to go over. To make sure that no cars are trapped on the crossing there are several steps in the sequence. These are:

step 1 − orange warning lights switched on;
step 2 − orange lights switched off, red lights switched on;
step 3 − motors to lower the gates switched on.

When the gates are lowered, a sensor turns off the motors and changes the railway signals to green. A sensor on the railway track detects when the train has passed and the system is then switched off and the gates are opened. (Why are these steps not part of the counting sequence?)

Because there are three steps in the process the counter system must count to **four**. There has to be a step in the system (a 'step 0' if you like) which is: 'everything is ready but nothing is happening yet'.

The counter controlling this has two bistables, so that it can count 00, 01, 10, 11 (i.e. step 0, step 1, step 2, step 3). Each bistable will have a Q and a 'not Q' ($\overline{Q}$) output.

How does the system know when the orange lights must go on? This is when the counter is at step 1. At step 1 the first bistable is set to 1 and the second bistable is set to 0, to give the binary number 01. Remember that the least significant bit (the *lowest*) is the *first* bistable in the counter. The orange lights have to be switched on when bistable 1 is at logic 1 **and** bistable 2 is at logic 0. This sounds like a simple AND gate, and that is, in fact, what is used. The 'Q' output from bistable 1 and the 'not Q' output from bistable 2 are connected to an AND gate and the output operates the lights (fig. 14.4). (Why is the 'not Q' output from bistable 2 used?)

In this system the AND gate is being used as the **switch** that operates the output. AND gates are very often used as control switches in this way. You will meet another example of this in chapter 19 on computers.

What about step 2 in the level crossing system, when the red lights come on? Remember that the red lights must stay on when the system goes to step 3. The lights must be on when:

either: bistable 1 is at logic 0 and bistable 2 is at logic 1
   or: bistable 1 is at logic 1 and bistable 2 is at logic 1 (step 3)

To do this we could use two AND gates, one to find step 2 and the other to find step 3 (in the same way as for step 1), and then use an OR gate so that the lights stayed on for both steps. In fact it is easier than that. For the red lights it does not matter what bistable 1 is doing. It can be either at logic 0 or logic 1. All that matters is that bistable 2 must be at logic 1. The output from bistable 2, in this case, **is** the control signal for the red lights. Fig. 14.5 shows this part of the system.

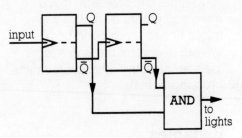

Fig. 14.4 Using two bistables and an AND gate to make the lights come on at step 1, when the counter output is 01.

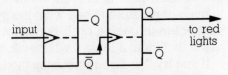

Fig. 14.5 Making the red lights come on when the counter is at steps 2 and 3 (binary 10 and 11).

On most level crossings there are two red lights that flash on and off alternately. How could this be made to work? The control signal for the red lights would also have to switch on the sub-system that operates the
⟦115⟧ two lights. All that is needed is a pulse generator and an AND gate. Can you devise the sub-system?

What about step 3 in the system, the closing of the gates? The arrangement is just the same as for step 1, but this time the AND gate must operate when bistable 1 is at logic 1 and bistable 2 is at logic 1. You
⟦116⟧ should work out for yourself how to do this. You should also work out the
⟦117⟧ logic system needed to change the railway signal to green ('clear').

How does the system know when to change from step 1 to step 2 or from step 2 to step 3? All that is needed is a pulse generator that sends pulses to the counter at the right time intervals. When the signalman operates the switch this turns on the pulse generator and the clock pulses from this generator take the sequence through its steps.

There is one problem left. Unless we stop the clock signals when the sequence is at step 3, it will keep going. As there is no step 4 it will go back to step 0. The crossing will open to cars and the train will have passed the green signal!

In much the same way as a 15-step counter can be made to count in tens, the counter can be made to stop at any number. All you need are further gates to control the clock pulses going into the counter and switch them off when the bistables are both at logic 1. A NOR gate could be
⟦118⟧ used this time, as in fig. 14.6 (why NOR rather than AND?).

The system described here is very simple, and the actual arrangement used by the railways could not be as simple as this. (What is missing
⟦119⟧ even from this simplified system? If you can, watch a real level crossing.) However, this example does show all the basic ideas in any sequential logic system. If you have equipment available you might like to try to build up a system to control the lights for a 'pelican crossing' (the green-man
⟦120⟧ crossing lights).

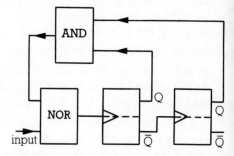

Fig. 14.6 Making the counter stop when it reaches step 3 (binary 11).

SUMMARY 14B

Counters can be used to control the steps in a process or the operation of a machine.

The parallel outputs of the counter are fed to logic gates which control the system and which give their signal when the right step has been reached.

The system is operated by sending clock pulses to the counter.

Bistables

Every sequential logic system uses bistables, but what is a bistable? How does it work? A bistable is a simple but clever arrangement of ordinary logic gates. The last part of this chapter explains what they are.

All the word 'bistable' means is something that can be set in either one of two positions. A light switch is a bistable device, because the mechanism locks the switch in either the on or the off position until you make the switch change over.

You can set up an electronic bistable very easily. All you need are two inverters connected together so that each one operates the other. A practical arrangement is shown in fig. 14.7. Indicators have been added to make it possible to see what the system is doing, and each input is also connected through a push-button switch to the zero line so that you can make that input a logic 0 whenever you want to.

If you try this arrangement in the laboratory you will find that, as long as you do not press both switches at once, only one of the indicators comes on. To make the other indicator come on you have to press the switch connected to its inverter but, when you do this, the other indicator

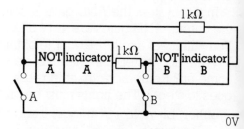

Fig. 14.7 Using two inverters to make a simple bistable. Pushing switch A makes the output of inverter A go to logic 1 and light indicator A. Indicator B is not lit, but lights when indicator A is not lit.

goes out. Once the circuit has changed over, pressing this switch again makes no difference, until you press the other switch and change the circuit back to its first state.

The explanation is very simple. If the input to one inverter (let us call it inverter A) is logic 1, then the output of inverter A is logic 0. This output is connected to the input of inverter B. Thus, the input of inverter B is logic 0 and its output is logic 1. This output goes to the input of inverter A, which is already at logic 1.

To change the circuit over you have to force the input of inverter A to be logic 0, and then the whole circuit switches over to the opposite set of conditions. The circuit can lock itself into either of two conditions. It is a bistable. (Can you explain what happens when both push-button switches are pressed at the same time?)

Push-button switches would be no use in a counter, so we must find some other way of making it possible to switch the bistable circuit. The answer is to use NOR gates rather than inverters. Fig. 14.8 shows two NOR gates connected in the same way as the inverters. If you connect a logic 1 to the unused input of the gate that is giving a logic 1 output, the circuit switches over. NAND gates could also be used. If you can, try out one of the arrangements in the laboratory.

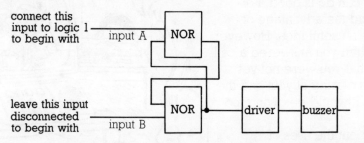

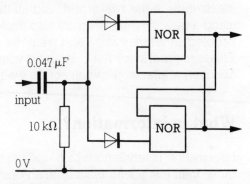

Fig. 14.8 A simple bistable using NOR gates. The buzzer should sound when the power supply is turned on, and stay sounding when input A is disconnected from the 5 V supply. Touching input B on the 5 V terminal will turn the buzzer off, and touching input A on the 5 V terminal will switch it on again. Two NAND gates could have been used instead of the NOR gates. What will turn the buzzer on and off then?

In the experimental system shown in fig. 14.8 the bistable is switched by connecting input A or input B to the power-supply line. This gives a logic 1 at the input. A logic 1 to switch the bistable could come from any other block that can give a logic 1 output.

When the bistable is made to switch over by sending a logic 1 to one of the inputs, we say that the bistable has been triggered. You have already met triggering in chapter 6 (in the triggered pulse producer), as well as in the earlier part of this chapter. You will remember that it is the rising edge of the pulse that triggers the bistable.

The arrangement in fig. 14.8 is called an RS-bistable. RS stands for *reset and set*. The latch used in chapter 2 was an RS-bistable.

This method of triggering a bistable is not always the most useful, because there are separate lines for set pulses and reset pulses. It would not be suitable for a counter. For a counter you want the bistable to turn on the first time that you trigger it, to turn off the second time, to turn on again the third time, and so on.

This is the T-bistable mentioned earlier in this chapter. The RS-bistable can be made into a T-bistable by using diodes to steer pulses to the set or reset line, as required. This arrangement is shown in Fig. 14.9.

Other types of bistable are used for the registers and the memories of computers. Some of these are described in chapter 19.

Fig. 14.9 Adding a steering network to the inputs of the bistable in fig. 14.8 turns the RS-bistable into a binary counting block called a T-bistable. The resistor and capacitor are a spike generator (see fig. 6.5).

SUMMARY 14C

A bistable system has two inverting logic gates (NOT, NOR or NAND) with the output of each gate connected to an input of the other gate.

Different kinds of bistable have different arrangements for triggering.

The RS-bistable has two signal inputs. One makes the bistable set (change over) and the other resets it (makes it change back).

A T-bistable has one input. Every input pulse causes the bistable to change.

15 INFORMATION BY ELECTRONICS

Making and using electronic systems is fun and many people treat electronics as a hobby. The real importance of electronics is **not**, however, as a game or as a hobby. The importance is in our use of it in all aspects of life. If you were left on an uninhabited island with no batteries and no electric generator, once you had got your food and shelter it would be the radio, television and telephone that you would miss first.

We use electronics to 'do things' with information. Electronics will store information, sort it, code it or send it from one place to another in a split second. So, to understand the way electronics is used, you will need to know something about 'information', something about communication and something about the processing of information by computers. Much of the rest of this book is about these things.

In real life, it is not enough to know what electronics is doing for us and what it could do. Not everything that electronics can do is good. For example, video-telephone is a real possibility, and the advantage of seeing the person you are talking to seems to be a useful idea. However, you might not think it was such a good idea if, when you answered a call from someone important to you, they could see that you were not yet dressed, the house was a mess, your mother was glaring at you, and the book that you 'never had' was lying on the table! It would be giving too much information.

Electronics can cause problems. In thinking about the uses of electronics in the real world, and all the new things that could be done using a new system, we must also think of all the disadvantages, the problems that may arise and what the proposed system will **not** do. These chapters are not only about what electronics can do, but also about what electronics will not do well.

ER...I'M SORRY...SHE'S IN A MEETING

What is information?

Information is anything which adds to what is already known. It is much more than just useful facts from an encyclopaedia, a railway timetable or a cookery book.

Information does not have to be useful. Millions of people watch television programmes such as 'Coronation Street' week after week. You know that Coronation Street does not actually exist, that the people are actors and that what they say is written by script writers. None of what is shown or said is useful, in the way that the word 'information' is usually used. However, the bits that go together to create Coronation Street are all bits of information. Indeed one of the problems that electronics has caused is that, because some of the scenes from programmes like Coronation Street can be made to be so lifelike, some people believe them to be real.

Information is not only words. Try turning your television set round so that you cannot see the picture but you can only listen to the sound. Places, movements, facial expressions, and colours all give information that you can no longer see. All these things are signals telling you what is happening or what people are thinking or doing.

Fig. 15.1 Can you identify at least twelve different ways of conveying information in ⟨123⟩ this photograph?

In the early parts of this book we were concerned with systems which had a signal input and a means of processing these signals to give an output. Many of the systems had simple input transducers that produced signals. To use electronics in real life we have to find ways of converting the information that we want to process, into electronic signals. Words, pictures, numbers, measurements, movements and even feelings all have to be changed into electronic signals that can then be processed.

There is a new area of technology, known as *information technology*, which is about using electronics to deal with information in complex forms. A computer can, for example, be programmed to identify who is speaking, to recognise words and print out a message, or even to translate words into another language. In these respects the computer is working like your brain, and using what is has 'learnt' to interpret the information at a high level. This book is only concerned with information at the lowest level, and does not attempt to consider the new developments coming from information technology.

Codes

Turning information into signals that can be understood is not special to electronics. Imagine a Russian worker or a Kenyan tribesman seeing 'Coronation Street' for the first time. The words would mean nothing to them because they are in a different language. Many of the gestures that were used would be misunderstood. Places and ideas such as a 'pub' would convey nothing. The clothes would not tell them whether it was night or day, or how the wearers lived and worked, because suits, pyjamas and curlers are not part of the life of the Russian Steppes or the plains of Kenya.

The Russian and the Kenyan do not understand because they do not understand the code. Language is a code. Written words are a code. Even the clothes we wear are a code. We have to learn these codes — everyone has to learn to talk, to read, to write and how to behave.

Electronic systems have codes too. Unfortunately the codes that have to be used in electronics are often not the same codes that we use in ordinary life. For example, electronic systems cannot read ordinary printed words (yet!) so more information has to be supplied to allow the electronic system to convert the letters into a number code (ASCII is the name of the most common code used at present). Some of the codes used in electronic systems are considered later in this chapter.

Carriers

Not only must there be a code for information, but there must also be something which will carry the code. You can, for example, think about something you wish to write, but unless you have pen and paper you cannot give that information to anybody else. If you wish to speak directly to someone, then the information is carried by a sound wave.

Every piece of information has a carrier. The information is imprinted on the carrier by changing the carrier in some way. The process of adding information to the carrier is called *modulation* and the block that performs this process in an electrical system is called a *modulator*.

At the point where the information is to be taken out of the electrical system there has to be a block which will separate the information from its carrier. This block is called a *demodulator*. Fig. 15.2 is the block diagram which shows the essential blocks needed for any information system.

Think about the telephone system as an example of this process. The carrier is the electric current in the wires. The microphone is the modulator: it causes variations of the electric current that correspond to the sounds reaching the microphone. The earpiece is the demodulator; it extracts the information from the electric current by making the variations in current produce a new sound wave.

What you are reading now is also coded information modulated onto a carrier. What kind of information is being used? What is the carrier? How is it modulated? Where is the information demodulated? Can you identify the second carrier in this system?

Turning information into electronic form

When we are turning information into electronic form, the electronic signal can be either a digital or an analogue signal. The difference between an analogue signal and a digital signal was introduced in chapter 3. If the information is something that is varying all the time, we can make the electrical voltage change in the same way. The electrical signal is then called an analogue signal. Digital signals are those which are either high or low, logic 1 or logic 0. In practice, digital signals are usually a series of pulses, and not just one change from logic 0 to logic 1 and back again. The series of pulses are used as a code for the information. Digital signals are always coded signals.

It is not only in electronics that information can be in digital or analogue form. Speech uses analogue signals, because the sounds we use vary continuously in both pitch and volume. Morse code uses digital signals, with the lamp, or buzzer, or hooter turning on and off as, for example, in the well-known SOS signal, which sounds like: dot-dot-dot, space, dah-dah-dah, space, dot-dot-dot ($\cdots$ $-$ $-$ $-$ $\cdots$).

At first sight it might appear that, because analogue signals can represent a wider range of values, they must be better. It is true that if we had to talk to one another in morse code we would have far less to

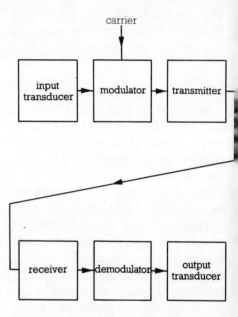

Fig. 15.2 Block diagram showing the essential parts of every information system.

An analogue signal is a signal whose magnitude varies in the same way as the information that it represents.

A digital signal is a coded signal. The code represents the information by a series of pulses. Most (but not all) digital signals use two levels only (on and off, logic 1 and logic 0).

say to one another because it is slow compared with spoken words. We would also not be able to show anger, thoughtfulness, doubt and so on, as we do by the way in which we say things. For human beings analogue communication is certainly better, but this is not true for electronic systems. The reasons for the difference are to do with speed and the number of things that can be handled at the same time.

Think about a television programme. As we watch, we take in the shapes and movement in the picture, the colours, and the sounds, all at the same time. The television receiver has, in addition, to 'know' where the top left-hand corner of the picture is, and how to position it correctly on the screen. All of these things are separate pieces of information, but the human brain deals with them all at the same time. For digital signals, each piece of information would have to be turned into pulses. You would need millions of pulses every second to deal with all this information. Human beings cannot sort out visual information coming faster than 15 items per second. A cine film is a series of still pictures shown at 16 'frames' a second, and the eye and brain 'sees' a continuously moving picture instead of 16 separate pictures. In the last 20 years, electronics engineers have learnt how to make electronic systems cope with tens of millions of pulses each second. There are big advantages in having information in digital form, and so most modern electronic information systems use digital signals.

Converting analogue information into digital signals

Much of the information that we are interested in starts as analogue information. For example, the daytime temperature varies continuously hour by hour and from place to place. When the weather forecast is shown on television or in the newspaper the weather map has temperatures given as a series of numbers. We are told that 'it will be 18 degrees in London today but in Manchester it will be only 17 degrees'. This information has already been 'digitised'. If we can work out what the weather forecaster does to digitise these temperatures we can also work out how to do the same thing electronically.

In the weather forecast the range of temperatures has been sampled, at certain places (London and Manchester) and at certain times of the day (noon, or mid-afternoon). As long as sufficient samples are taken, we can work out what will happen in our own district.

To convert an electronic analogue signal into digital form, the signal is sampled at regular time intervals and the information is turned into a digital code. Sampling has to be at a rate not less than twice the highest frequency in the signal. The sampling circuit measures the size of the signal at that time and then converts that measurement into a coded series of pulses. It repeats this for each sample. The code for the pulses is usually just a binary number. Fig. 15.3 illustrates this process diagrammatically. The block that carries out this process is called an *A-to-D converter*.

A code is only useful if it can be decoded when necessary. When using an A-to-D converter there are a number of things a system designer has to have in the system. For example, there needs to be a space between each group of pulses, so that the system has a way of knowing where one set of pulses ends and where the next set of pulses begins.

There also needs to be some method of checking that the individual pulses (or bits, which is an abbreviation for **bi**nary dig**its**) are correct.

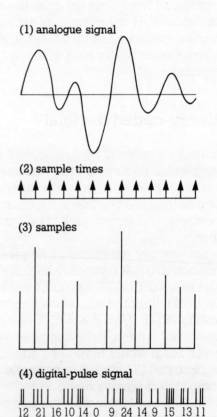

Fig. 15.3 The conversion of an analogue signal into a digital signal. The top graph shows an analogue signal. This is sampled by the A-to-D converter at the times shown in the second graph, and the third graph shows the samples the converter receives. The converter measures the size of each sample and turns that into a binary number. The bottom graph shows the pulses produced by the converter, and underneath each group of pulses is the number that each group represents.

Sometimes extra bits are added for checking purposes. The system designer needs to decide how many bits are needed in each group (or *word*, as these groups are often called). If a large number is used, the system will be expensive. If there are too few bits the samples will not be measured accurately enough or will not cope adequately with changes in amplitude.

Often the number of bits in a word is set by the components that the designer wants to use. Many microprocessor chips are designed to work with words of 8 or 16 bits. The designer will make the system fit the chips that are available.

Codes for numbers and letters

When you need to transfer information which is in the form of numbers or letters into an electronic system you do not need an A-to-D converter, because numbers and letters are already a kind of code. However, digital electronic systems usually have only two possible states (on or logic 1, and off or logic 0). There are ten numerals in our decimal number system and twenty-six letters in the alphabet (but each letter can be capital (e.g. A) or lower case (e.g. a), and there are also all the signs such as commas and question marks). There has to be a way of re-coding this information in binary form so that it can then be used in electronic circuits.

Binary-coded decimal

In theory it ought to be easy to deal with numbers. Any decimal number can be changed into a binary number, in the way that was explained to you in chapter 14. In practice, binary numbers are easy to deal with, as long as they are positive, not too large, do not involve fractions or decimals, and do not have to be converted back to decimal numbers too often.

You can see something of the problem by thinking about the decimal number 20 000 000 which, when changed into binary, becomes 1001100010010110100000000. There are twenty-five bits. The '2' in the decimal number might be the only significant figure (another way of writing 20 000 000 is 2×10^7). The binary number has seventeen significant figures. If the computer system used an 8-bit microprocessor, seven zeros would have to be added in front of the first '1' to give four whole bytes (32 bits). A very simple decimal number has become a very complicated binary one.

The answer to this problem is to code each decimal numeral in the number separately. This gives a code known as BCD, which is short for *binary-coded decimal*. Each numeral is turned into binary separately. The number 20 000 000 becomes 0010 0000 0000 0000 0000 0000 0000 0000. This still has 32 bits, but it is obvious that in every other way this is an easier code to use. Almost all electronic equipment for processing numbers (such as calculators) uses BCD or other codes (such as the 'Gray code') based on the same idea.

To turn a number into BCD, each numeral is turned into binary separately, and then the whole number is written down as a series of 4-bit words. For example, the decimal number 369 becomes 0011 0110 1001 in binary-coded decimal – 0011 represents the numeral 3, 0110 represents the numeral 6 and 1001 represents the numeral 9.

The ASCII code

There is no simple logical way of coding the letters of the alphabet, but it is important that everyone uses the same code when converting letters into electronic signals. (Why?) The agreed code is known as ASCII. These letters stand for *American Standard Code for Information Interchange*, but everyone calls it ASCII (pronounced 'ass-key'). All the letters and symbols of the typewriter keyboard have codes between 0000001 and 1111111.

How do these 7-bit words work when most computers use 8-bit or 16-bit systems. The extra bit is not wasted. It can be used in two ways. On simple equipment, normal letters have codes between 00000001 and 01111111 and then the codes from 10000001 to 11111111 can be used for the same letters but in italic style. On more advanced equipment the extra bit is used for checking for errors. It is called a *parity bit*, and the idea is very simple. If there is an even number of 1's in the 7-bit word, the parity bit is 0, whereas if there is an odd number of 1's in the 7-bit word, the parity bit is 1. The result is that the complete 8-bit words always have an even number of 1's. If one of the bits gets changed during the processing, the 8-bit word will not have 'even parity' and the presence of an error can be detected.

Table 15.1 Some examples of ASCII codes and parity bits

letter or symbol	ASCII code in decimal	ASCII code in binary	ASCII code with even parity bit
F	70	100 0110	100 0110 1
a	97	110 0001	110 0001 1
d	100	110 0100	110 0100 1
s	115	111 0011	111 0011 1
?	63	011 1111	011 1111 0

The advantages of digital systems

Whenever information is converted into a digital code the number of bits will be many more than the quantities they represent. Letters and symbols become 8-bit words and there are four bits for every decimal numeral if BCD is used. You may wonder why anyone bothers with digital systems. The reason is that once you have got signals in digital form they are easier to process and store. They do not suffer from electrical interference caused by outside factors, or by problems in designing good circuits. Digital systems are therefore reliable and cheap. To the user, it does not matter how complicated the circuits inside the blocks are. All the user wants is reliable equipment at the lowest possible cost.

SUMMARY 15

Information is anything that adds to what is already known. It may be numbers, letters, sounds, pictures, symbols, signs or anything else which conveys either facts or ideas.

Information always requires a carrier.

The process of adding the information to the carrier is called modulation.

The process of obtaining information from the carrier is called demodulation.

A signal is a modulated carrier.

Signals are either analogue or digital (or sometimes a hybrid of the two).

Analogue signals are signals where the voltage (or current) varies in step with the information being carried.

Digital signals are signals in which the information is coded.

Most digital signals in electronics use a series of binary pulses; the voltage switches between two levels, one being logic 0 and the other being logic 1.

An A-to-D converter converts analogue signals into digital signals by sampling the analogue signal at regular intervals and giving a binary code for the magnitude of each sample.

Numbers are usually coded using BCD. Binary-coded decimal turns each separate decimal numeral into its binary equivalent.

Letters and symbols are usually represented by an 8-bit code known as ASCII.

Digital systems are more reliable and cheaper than analogue systems. Digital systems are therefore preferred to analogue systems even though there are many more circuits in a digital system.

16 INFORMATION STORAGE

There is very little you can do with information unless you can remember what you have been told and recall what you know when you need it. We take memory for granted. You can read these words because you learnt and remembered the patterns of the letters and the meanings of the patterns when you were five or six years old.

Machines that will help the human brain must have this same ability to remember. They need memory to be able to store information for use later.

Ways of aiding man's memory are not all new. The early history of the Jews, as recorded in the Old Testament of the Bible, refers to Moses descending from Mount Sinai with the ten commandments on tablets of stone. Through the ages many people have learnt the ten commandments by heart but the tablets of stone are probably the first recorded example of a 'permanent, non erasable, read-only memory'.

If you have a microcomputer you will know that it has two kinds of memory, known as ROM and RAM. The letters ROM stand for *Read-Only Memory*. RAM stands for *Random Access Memory*, but this is not a helpful name. If you think of this kind of memory as a Readable and Alterable Memory that will give you a much better idea of what RAM does. RAM can have the information stored in it changed.

RAM and ROM are not special to computers. The words you are reading are a form of ROM. You cannot change what is printed. The information you obtain from a particular place in the book is the same every time you look at it.

Not everything written on paper is ROM. When you take notes during a lesson you are using a kind of RAM. You write new information down so that you can remember it, but you can rub it out or cross it through and so change sections that may be wrong or could have been better written.

Human beings have memories of both types. Decide for yourself which type of memory is involved when you are walking, or learning a formula in physics, or remembering the time of the bus to the next town.

In years gone by the most important form of memory was human memory, helped by books and written records. Even before the computer age there had been a need for new ways of storing information and for systems to store more than the brain could hold. Ways of recording sound information (on gramophone records) and visual information (on photographs) were both invented in the nineteenth century. Electronics helped to increase information storage by introducing electronic sound recording and playback in the 1930s. Magnetic tape was introduced in about 1950. Electronic video recording became a reality a few years later.

The gramophone record, cine films and photographs are all types of ROM; magnetic tape is a type of RAM.

The computer is a machine intended to assist and extend the mental processes of human beings. To do this the computer needs a memory that can be used in the way that a human uses the memory part of the brain. Thus it is the use of computers which has made us think about 'memories' more carefully. The computer needs more memory than earlier machines. It also needs to be able to use the memory (or *access* it, as computer people often say) very quickly.

Fig. 16.1 Part of the circuit board of the BBC model B computer. The arrowed chip is the microprocessor which controls the operation of the system. Most of the other chips are either ROM or RAM.

Memory is more than just learning facts. The person who learns a lot of facts for an examination, but does not know what to do with them, does not get a high mark. As well as knowing a fact (a piece of *data*) you have to know what to do with it (an *instruction*). You also have to know where to find the fact (its *address*).

All the words in *italics* in the last two paragraphs are words used by computer people to describe their machines. Why do they use all these new words? The problem does not lie with computer people but with the rest of us. We use words like 'remember' and 'learn' in many different ways. To make a computer do these tasks for us, we have to think out every step in the system very carefully. The words that are used in computing have exact meanings. These meanings help us work out each step and that is why they have appeared.

Let us now think about the process of using a memory in a little more detail. Suppose your teacher asks your class to look up the colours code for resistors.

Your brain changes (*interprets*) that instruction into a list (*program*) of other instructions you have remembered from previous times when similar questions were asked. So you get a book with the information in it (a *database*) and look up the list of chapters (*catalogue*) or look at the index (*database fields*). You turn to the right page and look up the information (*data*). You still have not finished. You now have to decide what to do with the data. You might write it down, shout it out, or just store the information in your brain for a short time (in a *register*) while you hold up your hand and wait to be asked. Your action will depend on what is stored in your memory about what you should do on such occasions.

It should be clear by now that memory is not special to computers, or even to electronics as a whole. What is special is that, without electronic memory, computers as we know them would be impossible — not because of the volume of information that can be stored but because of the time that it takes to get the information.

If you have used a cassette to put a program into a home computer then you know that it can take several minutes to 'load'. (To load in this sense means to transfer all the stored data and instructions from the tape into the computer.) If all the information is loaded at one time, the loading time is acceptable, but if the computer had to go back to the tape each time more information was required, this would be unacceptable because the tape would have to run through from beginning to end each time. Information can be loaded from a tape, typically, at about 120 characters (letters, numbers or codes) every second. Electronic memories can deal with information at speeds up to a million characters a second.

Volatile and non-volatile memories

Electronic memories have one major problem. They need power. When the power supply is turned off all the information is lost. This kind of memory is called *volatile*. Engineers have tried hard to find other types of memory that work fast enough to store vast amounts of information and yet do **not** lose the data when the power is turned off. The memory must also be able to be read directly by electronic machines. Such a memory is called *non-volatile*. The most common non-volatile memories in use at present are ROM chips and magnetic discs.

ROM chips are integrated circuits. The circuits are made so that they give signals which depend on the information they store. The computer can only read the information on the chip; there is no way that the computer can change the stored information. Because the information depends on the circuit, it is not affected when the power supply is turned off and will be exactly the same when the power is switched on again.

ROM chips – the chips that carry the operating instructions – are used frequently in computer systems. With some computers you can buy extra ROMs for different functions such as word processing, graphics, different computer languages or even for doing standard accounts.

Whilst most ROMs cannot be altered in any way, there are ROM chips for which it is possible to remove (erase) the information on them and start again (reprogram the chip). This type of chip is called an EPROM. EPROM is short for *Erasible Programmable Read-Only Memory*. To erase the data stored on an EPROM you have to remove the chip from the equipment and expose it to ultraviolet light for perhaps half an hour. You can then put new information onto the chip and it will stay there until the EPROM is next exposed to ultraviolet light. This is not a process that most people want to do very often!

RAM

Most random access memories in computing use integrated circuits. It does not matter if the information in a RAM is lost when the machine is turned off, as long as any important information has been 'saved' by writing it into a magnetic memory such as a floppy disc.

The name 'random access' can be a bit puzzling. It sounds as though the information you get is entirely random, but this is not the case. The tape used in a cassette recorder is a *serial access memory*. All the information is arranged one piece after another along the tape as a series of pieces of information. When the tape is used for recording music this is exactly what you want. The second line of a song must always come after the first one! When you are using a memory with a computer however, you need to be able to get the information you want without going through all the pieces that you do not want. You can do this with a random access memory. 'Random' is not quite the best word to use here, but it is the word that everyone uses.

Magnetic recording

Almost all the non-volatile storage of information in electronic systems uses magnetic recording. Video recorders and cassette tape recorders use magnetic tape. Many computers use 'floppy discs' which work in the same way as tape. The disc or tape is a plastic material with a layer of magnetic powder on its surface. The transducer (the recording head) is a piece of solid magnetic material with a coil wound on it. The material is shaped into a ring and there is a small gap (see fig. 16.2).

When information is being recorded ('written into memory') the transducer coil receives signals from the computer. The current in the coil magnetises the ring. The disc or tape passes very close to the gap in the ring so that the section of the disc or tape by the gap is magnetised too.

When you want to read the information that has been recorded, the transducer is used like a microphone. As the disc or tape passes the gap in the ring its magnetism produces magnetism in the ring, and this produces an electric current in the coil.

Discs have a greater advantage over tapes. Each bit of information can be found ('accessed') much more quickly. The disc is arranged so that information is written onto a series of circular tracks. A disc might have 40 or 80 of these tracks. The head (as the transducer is called) can read or write data onto one of these tracks as the disc rotates. A second motor can move the head across the disc so that any of the tracks can be selected. This second motor has to position the head very accurately and has to be under the control of the computer, so that a stepper motor is used for this purpose. Fig. 16.3 shows the principle of a typical disc drive.

Chapters 19 and 20 describe how you find information in a RAM.

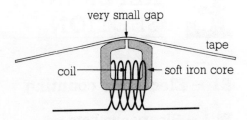

Fig. 16.2 The structure of the 'head' used in magnetic recording. The same head can be used for recording information and for reading the information back into the electronic system.

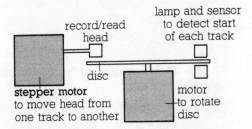

Fig. 16.3 The main parts of a disc drive system for a computer. Standard discs may be 3, 5, or 8 inches in diameter.

Recording sounds and pictures

Computer systems are not the only electronic systems that need memory. For example, very few radio or television programmes are broadcast 'live'. Most of them are recorded beforehand and replayed as needed.

Recording and replaying is just as much a matter of electronic memory as reading and writing information on floppy disc is in a computer system. The signals are analogue signals rather than the digital signals used in computer systems, and the electronic circuits connected to the transducer have to be suitable for processing analogue signals.

Video recorders are similar, and the methods of turning a picture into electronic signals are described in chapter 18.

SUMMARY 16

Information is stored in a memory.

Some memories provide information but the information stored in them cannot be changed. Such memories are called 'read-only memories' or ROMs.

Some memories can have information fed into them or read from them. If you can go directly to any position in the memory for information, the memory is called a 'random access memory' or RAM. If you have to go through all the information in order until you find what you want, then the memory is called a 'serial access memory'.

Information can be either data ('facts') or instructions. A list of instructions is called a program.

The whole collection of related data in a computer is called a database. The set of data on a particular topic is called a database field. A group of linked fields is called a file.

The position of an item of information in a memory is called its address. When a computer is linked to an address it is said to access that address.

The memory used in a processing unit is called a register.

Memory can be volatile or non-volatile. Information in a volatile memory is lost when the power supply is turned off. Information in a non-volatile memory is stored, even if the power supply is turned off.

ROM is non-volatile.

Most electronic systems use magnetic tape or magnetic discs as their main non-volatile memory.

EPROM is 'erasable and programmable read-only memory'. The contents of an EPROM can be removed using ultraviolet light and the chip can then have new information fed into it.

E REFERENCE SECTION

E1 — Electronic counting

E1.1 — Binary numbers

Binary is the number system, based on only two numerals (0 and 1), that is the basis of almost all mathematical operations carried out by electronics. It is what the mathematician calls 'numbers on base 2'. Each numeral is called a 'bit' (which is derived from **bi**nary digi**t**).

A binary number is a line of 1s and 0s. The bit at the right-hand end is the least significant bit (LSB) or unit bit. The places to the left of the unit bit have place values increasing in multiples of two. The values of these bits, from right to left, are: two, four, eight, sixteen, thirty-two, and so on, in the same way as a normal decimal number has the place values units, tens, hundreds, thousands, and so on.

E1.2 — Conversion of binary numbers to their decimal equivalent

To find the decimal number value of a binary number, the value of each 1 in the binary number is written down and then the values are added together. To do this, follow these steps.

1. First write down the number with the LSB (that is, the lowest value number) at the right-hand end.
2. Note the place value of each digit counting from the right (which are 1, 2, 4 (=2×2), 8 (= 2×2×2 or 2^3), 16 (=2×2×2×2 or 2^4), 32 (2^5), 64 (2^6), and so on.
3. For every bit that is a 1, write down its decimal value.
4. For every bit that is a '0', do not write anything down.
5. Finally, add up the list of decimal numbers.

An example of converting a binary number into its decimal value

Suppose we want to find the decimal value of the number 00110110.

To do this, check the place values of each bit in the number. To show how to do this the number has been spread out below:

bits	MSB	0	0	1	1	0	1	1	0	LSB
place values		128	64	32	16	8	4	2	1	

List the decimal values for each bit that is a 1:

$$
\begin{array}{r}
32 \\
16 \\
4 \\
\underline{2} \\
54
\end{array}
$$

And add them up: 54

Thus, binary number 00110110 is the same as decimal number 54.

Exercise 49 — Show that binary 110101 is equal to decimal 53.

Exercise 50 — Show that binary 10010111 is equal to decimal 151.

Exercise 51 — Find the decimal equivalents of 10110110 and 00011111.

E1.3 — Conversion of decimal numbers to binary numbers

To convert decimal numbers to binary, write down the binary place values (1, 2, 4, 8, etc.) until you reach a value bigger than the decimal number. Cross off that number and then:

1. subtract the largest place value left in your list from your decimal number, and write 1 as the MSB of the binary number;
2. try to subtract the next lower place value from the answer to the first subtraction — if you can do it write another 1 in the binary number, but if the place value is bigger than the decimal number write 0 in the binary number;
3. go on doing this all the way down to place value 1.

The list of 1s and 0s you obtain in this way is the binary equivalent of your decimal number.

An example of converting a decimal number into binary

Suppose you need to convert decimal 150 into binary.

Place values are, starting at the lowest, 1, 2, 4, 8, 16, 32, 64, 128, 256, etc. 150 is between 128 and 256. Cross 256 off the list. Start by subtracting 128 from 150, like this:

	150		
subtract 128	128		write 1
	22		
subtract 64	**	cannot do	write 0
subtract 32	**	cannot do	write 0
subtract 16	16		write 1
	6		
subtract 8	**	cannot do	write 0
subtract 4	4		write 1
	2		
subtract 2	2		write 1
	0		
subtract 1	**	cannot do	write 0

Thus decimal 150 is the same as binary 10010110.

In using this procedure you must work right through to the least significant digit, even if, several steps earlier, you get down to 0 and have nothing left from which to subtract numbers.

Exercise 52 — Show that decimal 93 is the same as binary 1011101.

Exercise 53 — Show that decimal 144 is the same as binary 10010000.

Exercise 54 — Find the binary numbers equivalent to decimal 77 and decimal 100.

E1.4 — Electronic counting systems

Electronic counting systems are based on bistables. One bistable circuit block is used for each bit of the largest binary number for which the counter is designed. Triggered bistables are used for counters. Fig. E.1 is the block diagram for a 4-bit counter. Note that the least significant bit is held on the bistable at the **left**-hand end of the chain of bistables as they are shown in this diagram.

E1.5 — Binary-coded decimal (BCD)

Binary-coded decimal is a method of using binary numbers to represent each digit of a decimal number. Each digit is converted separately into a binary number. All binary numbers are written as 4-bit groups. Thus, 150 in BCD is 0001 0101 0000, and the BCD code 1001 0111 0000 0100 is 9704 in decimal. It is important to note that BCD numbers are not always written with spaces between the 4-bit groups.

There are several other codes that code each digit separately. These are also used to convert decimal numbers into binary form that can be used for electronic computing.

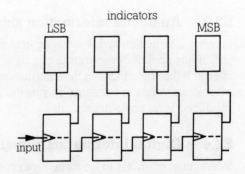

Fig. E.1 The block diagram of a 4-bit counter.

E2 – Information processing

E2.1 – Information systems

Every information system has the same basic blocks. An information system is like any other system in needing an input, a processing stage, and an output. However, in every information system there has to be a carrier for the information signals. The block that adds the signals to the carrier is called a modulator. At the output the modulated carrier has to go to a demodulator so that the information signals can be extracted from the carrier again.

Information systems may be used to send information from one place to another (e.g. the telephone), or to process information in some way (e.g. a word processor), or to store information (e.g. a tape recorder).

Fig. E.2 is a block diagram showing the essential parts of every information system.

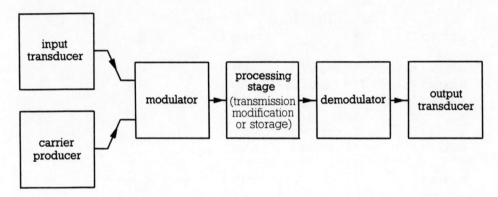

Fig. E.2 The block diagram showing the essential parts of every information system.

E2.2 – Information carriers

Every information system has to have a carrier. In electronic processing the carrier is the electric current in the circuit. In radio the carrier is the radio waves which travel through the air. The magnetic material is the carrier on a magnetic recording disc, and paper and ink are the carrier for written words.

To put information on to the carrier it must be changed in some way. The process of doing this is called modulation. Thus the size of the voltage or current in a circuit, or the amplitude or frequency of the radio waves, or the colour of the paper (with ink), or the direction of magnetisation of the magnetic material, must be changed.

E2.3 – Analogue information signals

In many information systems the input is some quantity that can vary in any way and at any speed. Temperature can have any value, and a car can move at any speed. If the transducer in the information system produces an output whose magnitude varies in the same way as the information it represents, the signal produced is an analogue signal.

E2.4 – Digital information signals

Information often has to be turned into codes. Letters on paper (or in any other form) are a code. Traffic lights give information as a code. Numbers are a code. Whenever information is converted into a form that is not an analogue signal it has to be coded so that you know the relationship between the information and the signal produced. A coded information signal is a digital information signal. Digital signals are characterised by sharp changes between one state and another, such as light and dark (in fibre optics), black and white (bar codes on paper), red and green (some railway signals), on and off (electrical circuits).

In digital electronic systems the circuits switch between two voltage levels, called logic 1 and logic 0. Logic 0 is usually (but not always) zero voltage. Switching to and from logic 1 produces a pulse. An electronic digital information signal is a chain or train of pulses.

E2.5 — Information codes

In electronic systems the following coding systems are commonly used:

for counting: binary numbers (chapter 14, page 138, and reference section E1.1).

for converting decimal numbers into electronic form: binary coded decimal (BCD) (chapter 15, page 148, and reference section E1.5). There are also other codes in use, such as the Gray code.

for processing letters in electronic form: ASCII (American Standard Code for Information Interchange) (chapter 15, page 149).

for instructions to computers: machine code, which is the set of basic instructions given to the system in a coded form. For most purposes a computer 'language' is used, such as BASIC and FORTRAN. These languages are word instructions which the computer interprets into machine codes and then into the individual steps of the process (chapter 19, page 193, and reference section G).

Pulse code modulation is a system where the input information is sampled at regular intervals and the size of each sample is then coded as a binary number. The binary number becomes a chain of pulses in the electronic system (reference section F2.5).

E3 — Memory

E3.1 — Bistables

The basic circuit used in any electronic memory or register is called a bistable. A bistable is a block in which the output depends both on the input and on the previous inputs to the block.

A bistable is made up from two inverting logic gates (NAND or NOR) connected so that the output from each of the gates is connected to one of the inputs of the other one.

A range of bistables is available. The differences are in the way the inputs are fed to the bistable.

An RS-bistable has two inputs. A logic 1 input to the S (set) input changes the output to logic 1 if it was logic 0 before. A logic 1 input to the R (reset) input changes the logic 1 output back to logic 0. A latch is an RS-bistable.

A T-bistable has a single input. Every logic 1 pulse to the input changes the output from whichever state it was in to the other one. Counters and timers use T-bistables.

A clocked bistable is any type of bistable arranged so that it will only react to its input signals when a clocking pulse arrives at its clock input. Computer registers are clocked bistables.

A D-bistable output changes to the same as the input signal when, but only when, it receives a clock pulse. This type of bistable is also called a data-latch and is used for storing data in electronic RAMs.

A JK-bistable has two inputs. It behaves like an RS-bistable when only one of the inputs receives a signal, but if there is a signal at both inputs at the same time it behaves like a T-bistable.

E3.2 — Types of electronic memory

Electronic memory can be either one of two types, ROM or RAM. ROM is short for Read-Only Memory. RAM is short for Random Access Memory (but it is easier to think of it as Readable and Alterable Memory).

ROM is a memory circuit that has been manufactured so that it will always give the same piece of information on demand. It is a kind of electronic reference book. ROMs are manufactured in the form of chips which, for example, store all the information a computer needs to convert instructions typed on the keyboard into codes which the computer can use.

RAM is used for storing data and instructions which may have to be changed as the computer works through a process.

It is possible to buy ROM chips that you can program (put information into) yourself. However, once you have programmed the ROM you cannot change the information. These chips are often called PROMS (Programmable Read-Only Memories). Some PROMS can have the stored information erased by taking them out of the circuit and exposing them to ultraviolet light for perhaps 30 minutes. This kind of chip is called an EPROM (Erasable and Programmable Read-Only Memory).

E3.3 — Types of peripheral memory

Peripheral memory is any form of non-electronic memory that can be used with a computer to store information when the power supply to the computer is switched off. Data and information can be 'saved' by transferring them from RAM to the peripheral memory.

Most peripheral memories use magnetic recording. Magnetic tape, as used in a tape recorder, can be used. Faster systems for transferring information are possible using discs. Simple systems use 'floppy discs'. Large systems use 'Winchester discs' which operate on the same principle as floppy discs. They are precision engineered discs which can be rotated at very high speed and therefore record or give back information very quickly.

17 WIRES AND FIBRES

This chapter and the one following are about the various kinds of communication systems. Much of this chapter is about telephone systems which use wires or optical fibres to carry signals and information. However, before thinking about the details of such systems it is important to know something about the things that all communications systems have in common.

Communication

Look around your home and make a list of everything you have that uses electronics. There will probably be a television, a radio or two, and perhaps even a home computer. If you have a washing machine it might have electronic controls. Don't forget the tape recorder, the portable stereo and the telephone answering machine.

Now tick every item on your list that can be made to make sounds like a person talking. You will have ticked almost everything on your list. All those that you have ticked are machines to help people communicate. Although electronics is very important for computing, the most important use of electronics is in communication.

How much does communication matter? It is the most important thing people need, after air to breathe, food, water and shelter.

One thing that makes humans different from all other animals is our ability to pass to one another, not only simple calls and signals, but also complex ideas. This means that each of us does not have to learn everything we need individually. We can ask someone else, and they can explain. Humans are animals that can communicate very efficiently.

Communication is not always a benefit. We can now place a tiny device (a 'bug') in someone's room and listen to everything that is said. We can pass on, from one person to another, all that needs to be known about the manufacture of nuclear weapons (in times past the limit was the elder tribesmen explaining to their younger braves how to make good spears!). Spies can send information halfway across the world by radio without leaving their hideouts. Although humans can do all these things, it does not mean that they **must** do them. It is human beings that **decide** whether electronics should be used for any particular purpose.

How has electronics helped us to communicate with one another? Electronics has changed our ability to talk to one another:

- by means of radio and television;
- by means of the telephone;
- by making it possible to record sounds.

Think about what it is like to be deaf. Most of us live in a world of sounds. There are sounds everywhere. We would be lost without them.

The day starts with the alarm clock; lessons end with a bell; horns, hooters and sirens warn us of danger. We enjoy the rustle of the wind in the trees, worry about the odd squeak from a new bicycle, and wince when the baby screams.

We use a sound to communicate. We listen to the teacher, ask questions, talk to our friends and listen to the radio and television.

What happens to someone who is deaf? They do not need to carry a white stick. How can they communicate? How important is communication for successful living? How far can electronics help someone who is deaf?

The essential parts of a communication system

In many ways, all communication systems are the same. There is a 'sender' and a 'hearer'. In electronics, the sender has to turn the message into electronic form, which needs a transducer. This electronic message is then sent to the hearer using a transmitter. The hearer has to have a device which collects the message; this is called the receiver. There is also another transducer to turn the message back into sounds to be heard, into pictures to be seen, or into printed words to be read.

We learnt in chapter 15 that all information has to have a carrier. In communication systems the carrier must be able to move, taking the information with it. The transmitter must modulate the carrier, and the receiver must include a demodulator. Fig. 17.1 shows a block diagram of a communication system.

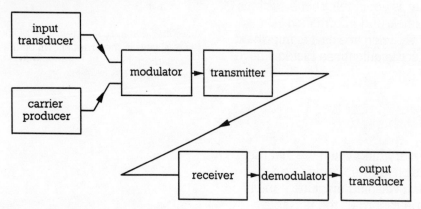

Fig. 17.1 A block diagram of a communication system. In most real systems the blocks that carry out the four functions in the transmitter may not be connected in the order shown here. Often the modulator controls the power supply to either the carrier producer or the transmitter.

Telecommunication

In the days before electronics there were plenty of ways of sending messages, although most of them were very slow. You do not have to use electronics for a communication system, but electronics has made a very great difference to communication.

Sending information by electronics, whether by radio, telephone or television, is given the name *telecommunication*. Recently, other ways of sending information using electronics have been developed. For example, organisations with offices in several parts of the country can use a system called 'electronic mail'. Letters and messages are typed into a computer terminal at one office and then transmitted to their destination so that they can be viewed on the computer display at the receiving end. Electronic mail is also a telecommunications system.

There are two kinds of telecommunication systems. One of them we normally think of as radio and television, where anyone can tune in to listen to the programme. This is called a *broadcast* system. The other kind of system is where two people can talk directly to one another. This is called a *two-way* system. The telephone is one example of this kind of system.

Person-to-person telecommunication does not have to be by telephone. Two-way radio is widely used. The fire and ambulance services, taxi drivers and the police all use two-way radio. There are many more radio systems for two-way communication than for broadcasting.

Broadcasting does not have to be by radio either. Hospital radio and cable television are broadcasting systems using wires and cables. Broadcast programmes are often sent from one station to the next by 'land-line' too. Land-lines are telephone cables.

SUMMARY 17A

A transmitter is the part of a communication system that sends a signal.

A receiver is the part of a communication system that receives a signal and converts it back into understandable form.

The blocks in a transmitter are an input transducer, a carrier generator, a modulator, a driver, and something to emit the signal.

The blocks in a receiver are something to receive the signal, a demodulator, an amplifier (if necessary), and an output transducer.

Communication based on electronics is called telecommunication.

Communication systems may be broadcast systems or two-way systems.

More about communication

Long before electronics had been thought of, people were able to communicate using light. Some of the latest developments in electronics use light too. The remote-control unit on many television sets uses light — infra-red light which the eye cannot see. Light signals are also used in computers. If two sections of a computer must not be connected electrically an *opto-isolator* is used. These systems using light are easy to understand and easy to set up in a laboratory.

What must you have for the light transmitter when you communicate using light? The simplest transmitting system has only three blocks: a power supply; a switch; and a lamp. Fig. 17.2 shows a simple laboratory arrangement for this transmitter.

For a communications system there must also be a receiver. In an opto-system the receiver has to sense the light and produce an electrical signal which will do something useful. There must be a light-sensitive transducer to detect the light. In a simple laboratory demonstration the transducer can be connected to an indicator. The arrangement is shown in fig. 17.3.

If you build this system in the laboratory, you should find that when the transmitter and receiver are close enough, the indicator will flash whenever the transmitter lamp is switched on. (You may need to shield the receiver from other light in the room.) This is the principle of the opto-isolator, but the kind of opto-isolator you buy is no bigger than a normal integrated circuit.

This system works if the transmitter and receiver are very close together. How can we improve the range? One possibility is to use a brighter (more powerful) lamp in the transmitter. Try it if you can.

Even with a more powerful lamp, most of the light is not falling on the LDR in the receiver, and is wasted. If more of the light were sent from the transmitter to the receiver, longer transmission distances would be possible. If you look at a torch you will see that there is a mirror (reflector) which makes the light from the bulb shine in a beam. If you are trying out this system in a laboratory you could use a torch reflector to make a beam of light which will, in a darkened room, transmit signals across several metres.

There is a way to collect more light for the receiver too. For this you need a lens. It must be a convex lens (one that is fatter in the middle than at its edges). If you fix it in the correct position it will focus the light onto the LDR.

Long-distance communication with light

Transmission of information by light beam has been used for hundreds of years. Bonfires on beacon hills and smoke signals are not used any longer, and the Navy makes much less use of signal lamps (like 'the Aldis') than it used to. In these examples the receiver is always a person, and electronics does not come into it.

Light rays travel in straight lines, and if there is anything in the way the ray is blocked. This did not stop the development by the Navy (almost two hundred years ago) of long-distance signalling between London, Portsmouth, Plymouth and other naval ports using visible signals. The system was called semaphore. Signal stations were set up on the top of the highest hills on the routes. To this day there is a 'Telegraph Hill' in a Hampshire village. However, it was not very good as a system. Rain

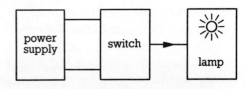

Fig. 17.2 The simplest possible opto-transmitter. Which of the three blocks is the carrier producer, the modulator, the [128] input transducer and the transmitter? Remember that in real systems the blocks are not always in the order shown on the block diagram in fig. 17.1. Remember, too, that with three blocks and four functions, at least one block must do two jobs.

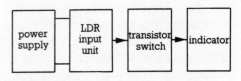

Fig. 17.3 The simplest possible opto-receiver. Which block is the receiver? Which block is the demodulator? Which [129] block is the output transducer?

clouds, fog, and even bright sunlight could easily close the system down.

It would be much better if you could use something other than light, which would not be stopped by clouds or fog, or if you could find some way of passing the light along a pipe. In fact, both ideas are being used. Radio waves behave like light in many ways but clouds and high hills are not so much of a problem. Optical fibres are light 'pipes' and they are now being used instead of telephone cables, even for underwater links between Britain and the rest of the world.

Optical fibres

Fig. 17.4 is a photograph of a telephone cable which uses optical fibres instead of wires. The fibres are only about 1 millimetre in diameter, and each fibre can carry up to 60 000 telephone calls. Continuous fibres of up to 40 kilometres in length are possible. For distances of more than 40 kilometres, regenerators are used to receive the feint light pulses and use them to operate the transmitter for the next length of fibre.

How do these fibres work? Once the light is inside the fibre it can only escape if it makes an angle of more than about 45° with any surface. Otherwise it is reflected back into the fibre each time it strikes the surface. Fig. 17.5 shows this diagrammatically.

If you have not been shown a real optical fibre working in this way, you can demonstrate the principle very easily at home. All you need is a drinking glass, a white plastic cup or beaker that will fit loosely inside the glass, and a torch. In a dark room, hold the glass as shown in fig. 17.6. Look at the top part of the rim while you shine the torch at the bottom part of the rim. The rim will be illuminated. The light coming to your eye has passed down one side of the glass, across the bottom and up the other side.

How is the light transmitted and received when an optical fibre is used? The transmitter is a laser. This kind of laser depends on much the same principles as a light emitting diode except that once light is emitted the processes taking place inside this special kind of diode lead to yet more light being produced. The word laser comes from **l**ight **a**mplification by **s**timulated **e**mission of **r**adiation.

The receiver is also similar to devices you have already met. The light-dependent resistor is not nearly sensitive enough, but the ideas it uses are similar to those used in photodiodes or phototransistors. These convert the flashing light signals back into electrical currents for processing in the ways you already know something about.

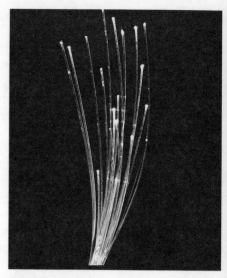

Fig. 17.4 A British Telecom fibre optic cable. The cable consists of a stranded steel wire (to give it strength) with several polythene tubes wrapped tightly round the steel. Each tube has eight fibres lying loosely inside. The whole cable has outer layers of aluminium and polythene to give protection.

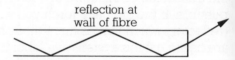

Fig. 17.5 The light inside an optical fibre is reflected by the wall of the fibre but passes out at the end where the angle between the light ray and the surface is more than about 45° This effect of reflection back into the fibre is called 'total internal reflection'.

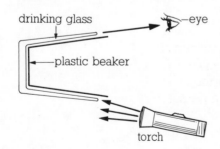

Fig. 17.6 A simple demonstration of transmission of light inside glass.

Telephone by wires

Although the main trunk routes in the telephone system which carry many thousands of calls are now being converted to optical fibres, the local networks use wires and electric currents to carry the information.

You may not have realised that the telephone system is a major application of electronics. It seems very simple. All you see is an instrument with a microphone (to talk into), an earpiece (to listen to), and a dial or some buttons (to call someone with). Two wires going to a pole seems to be the rest of it. In fact, there is a lot more to the telephone system than that.

The telephone is a system for person-to-person telecommunication. It is a two-way system because each person can speak to the other. To connect you to the person you want to talk to, there has to be an exchange. A telephone exchange is a very complex switching system which detects when you want to make a call, provides the power supply to make it possible, detects the number of the person you want to call, connects your line to the line of that telephone, rings the bell on that telephone, and then keeps the connection until you have finished the call. It also works out the charge that will be made for this service!

As if this is not enough, if you want to make a call to a place a long distance away, the exchange can pass your call on to other exchanges as necessary, and provide whatever amplification of the signal may be needed, even if you are calling someone in New Zealand. What is more, all of this is normally automatic.

In the early days of the automatic telephone system, exchanges used relays similar to those described in chapter 9, and other devices which also operated by electromagnetism. The system worked well, but the moving parts of these devices would wear out or get dirty after some time. Modern exchanges do the same things using electronic circuits. The first fully electronic exchange was called 'System X'. Even before all the old exchanges have been fully replaced by electronic exchanges, newer kinds of electronic exchange which will replace System X are being designed.

This is another example of the importance of understanding the system rather than the circuits involved. All the new types of exchange have got to do the same basic task as the equipment they replace. Whether your exchange is a System X exchange or the very old-fashioned 'Strowger exchange', it still has to detect when you want to make a call, supply the power, and so on. It does not matter to you whether the call is being sent by wire, or optical fibre, or satellite, or by microwave link. What does matter are the signals you send and what the system does with those signals.

Essential elements of a person-to-person telecommunication system

Every person-to-person system has the following characteristics:

- it is a two-way system;
- if there are more than two stations there must be a means of connecting the stations as required;
- there must be a calling signal;
- there must be a power supply for each station, one that is sufficient for signalling, sending and receiving.

For the telephone system the block diagram is shown in fig. 17.7 on the next page. In what ways is a two-way radio system (such as that used by taxis, the police, or the fire service) the same as the telephone system, and in what ways is the system different?

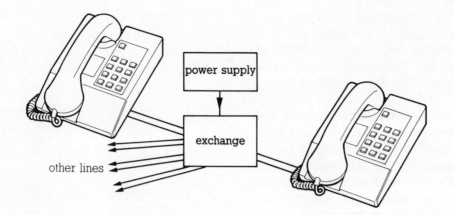

Fig. 17.7 A block diagram of the telephone system. The block diagram for any other two-way person-to-person telecommunication system will be very similar.

Telephone equipment

The telephone is a good example of a complex system that has been made easy to use and is automatic, so that no training is needed to use it properly. The instrument you use has to have power, an input transducer (the microphone), an output transducer (the earphone), a calling system (the bell), a switch to turn it on and a means of selecting the person you want to call. All these parts of the system have to be connected to the exchange by only two wires.

We take the telephone so much for granted that most people do not even realise the changes that have taken place over the last hundred years. Fig. 17.8 shows some of the changes in the equipment for the subscriber since 1890.

Until a few years ago, all telephones used relays and other electromagnetic components. Electronic circuits of the kind described in this book were not used, except for amplifiers which were used to amplify the signals on long-distance links. The bell was rung by sending an a.c. signal along the line. When you lifted the handset the bell was disconnected and the batteries or power supplies at the exchange were connected to your telephone. A capacitor prevented the d.c. from affecting the bell (see chapter 8). The microphone was a carbon microphone and as you spoke into it the vibrations changed the resistance of the carbon granules, which varied the current in the line. At the exchange, another capacitor separated the signals from the power supply and routed them to the person calling you.

When you made a call, the dial produced a series of pulses by switching the 50 volt d.c. supply on and off. These pulses operated relays and uniselectors at the exchange, connecting you to the person you wanted.

There is still a lot of telephone equipment that works in this way, but the system is now being converted to electronic circuits. It is always a problem changing a public service to a new system. With many millions of subscribers you could not change over the entire system at once, even if the cost of doing so was not too high. Nor can you turn off the system and let people do without telephones for a few months while you make the change. This means that you have to design the new equipment to work with the old equipment — the new must be *compatible* with the old.

The new designs of telephones are electronic. There is an electronic signal generator instead of a bell. The microphone is a better quality device because a transistor amplifier can provide the signal needed. The

Fig. 17.8 Typical telephones from 1890 (*top left*), 1905 (*top right*), 1925 (*bottom left*), and 1929 (*bottom right*). In the early days of telephones many users did not know how near they had to be when speaking into the microphone. How did the designers solve this problem?

dial is replaced by pushbuttons which switch on various tones. A logic circuit turns these tones into signals which the older exchanges can use. Because the instrument is electronic, it can be lighter and portable, and it can have extra facilities, such as a memory which remembers the last number that you called so that it can be called again; you don't need to push all the buttons again.

The way in which the pushbuttons are used to produce the same pulses as a telephone dial is an interesting electronic system. One type uses seven signal generators, each producing a different tone (musical note). Each row of buttons switches on one of the generators, and each column of buttons switches on another generator. When you press a button, you switch on two of the generators. The output from the buttons goes to seven amplifiers. Each amplifier has a filter which allows only one of the tones to reach that amplifier. For each button you press, two amplifiers give an output. These outputs are used to control a pulse generator which produces pulses in exactly the same way as the dial would have done. The block diagram is shown in fig. 17.9.

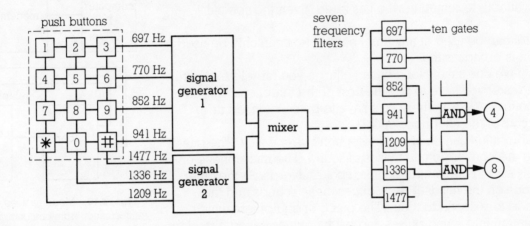

You may well be thinking that this is a very complicated system to use instead of a simple dial. It would indeed be possible to make the buttons control the final pulse generator directly without the need for all these blocks. The telephone dial is a very slow pulse generator. Electronic dialling could be much quicker but, in the old type of exchanges the equipment cannot work any faster than the way in which the old type of dialling mechanism did. Where all-electronic exchanges (such as System X) have been installed, the exchange can pick up the tone signals directly and dialling is much quicker. For all-electronic exchanges, the signals have to be tones because, at the exchange, they have to pass through capacitors which separate them from the power supply.

Fig. 17.9 A block diagram of the push-button dialling system used on some telephones.

Information services by telephone

Most of us use the telephone system only for speaking to our friends or for business contact. However, it is an information system, and not just a way of talking to someone. Any information that can be turned into electrical pulses suitable for the system can be sent by means of the telephone channels. Prestel uses the system in this way. Computers can be made to 'talk' to one another by connecting them to the telephone system through *modems*, and it is even possible to send pictures by telephone.

Prestel is an information service. At home you have an interface which connects your telephone to a television display. When you dial the correct call codes, your telephone is connected to the Prestel computer. You can then ask for the information that you want by sending the 'page numbers' of the information to the computer. The computer sends back signals which the interface can decode, and the information you want appears on the television screen.

The television information service *teletext* works in the same way, and you can obtain information from the BBC (*Ceefax*) or ITV (*Oracle*). However, Prestel has four advantages compared with teletext. The number of pages on teletext is limited by the fact that all the information has to be sandwiched between normal picture information, whereas there is no limit with Prestel. With Prestel you ask for the pages you want.

With Prestel you can send information to the computer, because it is a two-way system, but with teletext you can have only what the broadcasting station has put into the system.

Because teletext is broadcast, there is no way of controlling who uses the system, whereas Prestel can be used for confidential information which is only available to someone who has been given the special codes.

Finally, Prestel can be used at any time, but teletext can only be used when the station is broadcasting.

Prestel does have one snag! Nobody can charge you for teletext, but when you use Prestel you have to pay the cost of the telephone call, so the service is not free. (What other costs have to be considered in |132| addition to the cost of the telephone calls?)

Computer information can be sent by telephone very easily. The bits of the digital code are converted into pulses of sound. The microphone on the handset will send these sounds just like spoken words. At the other end, the earphone on the handset reproduces these sounds and the computer is made to respond to them. The piece of equipment which turns the information into sound pulses and back again is called a modem (see fig. 17.10). This name is a shortened form of *modulator-demodulator* The modem modulates the information onto a sound carrier and also demodulates signals sent in the other direction. To be able to 'talk' to the transmitting computer, the receiving computer needs to send signals back to confirm that it has got each section of information before the next section is transmitted.

Sending pictures by telephone seems more difficult. Only photographs (not moving pictures) can be sent in this way, but newspapers have used the system for many years as a way of getting photographs from one office to another.

The basis of the system is to scan the picture very slowly. For normal television the picture is scanned fifty times a second. The telephone system cannot accept information as fast as that, but it can cope with one picture every ten seconds or so. Equipment at the receiving end can either print the picture onto paper or display it on a screen, as required.

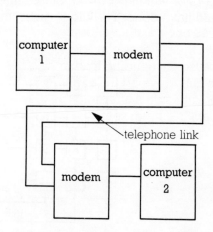

Fig. 17.10 Modems used to pass information from one computer to another. The information must be in serial form. |133| (Why?)

Which is better: wires or fibres?

The choice of a system for connecting telephones depends on many factors. The choice is not only between wires and fibres. Microwave radio is also used a lot for telephone channels. As far as the user is concerned, it does not matter which is used, as long as the information gets through.

Optical fibres are used where there are many calls to carry at the same time. New trunk lines between large towns and cities are often optical fibre links. They are very expensive, but they are better, lighter in weight and less prone to damage by water and corrosion.

Wires are used for connections to individual telephones. Wires are cheaper and easier to install, and do not need the special converters to turn the information into a form that can produce sounds at the earphone.

For international links, optical fibres that can be used over such large distances have not yet been developed. Undersea cables have to have repeaters every twenty miles or so, but reliable cables can now be made and laid fairly easily. The other alternative for international links is to send the information by microwaves to satellites. The satellites will transmit the information back to Earth using another microwave channel. However, because the satellite is about 30 000 kilometres above the Earth's surface, the information has to travel about 60 000 kilometres and this produces a time delay of about half a second (see fig. 17.11). For normal conversation this is just an annoying pause before the answer comes back, but for sending computer data in this way this half second slows the process considerably, because the sending station has to wait half a second for every checking signal after each section of data has been sent.

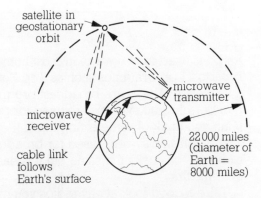

Fig. 17.11 International telephone links by cable and by satellite. Microwaves travel at the speed of light (300 000 km every second) and signals in wires travel at nearly this speed. It takes about half a second for signals to travel from transmitter to receiver via a satellite link.

SUMMARY 17B

The telephone system is a two-way system using wires or optical fibres to carry signals from one station to another.

The correct channel is selected by means of switches at an exchange.

Optical fibres carry information by pulsing a beam of light travelling along the fibre.

Telephone wires carry information by varying the d.c. current in the wires.

The telephone system can be used for Prestel, computer links, transmission of photographs, and other information systems.

18 RADIO

Radio is used in two ways. In most homes people use a radio to listen to broadcast programmes such as Top Forty or the news and traffic information. These are broadcast programmes, but by far the largest number of radio systems are used for person-to-person communication. [134] (Can you think of some examples of the use of person-to-person radio?) The electronic systems used for broadcast radio and person-to-person radio are basically the same but it is easier to think about broadcast radio systems first.

Take a good look at any radios you may have at home. Most radios have three controls: one to tune in the station; one to control how loud the output is; and one to switch from one band to another. There may also be a 'tone control' which adjusts the quality of the sound to suit the place in which you are using the radio. The volume control (the one that makes the output louder or softer) usually has an on/off switch built into it which controls the power supply to the radio.

If you turn the tuning knob, you can pick up a number of stations. If you switch the radio to the medium waveband in the evening you will hear many programmes, coming from all over Europe. Why can you not hear them in the morning? It is not because the French and the Germans transmit their programmes only in the evening!

Your radio may have a VHF band on it. If you use this band, you only pick up local stations, but if the radio is tuned carefully to the station the programme is very clear and you do not get the interference from other stations that you get on the medium waveband. Why are there various wavebands? What does medium wave mean? What is VHF? These are some of the questions that this chapter answers.

Radio waves

Radio waves are produced by alternating currents generated at the transmitter. The waves travel through space. They are one form of what is known as *electromagnetic radiation*. Because they are produced by alternating currents they have a frequency. This frequency can be anything between 100 kilohertz and 10 gigahertz (10 000 000 000 hertz). Table 18.1 shows the range of frequencies used and the names for each part of this range.

Different stations use different frequencies to transmit their programmes. When you turn the tuning knob on your radio you are adjusting the circuits inside so that they will respond to different frequencies and so give you the different stations. There is an international agreement that gives each station in every country of the world the frequency it can use. However, there are not enough different frequencies to make sure that stations do not interfere with each other.

The radio waves are the carrier for the information that is being broadcast. The equipment that produces the radio waves is called the *transmitter*. Inside the transmitter there are the following blocks (see fig. 18.1 on the next page):

● a carrier generator to produce the alternating currents for making the radio waves;

Table 18.1 The radio-frequency system

Frequency	Wavelength	Name of band
		VLF very low frequency
30 kHz	10 000 m	
		LF low frequency / long waveband is 1000 m to 2000 m (300 to 150 kHz)
300 kHz	1000 m	
		MF medium frequency / medium waveband is 200 m to 600 m (1.5 MHz to 500 kHz)
3 MHz	100 m	
		HF high frequency
30 MHz	10 m	
		VHF very high frequency / VHF radio is 90 to 100 MHz (3.3 to 3.0 m)
300 MHz	1 m	
		UHF ultrahigh frequency / The television channels are around 600 MHz (0.5 m)
3 GHz	10 cm	
		SHF superhigh frequency / Radar and microwave are around 10 GHz frequency (3 cm)

- an input transducer to pick up the information that is to be sent;
- a modulator to add the information to the carrier;
- drivers or power amplifiers, as required;
- an aerial to produce the radio waves from the electric currents.

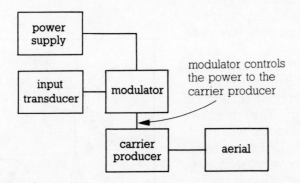

Fig. 18.1 The block diagram of a radio transmitter. Amplifiers and drivers have not been shown. You should compare this diagram with the opto-transmitter in the last chapter. In practical transmitters there are various ways in which modulation can be added to the carrier. Although all the blocks shown here would be required, they are sometimes connected differently.

Radio waves have to be modulated if they are to carry information. There are several ways of modulating the carrier in radio systems. Broadcast systems use either *amplitude modulation* (AM) or *frequency modulation* (FM). As computers become more important, another kind of modulation is being used, known as *pulse-code modulation* (PCM). Details of these various types of modulation are given in reference section F at the end of this chapter.

The equipment that picks up the radio waves and produces the signals that they are carrying is called a *receiver*. Fig. 18.2 is a block diagram of a radio receiver. You should compare this with the block diagram of a complete communication system given in chapter 17, page 160. Three of the blocks are ones that you already know about, but the blocks labelled *aerial* and *tuner* are special to radio systems.

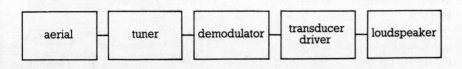

Fig. 18.2 The block diagram of a simple radio receiver. There is one other block, which every electronic system must have, that is not shown in this diagram. Which block is missing?

The aerial is a kind of input transducer for the receiver. It is where the radio waves are received and turned back into electric currents. The tuner is the part of the receiver that selects the station you want to hear, and rejects all the others.

The other blocks perform the same functions as they do in other systems. The demodulator separates the information from the radio frequency carrier. The loudspeaker turns the electric currents that represent this information into sounds that we can hear. The driver ensures that there is enough power to work the loudspeaker. There will, of course, also have to be a power supply for the system. (Can you remember what components are used as a demodulator? Look back to chapter 8 if you do not know.)

Two-way radio

What must you think about in setting up a two-way radio system? There are two answers to this question. One answer depends on the way the system is to be used. The other depends on the technical aspects of choosing and connecting together the right blocks to make the system. These two answers are linked. The way you use a system depends on what is possible. The blocks you need to use depend on what you want to do.

Suppose you need a two-way radio for three service engineers so that they can keep in touch with head office. What are the problems then?

If the radios are to be fitted into cars, then they must be small enough to go into the cars. They must work from the car battery. They must be usable at all places to which the engineers travel. The radios will need aerials both to transmit and to receive the radio waves, and these aerials must not be so big that they are dangerous or they hit every low bridge. The equipment must be easy to use. You need to know whether the engineers will have to talk to one another or only to the head office, and whether there needs to be a channel for talking and another channel for listening or whether messages can be transmitted in both directions over the same channel.

Before buying the equipment, the company will also need to know that the radios are the cheapest way of keeping in touch with the engineers. What are the alternatives? The cost is not only the cost of the equipment, but licence fees, maintenance, the lost money if the work cannot be completed quickly and efficiently, and the wages that have to be paid to the engineers when they have to spend time finding a telephone box to contact head office (base) instead of using the radio.

The first technical problem to consider is whether there should be one channel or two. The telephone system uses one channel which can operate in both directions. Where optical fibres are used, two channels are needed, one for each direction. In radio there are no wires or fibres to act as channels. A channel is a particular frequency of radio waves that you use as a carrier for the signals.

If you use one channel, all the engineers and the head office have transmitters tuned to produce radio waves of the same frequency. They both also have receivers tuned to this same frequency. If you use two channels, the base transmitter and the car receiver are tuned to one frequency, but to send signals in the opposite direction the car transmitter and the base receiver have to be tuned to a completely different frequency.

It does not cost any more money for equipment to use two channels [137] rather than one (why not?). The problem is the limited number of channels available. If there are three engineers and each station (including base) has to be able to talk to and listen to three others on separate channels, twelve channels are needed. Most companies using radio communication systems would have many more than three car-based stations. Having lots of separate channels is not a sensible idea.

If you use only one channel, then there is a different problem. You cannot use the transmitter and the receiver at the same time. The transmitter would be so close to the receiver that it would overload and damage the receiver. To overcome this the microphone of the transmitter is fitted with a switch so that when you want to transmit you press the switch and so turn off the receiver and turn on the transmitter. You can usually tell when a single-channel system is being used because at the end of each piece of the conversation the speaker says 'over' so that the person at the other end knows that he can turn off his receiver and start transmitting.

Things are easier if the three engineers do not need to talk to one another. Two channels can be used: one for the cars to talk to base, and the other for base to talk to the cars. In this system everyone will hear everyone else's messages.

What limits the number of channels that are available? Suppose a channel is set up on radio waves of frequency 100 megahertz. What will be the frequency of the next channel? Will it be 101 megahertz, or 1 000 001 hertz, or what? The answer depends on the kind of modulation being used.

When frequency modulation is being used, modulation changes the frequency of the carrier (as the name suggests). For voice signals the frequency is usually allowed to vary by up to 25 kilohertz from the original carrier frequency when the carrier is modulated. This means that there must be 50 kilohertz between channels. (Why 50 kilohertz and not 25 kilohertz?) The next channel to the 100 megahertz channel would be at 100.05 megahertz. We say that each channel needs a *bandwidth* of 50 kilohertz. Fig. 18.3 shows this diagrammatically.

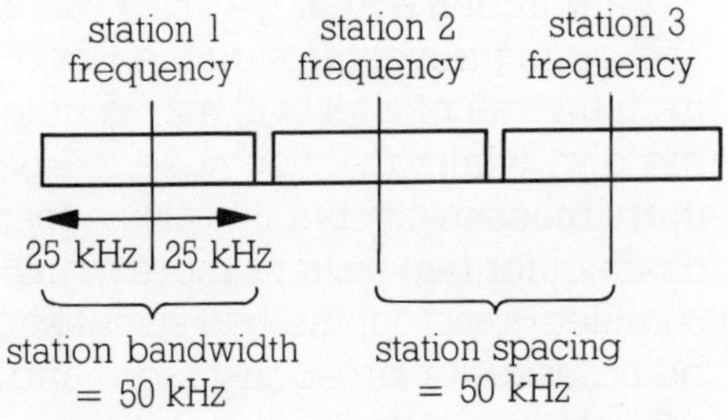

You might expect that with amplitude modulation there would be no problem, but this is not so. When a carrier is modulated, the modulation process produces *sidebands*. If the sound signal is a steady tone at 1 kilohertz, then an amplitude modulated carrier of 100 megahertz would produce sidebands at 100.001 and 99.999 megahertz.

For spoken messages (telephony), as long as sound signals up to about 3 kilohertz can be received the message will be clear enough to understand. For broadcast programmes, which may contain music, a bandwidth of 9 kilohertz (4.5 kilohertz either side of the carrier) is used. When AM (amplitude modulation) is used, channels can be closer together than when FM (frequency modulation) is used. For this reason, stations using the medium waveband use AM.

At VHF a lot more channels are available, because the carrier frequency is much higher. FM has a lot of advantages in that it avoids distortion and interference from other stations, so FM is used in the VHF bands even though it needs a bigger bandwidth and there can be less channels.

How far do radio waves travel?

Another problem to consider, if our three engineers are to have two-way radio, is the distance they might travel from their head office (base). How far do radio waves travel?

Radio waves travel from one place to another in three ways (see fig. 18.4).

All radio waves can travel directly through the air from the transmitter to the receiver. They can travel through most solid materials except metals, and they spread round obstacles. Because the Earth is round and the surface is, therefore, not flat, the maximum range for radio waves travelling direct to the receiver is about thirty miles.

For some radio waves, the outer layers of the Earth's atmosphere (called the ionosphere) can reflect the waves back to the Earth.

High-frequency (HF) waves are reflected strongly by the ionosphere, so that it is possible to contact places on the other side of the world using what is known as short wave radio. A receiver tuned to the short wave band will pick up stations from America, Russia or Australia, but

Fig. 18.3 With frequency modulation each station needs a band width of 50 kHz. Channels are therefore not less than 50 kHz apart.

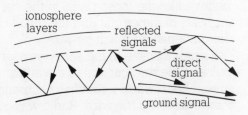

Fig. 18.4 The three ways in which radio waves travel from the transmitter.

you cannot listen to stations only a few hundred miles away because you are too far away for the waves to reach you directly, but not far enough away to receive the reflected signals.

The third way in which some radio waves can travel is along the Earth's surface. It is only the medium- and low-frequency waves that can travel as 'ground-waves'. Broadcast stations in Europe use these bands (the medium and long waves) because one station can broadcast to a large part, or even the whole, of a country. Because they are so useful for broadcasting, these parts of the radio spectrum are not available for two-way radio communications, except for special purposes (such as for aircraft).

Very high-frequency (VHF) waves are not reflected by the ionosphere and do not travel through the Earth. Anyone more than 30 miles away from the transmitter will not be able to receive the signals at all. This is a big disadvantage if you need to keep in contact with someone more than thirty miles away, but it is also a major advantage: you can use the same channel for two stations more than 60 miles apart (why 60 and not 30 miles?) without the two stations interfering with one another. This is being used for broadcast radio and television, as well as for two-way radio links.

Aerials

The aerials can be a problem for two-way radio too. In theory, any piece of metal will do as an aerial for the transmitter or for the receiver. In practice, the transmitter must turn as much as possible of the electrical energy into radio waves, and the receiver has to be able to sort out the required station from all the rest that will also be picked up by the aerial. In both cases, the system uses *resonance.*

To understand what is meant by resonance, an example (which is nothing to do with electronics) will help. In many cars (especially old ones!) you often hear an annoying rattle or vibration when the car is travelling at certain speeds. There is something which can vibrate in the body of the car, such as a loose panel. At one particular speed the vibration produced by the engine or by the wheels on the road is at the same frequency as the natural vibrating frequency of the panel. At this speed the panel vibrates because, we say, it resonates with the vibration from the wheels or the engine.

Electrical systems can resonate in the same way. The frequencies are usually much higher and electric currents are produced instead of sounds.

You will remember from chapter 9 that a capacitor and an inductor connected together are used as the tuning block for a radio. They behave like the loose panel in the car. They will resonate with alternating currents in the circuit and the result is that, at that resonant frequency, the currents are much larger.

Aerials behave in the same way for radio waves. It takes time for a pulse of electric current to travel from one end to the other. If the current is sent back when it reaches each end it will go backwards and forwards along the wire. Radio waves cause currents in a piece of wire, so if the frequency of the current flowing up and down the wire is the same as the radio wave causing it, the currents are much larger. At the transmitter, if the alternating voltage producing the currents is resonant with the natural frequency of the wire, the currents will again be much larger. For maximum efficiency, aerials must be made the right length.

How can we find out what the right length is? To do this we need to know a little more about radio waves.

Suppose you could see the peaks of a 1 megahertz radio wave as it travelled through space. As you watched, 1 000 000 peaks would pass you every second. Radio waves are electromagnetic radiation; they travel through space at 300 000 000 metres per second.

By the time the last radio wave in any particular second went by, the first one would be 300 000 000 metres in front (if it could go that far!). A million peaks spread out over 300 000 000 metres means that the peaks would be 300 metres apart. We call this 300 metres the *wavelength* of the wave. Fig. 18.5 shows this diagrammatically.

You do not have to work out the wavelength each time in this complicated way. All we have done is to divide the wavespeed by the frequency, and the wavelength is the answer. This statement can be written as the wavespeed formula. The formula is given in the panel to the right. There is more information about this formula in reference section F2.8, on page 184.

For most purposes, the best length for an aerial is about half a wavelength long. Receiver aerials that are not the right length will work. However, unless transmitter aerials are the right length they waste most of the electrical energy fed to them.

Think again about our three engineers with radios in their cars. A large aerial fitted to the roof of a car would cause problems (what problems?). The limit for the length of such an aerial would be about 1 metre. This will transmit radio waves with a wavelength of 2 metres and a frequency of 150 megahertz. This length of aerial could be used to transmit down to about 100 megahertz efficiently. Thus for two-way radio which is to be used in a car or which has to be portable, the frequency used will usually be 100 megahertz or more.

A two-way radio system where both stations were at permanent locations could use much longer aerials. Amateur radio enthusiasts use high-frequency rather than VHF for two-way radio so that they can contact other parts of the world. They can mount the aerials on masts in their gardens, so the aerials can be much longer than 1 metre. Apart from amateur radio, almost all two-way radio is in the VHF or UHF bands. Most stations working below VHF are broadcast stations. (Which is the UHF band? What would be the typical length of a UHF aerial? Can you think of other advantages (besides aerial length) of using VHF for two-way radio? What bands would you expect to be used by the fire service, the army, and the navy?)

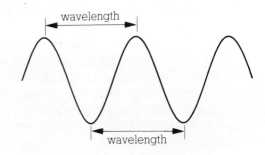

Fig. 18.5 The wavelength of a stream of waves is the distance between any point on one wave (such as the top of the wave) to the same point on the next wave.

The wavespeed formula

$$\lambda = \frac{c}{f}$$

where:

λ (the Greek letter called lambda) is the normal symbol for wavelength;

c is the normal symbol for the wavespeed of electromagnetic radiation;

f is the normal symbol for frequency.

(See reference section F2.8, page 184.)

SUMMARY 18A

There are two kinds of radio systems: broadcast systems and two-way radio.

Radio waves are one form of electromagnetic radiation. They travel through space at a speed of 300 000 000 metres per second.

Information is encoded on the radio carrier by modulation. Modulation can be amplitude modulation (AM), frequency modulation (FM) or pulse code modulation (PCM).

A transmitter comprises a signal generator to produce the carrier, an input transducer, a modulator, suitable amplifiers or drivers, and an aerial. A power supply is also necessary.

A receiver comprises an aerial, a tuner to select the required station, a demodulator, suitable amplifiers and drivers, and an output transducer. A power supply is also necessary.

Each station has its own allocated transmitting frequency (channel). Modulation adds sidebands to the carrier frequency. The range of frequencies required on either side of the carrier frequency to avoid stations interfering with one another is the bandwidth of the channel.

Radio waves travel on direct path, by reflection from the ionosphere, and as ground waves.

$$wavelength = \frac{wavespeed}{frequency}$$

The essential parts of a radio receiver

If you look back to fig. 18.2 you will see that there are five basic blocks in a radio receiver. What has to go into each of these blocks?

The aerial could be any piece of metal, so long as it is not connected electrically to the ground. Good aerials are usually a length of insulated wire suspended in the air as high as possible. On modern radios, an aerial like that would be a major problem, and most radios use either aerial rods perhaps 50 centimetres in length, or a ferrite aerial fitted inside the receiver. If a short aerial is used, then the receiver must have amplifiers with high gain. Ferrite aerials make use of the magnetic properties of electromagnetic radiation.

The tuner is a capacitor and an inductor connected in parallel. It behaves like a high resistance for the frequency to which it is tuned, but like a low resistance for all other frequencies. It therefore shorts out all the signals from the aerial, except the one that you want. Fig. 18.6 shows the simplest tuning circuit. To tune to different stations the resonant frequency of the tuner has to be varied. This is normally done by making the capacitor a variable capacitor.

The simplest form of demodulator uses a diode. The diode rectifies the alternating currents coming from the tuner, but the way in which the output from the diode is smoothed is very clever. If you used a very large capacitor, then the output would be a steady d.c. and all the information in the signal would be smoothed away. If you used a very small capacitor, all you would get is the positive half of each cycle of the alternating current, and because this is at high frequency it would not work the loudspeaker and you would not get any sound. The trick is to smooth the output enough to remove all the high-frequency a.c., but to allow the output to vary in step with the information modulated on the carrier. The value of the resistor and capacitor **together** is what matters.

Fig. 18.7 shows the circuit of the diode demodulator block and the values of the resistor and capacitor that you need for medium frequencies. (Why would you need a smaller capacitor for high frequencies?) Fig. 18.8 shows, by means of graphs, what the demodulator does to its input.

Neither the diode demodulator nor the tuner need a power supply. They are passive circuits. The signals for these two blocks come from the aerial. The currents in the aerial are only a few microamps and the voltages obtained are a fraction of a volt. This is enough to make a very sensitive earphone work, and that was done in the early days of radio when crystal sets were used (see the photograph in chapter 8, page 72). To get sufficient power to drive a loudspeaker, the signals must be amplified, and so the fourth block in the system is an amplifier. There are often two amplifiers: a voltage amplifier to make the signal larger and a power amplifier to drive the loudspeaker.

Better radios: the TRF receiver

The biggest problem with the simple radios based on the system just described is that the stations cannot be separated properly. How can we make a better tuned filter to remove all the unwanted signals?

The simple answer to this problem is to add another tuning filter. The way in which this is usually done is to add another amplifier too. The new amplifier is used to amplify the radio frequency signals before they are demodulated. This helps to make the second tuning filter work better.

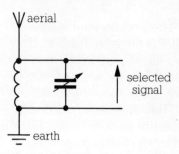

Fig. 18.6 The simplest form of tuning circuit for a radio. A connection to earth is shown in this diagram, and for simple radios this would be necessary. Modern radios use high gain amplifiers and do not need an earth connection to which the currents in the aerial would go.

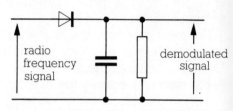

Fig. 18.7 The circuit of the demodulator block. The values of the capacitor and resistor are chosen to remove the high-frequency ripple from the radio carrier but not to smooth out the wanted signals. The graphs below show what the demodulator does to the signals it receives.

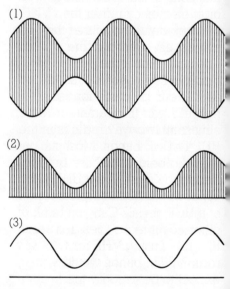

Fig. 18.8 These graphs illustrate the demodulation process for an amplitude modulated radio signal. The top graph shows the signal reaching the diode. The second graph shows the effect of the diode (by itself) on this signal. The third graph shows what happens to the signal when the resistor and capacitor are included too.

The second tuning filter has to be identical to the first one, so that each selects the same station. This means that the variable capacitors for the two filters must work in exactly the same way. To do this, a *two-gang* variable capacitor is used. This is two variable capacitors mounted so that one spindle operates both sections.

The whole arrangement is known as a TRF receiver. TRF stands for **t**uned **r**adio **f**requency. Fig. 18.9 is a block diagram for the TRF type of receiver. In the days when devices known as *valves* were used to give amplification, cheap radios used the TRF system because it needed fewer expensive valves. Transistors and integrated circuits are much cheaper devices than valves, so that now it costs very little more to make a much better radio. Most radios now made are *superhets*, and the TRF system is rarely used.

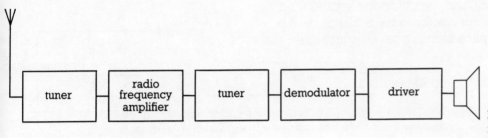

Fig. 18.9 A block diagram of a TRF receiver. Nowadays almost all radios are superhets and the TRF system is not often used.

The superhet

As the number of radio stations increased, designers looked for better ways of selecting stations and avoiding interference between them. It is possible to use more tuned circuits, but they would need three, or four, or even more ganged tuning capacitors. In practice, the problems of making identical coils and identical variable capacitors are impossible to solve at an economic price. (Why does the **price** matter?)

To solve the problem, a new type of system called a *superheterodyne*, or *superhet* for short, was invented. What it does is to select the signal from the wanted station using a tuned circuit, and then change the frequency of the signal and pass it to a series of amplifiers all tuned to the new frequency. This new frequency is called the *intermediate frequency* (IF). The trick is that, whichever station is selected, the IF to which it is changed is always the same. The amplifiers only have to be tuned to this frequency when the radio is first made and because there is no variable capacitor you can have four, six, or even eight tuned circuits.

How is the frequency changed? It depends on what happens when you mix together two a.c. signals of different frequencies. All you need in order to show what can happen are two pulse generators and a summing amplifier (feeding a driver and loudspeaker) as shown in fig. 18.10. One of the pulse generators is adjusted to give a sound in the middle of the normal music range, and the second generator is adjusted to give a sound a few notes (tones) different from the first generator. The two generators are then turned on together. New frequencies are heard when the two notes are mixed. Varying one generator changes the extra frequencies heard.

When two frequencies are mixed, they produce new frequencies equal to the sum of the original frequencies and to the difference between the two original frequencies.

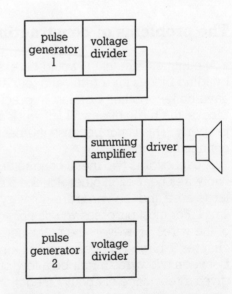

Fig. 18.10 An experimental arrangement for mixing pulses of two different frequencies. The output will contain new frequencies (equal to the sum of, and to the difference between, the input frequencies). Because the pulses are square waves some other new frequencies will be produced as well.

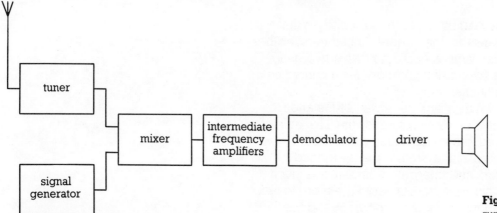

Fig. 18.11 The block diagram of a superhet.

In a superhet, the signals are at much higher frequencies than in the experiment but the principle is the same. One of the two frequencies to be mixed is the signal from the aerial, and the other one is produced by a generator inside the radio. The generator (or local oscillator, as it is often called) is tuned to give an output which is a set amount higher than the station frequency. The tuning control is a two-gang variable capacitor designed to make sure that the difference between the two does not change. In this way it gives a constant intermediate frequency.

Fig. 18.11 is a block diagram for a superhet receiver.

SUMMARY 18B

A tuner comprises a capacitor and an inductor in parallel. It resonates at one frequency and has a high resistance to signals at that frequency.

A demodulator for AM uses a diode with a resistor and a capacitor as a filter.

A TRF radio system has two tuning circuits. The second one follows a radio frequency voltage amplifier.

A superhet radio system changes the frequency of the wanted station to an intermediate frequency which can then be passed through several tuned filters.

The problems of constructing radios

You might expect that it would be easy to collect together the various building blocks for a radio and join them together in the same way as you have done for other systems. In practice, even if you have got all the right blocks, the radio often will not work at all or, if it does, it does not work properly. This is **not** because the basic idea is wrong. The problem is the connecting wires.

A capacitor is two metal conductors separated by an insulator. Thus two wires near each other act like a capacitor. If the wires do not have a large area and the wires are not very close, the capacitance is very small. For most purposes you do not notice any effect from the capacitance of the wires. However, the reactance (the effective resistance – see chapter 9, page 77) goes down as the frequency goes up. The capacity between two wires might be a few picofarads, but at 1 megahertz this gives a reactance of about 1 megohm, and at 100 megahertz (the frequency used by VHF radio broadcasts) the reactance is only about 10 kilohms. The connecting wires behave like resistors connected between the various terminals and so interfere with the way in which a radio works. Because of this, the layout of wires in a radio has to be worked out carefully. The systems ideas still work but there is another factor to take into account in making the systems work. The higher the frequency, the larger are the problems that have to be solved.

Modern developments in radio

Most people watch television these days, so how important is sound radio? It is true that the use of broadcast radio has decreased over the past twenty years, but other uses have increased greatly. Think about aircraft control, pocket radios carried by police, satellite links to other parts of the world, radio links used for sending messages automatically from remote weather stations, links between ships and shore, and even the cordless telephones you can now buy. Radio is used wherever a link between two or more people cannot use wires or a normal telephone.

There are several ways in which radio systems have been improved so that more people can use these systems.

Modern radios are much more efficient and are therefore smaller. Using integrated circuits, more of the power from the power supply is used in transmitting the radio waves or producing sound in the loudspeaker. Designers do not have to allow for large amounts of energy wasted as heat.

Radios cost about the same as they did ten, twenty, thirty, forty and fifty years ago. You may say 'so what?', until you remember that in 1950 it cost just over 1p to send a letter, a school dinner cost 3p, petrol cost about 15p per gallon, and a new family car cost around £500. Cheap integrated circuits, the use of printed circuits to make the connections, mass production (often in South East Asia) and plastic cases have reduced the real cost of manufacturing a radio by very large amounts.

The other main change has been in the use of higher and higher frequencies. The basic ideas are the same, whatever the frequency at which the radio is working. However, the techniques used in practice to make the various blocks work at higher frequencies have to be different from those used at lower frequencies. The use of microwaves (the highest radio frequencies now used) is a recent development.

Television

What has to be changed if you want to send pictures rather than sounds using radio waves? The Chinese say that "a picture is better than a thousand words". There is a lot more information in a picture than in sound, and a television system has to be able to deal with all that information.

The television transmitter does not send all the information in the picture at the same time. In the television camera, the picture is broken down into small units or cells (often called *pixels*) and the camera sends information on each cell in turn. At the receiver, the information for each pixel has to be put back together to make the picture again.

This method of sending information in a stream of single units one after the other is called a *serial* method of transmitting information.

Both the television camera and the cathode ray tube that produces the picture on a television receiver depend on the properties of beams of electrons in a vacuum. This beam is made to scan across the picture in a series of lines, following a pattern called a *raster*. For British television the complete raster is scanned twenty-five times a second. The picture is made up of 625 scanning lines, giving about half a million pixels. America uses 525 lines and France uses 805 lines. Fig. 18.12 is a simplified diagram of a raster pattern.

Why do you not see the moving beam and the lines on the picture when you watch television? The human eye does not see separate

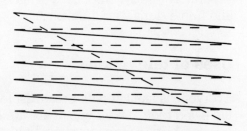

Fig. 18.12 A simplified diagram of a television raster pattern. The solid lines are the scanning lines forming the picture. The dotted lines show where the beam goes back ('flies back') to start a new line.

pictures if they change faster than fifteen pictures a second. Because the eye cannot see things that change very quickly, you see a complete picture.

If you use an ordinary camera to take a photograph of the picture on a television screen, the photograph shows what is actually visible on the screen at the time. Fig. 18.13 is a photograph of a television picture taken with a hundredth of a second exposure time. (What will come out on the photograph if the camera exposure time is a twentieth of a second?)

Fig. 18.13 A photograph of the picture on a television set, taken with an exposure time of a hundredth of a second. There is more of the picture than might be expected because the television raster scans 312 lines across the screen and then goes back and scans another 312 lines in between the first ones, to complete the raster. In addition, the picture does not disappear immediately the electron beam has passed by. The screen continues to glow for a small fraction of a second.

To transmit television pictures the signal has to include all the following information:

- where each line of the raster should start;
- where each new raster ('frame') should start;
- how bright or dark each pixel should be;
- information on the colour of the pixel (in practice this means that the signal must have information on how much red there is in the pixel, and on how much blue there is in the pixel, leaving the receiver circuits to compute the rest of the information);
- sounds to accompany the pictures.

All of this information is coded onto a single carrier by a clever combination of all the separate parts of the signal. The receiver decodes the signal to obtain the sound, vision, colour and synchronising signals separately (the synchronising signals − or sync for short − are the line and frame signals for the raster).

Uses of television

Everyone is familiar with broadcast television as seen on the TV set in the living room. Like radio, there are lots of other ways that television can be used besides broadcasting. Unlike radio, two-way television communication is not used.

The most important use of television, other than for broadcasting, is in what is known as *closed-circuit television* or *CCTV*. For CCTV there is a camera (and all the transmitting circuits) and a receiver (and all the decoding circuits) but the signal from the transmitter to the receiver is sent along cables instead of by radio.

The most common place to see CCTV in use is in large supermarkets where it is used to watch for thieves. However, you can see cameras on motorways being used to check on traffic problems, on railway stations being used to display details about arrivals and departures, and to allow the guard to see along the entire platform, and in all sorts of other places where surveillance is needed. (Can you think of some more examples?)

It is important to remember that the CCTV system does not catch thieves and criminals. It is the people watching the screen who have to think about that. You should work out why it is often better to use CCTV and have someone watch a television screen than to put that same person in, say, the shop itself to watch for shoplifters in person. What other communication system would the person checking the screen need to have to make the system effective?

Another use for CCTV is in inspecting places where it would be too dangerous for a person to go or where there would not be enough room. For example, a sewer can be inspected by sending a camera (in a suitable capsule with lights on it) through the sewer. The same idea has been used on spacecraft to obtain pictures of distant planets, and is used in medicine where tiny cameras can be used to see what is happening inside the body and produce a much-magnified picture on a screen.

Not every television screen you see is part of a CCTV system. In computing, television screens are used as visual display units (VDUs) to provide information from the computer. There is no camera, and the signals are produced inside the computer. However, the signals from the computer to the VDU must still carry the same information, so that the raster and the picture information are all correctly arranged.

SUMMARY 18C

Television uses the same principles as radio but it transmits picture information.

The picture is scanned in a series of lines. The scanning pattern is called a raster. Each bit of the picture is called a pixel.

A television signal must include information on line and frame synchronisation, brightness and colour for each pixel, and sound.

F REFERENCE SECTION

F1 — Communication systems

F1.1 — Duplex and multiplex

In telecommunications the terms duplex and multiplex are used to describe systems which carry more than one channel of information.

A duplex system is a system which carries two channels on the same set of wires (or whatever is carrying the information). The two channels are usually one in each direction so that the person at each end can both send and receive signals at the same time on the same channel.

A multiplex system is one in which there are many channels using the same line at the same time. This can be achieved by giving each channel a different carrier frequency (known as frequency division multiplex, FDM), or by allowing each channel to use the line for part of the time (known as time sharing or time-division multiplex, TDM).

F1.2 — Person-to-person communication

A person-to-person system is a two-way system. Each transmitter has a prearranged channel to which the receiver is switched. The transmitter has to produce only enough power to send the signal in the required direction. Most duplex systems use wires and cables (e.g. local telephone connections) and in these cases the channels are selected by switches in an exchange. Duplex systems can, and often do, use VHF or microwave radio. The system then has a series of agreed channels to which both transmitter and receiver are tuned. If one channel is used for communication in both directions, then each station must transmit and then receive in turn. ("Calling Oscar Bravo, Over" "Receiving you, Charlie Delta, Over".) Often, two separate channels are used so that it is possible for communication to take place in both directions at the same time.

F1.3 — Broadcast systems

A broadcast system is a communication system where the transmitting station sends out signals to anyone who wishes to receive them, but it cannot receive signals back. The transmitter needs to produce high-power signals and radiate them in all directions in which listeners might be expected to be. Receivers must have a means of selecting the required transmitting station. Most broadcast systems use radio waves, but cable broadcasting systems are also used (e.g. 'cable' television, hospital radio stations).

F1.4 — The telephone system

The telephone system is a duplex communication system based on direct links by wire, optical fibre or microwave beam. It uses exchanges to switch circuits to make the necessary links. The essential parts of the system are the telephone instrument (which is a combined input transducer and output transducer), exchanges and the required connecting lines.

The system includes seven kinds of signal (eight signals in all). These are given below:

• signals to turn the power on and off (a switch operated by lifting the handset which connects the caller to power supplies at the exchange);

- codes to select the required routes at each exchange (a series of pulses produced by the dial or push-buttons);
- a calling signal (an a.c. signal which rings the telephone bell);
- a means of switching off the calling signal when the person being called answers (another switch operated by lifting the handset);
- two sets of voice signals (modulated onto a steady direct current by the microphone and demodulated by the earpiece at each end);
- feedback signals from the exchange to tell a caller what is happening and what must be done next (the dialling tone, ringing tone, engaged tone, number unobtainable tone, and 'put your money in now' tone);
- codes to allow the correct charges to be made.

The British telephone system operates on 50 V d.c. It is designed for voice frequencies up to 3 kHz. This is sufficient for normal spoken conversation but it puts a limit on the use of the telephone for transmitting other signals. Computer information is sent by using a modem which transmits codes as pulse-modulated sounds and decodes incoming signals into serial pulses that a computer can use. Prestel and other telephone information systems work in a similar manner to this.

Each telephone is connected to the system by two wires which carry all the signals in both directions. Most local telephone cables are buried underground and are bundles of wires. Wires are twisted together in pairs and each phone uses one 'twisted pair', connecting the telephone to the local exchange or distribution point.

Main exchanges are connected by lines which can carry many sets of information on the same cables. The signals are modulated onto different carrier frequencies and the frequencies are mixed together on the same line. This is called frequency multiplexing. The various frequencies are separated and demodulated at the receiving exchange. The signals may either be sent as analogue signals or they may be converted into digital codes before modulating the carrier.

Trunk telephone connections of this sort could be twisted pairs. More often a special kind of cable (known as coaxial cable) or microwave radio, or optical fibres is used. Each of these can carry very high frequencies, so that the number of channels can be much larger. Table F.1 compares the various kinds of system that are available.

Table F.1 Comparison of various kinds of telephone link

	Standard twisted pairs	Microwave radio link	Low-loss coaxial cable	Optical fibres
Maximum number of telephone channels	25	1000	2000	7000
Maximum number of hi-fi channels	3	140	200	1000
Maximum number of TV channels	–	1	2	7
Distance apart of repeaters in km				
a) if analogue signals are used	1.5	15	1.5	not used
b) if digitally-coded signals are used	2	15	2	40

If telephone lines are too long, the signals will become too weak to be able to use them. All types of telephone line need repeaters at regular intervals to boost the signals.

Trunk telephone lines are not only used for normal telephone calls. Both sound programmes and television are distributed through these lines. In such cases, the frequencies involved are much higher and fewer channels can be included on the same line.

Optical fibre systems can carry much more information along a single fibre than is possible using other means such as wires. Optical fibre lines are used only with digitally-coded signals.

A standard telephone link responds to frequencies up to about 3 kHz and needs about 70 000 bits per second. To send music, a hi-fi channel must respond to frequencies up to 16 kHz. A digital system needs 0.5 megabits per second. Television needs 5 MHz or 70 megabits per second.

F2 — Radio and television

F2.1 — The superheterodyne principle

The superheterodyne principle is concerned with the interaction of signals of different frequencies.

Radio waves of different frequencies do not affect one another as they pass from the transmitter to the receiver. A signal is therefore not affected by the other signals being transmitted at the same time.

When signals from different stations are received on the same aerial, they do not interfere with one another and each signal can be separated from others of different frequency.

If a circuit has any component with a non-linear characteristic, such as a diode or a transistor, then the signals do interfere with one another. (A resistor has a linear characteristic. It obeys Ohm's law.)

When two signals of different frequencies interfere with one another, the effect is that the output contains not only the original two frequencies but also two new frequencies. One of these is equal to the **sum** of the frequencies of the original signals, and the other is equal to the **difference** of the two signal frequencies. For example, signals of 1.5 MHz and 1.9 MHz, when mixed, will produce an output containing four frequencies: 0.4 MHz, 1.5 MHz, 1.9 MHz and 3.4 MHz.

This principle is used in the superhet receiver. The incoming signal is mixed with an internally-generated signal in a block which is deliberately non-linear. This block is called a *mixer*. The difference frequency is separated at the output of the mixer.

When amplitude modulation is used, the modulator stage depends on similar principles.

F2.2 — Modulation

Modulation is the process of adding the information signals on to a carrier.

The signal is a series of changes (e.g. in voltage). To describe the signal the size of the changes (their *magnitude*) and how often the changes occur (their *frequency*) have to be known.

There are three main methods of modulation. They are known as amplitude modulation (AM), frequency modulation (FM), and pulse code modulation (PCM).

In amplitude modulation, the magnitude of the signal changes becomes changes in the amplitude of the carrier, and the frequency of the signal becomes the *frequency of the changes in amplitude*. The frequency of the carrier does not change.

In frequency modulation, the magnitude of the signal becomes the change in frequency of the carrier, and the frequency of the signal becomes the *frequency of the changes in frequency*. The amplitude of the carrier does not change in this case.

In pulse code modulation, the signal is not modulated continuously on to the carrier. At regular intervals the amplitude of the signal is measured and this value is converted into a digital code. In this system the carrier has two states, corresponding to logic 0 and logic 1. These can be different amplitudes or different frequencies. The 1s and 0s of the digital code are modulated onto the carrier, together with marker codes. At the receiver the digital codes are decoded and the original signal is regenerated.

F2.3 — Amplitude modulation (AM)

The three graphs in fig. F.1 show the principle of amplitude modulation. The first graph is the signal to be transmitted. It might be the amplified signal from a microphone. The second graph shows the unmodulated carrier. It might be a continuous a.c. at perhaps 1 MHz. The third graph shows the output from the modulator, in which the signal and carrier are combined.

(1)
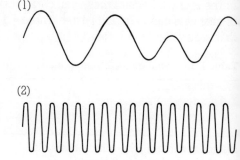

(2)

(3)
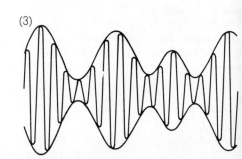

Fig. F.1 Amplitude modulation. The top graph shows a signal and the middle graph shows an unmodulated carrier. The lower graph shows the carrier with the signal modulated on to it.

The advantages of amplitude modulation are that the circuits needed are simple, and the bandwidth required is less than for other methods of modulation.

However, amplitude modulation has several disadvantages compared with other methods of modulation. Any interference due to, for example, thunderstorms, behaves as changes in amplitude and affects the received signal. Because modulation produces 'sidebands' (by the superheterodyne principle), as well as changes in the carrier itself, signals from adjacent stations can overlap and the tuning circuits can distort the signal.

F2.4 — Frequency modulation (FM)

The three graphs (fig. F.2) show how a frequency-modulated signal is produced, although for clarity the changes have been very much exaggerated, and square and triangular waves have been used for the signal. The first graph is the signal, the second graph is the unmodulated carrier, and the third graph shows the output from the modulator, in which the signal and carrier are combined.

Because the amplitude of the carrier is constant, interference and distortion can be removed in the receiver by clipping the received signals to a constant amplitude.

Frequency-modulated signals use a much bigger bandwidth than amplitude-modulated signals. AM broadcasting stations use a bandwidth of 9 kHz, whereas FM broadcasting stations use 50 kHz.

F2.5 — Pulse code modulation (PCM)

Fig. F.3 shows the principle of pulse code modulation. The first graph shows the signal to be transmitted. For PCM the signal is made so that the whole of the signal is positive, and the zero signal is (in this case) 2.5 V instead of 0 V.

The second graph shows the timing points at which the signal is to be sampled and the numbers at each point are the magnitudes of the signal at those points.

The third graph shows the digital code for each of the samples. In a real system both the number of sampling points and the range of binary numbers used for coding would be larger than those shown in these diagrams.

The fourth graph shows the unmodulated carrier, and the fifth graph shows the carrier with the code added to it by changing the frequency. The amplitude could have been changed instead of the frequency.

The advantages of PCM are that you can use cheap digital integrated circuits to process the signals and you can interface the signals directly to computer systems.

The disadvantages are that the systems are much more complex and, because the system depends on sampling, there are limits to the match between the received signal and the transmitted signal because of the number of steps in the digital code and what might have happened between samples.

F2.6 — Aerials

Any piece of metal acts all the time as an aerial, collecting energy from radio waves. However, for an aerial to be useful for radio reception it needs to be at right angles to the path of the waves and vertical or horizontal, to match the transmitting aerial. Except in specially designed systems there is no advantage in having an aerial that is more than half the wavelength of the radio waves being received.

The reason for the limit in length is that the signals received at the far end of the aerial take time to reach the receiver. If the aerial is too long the signals from the far end are cancelled out by the following part of the signal before they have had time to get to the receiver circuits.

If an aerial is exactly half a wavelength in length, it resonates with the radio wave and so collects more energy from that wave. Television aerials are made half a wavelength in length to obtain the stronger signal this gives. The same

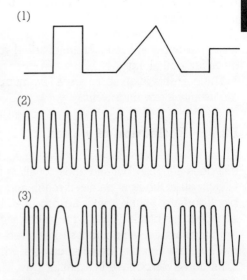

Fig. F.2 Frequency modulation. The top graph shows a signal made up of a square wave and a triangular wave. The middle graph is the unmodulated carrier and the lower graph shows this carrier after modulation with the signal.

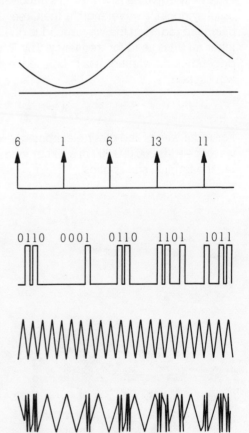

Fig. F.3 Pulse code modulation. The five graphs are explained in the text.

would happen at medium frequencies, but an aerial 150 m long for a 300 m wave is not usually practicable!

VHF radio is used for radiocommunication between cars or other vehicles and a base, partly because the length of aerial you need (half a wavelength) is not inconveniently long.

The currents in an aerial are a few microamps and the voltages of the signals are usually a few microvolts.

F2.7 — Reflection of waves

All waves can be reflected. Reflection occurs when the wave reaches something that does not absorb it and does not allow the wave to pass through it. When light falls on glass the light passes through and is not reflected. When light strikes a black surface, all the light is absorbed and none is reflected. That is why the surface looks black. When light strikes a shiny surface, the light is reflected back from the surface. When light strikes a red surface, the red substance reflects the red light but absorbs the other colours, which is why it looks red.

Radio waves behave in a similar way. They pass through almost all non-metals. They are reflected by pieces of metal which are insulated from their surroundings. They are absorbed by pieces of metal which are earthed, because the currents produced in the metal by the waves go to earth. They are absorbed by an aerial because the currents produced go into the receiver.

F2.8 — The wavespeed equation

For any wave the speed with which the wave travels is related to the frequency of the wave and its wavelength by the formula:

wavespeed = frequency × wavelength

When this equation is written in symbols, the usual symbol for frequency is f, the usual symbol for wavelength is the Greek letter lambda (λ), and for electromagnetic radiation the wavespeed is given the symbol c. Sometimes the Greek letter nu (ν) is used for frequency. The formula can be written in three forms, depending on whether it is to be used to find frequency, wavelength or wavespeed:

$$c = f \times \lambda \qquad f = \frac{c}{\lambda} \qquad \lambda = \frac{c}{f}$$

For radio waves and other electromagnetic waves travelling in air or space, the wavespeed is 300 000 000 m/s. Other kinds of wave have their own wavespeed, but the formula still applies.

Example of the use of the wavespeed equation

Light is a form of electromagnetic radiation. The speed of light in an optical fibre is about 210 000 000 m/s. If light pulses are sent down the fibre at a frequency of 500 MHz, how far apart are the front edges of each light pulse along the length of the fibre?

The distance between each pulse is the wavelength of these pulses (**note**: it is the pulses we are interested in, not the light waves themselves). To find wavelength we use the wavespeed formula in the form:

$$\lambda = \frac{c}{f}$$

Substituting the numbers for wavespeed and frequency (and remembering that 500 MHz is 500 000 000 Hz) we get:

$$\lambda = \frac{210\,000\,000}{500\,000\,000}$$

$$\lambda = 0.42 \text{ m}$$

The distance between the front of one pulse of light and the front of the next pulse of light is 0.42 m.

Exercise 55 — What is the frequency of the Radio 2 transmission on the long waveband which has a wavelength of 1500 m (remember $c = 300\ 000\ 000$ m/s)?

Exercise 56 — One of the bands used for licenced amateur radio transmissions has a frequency of 7 MHz. What is the wavelength of 7 MHz radio waves?

Exercise 57 — Sound waves travel very much more slowly than radio waves. If a sound wave of frequency 500 Hz has a wavelength of 60 cm, what is the wavespeed of sound?

F2.9 — Resonance

If two vibrating systems can vibrate at the same frequency, then the vibration of one will start or increase that of the other one. The two systems are in resonance. The same interaction will occur between a vibrating system and a wave striking the system, if the frequencies are the same for both the wave and the system.

In an electrical circuit with inductance and capacitance, currents can flow between the two as the inductance produces a current to charge the capacitance, which then provides a voltage to feed a current back to the inductor. This happens at a frequency which depends on the sizes of the capacitance and inductance.

If an a.c. supply is connected to a circuit containing both capacitance and inductance, there will be resonance if the resonant frequency of the circuit and the frequency of the supply are the same. This is the principle of the tuning circuit in a radio (see also reference section F2.13).

F2.10 — The uses of radio

This section summarises the various purposes for which radio is used.

(i) **Broadcasting**

National networks
Services to other parts of the world
Local radio
Private systems (e.g. university students' radio)
Beacons for navigational purposes
Time signals for synchronising time throughout the world

} for news, for opinions and comment, for advertising, for entertainment, and for education.

(ii) **Two-way radio**

Air-traffic control, ship-to-shore radio, coastguards, etc.
Mobile radio (e.g. police, fire services, taxis)
Telephone links
Cordless telephones, radio microphones
Amateur radio
Citizen's band radio

(iii) **Telemetry (use of radio for measurement or control)**

Radio control of automatic vehicles, etc.
Continuous monitoring of weather conditions, water supplies, etc.
Radar

F2.11 — Block diagram of a TRF receiver

TRF is an abbreviation for *tuned radio frequency*. Receivers using this system have at least two tuned circuits and an amplifier to amplify the signal while it is still at the frequency of the incoming radio wave and before it is demodulated. The block diagram of a basic TRF receiver is on page 175.

F2.12 — Block diagram of a superhet receiver

A superhet receiver is one in which the frequency of the incoming radio waves is changed to an intermediate frequency. This is then amplified using tuned amplifier circuits. The amplified intermediate frequency signal is then demodulated. The block diagram of a basic superhet receiver is on page 176.

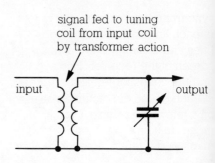

Fig. F.4 A standard tuned circuit as used in radio receivers.

F2.13 — Tuning circuits

The normal tuning circuit used in radio uses a capacitor and an inductor in parallel, and this combination is connected between the signal line and earth, as shown in fig. F.4. Used in this way the tuning filter rejects all signals except the signal of the required frequency. The resonant frequency of the circuit depends on the values of the capacitance and the inductance, and is given by the formula:

$$f = \frac{1}{2\pi\sqrt{(L \times C)}}$$

where L is the inductance value and C is the capacitance value.

Whenever inductance and capacitance are used together in a circuit it can behave as a resonant (tuned) circuit.

F2.14 — Simple demodulator for amplitude-modulated radio frequency signals

The simplest demodulator for amplitude-modulated signals uses a diode and a capacitor. The value of the capacitance depends on the load resistance of the circuit. If the resistance of the circuit connected to the output of the demodulator is very high, then a separate resistor is sometimes added. The circuit of the demodulator is shown in fig. F.5.

The capacitor removes the radio frequency currents, but not the lower frequency currents, from the signal. The value of the capacitor (in μF) multiplied by the value of the load resistance (in kΩ) should be between 0.01 and 0.1.

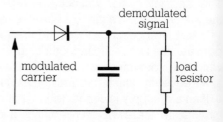

Fig. F.5 The circuit of a demodulator block for an amplitude-modulated radio signal. If the load resistance is very high a separate resistor is sometimes added in parallel with the load.

F2.15 — Uses of television

The main purposes for which television is used are as follows:
- broadcasting;
- information services (viewdata, teletext, etc.);
- surveillance and traffic monitoring;
- advertising;
- inspection of remote, inaccessible or hazardous locations;
- relay of conferences, etc;
- analysis of events by recording and replaying;
- facsimile transmission (information relayed by television instead of making and sending photocopies of text or pictures).

F2.16 — The television raster

In order to transmit pictures, the pictures are converted into a string of information that can be modulated on to a carrier by scanning the picture. This is achieved by scanning the picture in a pattern called a *raster* (see fig. F.6).

For British television pictures, the scanning process is repeated 25 times every second, so that 25 *frames* are transmitted each second. For each frame there are 625 scanning lines. To reduce flicker of the picture for the viewer, instead of scanning all 625 lines straight down the frame, the scanning system scans 312.5 lines down the frame and then scans the remaining 312.5 lines in between the lines it has already scanned. This arrangement is known as interlacing. To achieve this, the frame scanner must run at 50 scans a second to give 25 complete frames a second.

At the end of each line and of each frame, the scanning spot on the display must move back across the screen very quickly in order to start the next piece of the scan. This is called *flyback*.

The transmitted signal must include information so that the receiver circuits 'know' when to start a new line or a new frame. The pulses that do this are called

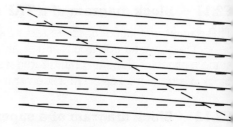

Fig. F.6 The raster pattern used for British television.

synchronisation pulses (sync pulses, for short). They are included at the beginning of each line and of each frame. The frame sync pulses are several of the picture lines and these lines are arranged in such a way that they do not show on the screen of the receiver. However, they can be used for sending other information, and the codes for teletext are transmitted on these 'blank' lines.

Each dot on the picture is called a pixel. It is possible to see the separate lines on a television picture if you look closely but the way the information is sent means that on a black-and-white picture there are no separate dots. Computer displays do generate separate dots. A television picture is about five million pixels.

In order to receive television pictures, all receivers must use the same standard as the transmitter. The frame scanning system works at 50 Hz because the a.c. mains supply is 50 Hz. However, closed circuit systems, computer displays and television systems in other countries can, and in some cases do, use different standards.

19 CONTROLLING THE WORLD WITH A COMPUTER

Can computers control the world? It depends what you mean by controlling the world. What is clear is that we can use computers in many ways. Most of the things we now do with computers were difficult or impossible a few years ago. However, computers are only as good as the people who make and program them. The computer will not take over from humans.

This chapter is about the way that computers are used, and what facilities they have. Electronics is about doing useful things in the real world. It is no use thinking about computers unless we think what job we want them to do. And it is no use thinking about that job unless we think about whether it is worth doing.

What is a computer? It is an electronic system using standard building blocks in the same way as has been described already in this book. Computers use large numbers of these standard circuits, and as a result they are powerful machines, but there is nothing in the electronics of a computer which is different from the electronics in this book.

Who uses computers? What do they use them for? Almost all of us use computers in some way or other. A computer does not have to be large and expensive, although large and expensive computers can do more than small, cheap ones. A calculator is a simple computer that most people are familiar with, but many homes now have teletext, or a home computer, or appliances such as washing machines with microprocessor control.

You will remember that a system has various kinds of inputs, a processing stage and an output. A computer is a system in which:

- the signal input is information or *data*;
- the control input is by means of a *program* containing coded instructions;
- the processing stage can be made to process the information it receives in a number of ways, depending on the program it receives (such a processing stage includes a device known as a *microprocessor*);
- the output is in the form of information.

Anyone who is interested in dealing with any form of information might be expected to use a computer. Your electricity bill and the bank cash dispenser are obvious examples. Many supermarkets have computerised tills, and some use them for keeping a check on stock, often using the bar codes printed on the containers. Travel agents and hotels use computers for storing information and making bookings. Offices use them in word processors. Machine shops use them for controlling lathes, and drawing offices make use of computer-assisted draughting. The doctor may have you listed on a computer and a librarian finds a book for you by consulting a computer. The list is almost endless.

Do all these computers do the same thing? The answer is yes, but there are many ways in which you can use the skill of a computer, just as there are many ways in which you can use the skills of human beings. If you think about the list of users you will see that some are using them to store information, like the doctor and the librarian. Some are using the machine to process information, in tasks like stock control and word

Fig. 19.1 Can you identify the use being made of a computer in the above [151] photograph?

processing. The Electricity Board is also processing information, but is using the machine as a very clever calculator too. The industrial users want something different. They are interested in using the computer to control other machines. We will think about each of these uses in turn.

Information storage and retrieval

If a library has not got a computer, how does it keep its records? Many public libraries do not have computer facilities and neither do most school libraries. The records are kept on cards. Each card has details of one book and the cards are filed in boxes or drawers (fig. 19.2).

The books themselves are usually given two numbers. One is an *accession number*. The five-thousandth book to be put in the library will have 5000 as its accession number, and there will be a record book in which each title is recorded against its accession number. The second number (for non-fiction books) is the subject classification, and it shows the subject area with which the book is concerned. The books on the shelves are usually arranged in Dewey number order so that all the books on a particular subject are in the same part of the library.

There will probably be two, or even three, sets of record cards. One will be the author index, in which the books are arranged in alphabetical order of their authors. The second set of cards will have the same information as the first set, but will be a title index, in which the cards are in alphabetical order of titles. The third index would be a subject index, with the same cards arranged this time in subject order.

However, these are not all the records the library has to keep. There will be cards to show which books have been borrowed, and by whom. If the library is a branch library ' as many are ' then there will be yet another set of record cards at the headquarters library.

Instead of cards and lists some libraries are now using a computer system to do the same job. By comparing the two ways of doing this we can see what it is that the computer has to do, and we can begin to see how it does it. We can also check some of the words used in work with computers and see what they mean.

The whole system with all its information is called a *database*. Each card is replaced by a *record* in the computer. Each branch library has a *file* of records.

For each book there are several items of information such as the title,

```
                                              621.381
                                              WAT


       WATSON, John


       Mastering Electronics

       (Macmillan Master Series)


       Macmillan Education

       1983                                    01971
```

Fig. 19.2 A typical library record card. The number on the right at the top is the subject classification which is a code for the subject of the book, and the number on the right at the bottom is the accession number, showing when the book was obtained.

the author, and the subject. Each item of information is called a *field*. The author information is a field in the database; the title information is another field.

Each record refers to a book. In computerised libraries the books are kept on shelves in the normal way, but it would be possible to type the whole book into the computer, if required. In this case the record would refer to a *data-file* and the computer could be made to display the whole book (data-file) if required.

The computer needs to keep only one set of records, and it does not need to keep them in any particular order. There do not have to be two, three, or even more, alphabetical indexes. The computer can pick out the records needed using any of the fields to find them.

How does the computer achieve this retrieval of information? Each file and each field has a separate code. The computer **could** be programmed in such a way that the code for the authors was AUTHOR INDEX (just like the label on the front of the drawer full of cards in the non-computerised library), but in practice there would be a number code for each field.

Having identified the field required, the computer is programmed to search that field. Suppose you want a book on electronics. The computer will look for the records with electronics in the subject field and note them in another part of its memory, rather like jotting them down on a note pad. Suppose you want only books on GCSE electronics. As long as the records have a field for the various examinations, the computer will now search that field and find records which are GCSE *and* electronics. This process could be used for each field in turn. When you have finished sorting the information you want, you can ask the machine to display or print what it has found.

What are the advantages of using a computer database instead of a normal filing system with cards and indexes? A typical county library system might have 1 000 000 books and 50 branches. This means that there might be as many as four million record cards kept. That number of cards would need 2000 drawers, or a total of about 800 cubic metres of storage space (all the space in 15 typical houses). To find one particular card could take several minutes. By comparison, the computer would need less space than that in an average sitting room and it could produce the required record in a few seconds.

Your address book is a much simpler example of a database, and if you have a home computer you might want the details in the address book stored on it. Suppose you have 200 addresses. In an address book the addresses would be stored in alphabetical order of names, and this is the only field you would need. By the time you have switched on your computer and typed in the instructions, you could have found the address in a normal address book. To buy an address book costs about £2. To buy even the cheapest computer system, complete with the program, the display, and a tape recorder used as a memory, you would have to spend about £250.

There is one other disadvantage of electronic storage of information. It would not be easy to steal 2000 drawers of file cards and their loss would be noticed. It is much easier to copy the information held in a computer and send that copy, by telephone, to some other computer anywhere in the world, without anyone even knowing that the theft of information had taken place. Such a theft might not be important with library books, but it would certainly be important in matters such as national defence or police records.

Would it be sensible to put a school library's records on to a computer? Explain the arguments both for and against such an idea.

> A database is a complete information system.
>
> A record is the set of information about a person, item or event.
>
> A field is all the information in one category.
>
> A file is a set of records.
>
> A data-file is a set of data.

Information processing

There may be other things that you want to do with information besides storing it and searching through it. You may want to modify it and be able to rearrange it in some way. The best example of this is word processing.

This book could have been prepared in two ways. The handwritten words could have been typed using a typewriter and then checked, edited and altered as necessary. Soon the whole text would have pages cut up to make space for diagrams, new pieces stuck over old sections and many inked corrections. It would be such a mess that it would have to be retyped before it was sent to the printer. The other way was to type the words into a computer, type in all the corrections and alterations, and when the computer had got the whole text rearranged in its memory instruct it to print the final version. Not a word would have had to be typed on paper until all the corrections had been made.

Many computers are adapted to do this job and nothing else, and they are then called word processors, but with suitable programs any computer can be used as a word processor. The trick which the computer is using is its ability to shunt information in and out of various parts of its memory at will. It is the large memory capacity of a computer that makes it so much faster and neater than a human in processing information.

The advantages of such a system are obvious, and this book was indeed prepared using a word processor. But are there any disadvantages? If the machine saves on the amount of typing then fewer typists are needed. Is that a bad thing, or is it good to release typists from boring retyping to do more interesting things? Electronics cannot answer that question, but anyone buying word processors for an office in order to save staff has to ask such questions.

Would it be worth adding a word processing program to a home computer? If all you are going to do with it is to correct the spelling mistakes in your once-a-year letter to Granny to thank her for the Christmas present, then even the cheapest program at over £10, and all the time needed to learn how to use it, would make a dictionary and a large pad of writing paper a better proposition!

153 Why are magnets a big problem anywhere near equipment used for word processing? For what kinds of work done in school do you think a 154 word processor might be a sensible choice?

Calculating by computer

The bill asking you to pay for the electricity you use (see fig. 19.3) is produced by a computer, but why does the Electricity Board work out your bill on a computer? Wouldn't it be better if the meter-reader worked out your bill when he came to read the meter, just as the milkman collects money for the milk each week? The problem is that the charges are different for different users. The amount of money can be quite large, and the calculations involve multiplying decimals. Also, the meter-reader

Fig. 19.3 A typical electricity bill

electricity bill   WINTER QUARTER

MR D BROWN
4 GREEN ROAD
ANYTOWN

DESCRIPTION	METER READING		UNITS USED	PENCE PER UNIT	AMOUNT £		V C A O T D
	THIS TIME	LAST TIME					
DAY UNITS TO 23 MAR	13725	12860	865	5.64	48.	79	
NIGHT UNITS TO 23 MAR	27094	23471	3623	2.04	73.	91	
STANDING CHARGE					9.	31	

YOUR CUSTOMER NUMBER	YOU CAN PHONE US ON	PERIOD ENDING	AMOUNT DUE NOW
		30 MAR 1985	£ 132.01

would not know, for example, if you were paying for, say, an electric cooker through your Electricity Board account.

Why do supermarkets use computerised cash tills? Computers can do the calculations quickly and without mistakes, and they do not get tired.

How does a computer do arithmetic? In chapter 15 you were introduced to the idea that computers use binary numbers or number codes such as BCD (binary-coded decimal).

The trouble with binary numbers is that whilst it is fairly easy for a computer to cope with them, they are not easy for we humans. Remembering that there are 454 grams in a pound is bad enough, but 111000110 grams to the pound is mind-stretching! 111000110 is, of course, the binary number for decimal 454. (For methods of changing numbers between decimal and binary see reference sections E1.2 and E1.3.)

It is not only when computers are doing calculations that they need the amounts in binary numbers. Everything that goes into the computer has got to be converted into a binary number code before the computer can do anything with it, because binary numbers are the only thing that the microprocessor can understand. Letters, numbers, patterns, instructions all have to be in a binary form.

It is possible to 'talk' to a computer in its own language, and there are certainly times when you have to use *machine code* to make the computer work as you want it to. But if you had to play computer games in that way, or had to turn everything into binary numbers and machine code binary instructions before your calculator would give you an answer (in binary!), you would reach for paper and pencil instead.

To make life easier we use a special 'language' to give our instructions to a computer, and we either make the computer turn ordinary numbers into binary for us, or use a number system called *hexadecimal* ('hex').

There are a lot of different computer languages. Most home computers use one of the forms of a language called BASIC, but there are many others, such as FORTRAN, COBOL, and PASCAL. Each language has a set of word instructions which the computer has been programmed to 'understand' by converting them into binary codes. For example, if you need to tell the computer to follow a particular set of procedures in its program, one version of BASIC uses the word PROC to indicate where the procedure must begin.

There are different languages because larger computers can cope with more complex instructions. A simple computer needs a low-level language to take it through the processes a few steps at a time. A large computer has the capacity to work out the long series of instructions that would be included in the words of a high-level language.

Hex is a way of dealing with binary numbers in a more convenient way. Hex numbers count in sixteens rather than tens or twos. You may wonder how that helps if a computer cannot manage anything other than binary. It works by grouping four binary digits (bits) to make sixteen patterns for the sixteen numerals in the hex system. When hex numbers are written down we need extra symbols for the numerals between ten and fifteen, and the first six letters of the alphabet are used. Table 19.1 shows hex, binary and decimal forms of some numbers.

Doing actual arithmetic in a computer is easy as the only numerals are 0 and 1. For example, multiplying 13 by 23 in decimals is multiplying 1101 by 10111 in binary. Fig. 19.4 shows the process. It is exactly the same process as long multiplication of ordinary (decimal) numbers. There are more steps in the binary calculation, but each step is very simple.

A calculator is a *dedicated* computer which can carry out certain programs chosen by the buttons you press. This makes the calculator

Table 19.1 Numbers in decimal, binary and hex notation

decimal	binary	hexadecimal
1	0001	1
2	0010	2
3	0011	3
	. . . .	
8	1000	8
9	1001	9
10	1010	A
11	1011	B
12	1100	C
13	1101	D
14	1110	E
15	1111	F
16	0001 0000	10
17	0001 0001	11
18	0001 0010	12
	. . . .	
25	0001 0101	19
50	0011 0010	32
75	0100 1011	4B
100	0110 0100	64
125	0111 1101	7D
150	1001 0110	96
175	1010 1111	AF
200	1100 0100	C8
255	1111 1111	FF
256	10000 0000	100
257	10000 0001	101

(We do not normally leave a space in the middle of binary numbers but the space has been included to make the relation between binary and hex clearer.)

```
    1101   ×   10111
  _____
  11010000   (do 1101 × 10000: put
             four 0s down and do
             1 × 1101)
       000   (do 1101 × 0000)
    110100   (do 1101 × 100)
     11010   (do 1101 × 10)
      1101   (do 1101 × 1)
  _____
 100101011   (add the parts)
```

Fig. 19.4 The steps in multiplying 13 by 23 using binary numbers. 100101011 in binary is the same as 299 in decimal

easy to use and cheap to manufacture. It is possible to make other computers do the same things but they have to be programmed each time to do each task. In theory you could adapt a calculator to do other computing tasks but in practice the microprocessor chip has all the programs built on to the same chip in the form of ROM (what does ROM stand for? – see chapter 15) and they cannot be modified.

There are plenty of other examples of a system using a dedicated microprocessor. Can you name the example already mentioned in this chapter? What do you think are the advantages and disadvantages of having systems with dedicated microprocessors?

Control by computer

There are more microprocessors being used for controlling machines than for all the other uses put together. This may seem surprising, as you do not see lots of robots about as you walk around town! Although robots are good examples of using computers to control machines, most computer-controlled machines are much less exotic.

The main use of microprocessors is for controlling processes in factories. Suppose you are manufacturing biscuits. The mixture is made by feeding in the ingredients continuously, mixing, and then measuring the right amount for each biscuit onto the conveyor. The conveyor moves through the oven at a steady speed. At the other end the hot biscuits are cooled, counted and packed. If any part of this process goes wrong then production stops and all the biscuits on the production line may be wasted. Someone has to watch each part of the process, carefully, all the time, day and night.

There is no problem in getting transducers which can measure the flow of ingredients into the mix, the speed of the conveyer, the oven temperature, and so on. Each transducer could feed its input to its own system in the way that was described in chapters 3 and 4. All control systems have the same basic building blocks (see fig. 19.5).

Some of the factors depend on one another. If the conveyer is going more slowly the biscuits would still be all right as long as the oven temperature was turned down. A microprocessor can be programmed to allow for all these factors at the same time. Now that microprocessors are so cheap they are in great demand for tasks of this sort.

The microprocessor has one other advantage over the use of separate control systems for each part. If you want to change the conditions, perhaps to make Morning Coffee instead of Rich Tea biscuits, then you can do this by adjusting the program. You do not have to go round and alter the settings of each section of the system, one by one.

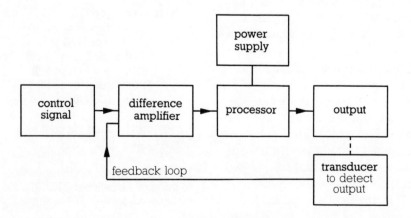

Fig. 19.5 Block diagram of a control system. All control systems have a feedback loop to pass signals (giving information about what is happening at the output) back to the input. By comparing what is meant to happen (the input) with what is actually happening (the feedback signal) the system can adjust itself to do what its input tells it to do.

When a machine is controlled by a microprocessor, the system has to have a means of making the machine respond to its commands. There has to be something which takes the information at the output of the microprocessor and turns it into action. In earlier chapters we found that you often needed a driver stage, or a power amplifier. You need something like this with a microprocessor system. The name that is used for this block in the system involving computers is an *interface*. Interfaces come in many forms, depending on what is being controlled. A driver stage of the type we have already met could be a suitable interface, but often there are several pieces of information coming from the computer and the interface has to sort these out, and drive the various controls.

This is where another of the ideas we met earlier comes in. In the chapter on amplifiers (chapter 5) the idea of *feedback* was introduced. Feedback was used to control the gain of the op-amp. Many computer control systems use feedback. The feedback is not to control the microprocessor but to control the whole system. Here is one example.

The biscuit oven should be at the correct cooking temperature. The computer has been programmed to know what that is. It also has an input from a temperature transducer (or probably more than one) so that it knows the actual temperature in the oven. The output of the computer will be fed through an interface to a motor which turns the gas supply to the heaters on or off. The computer will be programmed to check the temperature (the feedback signal) against what it ought to be, and to work out the difference. It will use that piece of information to work out how the gas supply needs to be adjusted. In fact it can do even better, because it can be programmed to work out how long to turn the gas full on to get the temperature correct, before adjusting the gas to keep the temperature correct.

There are plenty of examples of this sort of process in industry. The number of uses of microprocessor control in the home is rapidly increasing too. Washing machines and central heating systems are the most common uses so far, but others will follow. Microprocessors are now being used in cars, too, to keep a check on all functions and warn the driver of any problems.

Many of these uses are worthwhile, but you must not assume that because a task is done by a microprocessor, the task must be good. Table 19.2 lists some advantages and disadvantages.

So far we have thought about what computer systems can do and how they do it. As with all systems you do not need to know much of what is inside the system to be able to use it. That is why there has been very little detailed electronics in this chapter. In chapter 20 we look inside microprocessors and find out about the electronics of these devices.

Table 19.2 Advantages and disadvantages of microprocessor control

Advantages
Cheap integrated circuits
No moving parts
Easy to replace if faulty
Small size
Can control many functions
Can be individually programmed

Disadvantages
Need separate d.c. power supply
Need interfaces and transducers
Difficult to diagnose faults
Will not operate at high or low temperatures, or in wet conditions
Prone to electrical interference

SUMMARY 19

Computers use standard electronic circuit blocks.

A computer takes in data and a program. It processes these using a microprocessor to give an output in the form of information.

Computers are used for: storage and retrieval of information; processing of information; calculations; and control of machines.

Computer information storage is usually based on a database system. Information is stored in a range of fields within each record, and it is retrieved by searching fields in turn.

Computers are fast, accurate, and they never get tired, but they are expensive and they need to be programmed.

All processes within a computer are carried out using binary numbers; machine code is computer instructions in binary numbers.

Decimal numbers, words, letters, patterns and instructions must all be turned into binary form. A computer language, such as BASIC, is used so that the computer can do this conversion for instructions.

Numbers are often written in hexadecimal (hex) and keyboards turn letters into a code called ASCII.

When a computer is used for controlling a machine the input data comes from transducers. The output requires an interface to enable it to operate a machine. Most control processes use feedback.

20 INSIDE A COMPUTER

The computer is a machine designed to increase our brainpower, but how does it do it? A computer is a system. It has an input, which it processes to produce an output. It needs a power supply. It needs control signals to tell it what to do and when. The input is information, and the output is more information.

A computer can only do what it has been designed to do. It does not have mental abilities which people do not have. It can, however, cope with much more information than any one person could manage, and it can work much faster than a human being. When people blame computers for making mistakes they forget that it is the programmer who prepared the routines for the machine or the operator who fed in the wrong data who really made the mistake.

The whole of the inside of a computer is based on the blocks which you have already met in this book. The main difference between a computer and most other pieces of electronic equipment is the number of these blocks that have to be used. Even so, it is possible to make a working computer using only three chips − three integrated circuits which between them have all the blocks necessary for a complete and working computer. All useful computers have more integrated circuits than this, but the extra chips are there to increase the speed, to increase the amount of work the machine can do, to increase the number of processes that it can carry out at the same time, or to increase the number of inputs it can cope with.

If the computer is really as simple as that, then it should be possible to draw a simple block diagram to show what the system is. This is indeed the case. Fig. 20.1 is a block diagram of the main structure of a computer, any computer. Computer engineers often call this the *architecture* of the computer. The blocks on this diagram do not have familiar names because each contains many of the basic blocks that you have learnt about. In this chapter we shall find out what is inside each of these blocks in turn.

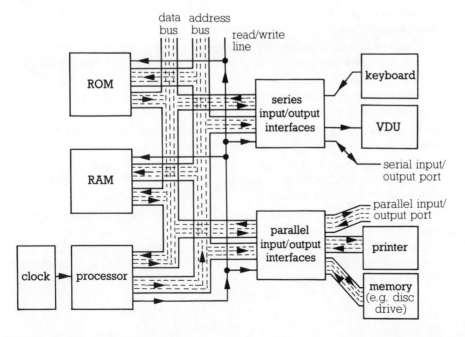

Fig. 20.1 A block diagram of the main architecture of a computer. The wide 'buses' joining the various blocks together contain a number of parallel information channels.

The input/output port

A computer may have to deal with information in many forms. The information may be analogue or digital. You will remember from chapter 14 that an analogue signal is one for which the size of the signal depends on the magnitude of the quantity it represents. For example, if you wanted to feed some information about the temperature inside a furnace into a computer, then the input transducer would produce a voltage which depended on the temperature. On the other hand, if you wanted to use the machine for word processing, then each letter would have a separate code of pulses to identify it, so that digital signals would go to the computer.

Inside the computer, all the information is processed in the form of digital codes. The purpose of the input/output port is to convert all input signals coming from outside the computer into the form that the computer requires, and to provide suitable signals to go from the computer to whatever device the computer is controlling.

Some of the equipment connected to the computer will be part of the computer system itself. There will normally be a keyboard, a display unit, a printer to produce *hard copy*, and a disc drive or tape recorder. These items are often called the *peripherals*. The blocks needed to make the signals from these peripherals suitable for the computer are usually included inside the computer itself (see fig. 20.2).

If the computer is being used to control something else, then there will be both input transducers (such as thermistors) and output transducers (such as stepper motors) connected to the computer. These devices will also have to be matched to the computer, and they will each be connected to the computer through an *interface*. For the input transducer, the interface will change the signals into a form that the computer can use, and for the output transducer, the interface will change the computer signals into the form necessary to drive the transducer. One important task of the interface at the output port is often to provide the *power* needed by the output transducer.

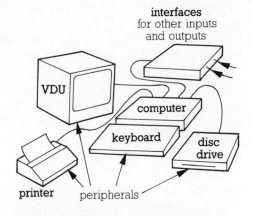

Fig. 20.2 The interfaces for the peripherals are built into the computer.

One kind of input interface often used is an *A-to-D converter*. An A-to-D converter codes analogue signals into digital signals for the computer. You have already met this kind of block. The comparator (chapter 2, page 10) is a very simple device for getting a digital signal from a signal that is varying in size, but for most purposes the computer needs to know not only whether the signal has reached a certain size but also how the signal is changing. You have already met that kind of A-to-D converter too. In chapter 12 (page 117) there are details of how the digital voltmeter works. That system is one standard type of A-to-D converter. The number of pulses counted by the counter can be the input to a computer, just as it can be the input signal to the seven-segment display.

The input to the computer would be a series of binary pulses, which the computer would 'count' and register as a binary number. This is called a *serial input* because the pulses come one after the other. There are two problems with serial data of this kind. One is that, although in decimal numbering there may be three or four digits in the number, in the binary system there are many more bits in the number. For example, the decimal number 1230 has four digits but when that number is written in binary it is 10011001110 and has eleven bits. The second problem is that if there are a lot of bits it will take the computer longer to read the information.

If all the information has to be sent along one pair of wires the only way of sending data to the computer in digital form is to send it in serial form.

If the time it takes to read serial information matters, then it is possible to have a different wire for each bit in the number, and then all the information can be sent at the same time. *Parallel inputs* like this are very often used in computer systems, and all the movement of data inside a computer is by means of parallel circuits called *buses*.

You may wonder why this is so important. At first sight it seems wasteful to use nine or seventeen wires to connect things together when

158 two would do the job. (Why nine and seventeen particularly? Why might

159 the buses have only eight or sixteen of these wires in them?) For a home computer using an 8-bit microprocessor the parallel system is about ten times faster than the serial system, and with larger computers that can handle more bits at one time the advantage is even greater. With serial systems time also has to be allowed for the machine to check that it has all the data. With parallel data, the part of the system receiving the data either has all of the binary number or none of it. With a serial system there has to be a way of telling the receiving end that the pulses it has just received were one number and the next lot of pulses are another number.

Although the circuits inside a computer can operate at phenomenal speed, the speed with which a computer can produce the answers or the effects that you want usually depends on how fast you can feed information into it or use the information coming out. The speed with which information can be fed in using a keyboard depends on how fast the typist can work. The speed with which information can be fed out to a printer depends on how fast the mechanical parts of the printer can produce letters on a piece of paper.

Table 20.1 sets out some typical speeds for common systems. These speeds are measured in two ways: the *baud* rate, and the number of characters per second. A baud rate of 1200 means that each second has been divided into 1200 equal intervals during which a signal can be logic 1 or logic 0. Characters refer to the letters or numbers (or spaces) on a typewriter keyboard or their binary, hex or ASCII equivalent. A character requires eight bits, plus the spaces between each character and the next one, so that in a **serial** system a baud rate of 1200 is usually 120 characters a second.

Table 20.1   Operating speeds for some typical systems

Good, fast typist	6 characters per second
Electric typewriter with letters on a 'daisywheel'	
	30 characters per second
Electric matrix printer (prints by making separate dots)	
	150 characters per second
Tape recorder used as a memory for a computer (serial data)	
record or replay 1200 baud =	120 characters per second
Floppy disc memory for a computer	10 000 characters per second
Stepper motor (1 baud typically rotates the motor by 7.5°)	
1200 baud =	50 revolutions per second
Television picture 6 000 000 baud	
Video monitor for a computer (high resolution)	
2 000 000 baud	
Internal circuits of a microcomputer, typically	
4 000 000 baud	

160 (Why have the last three figures been given only as baud rates?)

The central processing unit

The input and output ports, with their interfaces, are concerned with the input to the system. They turn the input into a form that the system can process. The central processing unit (CPU) is where the actual processing takes place. In a typical microcomputer the CPU is one chip with all the circuits on it, called a microprocessor. Larger computers may have a number of microprocessors.

A microprocessor is basically a set of logic gates, each of which can be switched to be an AND gate, OR gate or NOT gate by control signals. The control signals come from the program that the computer is given. In this way the microprocessor can be made to do whatever is required with the input signals (the data) that it receives.

A complete microprocessor chip would also need a number of *registers* which will store ('remember') the various bytes coming into the processor or being moved around the processor, in exactly the same way as you write down your steps of working as you work out a mathematical problem. To distinguish the two main parts of the processor the programmable logic gates are often called the *arithmetic and logic unit (ALU)*. The operation of the ALU is described later in this chapter.

Microprocessors can be made to deal with just one string of bits at a single data input or with a number of data inputs in parallel. Most microprocessors being manufactured at the present time are designed for either eight or sixteen parallel inputs, although some of the latest chips can deal with 32 parallel inputs. There is no reason why microprocessors with six, or thirteen, or any other number of parallel inputs could not be made, but bytes with four, eight and sixteen bits in them are particularly useful. Coding the numbers from 0 to 9 in binary needs four bits. Coding the letters of the alphabet using the ASCII code needs eight bits. A microprocessor that has eight parallel data inputs is called an *8-bit* microprocessor.

The control signals to the microprocessor will also be in the form of binary codes. These codes are called *machine codes.* The microprocessor chip will include logic gates which can sort out the various codes and control the processing gates to do what is required.

Memory

The third block in every computer is its memory. We have already referred to the registers in the CPU, but a computer also needs a separate memory to store programs, instructions and data. A calculator needs only enough memory to keep instructions for each process it may have to do, and the memory can be in the form of a chip. Most other computers need much more memory and so they have magnetic discs or some other form of peripheral memory. Chapter 16 is about memory systems; later in this chapter we shall consider the kind of electronic circuits used in computer memories.

SUMMARY 20A

A computer has an input/output port, a central processing unit, and a memory.

The keyboard, display screen, disc drive (or tape recorder) and printer are peripherals.

External devices must be connected to the computer through an interface. The interfaces for the peripherals are included on the computer circuit boards.

Internal circuits in a computer use parallel data lines (called buses) so that they can operate at higher speeds.

The central processing unit comprises an arithmetic and logic unit (ALU) and several registers, including the accumulator.

Experimental work with processors

It is easy to set up a simple system which will show you how the programmable logic gates of the ALU operate. This section describes such a system. It is a 1-bit processor which can be made to do any one of seven functions using control codes.

You will remember from chapter 4 that all logic processes can be broken down to the AND decision, the OR decision, and the NOT decision. The first step is to find out how to make a controllable version for each of the gates with these functions. The gates should only give an output if the control signal allows the signal to be given.

The AND gate is the easiest gate to control. Suppose we have two inputs to the gate and we want the gate to give a logic 1 output only if there is a control signal present. This means that we only want the gate to give its logic 1 output when there is a logic 1 **and** a control signal. This is obviously another AND function and a second AND gate will give the control we want. Fig. 20.3 shows the arrangement.

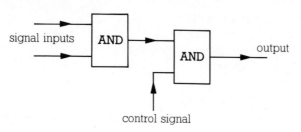

control signal

Fig. 20.3 A simple controlled AND gate. This gate will only give the AND output if the control signal is logic 1. There is an even simpler way of doing the same thing, using only one gate. Can you suggest what it is? [161]

A controlled OR gate can be made in exactly the same way. The output from the OR gate passes to a two-input AND gate. The other input to the AND gate is the control signal. Fig. 20.4 shows the arrangement.

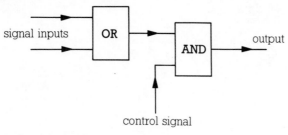

control signal

Fig. 20.4 A controlled OR gate.

The controlled NOT gate is not quite so easy to deal with, so before we do, let us find out how to combine the controlled AND gate and the controlled OR gate. This will give a system which can give either the AND of two input signals, or the OR of these inputs, or no output at all, depending on the control signals that the system receives. To select one of three different possiblities we need three **different** control signals, but we need only **two** control inputs to do this. If there are two control lines, which can be at either logic 0 or logic 1, then:

both can be at logic 0	code 00
line 1 can be at logic 0, and line 2 at logic 1	code 01
line 1 can be at logic 1 and line 2 at logic 0	code 10
both can be at logic 1	code 11

A group of logic gates can be used to sort out the three control signals that we need from the two lines. The easiest way of doing this is to connect inverters to each line and then to pick out the combinations needed using AND gates. Fig. 20.5 shows how this can be done. (If there were three control lines, how many control signals could be obtained by the same method?) [162]

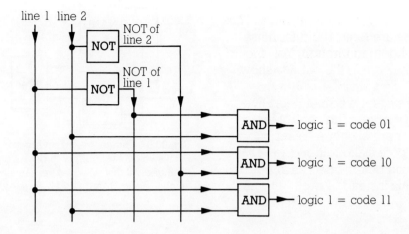

line 1 line 2

NOT of line 2

NOT of line 1

logic 1 = code 01

logic 1 = code 10

logic 1 = code 11

163

Fig. 20.5 Generating three control signals from two control lines. How could a fourth control signal be obtained from these two control lines?

It is now a simple matter to combine all these ideas to make a programmable logic gate. We will use code 01 to make the AND gate operate, code 10 to make the OR gate work and code 00 to make neither of the gates work. In computer language, code 00 *disables* the gate. Code 11 is not being used at this stage. We do not need to get a logic 1 for code 00 in this case because the system will be disabled anyway if neither gate is switched on (*enabled*). Fig. 20.6 shows the system. The final OR gate in the system prevents the output from one AND gate reaching the other AND gate.

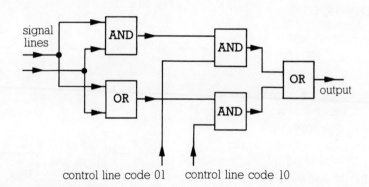

signal lines

output

control line code 01   control line code 10

Fig. 20.6 A programmable AND/OR gate. The control codes come from a system of the type shown in fig. 20.5.

If we could control the NOT gate, it could be added to the system in fig. 20.6 to change the function to NAND or NOR as well as AND or OR. The NOT gate inverts the signal, so that it really needs to work both when the output is logic 1 **and** when the output is logic 0. Feeding a control signal to an AND gate will work only when we want to control a logic 1 signal.

What we want is a gate which gives an inverted output when the control signal is logic 1 and gives a non-inverted output when the control signal is logic 0. A truth table will show what the system has to do (see fig. 20.7).

If you look at the truth table you can see that the output is logic 0 if the input signal and the control signal are the same but is logic 1 if those two signals are different. This is the function of the Exclusive OR (EOR) gate described in chapter 4, page 33, and reference section B3.7.

	Input signal	Control signal	Output	
1	0	0	0	} output not
2	1	0	1	inverted
3	0	1	1	} output is
4	1	1	0	inverted

Fig. 20.7 The truth table for the controlled NOT gate.

There are several ways of combining gates to give an EOR function. Fig. 20.8 shows one of these. In this arrangement, the OR gate will give lines 2 and 3 of the truth table but it will also give a logic 1 for line 4. Thus we use an AND gate to find when both inputs are logic 1 and then use that output to stop the logic 1 signal for line 4 getting through. You should satisfy yourself that this arrangement does really give the outputs shown in the truth table.

To add the inverter to our programmable system we shall need five control codes (AND, OR, NAND, NOR, and disable). The control input will have to have three parallel lines so that there are three binary control bits. The three bits could give eight codes altogether. Fig. 20.9 shows the basic system. The control codes can be obtained as in fig. 20.5, but all the AND gates would have three inputs instead of two.

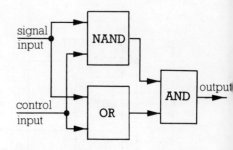

Fig. 20.8 The controlled inverter or Exclusive OR system. Try to devise an arrangement that will give the same function using NAND and NOR gates. [164]

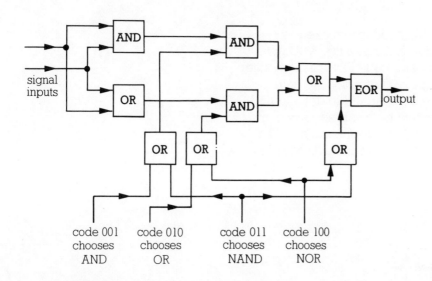

code 001 chooses AND   code 010 chooses OR   code 011 chooses NAND   code 100 chooses NOR

Fig. 20.9 Programmable logic gate giving AND, OR, NAND, NOR and disable. What is the purpose of the three OR gates on the control lines? [165]

The ALU (arithmetic and logic unit) of a microprocessor might be required to carry out at least one other process. Sometimes two numbers have to be added together. In binary numbers this is a very easy process, but the programmable logic block will not do it without using several of these blocks. It would be much better to add another section to the programmable unit with another code to make it operate.

When you add together two bits there are only four possibilities. They are:

0 + 0 = 0
0 + 1 = 1
1 + 0 = 1
1 + 1 = 10 = 0 down, carry 1

Apart from the carry, this table is just like the truth table in fig. 20.7. In other words, an exclusive OR gate will act as an adder. The carry can be obtained by using a second logic block as an AND function (fig. 20.10).

In practice, if you have to add a series of numbers each addition stage needs two of these adder units (and an OR gate): one to deal with the two bits and the other to deal with the carry number from the next column. For that reason, the arrangement just described is known as a half-adder. Fig. 20.10 shows both the half-adder arrangement and how two half-adders are combined to make a full adder. (What is the purpose of the OR gate in the carry output line of the full adder?) [166]

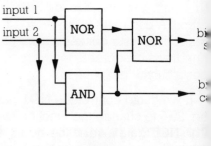

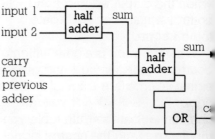

Fig. 20.10 The half-adder (*top*) and a full adder made from two half-adders.

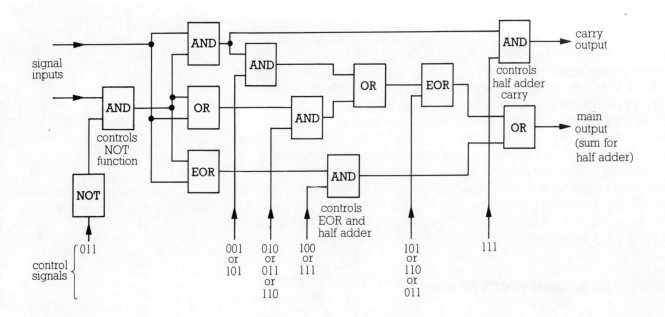

signal
inputs

AND
controls
NOT
function

NOT

AND

OR

EOR

AND

OR

AND

AND

OR

EOR

AND
controls
EOR and
half adder

AND
controls
half adder
carry

OR

carry
output

main
output
(sum for
half adder)

control
signals {
011

001
or
101

010
or
011
or
110

100
or
111

101
or
110
or
011

111

The output of the half-adder can be controlled by control signals, in exactly the same way as the AND and OR gates, using an AND gate in the output as a control switch. Fig. 20.11 shows the complete system of a programmable logic block with a half-adder included and with a controlled AND gate used to produce the carry signal for addition. You may need more logic gates than you have available to make up this whole system, but the system will work if you are able to construct it. (This design is based on earlier systems and is not the simplest 1-bit processor.)

No-one makes computers by assembling these programmable logic units from separate gates. Integrated circuits are so cheap and easy to make that systems of this kind are always made on chips. A complete 8-bit microprocessor containing many hundreds of separate logic gates costs only a few pounds.

Fig. 20.11 The complete system for a 1-bit arithmetic and logic unit. This system is made up from the sub-systems already described in this chapter. The codes are: disable 000; AND 001; OR 010; NOT 011; EOR 100; NAND 101; NOR 110; half-adder 111.

SUMMARY 20B

The ALU (arithmetic and logic unit) of a microprocessor is made up of programmable logic gates, each of which can act as AND, OR, NAND, etc, depending on the control codes received.

Programmable gates can be controlled by using an AND gate in the output lead as a switch turned on or off by the control signal.

An exclusive OR gate is a gate that gives an output if one of its two inputs is at logic 1 but not if both inputs are at logic 1.

An EOR gate can be used as a programmable inverter or as part of a half-adder.

A full adder uses two half-adders plus an OR gate to generate the 'carry'.

Registers in microprocessors

So far we have considered only the ALU (the arithmetic and logic unit) in the microprocessor chip. No microprocessor can work without having several registers in addition to the ALU. Think how you do arithmetic. You learnt at a very early age the basic 'number bonds' (as they are called), which are 2 + 2, 3 + 5, 9 + 8 and so on. These are like the adders in the ALU. For you to add 25 and 32 your brain works out 5 + 2 and remembers it while it works out 2 + 3 and decides how to combine the answer with the answer of 5 + 2. If you had to add together 4957 and 7235 you would probably use a piece of paper to jot down your working.

A microprocessor has these three levels too. It can cope directly with single bits, but for numbers with more than one bit it needs a working memory to hold one part of the data while it is dealing with another part. Any set of circuits that hold data in this way is called a register. The working register for the microprocessor is called the *accumulator*. The microprocessor also needs other registers to serve in the same way as the rough paper on which you would do your working out. In fact some computer designers call these registers the 'scratch pad'!

Do not confuse these registers with computer memory. A computer system needs memory to store programs, instructions, and data. That sort of memory is separate from the microprocessor chip itself. Comparing the computer system once again with the way you do arithmetic, the registers are where you do the rough working but the memory is like the textbook, because it has the instructions on how to do the sums. The memory is also like the answer book in which you write out neatly what you want the teacher to see.

Memory in a computer system

The block diagram of the computer system given in fig. 20.1 had three main sections: input/output interfaces; the microprocessor; and the memory. In practice, it is the memory that takes up most of the space inside a computer.

As with all the other parts of a computer, the principles are simple but there are a lot of circuits all doing the same thing. Chapter 14 described the bistable, the basic block of every electronic memory system. Chapter 15 described the various types of memory, such as RAM, ROM and so on. (What do these letters stand for? If you do not remember, turn back to chapter 15.)

The use of bistables in a computer presents the same problems as using logic gates in a computer does. You have to be able to control the bistables by instructions from the microprocessor. It would be no use having each memory unit working separately from all the others.

For a controlled bistable, the bistable itself is the same, but the inputs are connected through a control gate. The control gate can be an AND gate in the same way as for the controlled logic gate in the ALU. Fig. 20.12 shows how this is done for an RS-bistable. (Refer back to chapter 14 if you do not know what an RS-bistable is.) Controlled bistables are known as *clocked bistables.* This is because the control signals for the bistable are usually the clocking pulses which control all the processes in the computer.

For the random access memory (RAM) of a computer, the bistables have to store whatever signal they are asked to remember. Neither the RS-bistable or the T-bistable will respond to a logic 0 input, so another type of bistable with a different input arrangement has to be used. This is the D-bistable or *data latch.* The data latch is like the clocked RS-bistable except that input B is connected to input A through an inverter. This makes the bistable output always change to be the same as the data signal at the input, whether that signal is logic 1 or logic 0. Of course, the D-bistable does not change until the control signal from the clock arrives. Fig. 20.13 shows the block diagram of a D-bistable.

It is the RAM that stores the data and programs on which the computer will work. A typical home computer might have anything between 20 K and 100 K of memory. A memory of 1 K is able to store 1024 bytes of data. A byte of data has eight bits in it. Each **bit** needs a separate D-type bistable to remember whether the bit is logic 1 or logic 0. This means

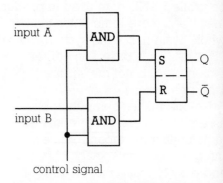

Fig. 20.12 The clocked RS-bistable. The bistable will not change over until a control signal is received. This control signal is usually the clocking pulse that controls all the processes in the computer

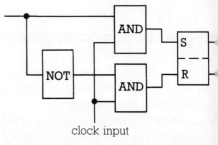

Fig. 20.13 The D-bistable. An inverter between the two inputs of an RS-bistable always makes the bistable change to give an output that is the same as the last input signal it received. For this reason this kind of bistable is often called a data latch.

that a home computer with 20 K of memory has 163 840 separate
bistables in its memory. It is not possible (yet) to get this many bistables
on one chip but chips with 8 K of memory (65 536 bits) are common.

How does the computer know which part of the memory has the piece
of information that it needs? The memory units are arranged so that each
one can have a separate *address* on the chip.

The word 'address' makes you think of streets and house numbers, but
there is no High Street in an electronic memory! The address is simply a
number. (It would be possible to give every house in a town a different
number and you would not then need street names in the addresses).
These numbers are, of course, binary numbers, so that the computer
does not have to search every address in turn until it finds the right one.
By sending an address code through a series of gates it is possible to go
straight to the required place in the memory. It is exactly the same
system as is used in the postal service. Your address has your house
number or name, the street or village name, a town name, the county,
and, if the letter is from overseas, the name of the country has been
added too. Until the letter arrives in your town no-one is interested
whether you live in High Street or Town Lane!

Most computers do not store information as separate bits but in bytes
(eight bits) or in *words* of 4, 16, or some other convenient number of bits.
(Byte is just the special name for the length of 'word' a computer is
designed to use. It is almost always eight bits.) This means that there
does not have to be so many addresses for the computer to cope with. If
a 65 536 bit memory is arranged to take bytes (8-bit words), then you
need only 8192 addresses. The number 8192 is 8 K in computer language.
Fig. 20.14 shows this diagrammatically.

How many wires would there be going to such an 8 K memory? The
decimal number 8191 is 1 111 111 111 111 in binary (remember 0 000 000
000 000 is the 8192nd address), so that thirteen wires would be needed to

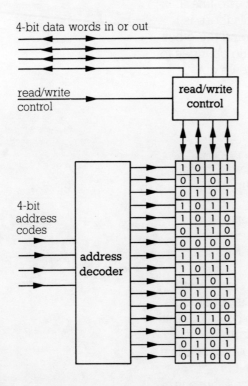

Fig. 20.14 The structure of a 64-bit RAM
arranged to store sixteen 4-bit words.

carry thirteen logic signals. That is not all. The data will be in bytes of eight bits, so that eight more wires would be needed for this, assuming that you need only one wire both to get a bit of data into the chip and to get it out again. The number of connections is obviously a problem! The next section explains some of the ways in which that problem is managed.

Buses and the read/write line

You cannot turn a microprocessor chip into a computer unless you can connect the chip into the rest of the system. The connections between the various parts of the system are parallel systems in which, typically, eight bits of data are transferred simultaneously down eight wires. Connections of this sort are called *buses*. The computer has to know whether the information going along a bus is data, or instructions, or just the address of a memory location. Address signals for memories have to be kept separate from the data and information, so that there will be two buses going to the memory – a *data bus* and an *address bus*.

There is another point that you must not forget about all these connections in a computer. It is usual to think only about the wire carrying the signal, but there have to be two wires to complete the circuit – one to carry the current to the device and the other to complete the circuit back to the source. The return path would be the same wire for all the channels. All the parts of the computer would be connected to a *common return* or earth connection, and this common return completes all the circuits.

Some of the buses have to carry signals both ways. You cannot feed information into a ROM (read-only memory), but information can go both to and from a RAM. How does the computer know which way the information is going? In addition to the buses there is one other connection between the various units. It is called the read/write line. It is arranged so that when the microprocessor is sending signals there is, say, a logic 1 on the read/write line, but if the signals are going the other way along the bus (to the microprocessor) the read/write line changes to logic 0. The microprocessor then knows that it is has to receive any signals there may be on the data bus concerned.

Tristate buffers

The read/write signal tells the parts of the computer which way signals are going, but how do we stop signals from getting mixed up on the buses?

For signals going from the bus **to** one of the blocks, the answer is simple. You have seen how AND gates can be used as switches for controlling signals in the processor. The same idea can be used in routing signals from a bus to the input of a block.

It is not quite so easy to route signals from the outputs of blocks onto the bus. Output circuits have a much lower resistance than input circuits. When you do not want the output from a particular block to go onto a bus you have to disconnect it altogether, to prevent it 'short-circuiting' the other signals. There are thus **three** possibilities: either the output sends a logic 0 down the bus; or it sends a logic 1 down the bus; or it is disconnected from the bus altogether. The block that gives all these is called a *tristate buffer*. Tristate means 'three possible states'.

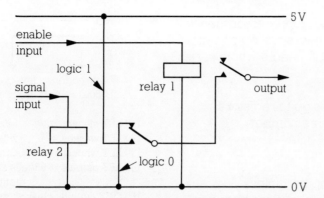

Fig. 20.15 The principle of the tristate buffer, demonstrated using two relays. Relay 1 connects the buffer output to the bus and relay 2 gives a logic 0 or logic 1 signal at the buffer output.

To get three possibilities in a digital circuit you must have two bits in the signal. For the tristate buffer, one of these bits is the signal from the output of the previous block. The other bit comes from the processor along the read/write line, and is called an *enable* signal. If that signal is logic 1, the output goes onto the bus, but if it is logic 0, the output is disconnected from the bus.

To see what the tristate buffer does think of it as two relays, as in fig. 20.15. The enable signal makes one of the relays connect the buffer's output to the contacts of the other relay. The input signal operates the second relay and sends logic 1 to the buffer output when the buffer input is logic 1. (Why are relays not suitable in practice?)

The electronic tristate buffer also has two parts. It has logic gates for the enable function, and electronic switches to switch the output either to logic 0 or to logic 1. Fig. 20.16 shows a circuit you can try out in the laboratory. It uses one n-p-n transistor and one p-n-p transistor as the switches, but in a tristate buffer chip CMOS devices are used.

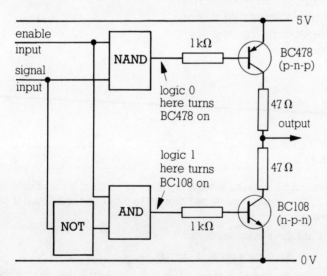

Fig. 20.16 Block diagram of a tristate buffer that you could build in the laboratory. Note that one of the transistors is a p-n-p transistor.

Programs

A computer system uses a microprocessor that has programmable logic gates, tristate buffers that can be controlled, and memories with lots of addresses. How does the computer know what to send where, and when? The answer is that the computer is given a program, which it will then follow. The program will tell the computer what to do, step by step.

The program is written in a computer language such as BASIC. Fig. 20.17 on the next page is a simple program written in BASIC for a ZX Spectrum computer. It operates a flashing sign. The top line comes on, the second line comes on and then the third line flashes on three times. The sequence then repeats.

By the time the instructions have reached the microprocessor they will have been converted into single steps which the microprocessor can actually do. For example, the PAUSE command will need a whole series of steps, such as:

set register A to 1100100 (i.e. 100 in binary)
send logic 1 to control gate so that timing pulses go to register B
find out if register A and register B have the same number
when they are the same, send logic 0 to control gate
read next line in the program
clear register A
clear register B

Each of these steps will have a series of machine codes. When the program is given to the computer these steps will be held in memory at specific addresses. When the program runs, the microprocessor will find the first address in the memory and read the instruction or data it finds there. At the next step it will go to the second address and repeat the procedure.

This process will go on until the microprocessor reaches an instruction telling it to stop. The microprocessor will do only what it is told to do. The memory will contain only a faithful list of the programmer's wishes. It is the programmer who chooses what to do.

How does the microprocessor know which step it is on and when to go on to the next one? Built into the system is a *clock*. The clock produces pulses at a steady rate – perhaps as many as 4 million pulses every second. Each pulse can be used by the computer as a control signal to the various gates which have to be operated.

To find out which step the microprocessor has got to, there is a counter which counts the number of clock pulses from when the program started. This is called a *program counter*. The microprocessor knows that it is at, say, step six. When the next clock pulse arrives the actions for step six take place and the program counter then moves on to step seven.

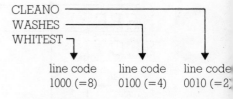

	line code	line code	line code
	1000 (=8)	0100 (=4)	0010 (=2)

110 **LET cleano = 2**/   tells the computer
120 **LET washes = 4**/   what it is
130 **LET whitest = 8**/   controlling
140 **LET outputs = 63**/tells address of
                                    output port
150 **OUT outputs, cleano**/top line turned on
160 **PAUSE 100**/wait two seconds
170 **OUT outputs, washes**/line two turned
                                    on
180 **PAUSE 100**
190 **FOR c = 1 TO 3**/count three flashes
200 **OUT outputs, whitest**/line three on
210 **PAUSE 30**
220 **OUT outputs, off**/end of flash
230 **PAUSE 20**
240 **NEXT c**/go to next flash
250 **GOTO 150**/go back to line 150 and do
                                    it all again

Fig. 20.17 Program for a flashing sign using BASIC suitable for a 'Spectrum' computer.

The complete computer

At this stage you should refer back to the diagram of the complete computer system shown at the beginning of the chapter. You will then see how the various separate parts fit together to make the complete system.

A computer is a complicated system, but always remember these three points:

- the only clever part of the computer is the programmer;
- you do not need to know how the system works to use it. You need to know only what inputs you must provide to get the outputs you want; and
- the circuits inside the computer are all simple logic systems you can understand.

SUMMARY 20C

A microprocessor contains several registers, in addition to the arithmetic and logic unit (ALU). The register connected directly to the output of the ALU is called the accumulator.

Registers are short-term memories.

Electronic memories use bistable circuits.

In a computer the bistables are clocked bistables so that they can be controlled by the clock signals of the computer.

RAM uses D-type bistables (data latches).

The read/write line of a computer controls whether information goes into memory or is collected from memory.

A tristate buffer is a controlled gate which passes a logic 0 or a logic 1 signal from a block to a bus, or disconnects the block from the bus altogether, as required.

All the processes within a computer are controlled by a program. The computer converts the language (e.g. BASIC) into machine codes which it can use.

A computer uses clock pulses and a program counter to make it go through the program one step at a time, in the right order.

G1 — Computing

G1.1 — Uses of computers

Computers are used for four different purposes:

- storage and retrieval of information;
  (Typical applications might be library records and hotel booking systems.)
- processing of information;
  (The most obvious application is the word processor, but machines used, for example, to plan integrated circuit layouts are also processing information.)
- computation;
  (Typical examples are statistical analysis and as a tool in scientific research. Calculators and simulators use the computer in this way too.)
- control.
  (Good examples are computer numerical controlled lathes, automatic production lines and robots.)

G1.2 — Micros, minis and mainframes

The size of a computer installation is sometimes described using one of the following terms: microcomputer, minicomputer and mainframe computer. The differences are not specific, but are related to the number of separate processes the central processing unit can carry out at the same time, the size of memory the computer has, and the range of peripheral equipment it can operate.

In general, home computers are microcomputers. They rarely have more than one microprocessor. At the other extreme, the large permanent installations used by large companies are mainframe computers. They are operated by specially-skilled staff and they usually have a number of stations connected to them where data can be input or obtained. In between these two extremes are the minicomputers which are used by many businesses and which are more powerful than home computers but otherwise similar to them in many ways.

G1.3 — Languages

Computer languages are series of words that can be used to tell a computer what to do. The computer itself uses number codes, called *machine codes*, for each and every step of every procedure, but these are extremely tedious to work out. The computer is therefore made to recognise the words and to convert them into the necessary machine code itself.

There are many languages in use. Different machines and different applications use different languages. Most home microcomputers use a form of the language called BASIC, but the BASIC for a BBC computer, for example, is not the same as the BASIC used for a Sinclair computer. Other common languages are FORTRAN, COBOL, PASCAL. In order to use any language on any computer, that computer has to have the correct *interpreter* to convert the language into its own machine codes.

Although computers can work at very high speeds, the time taken to convert instructions in a 'high-level' language into machine code can be important, because there are many steps involved. For control applications computers are often programmed in *assembly language*. Assembly language is a set of simple-to-remember codes which the microprocessor can interpret directly. An example of a typical code is LDA, which is an assembly language code meaning 'load data from memory into the accumulator'. There would be a binary number with this code to tell the microprocessor the memory address from which to get the information.

G1.4 — Hex

Hex is an abbreviation of 'hexadecimal'. Hexadecimal numbers are numbers to base 16. There are sixteen digits:

0, 1, 2, 3, 4, 5, 6, 7, 8, 9, A, B, C, D, E, F.

Digits A to F have the same value as decimal numbers 10 to 15.

Places values are powers of 16 instead of 2 as in binary or 10 as in decimal. The place values are therefore units, 16's, 256's, 4096's and so on. Thus, 222 in hex is equal to (working from the **right**) $(2 \times 1) + (2 \times 16) + (2 \times 256)$, which is 546 in decimal.

Hex is important as it is an easy way to deal with binary numbers. Counting from the least significant bit, each group of four binary digits can be replaced by one hex digit.

Exercises in finding the decimal values of hex numbers

Exercise 58 — Show that the decimal value of the hex number 3B6 is 950.

Exercise 59 — Find the decimal value of 10AF.

G1.5 — Converting between binary and hex

To convert binary to hex, mark off the binary number in groups of four bits starting from the LSB. Replace each group of four by its hex equivalent. The hex equivalents are given in table G.1.

To convert hex to binary, write down the binary equivalent of each hex digit in turn. The result is the binary number that has the same value as the hex number with which you started.

Table G.1   The binary and decimal equivalent values of hexadecimal numerals 1 to F

hex	binary	decimal	hex	binary	decimal	hex	binary	decimal
0	0000	0	6	0110	6	C	1100	12
1	0001	1	7	0111	7	D	1101	13
2	0010	2	8	1000	8	E	1110	14
3	0011	3	9	1001	9	F	1111	15
4	0100	4	A	1010	10			
5	0101	5	B	1011	11			

Examples of changing numbers from binary to hex and hex to binary

Example A: Change the binary number 10010011100 into hex.

The first step is to group the bits in fours from the **right** (LSB):

100 1001 1100

Now write the hex equivalent under each group (use table G.1):   4   9   C

(Note that if you find it difficult to remember that the 100, with only three bits, is the same as 0100 in the table, then where there are less than four bits you can make the number into a four-bit number by adding 0's to the **left** .)

binary 10010011100 is the same as hex 49C.

Example B: Change hex F2C into binary.

Write the hex numbers down and write the binary number for each hex digit underneath:

```
F    2    C
1111 0010 1100
```

Hex F2C is the same as binary 111100101100.

Exercise 60 — Show that A7D is the same as 101001111101.
Exercise 61 — What hex number has the same value as 1001001110?
Exercise 62 — Change ABCD into binary.

G2 — Computer systems

G2.1 — Computer architecture

The architecture of a computer is the way in which the various blocks in the computer are related together. The essential blocks in any computer are: a processor containing registers, an arithmetic and logic unit (ALU), and a program counter; a clock pulse producer; memory; and input and output ports to allow the computer to accept inputs and give outputs. The diagram in fig. G.1 shows how these blocks are interconnected. The connections shown as two parallel lines are buses containing a number of parallel signal lines. The arrows show the direction(s) in which signals can pass along the signal lines.

There must also be a power supply, but this has not been shown.

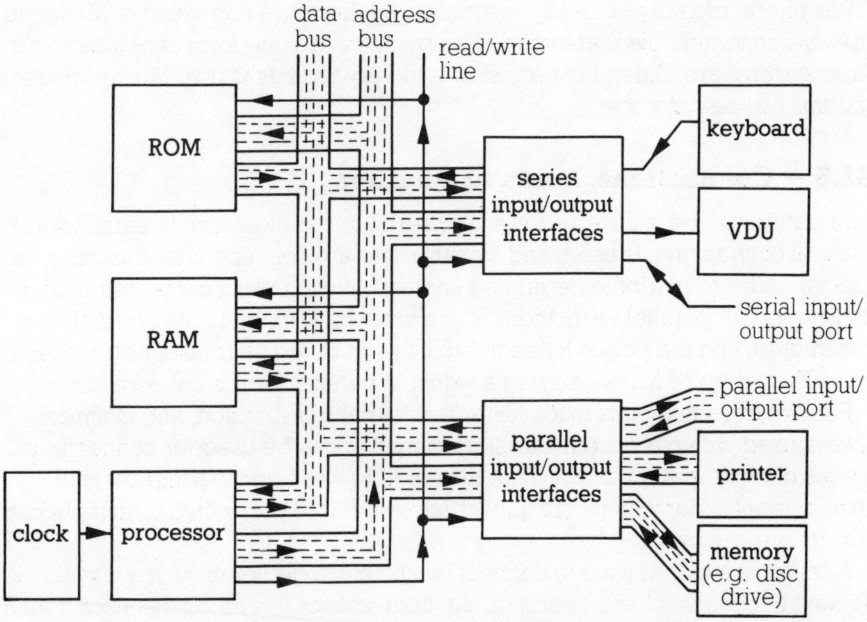

Fig. G.1 The architecture of a small computer. Larger computers have more than one central processor.

G2.2 — Input and output ports

The input and output ports are the interconnecting points between the computer and other equipment. Items of equipment which are part of the complete computer system but not part of the computer itself, such as the keyboard, are called *peripherals*. Most computers have input or output ports for a keyboard, display unit, printer, and tape or disc memory, as part of the computer circuits.

Many computers have a means by which other equipment (such as transducers) may be connected to the computer using a plug and socket. This port is connected to buffers, to protect the main computer circuits, and may include analogue-to-digital (A-to-D) converters.

Not all electronic equipment can be connected directly to the input or output port of a computer. Often it is necessary to use an interface unit to match the equipment to the computer. The type of interface used depends on what is being connected.

G2.3 — The central processing unit

The central processing unit (CPU) is the processor of the computer. A microprocessor is a processor made as a single integrated circuit.

The processor has three main parts. These are: the arithmetic and logic unit, which actually processes the signals; several registers, including an accumulator for storing data and instructions; and control systems, which include a program counter, flags for detecting when registers have reached certain values, and circuits for interpreting instruction codes.

G2.4 — Computer memory

A computer has three levels of memory. These are the registers within the central processing unit, the addressable memory within the computer system, and peripheral memories, such as disc units.

Registers are used by the ALU during the processing of information. The accumulator is the register containing the data which is being processed at that time.

Addressable memories are of two kinds, RAM and ROM. Data and instructions can be transferred to and from RAM, but can only be transferred from ROM to the processor. Information in RAM is described as volatile because it is lost when the power supply is switched off. ROM is non-volatile.

Peripheral memory is usually magnetic and therefore non-volatile. Magnetic tape and magnetic discs are used. 'Floppy discs' are one form of magnetic disc. Tape systems are cheap but very slow and very tedious to use. Most professional systems use disc storage.

G2.5 — Connections, buses and buffers

Information can be transferred in either serial or parallel form. In serial form, one channel of two wires is used, and signal pulses are sent one after the other, with special codes to mark the beginning and end of each word in the information transmitted. In parallel form, there is one wire for each bit in the words being transmitted, and the pulses for each bit of the word are all transmitted at the same time. The group of wires carrying a signal in parallel form is called a *bus*.

Parallel transmission is much faster than serial transmission, and is almost always used within a system. Serial transmission can be used for connecting pieces of equipment which are not designed to work on the same parallel arrangements. Many home computers have an RS232 port which is an input/output port for serial signals.

A buffer is a circuit used to connect two blocks together in such a way that they do not affect each other's operation. An opto-isolator is a block that uses light to make the connection when no electrical connection should be made between two systems.

A tristate buffer is a circuit used so that the same bus can be connected to the outputs from many blocks without them interfering with one another. It can connect an output to a bus, or it can isolate the bus from the output circuits. Which of these 'states' it is in depends on the control codes sent to it.

A modem is a device which converts serial signals into a form that can be sent over circuits designed for speech. The telephone system is used most frequently. There must be a modem at each end, one to modulate the signal on to a sound carrier and the other to demodulate it at the other end.

21 MAKING MEASUREMENTS

Electronics is about making real systems that will do things that people want them to do. So how do you find out whether a system is doing what it is meant to be doing? "Test it", you might well say. There are some systems where you can indeed get most of the answers that you want just by letting the system do what it is meant to do. Sooner or later you find that you cannot get all the information you need just by switching on and playing with the inputs or controls. You will need to make measurements.

Engineers sometimes say that "to measure is to know". You can get two kinds of knowledge from measurements. Measurements can answer the question "is this system doing what it is meant to do?".This is called *evaluation*. Or measurements can answer the question "why is this system not working properly?" This is called *fault-finding*.

What can we measure in electronics? There are ways of measuring anything that you might want to measure, but in practice there are five quantities which we often need to measure: voltage, current, frequency, waveshape and resistance. You do not need five different instruments to measure these five things. An electronics engineer will normally have two measuring instruments: a *multimeter* to measure voltage, current and resistance; and an *oscilloscope* to measure frequency and waveshape.

The engineer will probably have one other instrument as well. You cannot get outputs that you can measure, unless you have given the system the right input. To provide inputs for the systems being tested, the engineer will use a *signal generator*.

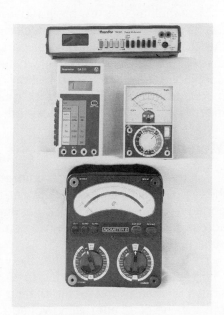

Fig. 21.1 Four typical multimeters. Two are digital meters and two are analogue meters. The larger meters are for bench use and the smaller ones are for use by service engineers. The larger analogue meter would be more accurate than the smaller one, but size does not affect the accuracy of digital meters.

The multimeter

Multimeters come in all sorts of shapes and sizes, and at various prices. Some are digital meters, giving their measurements as numbers displayed on three or four seven-segment displays. Some are analogue meters, with a scale and a needle that moves across that scale. All of them will measure voltage, current and resistance, and all of them have one or more switches to select the *range* to be used. Fig. 21.1 is a photograph of some typical multimeters.

Many people still call multimeters 'Avometers'. The first company to make and sell multimeters called themselves the AVO meter company. They got this name from Amps, Volts and Ohms. Current is measured in amps, voltage is measured in volts, and resistance is measured in ohms.

Table 21.1 is the table of ranges on one typical multimeter. There are 26 ranges in all. You may wonder why one range for voltage would not do. Suppose you need to measure a voltage that is about 1 volt, and all that you have is a meter with a 300 volt range. A 300 volt range means that when the needle is at the right-hand end of the scale, at *full-scale deflection* (FSD), the voltage at the terminals of the meter is 300 volts. For 1 volt, the needle will hardly move at all. You would be lucky to see the movement and you could not tell whether it was 0.9 volts or 1.1 volts. On the other hand, if you used a meter having a range with a FSD at 3 volts, it would be fine for measuring 1 volt, but using it to check your 9 volt battery would damage the meter.

Table 21.1 Ranges on the Avometer Model 73

d.c. voltage: (volts)	0.15, 0.75, 1.5, 3, 7.5, 15, 30, 75, 150, 300, 750 (at FSD)
a.c. voltage: (volts r.m.s.)	7.5, 15, 30, 75, 150, 300, 750 (at FSD)
d.c. current:	75 µA, 300 µA, 3 mA, 300 mA, 3 A (at FSD)
resistance:	1 Ω to 2 kΩ, 100 Ω to 200 kΩ, 10 kΩ to 20 MΩ

What do you do if you have no idea how large the voltage you are measuring might be? The answer is simple. When you use a multimeter you always start with the meter switched to a high range. You then switch to the lower ranges one after the other until you have a good deflection on the meter that you can then read off on the scale.

Most multimeters are provided with special *test probes* for connecting the meter to the circuit being tested. These are specially insulated so that they do not touch any other part of the circuit when a test is being made, and also to ensure that, whatever the voltage might be, the user does not get a shock. Good test probes have a clip or clamping mechanism so that they can be clipped onto the points being tested, leaving your hands free to make adjustments or to operate switches.

Measuring voltage

A voltage is always a **voltage difference between two points**. One of these points is often, but not always, the zero line of the system or the negative connection to the power supply. You always connect the meter **across** something, between two points where there is meant to be a voltage difference (see fig. 21.2).

You have to decide whether the voltage you are measuring is a steady (d.c.) voltage or an alternating (a.c.) voltage. Most meters have different scales for steady and for alternating voltages. The meter measures the r.m.s. value of an alternating voltage. (Refer back to chapter 13 if you do not remember about r.m.s. voltages.) If you do not know which type of voltage it is, use the a.c. volts scales first. A large a.c. voltage will give no deflection on the d.c. scales but it might damage the meter. A large d.c. voltage will give a deflection on the a.c. scales but the reading will not be the correct voltage.

For d.c. voltages the meter must be connected the right way round. One lead will be labelled + (or coloured red) and the other lead will be labelled − (or coloured black). The red lead goes to the positive side of the voltage difference. The black lead often, but not always, goes to the zero line because this is the most negative part of the circuit. If you connect the meter the wrong way round, the needle will try to move down below the zero on the scale. If you start by using the high-voltage range as advised in the previous paragraphs, then you will notice this backwards movement before it becomes powerful enough to harm the meter. If the needle does deflect backwards, change the leads round so that the red one goes to where the black one was connected, and vice versa.

When you connect a voltmeter to a circuit, it does not, in theory, affect the circuit in any way. In practice, it can make the voltage lower than it was before the meter was connected. This is more likely to happen where the voltages are low, where the resistances in the circuit are high, or when a cheap meter is being used. You can tell whether the effect is likely to be large or small by finding out the *sensitivity* of the meter. A poor meter will have a sensitivity of 1000 ohms per volt (or less). A good analogue meter will have a sensitivity of 20 000 ohms per volt or more. Some digital meters have sensitivities as high as 100 000 000 ohms per volt on some of their ranges.

Although an electronics engineer would use a multimeter for measuring voltages, there is nothing wrong in using a voltmeter that measures just one range of voltage, if it is the range you need. Many schools use voltmeters for science experiments and these will do just as well for electronics work.

If you do not know what voltage to expect, turn the multimeter to the highest range and then switch down through the ranges until you can measure the voltage.

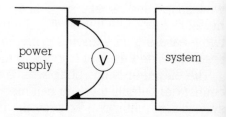

Fig. 21.2 You always connect a voltmeter across between the two points where you expect the voltage to be.

Measuring current

Electric current flows along a wire or along a resistor. To measure current you have to make a break in the circuit and connect the meter to the two sides of the break so that the current will flow through the meter as well.

Because of the need to disconnect something to measure the current, electronics engineers use voltage measurements wherever they can when tests are being made. However, the current from the power supply to the circuit board is often measured as it is easy to disconnect the lead to the power supply and connect a meter and extra lead so that the power-supply current goes through the meter (see fig. 21.3).

You may be surprised that a meter which measures voltage can be changed by turning a switch into a meter that will measure current. In fact, analogue meters measure current but they can be made to give measurements of voltage by connecting resistors to them. Digital meters measure voltage but they can be made to measure current by adding extra resistors to them. These extra resistors are inside the case and the switch determines which resistors are used. These resistors are often called *shunts*.

In electronics, the currents are usually quite small, perhaps a few milliamps. Table 21.2 lists some typical currents in electronic circuits. When you use a multimeter to measure current, **always** start with the meter switched to the **highest range**, in exactly the same way as for measuring voltages.

Currents can be a.c. or d.c. However, you rarely need to measure alternating currents. Almost all the currents in an electronic circuit are d.c., and the only a.c. currents will be those in the mains supply. In general, you should avoid making measurements on any part of the circuit that is directly connected to the mains. The risk of a dangerous shock is great, and the risk that the shock will make you jerk and knock your circuit board and the meter onto the floor is also great. Such mistakes can be costly. A good multimeter costs well over £100.

When you measure direct currents, the meter has to be connected the right way round. The current goes into the meter on the red (or +) lead and comes out of the meter on the black (or −) lead. If you were measuring the current from the power supply, the red lead goes to the power-supply positive terminal and the black lead of the meter goes to the **positive** connection on the circuit board.

As with voltmeters, there is nothing wrong with using an ordinary ammeter to measure currents, providing the ammeter has the range you require.

Measuring resistance

Most multimeters are made so that they can measure resistance as well as voltage and current. Resistance measurement is used in fault-finding.

Using a multimeter to measure resistance is different in many ways from using a multimeter to measure voltage and current. The most important differences are as follows.

- The scale for resistance (on an analogue meter) has the zero at the right-hand end instead of the left-hand end (see fig. 21.4).
- The divisions on the resistance scale are not equally spaced across the scale.
- All voltage and current measurements are made with the power-supply turned **on**. All resistance measurements are made with the power

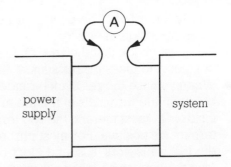

Fig. 21.3 To measure the current from the power supply one lead is disconnected and new connections are made so that the current goes through the meter.

Table 21.2 Typical currents in electronic circuits

A gate on a logic IC (TTL)	3 mA
Output of an op-amp	15 mA
Collector of a transistor (e.g. BC 108)	10 mA
Base of a transistor (e.g. BC108)	50 μA
LED	10 mA
7-segment LED display	20 mA
Relay (6 V type)	100 mA
Power amplifier for portable radio	100 mA

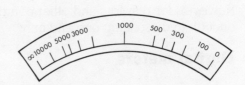

Fig. 21.4 A typical resistance scale for an analogue meter. The zero is at the right-hand end. The divisions are not equally spaced.

supply turned **off**. The power for resistance measurements comes from a battery inside the meter.

- You must check that the zero on the scale is correct every time you use the meter to measure resistance.
- When you use the resistance ranges there is a voltage difference between the terminals of the meter. This is produced by the battery inside. On most meters, the red terminal is **negative** and the black terminal is **positive**. For most purposes this does not matter, but with diodes, transistors, ICs, and electrolytic capacitors this does matter (see the section on testing diodes in chapter 8).
- A correctly-connected voltmeter or ammeter cannot damage the circuit being tested, but when measuring resistance the voltage of the battery in the meter can be too high for some components. For example, some multimeters use 9 volt batteries: TTL logic chips are damaged by voltages larger than 5.5 volts.

Before you connect a multimeter to measure a resistance, you have to:

1 choose the range you need to use;
2 check that, with nothing connected to the meter, the needle is at the left-hand end of the scale (0 on voltage and current scales, ∞ or infinity on the resistance scales);
3 touch the ends of the two test probes together to 'short' them. The needle should go to the right-hand end of the scale. There will be a control on the multimeter which you can adjust to get the needle exactly on the zero of the resistance ranges;
4 recheck step 3 every time you change the resistance range you are using on the meter.

You can use the resistance test for several applications. You can use it as a *continuity tester*, to see whether parts of a circuit that ought to be connected are really connected together. To do this, connect the two probes to the two points that should be connected. The needle will go over to the right-hand end (zero ohms) if the parts are connected.

You can also use the meter for checking the value of resistors. All you have to do is to connect the test probes to the two ends of the resistor. The number the needle points to on the scale is the value of the resistance.

Diodes and transistors can be checked too. A diode has very low resistance when connected one way round, but very high resistance when connected the other way round. In a transistor, the base and the emitter by themselves (with no connection to the collector) behave as a diode. Similarly, the base and the collector by themselves behave as a diode. If you test between the collector and the emitter there should be high resistance, whichever way round you connect the probes. (Can you explain why this is so?) Fig. 21.5 shows these tests diagrammatically.

When testing components you usually have to disconnect them from the circuit which contains them. This is because the rest of the circuit acts as another resistor connected in parallel with the one that you are testing. However, for resistors and other components with two leads it is good enough to disconnect one end only.

Digital meters

Digital meters are meters which have, instead of a scale and a needle that moves over the scale, a number display like that used on a calculator. The voltage (or current or resistance) is shown as numbers on the display. Inside the meter there are electronic circuits that measure

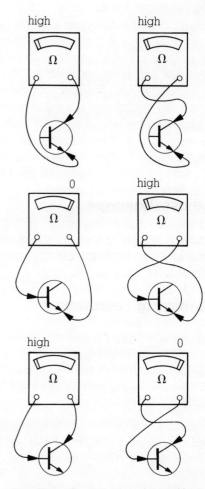

Fig. 21.5 Testing a transistor with an ohm-meter.

the voltage and compute the numbers to be shown on the display. Even though the circuit is quite complex, ICs have been made with the whole circuit on one chip. There is a block diagram of a digital meter given in chapter 12, on page 117. Digital multimeters are now so cheap that they are steadily replacing analogue meters.

Digital meters are used in the same way as analogue meters, but you have to remember two things. Firstly, because there is an electronic circuit inside the meter it needs a power supply and it has to be switched on (and switched off after use!). Secondly, although a digital meter shows three or four figures on the display this does not mean that it is more **accurate** than an analogue meter.

As an example of the accuracy problem suppose that a digital meter has been used to check a dry cell. The digital meter might show a reading of 1.559 volts. On a cheap digital meter, the real voltage could be anywhere between, say, 1.52 and 1.58 volts. An analogue meter that shows 1.55 volts has given just as accurate an answer.

Table 21.3 compares digital and analogue meters.

Table 21.3 A comparison of analogue and digital meters

Digital meters	Analogue meters
The basic system measures voltage	The basic system measures current
Current is measured by passing it through a standard resistor; the meter measures the voltage across it.	Voltage is measured using a resistor in series with the meter
The meter needs its own power supply	The meter needs no power supply
Resistance measurement uses the same system and scales as the other ranges	Resistance scales go from right to left, are not linear, and require a separate battery
Only gives steady readings if the voltage being measured is completely steady	The meter measures average voltage, even if the voltage is not steady
When used as a voltmeter, the meter resistance is very high and constant (typically 10 MΩ)	When used as a voltmeter, meter resistance depends on the range used (typically 1000 to 20 000 Ω per volt)

The oscilloscope

The oscilloscope is an instrument that looks like a small television set with a lot of controls on the front panel. It is, in fact, a voltmeter that can show you the changes in voltage of an alternating voltage during a short period of time. It is possible to use an oscilloscope as an ordinary voltmeter, but it takes a long time to make a measurement so that no experienced electronics engineer would use one instead of a multimeter. What an oscilloscope can do, which a multimeter cannot do, is show the shape of a wave or a pulse, and also measure its frequency. Its main use is in finding out what happens to a signal as it passes through a system.

When you are checking signals, you often need to know the waveshape of the signal at the input to a block **and** the waveshape at the output. To make this easy, many oscilloscopes are *dual-trace* oscilloscopes. (Dual-trace oscilloscopes are also known as *double-beam* oscilloscopes.) This means that inside the oscilloscope there are two sets of circuits, each of which can trace a waveshape on the screen. That means you can display both the input and the output on the same screen at the same time. It is then very easy to compare the two waveshapes.

The easiest way to understand what the oscilloscope is doing is to think of it as an electronic graph-drawing machine. In normal use, it plots voltage in the vertical direction (up and down). This is called the *y-direction* (just as it is in mathematics). The horizontal, or *x-direction* (side to side) is used for plotting time. The line on the screen thus shows how the voltage changes over a period of time (fig. 21.6).

The input to the oscilloscope from the system being tested is used to move the trace up and down. The horizontal movement of the trace is controlled from inside the instrument. The circuits which produce the horizontal timings are called the *time-base* of the oscilloscope. These circuits generate a ramp waveform (see chapter 12). When the ramp reaches its maximum and the trace is at the right-hand edge of the screen, the ramp-generator output switches back to its starting voltage very quickly and the spot producing the trace *flies back* to the beginning of the trace, to produce it all over again.

On a good oscilloscope it is possible to produce the complete trace from side to side in as little as one microsecond. The complete trace is drawn a million times every second. We say that the time-base frequency in this case is 1 megahertz. If the screen is 10 cm wide, then the spot which produces the trace is moving across the screen at a speed of 10 cm every microsecond, so that each centimetre division on the screen represents a period of one tenth of a microsecond.

You could not see anything moving at a speed of 10 cm every microsecond. That is the same as 360 000 kilometres per hour! This is why you do not see the spot of light which is producing the trace. You can see the trace because the time-base circuits are made so that they can be *synchronised* with the waveshape being investigated and so always trace the same path across the screen. (The trace also takes a little time to fade, which helps make it visible, too.)

Setting the oscilloscope controls

Most oscilloscopes have a lot of controls but if you remember what the oscilloscope is doing and use the controls in the right order, it is not difficult to use them properly. Fig. 21.7 is a block diagram of the oscilloscope, showing where the various controls operate in the system.

When you turn on an oscilloscope, the first thing to do is to set all the controls at the middle of their range. The trace does not appear immediately but takes between fifteen seconds and a minute to appear. It will probably be a horizontal line at this stage. As soon as the trace is visible, adjust the brightness control to give a trace which is bright enough to see easily. The spot is then focussed to give a sharp trace.

You can now connect the circuit that you want to test to the Y-input. For a dual-trace instrument there are two Y-inputs, labelled Y1 and Y2. Use only the Y1 input while you are setting up the instrument. Adjust the Y-gain (Y1 gain if it is dual-trace) so that the trace fills most of the screen.

The next step is to adjust the sweep frequency. You will probably want to have two complete waves displayed on the screen. If you have more than two complete waves then you need to increase the sweep frequency. If the trace is a jumble of horizontal lines or only part of a wave you need to reduce the sweep frequency. Fig. 21.8 shows these three conditions.

You should be able to get the trace steady on the screen. If it will not lock to a steady display, you will need to adjust the sync control to get it steady. Some oscilloscopes lock very easily, whereas others have to be

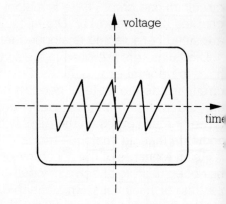

Fig. 21.6 The trace on an oscilloscope is like a graph. Voltage is the vertical axis and time is the horizontal axis.

Brightness, focus;
Input linked.
Gain and timebase;
Shifts and sync.

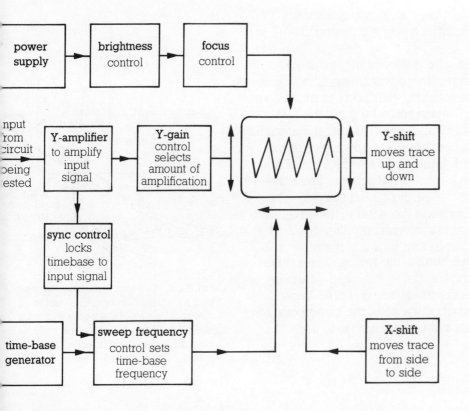

power supply	brightness control	focus control

input from circuit being tested

Y-amplifier to amplify input signal

Y-gain control selects amount of amplification

Y-shift moves trace up and down

sync control locks timebase to input signal

time-base generator

sweep frequency control sets time-base frequency

X-shift moves trace from side to side

Fig. 21.7 The block diagram of an oscilloscope, showing the function of the various controls.

adjusted quite carefully to get a steady trace. (On some oscilloscopes the sync control is called a *trigger* control.)

If you started with all the controls at their mid position, then the trace is probably fairly well centred on the screen. If it is not, or you need to move it to another part of the screen, the two shift controls will do this. The Y-shift moves the trace up and down; the X-shift moves it from side to side. There will be two Y-shift controls if you have a dual-trace oscilloscope. (How do you know which shift control is which?).

Fig. 21.8 The left-hand photograph shows a clear trace. The middle photograph is the same input but too high a sweep frequency, and the right hand photograph is the same input with too low a sweep frequency.

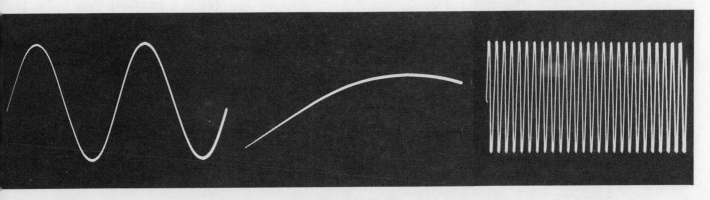

Using the oscilloscope to check a waveshape

If you have used the procedure given above, you should get a trace which shows the waveshape at the point which you are testing. There are a few things to remember.

The amplifiers in an oscilloscope can give a very high gain. If you touch the Y-input terminal with your finger, there will be enough signal picked up from the mains wiring in the room by your body to produce a trace of the 50 Hz mains on the screen. Unless you take care, the test leads will also pick up these signals from the mains. The test leads should be of *screened cable*. Screened cable has the insulated wire carrying the signal to the Y-amplifier in the middle; the other lead is a set of fine wires wrapped round the inner wire to form a metal screen. The screen is connected to the negative rail and to the earth point of the oscilloscope. Because the signal wire is inside the screen, the unwanted signals cannot get to it and so they do not reach the amplifiers. Fig. 21.9 shows the end of a piece of screened cable and how it is made.

Because one of the leads is a common return, the test leads must be connected the right way round to the circuit being checked. Make a habit of connecting the earth lead first. If you are using a dual-trace oscilloscope, the earth lead for both inputs must go to the same point on the circuit board. The earth leads often, but not always, go to the common (negative) line on the board.

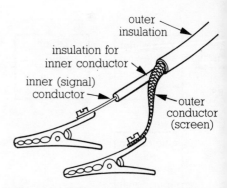

Fig. 21.9   The end of a screened test lead for an oscilloscope. The diagram shows clearly what a screened cable is like. Special test clips would usually be used instead of the crocodile clips shown here.

Specifications

At the beginning of this chapter the engineer's maxim that 'to measure is to know' was quoted. As part of your course you will probably do a project in which you have to produce a piece of equipment to do a particular task. How will you know if you have succeeded?

Every piece of engineering work starts with a *specification*. A specification is a statement of what a system has to do. It is concerned, not only with what the output will be, but also with the full range of conditions under which the system will work properly.

A good specification will state:

- what the inputs have to be and what output will result;
- how far the inputs can vary from the intended values and yet still give a correct output;
- within what range the output is to be expected to vary (e.g. what levels of distortion are to be expected);
- what power supplies are required, how much the voltage can vary and how much power the system uses;
- what the various controls do and what the range of control is (i.e. what effect a control has at minimum and maximum settings);
- limits on size, weight, cost, insulation, effect of weather or other outside conditions, colour, strength, method of fixing, or anything else of a non-electronic nature which is important to the functioning of the system.

When a system has been completed, it is checked; measurements will be made to test each point in the specification.

Table 21.4 is an example of a real specification. It is the specification for an LED digital meter. (Because it is a fairly simple unit the specification is shorter than one for, say, a radio or a hi-fi system.) This specification tells you what the meter is meant to do (measure voltages between −2 volts and +2 volts) and what the output will be (a red

display of four digits showing up to 1999). The accuracy is stated, and it should be tested, not just at 1.999 volts, but at several values between −2 and +2 volts, including zero. The power supply is stated, and the meter would be tested at 4.75 volts and at 5.25 volts.

Table 21.4 Specification of the Farnell type DPM2A LED digital meter

Range: nominal	± 2 V FSD ('nominal' means the stated range of the meter)
actual range displayed	± 1.999 V at FSD
Accuracy	± 0.05% of FSD, at 23 °C, to ± 1 digit in the display
Reading rate	4 per second
Display	red 4-digit LED display, 10.92 mm character height; anti-glare filter
Power supply: voltage	5 V ± 0.25 V
current	150 mA typical

If you were making and selling these meters you would need to find out how to test each of these statements for all your instruments. It is no use connecting one to a power supply, connecting a battery across its input and saying "it must be all right − the reading is about 1.55 volts".

All electronic systems are made to do a particular job. When you make a system you should decide what it is meant to do before you start, and keep this in mind throughout the design stages. Test each block or section in the system to make sure that it is functioning correctly. Then, at the end, check that the system does do what it is meant to do, safely, in every respect and under all likely conditions. That is what measuring in electronics is really about.

APPENDIX
TEACHERS' NOTES ON USING THE SYSTEMS APPROACH IN THE CLASSROOM

The first part of this book describes the nature of systems and how systems ideas can be applied to electronics. How can these ideas be used in the classroom? Where in the course should they be introduced? How can the basic theory of the subject be incorporated with the work on systems? The purpose of this Appendix is to describe the classroom strategies which can be successfully used to exploit systems ideas.

'Systems' is not just another piece of theory to be tacked on at the end of an otherwise traditional course in electronics. It implies a wholly different approach. The power of the systems approach is that it unifies the subject, motivates the students, and almost makes a virtue out of the extreme complexity of modern electronic devices.

As a teacher, what do you want your students to gain from your course in electronics? We are talking about a first introduction to the subject, so that there is no suggestion that they will be able to design mainframe computers or build approach radars for airports. However, it is a reasonable guess that you expect the students, at the end of the course, to be able to understand simple circuits, to construct simple circuits, to do elementary calculations (such as using the Ohm's law equation), to have basic ideas about circuit design and to be able to design simple systems.

Electronics teaching has traditionally sought to achieve these five objectives, and it has approached them in the order given in the last paragraph. The result has been that few have got beyond the third objective and many less numerate students have failed to master even the simplest of calculations. Even if they reach the stage of designing simple systems this work comes right at the end of the course and the systems they can cope with are often only the extremely simple ones. The motivation that persuaded the student to start the course was the possibility of actually making some of the exciting systems that are the focus of modern electronics. If their motivation lasted to the end of the course and, in addition, they were able to master the intervening stages, they will still finish the course frustrated because the extent of their work on systems design is minimal. Hopefully this does not describe your own teaching, but you will know of many places where it is often too accurate a description of what happens.

So how can adding some work on systems change all this? How is it possible to do all the difficult things, like designing systems, without first mastering the basic things, like simple calculations?

How do children master high technology?

Think back to when you learnt to drive a car. A car is an object which, for most purposes, can be treated as a point mass operating on a low friction surface and propelled by a heat engine. However, mastery of the laws of Newton and the principles of thermodynamics are not prerequisites either for taking or for passing the driving test. The roads would possibly be a lot safer if they were requirements, but it is unlikely that the few licensed drivers would be any better at their skill as a result of their study. There is no evidence that physics graduates are any better at passing the driving test than anyone else.

To learn to drive, you first spent some time learning how to make the car go where you wanted to go. You then mastered the control of the clutch and gears so that it moved smoothly, and finally you learnt, by experience, how to apply these skills in heavy traffic. Knowing what happens when you depress the clutch pedal helps a little in understanding why it behaves as it does, but it is little protection from 'kangaroo petrol' for even the cleverest learner driver. It is later, perhaps only when you have a car of your own, that you learn how to put petrol in, check the oil, and maybe undertake routine servicing. A few motorists attempt major repairs, and the occasional enthusiast will know enough to modify the car. None of these additional skills make you any better at using this piece of high technology. They are added as required, by those who wish to acquire them, to increase the scope of what can be achieved. The car accessory shops in every High Street are ample evidence that these extra skills are the product of motivation and enthusiasm, rather than of academic ability.

In real life, electronics is no different. Many three-year olds have mastered the basic skills of using complex electronic equipment. Watch a toddler select the programme on a television, turn up the volume, or get an adult to plug the set into the mains if it will not work. To set a complex piece of electronics like this into operation, all a child needs to know is what the system is supposed to do, and what to supply to the system to make it do it.

That this is not the extent of the electronics that we hope to teach is self evident. However, it is a golden rule of teaching that you start where the students are when they come to you, and you seek to build on the experience and interests that they already have. Children come to the course knowing that systems have inputs, controls and outputs, and that electronics is a powerful tool for doing clever things, although they may not use these words to describe their knowledge. The skill of the professional teacher is to start from this point.

The starting point

The systems approach to electronics starts with systems. Not only does it start with systems, but the route through the rest of the required concepts, skills and knowledge is based on that starting point. What is being proposed in this approach is that, compared with traditional approaches, the order in which topics are covered, in which knowledge is incorporated and in which skills are mastered is reversed.

There are many areas of human endeavour where the idea of starting at the other end would be incredible. You could not make much of the Theory of Relativity without some basic understanding of Newtonian mechanics, because the concepts of relativity build on the concepts of Newtonian mechanics.

You could not ask a student to paint a masterpiece before that student has developed, or you have taught, the basic skills of manipulating paint on canvas with a brush, because the masterpiece is an extension of these basic skills.

Technology is different. Although the design of technological artefacts depends heavily on the principles of science, the user (and even the designer) does not need to master these principles. Electrical engineers use devices rather than enquiring into their inner circuit design. Transistors work very well and they are manufactured in millions, even though physicists have yet to perfect their theories as to how a transistor operates. Electronic devices are treated as systems and the important knowledge is what you have to know in order to use them.

So far, it sounds perhaps as though only the last of the objectives (listed earlier) is of interest. This is not so. The electrical engineer cannot use devices without knowing something about circuits and how to connect the devices into circuits. Similarly, the student needs to know not only what the devices will do, but also how to connect them into circuits.

The systems approach embraces all five of the objectives listed earlier. One of the essential skills of the teacher is to select the order in which material is presented to the students so that the degree of complexity increases in step with the students' increasing ability **and** to present the range of necessary experiences, skills and concepts which are the purpose of the course. In many traditional subjects (physics being a good example) the approach and the order of the topics are both prescribed by many years' experience of the subject as it has been taught in school, but it is important not to fall into the trap of assuming that the 'correct' order for science is necessarily the 'correct' order for electronics. Indeed, experience of using the systems approach for electronics in the classroom has shown that deviating from conventional wisdom produces remarkable results. We shall consider the order in which topics can build one from the other, starting with complete systems. However, before doing so, we shall consider how complete systems can be used as a starting point without encountering paralysing gaps in a student's knowledge and experience.

Introducing systems without Ohm's Law

It will be evident from the students' text that the use of 'building blocks' — manufactured circuit blocks with a single specified function — is a major part of the initial approach. The problem that many teachers have encountered in starting with basic circuits and working towards more complex systems was that students could not construct systems fast enough and reliably enough to understand what the system was meant to do. They got lost in problems such as which leg of a particular type of transistor is the base and 'please, sir, I've done what you said and it doesn't work'. The intention of the building blocks is to take all these problems away in the initial stages and to allow the student to concentrate on the function of the system and on what the parts of the system are doing to the signals as they pass through. There is nothing in the nature of the blocks that the student will not be able to understand. However, the necessary understanding of what is going on within each block is reserved for later.

Each block has a single circuit function. It might be an inverting amplifier, or an OR gate, or a voltage divider. The important feature is that the blocks can be connected together easily and quickly on the boards, without fear of error, so that not only the signal but also the power supplies are provided to each block without using flying leads. Such boards can easily be constructed in school if time is available, but it is recognised that this can be a major

Examples of 'building block' boards for teaching electronics using the systems approach, manufactured by E & L Instruments Ltd (right) and Unilab (left)

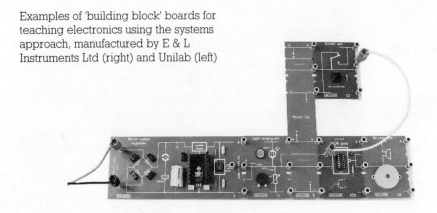
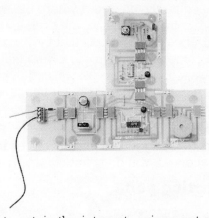

task. An alternative strategy is to purchase suitable boards from equipment suppliers. The photograph below shows two examples of the type of boards that are currently available.

The advantage of using boards of this type is that by the end of the first lesson with a new group of students all doing electronics for the first time, each student can have constructed and tested several electronic systems. All of the students will have convinced themselves that they can make interesting electronic systems that will actually do things for them. The biggest problem is getting the students to go away at the end of the lesson!

Although it is not recommended, it is feasible to invite the students to connect any block to any other block to see what happens, as the blocks are (virtually) childproof so long as the power supply is correctly connected and the boards are plugged into one another in the approved manner. Rather than recommend such unbridled learning, it is strongly advised that, without apparently removing the freedom of enquiry, some deliberate structure and direction is adopted. The simple burglar alarm, so popular as an application of basic transistor circuits, can be used here to good effect. A system that will respond to an intruder requires four blocks; a power supply, an input transducer, a switch or comparator, and an output device. The input and output devices can both be varied; the advantage of using a comparator can be checked; the effect of inverting the input signal can be tried; the function of a latch can be determined; and the combination of signals from two input transducers can be investigated. Other examples will no doubt come to mind, and the first group of work sheets in the practical book (which is the companion to this book) have the same intention. Additional material for this stage of the course will be found in 'Electronics Through Systems' by Mike Geddes, published by Peter Peregrinus.

The students will enjoy this 'electronic Lego' stage, and the movement on to other aspects of the course

must seek to retain the interest, enjoyment and motivation that this introduction will have engendered. The blocks can serve a variety of purposes throughout the course. It is very desirable that they should do so, because the link with the initial introduction will be maintained and, much more importantly, the emphasis on understanding electronics by identifying the system function of the various blocks will be reinforced. Consequently, the route through the remainder of an introductory syllabus in electronics is governed by the order in which the various ideas are required so as to extend the understanding of systems. The next section outlines a teaching order, and subsequent sections discuss some of the topics and their treatment in more detail.

Introducing other topics

The development of ideas concentrates first on the signal passing from stage to stage. It then considers the additional functional elements needed in system turning subsequently to discrete components, constructional techniques, power supplies, and final a broader look at electronics as it is used in real life. Subject topics, such as voltage and transistor circuit configurations, are woven into this progression.

All the simple circuit blocks operate on voltage signals. It is therefore easy to track a signal through system using a voltmeter. This allows, as the first step, the introduction of ideas of voltage difference, of digital and analogue signals, and of fault-finding. is particularly useful to introduce fault-finding at this stage because it reduces the dependence of studen on that non-productive aspect of teachers' attention − making equipment operate when the student is unable to get results!

A closer look at input and output transducers allows three extensions of the theme: into logic, as a means of combining input signals; into voltage amplification, in order to cope with signals that are too small; and into ideas of power, in order to cope with output transducers.

Ideas of power lead naturally to a treatment of current and conduction. It is not necessary to introduce resistance at the same time; ideas about resistance can come in any one of several places in this part of the course. Resistors will be encountered in voltage divider networks (such as the load resistor for an LDR), and in operational amplifier networks.

Voltage amplification is carried out by operational amplifiers. It is suggested that, if your examination syllabus allows it, you do not attempt to deal with transistor voltage-amplifier circuits at all. The reasons for this are that the design parameters of such circuits are far more complicated than simple analysis implies and that, in any case, no-one working in the field of electronics would now use a transistor amplifier for voltage amplification in preference to an operational amplifier. Details of transistor voltage amplifiers are included in this book but the section can readily be omitted!

Introducing the operational amplifier is a good place at which to introduce ideas of resistance or at least the necessary familiarity with resistors, including colour codes, choice of components, and ratings.

Whilst the emphasis throughout is on using circuit blocks and integrated circuits without worrying about how each unit carries out its function, it is important that students have some idea of basic circuit design. The transistor used as a switch or as a current amplifier can provide this, and having considered the operational amplifier in conjunction with its network of resistors, the step to transistor networks is not too large. It is suggested that simple diode-transistor logic gates are the best choice for this, because they carry out a useful function, and they provide the right size of task for introducing construction techniques. They also introduce the diode.

Meeting the diode for the first time as a steering device, rather than in conjunction with a.c. and rectification, helps to break the new material into manageable parcels. When power supplies are used as the medium for introducing the diode the student is also meeting the transformer, a bridge network, the capacitor, and a.c. — all at the same time.

The capacitor can be introduced during the construction stage too. Construction should not be limited to transistor circuits, and a simple timer using a 555 chip is a good way of introducing both the capacitor and constructional work with integrated circuits. Once again, the reason for choosing this particular circuit is that it does something interesting.

There are two areas of basic ideas left: power supplies, and systems involving pulses, pulse generators and counters. The way is open to treat both these areas of basic ideas in either order.

In considering power supplies there is a good opportunity to discuss safety practices with the students. Whilst it is assumed that safety procedures and good practice will have been introduced from the beginning, at some stage these ideas need to be drawn together and the student needs to be made aware of the particular dangers of mains electricity.

Electrical measurement has been implicit from an early stage, when the voltmeter was introduced for tracing signals. It is assumed that the ohm-meter would be introduced when resistors are being discussed. The oscilloscope should also find a place in the course, and, clearly, both power supplies and pulse circuits are ideal topics for the inclusion of this instrument. Although it is not included in the main text, students should be made aware of the practical problems arising from the reverse polarity at the terminals of some multimeters when they are switched to the resistance ranges. This is a practical point of some importance, as some chips, LEDs and even capacitors could be damaged by the voltage differences at the terminals of some multimeters under these conditions.

The social implications of electronics

It is hoped that the way in which electronics is applied in the real world will not be left to the end of the course. Approaching electronics through systems provides an abundance of opportunities to relate the classroom systems to real applications. However, students will not be ready to look at either communication systems or computing until the latter part of the scheme. It is suggested that the introduction of these two areas should be done in such a way that the electronics and the applications are integrated and interwoven. The reason for including the social implications of electronics in the scheme is to demonstrate that what the student is learning is relevant to real life, and to separate out this topic at the end of the course largely defeats the intention.

Practical work

Some reference has been made to construction but little comment has been made about other forms of practical work. Electronics is a practical subject, and it is assumed that practical exercises will be included throughout the course. Although the companion practical book is a separate publication the intention is that the suggestions and exercises included in that book will be integrated with the topics included in the main text of this book.

The other aspect of practical work in most courses is a project. At first sight the right place for a project might seem to be at the end of the course, but there is no reason to make such an assumption. As the development has been from complete systems through functional blocks to discrete components, this matches the development of ideas implicit in successful project work. It is suggested, therefore, that the project is started fairly early in the course and allowed to progress side by side with the other elements.

The following sections deal in more detail with certain topics referred to earlier.

Voltage difference

Confusion between voltage and current is one of the most common faults in students' understanding of electrical concepts, a fault which extends to many adults too. Introducing the concept of voltage in terms of signals should help in some ways, because it introduces the idea outside the context of Ohm's law and therefore separates ideas of voltage and ideas of current more firmly than in traditional teaching approaches. However, treating voltage as a parameter of a signal assumes implicitly that the negative supply line is the zero reference point. (The assumption is very often made in traditional approaches too. When did you last see a battery labelled + on one terminal and −1.5 V on the other?). Students do not realise that voltage does not exist at a point but only exists between two points. In this book the term 'voltage' is not generally used; the term 'voltage difference' has been used instead. The purpose of this is to emphasise that voltage only exists between two points, and it is suggested that in adopting the systems approach it would be wise for teachers to adopt this terminology too and to make it quite clear that the negative rail is an arbitrary reference line used for convenience.

The need to do this is emphasised by the fact that one of the manufacturers of circuit boards has employed operational amplifiers which will work on very low supply voltages and has therefore designed the circuits for +2.5 V/0/−2.5 V operation. The −2.5 V supply is the zero rail of the power supply and the +2.5 V supply is the 5 V rail of the power supply. This makes the whole system operate on a 5 V power supply. The arrangement works well electrically, and causes no bar to students' understanding, providing they have not acquired a sloppy, half-understanding of voltage difference.

Fault-finding

Fault-finding on a circuit constructed of discrete components can be a nightmare, as anyone will know who has tried to find out why a gadget constructed from the latest edition of 'New Electronic Constructors Monthly' does not work. The process is, nevertheless, an important aspect of electronics, and an important training in logical thinking. Using prefabricated circuit blocks takes away the need for tracing circuits, as the input and output signals come to clearly defined terminals on the connectors between the blocks. Knowing what the function of the block should be, it is an easy task to find out whether a particular block is functioning, independent of the rest of the system. Students thus receive an introduction to fault-finding at a level which they can handle.

It is not suggested that students should be given deliberately faulty units to identify. (It will happen soon enough that they have to find a genuinely faulty block!) Students should be encouraged to monitor the signals and supply voltages between the blocks in their systems in both operated and non-operated conditions, so that they learn by experience what each block should do to the signals it receives. It will not be long before many of the students set up systems which do not do what they intended. At that stage they should be encouraged to use their experience of monitoring signals to find out where the unexpected occurs. They will soon learn that, very often, the answer is to put an inverter in the system at the appropriate point, but this is just as valid a fault-finding process as identifying a faulty component (and a little easier!). The cleverer aspects of fault-finding can come later.

Power

In a systems-based approach, power becomes a more important concept than it is in a more traditional approach. Systems have to fulfil a function. They will not do this if the power supplied is less than the power required. This is, of course, a fundamental law of nature applicable to all systems, electronic and non-electronic alike. There is no harm in the student realising this.

The approach adopted in this text is to establish the requirements of output devices, particularly those which operate as actuators rather than information displays, and to match the devices to the systems by arranging that the systems provide the necessary power. Because the number of functional blocks is finite, the choice of ways of matching is also finite, so the task is easy. However, it is important that, because it is easy, teachers do not gloss over this part of the process and leave their students not realising fully what they are doing.

While on the subject of power, it is important that students should be aware of the difference between energy and power, and realise that the power supply is really an energy source. The term 'power supply' is so ingrained in the jargon of electronics that it is impossible to change it, but we should not leave students unaware of the confusion of ideas that is implicit in this misnomer.

Voltage amplification

Reference has already been made to some of the reasons for specifying operational amplifiers for this section of the course, and to those reasons already given can be added the advantage of being able to specify the gain of the system within a close tolerance. However, there are hidden problems to the introduction of ideas of amplification if the ideas are to be developed in a realistic context. The problems are twofold.

One area of difficulty is that most simple systems are digital and the majority of analogue systems are more complex than they appear. Thus, in most of the systems the students will meet, the output from a transducer will be converted into a digital signal as soon as possible.

The second area of difficulty is that, although many transducers give small enough signals to warrant amplification, the characteristic of many transducers is such that you do not get zero output for zero input. With experience, the idea of amplifying the change in voltage level is not difficult to master, but it is an added complication when you are trying to convince the student that the gain of a system is, say, ten and hence the output signal is ten times the input signal. For demonstration of the behaviour of an amplifier, the input transducer should therefore be one that generates an e.m.f. proportional to the input imposed on the transducer.

There are thus few suitable transducers. The thermocouple and the Hall probe are the only feasible ones at this level. Of these, the thermocouple is not very suitable because the e.m.f. is low, the input resistance is very low, the temperature ranges used in elementary work are large, and serious electronic engineers would not use a simple operational amplifier with a thermocouple as they would expect to employ a compensated bridge network and pick up the out-of-balance signal.

The Hall probe is a good alternative. Semiconductor probes are available which give signals up to 0.5 volt, and which are easy to use with an operational amplifier. The size of the signal is such that amplification is necessary before converting the signal to a digital signal, but the gain needed is relatively small, allowing the use of normal voltmeters to monitor what the amplifier is doing. This arrangement is featured in the main text.

Transistors

No attempt has been made to include a treatment of the semiconductor physics of the transistor. This is thought to be neither relevant to a modern systems-based approach to electronics nor appropriate at this level. The physics of the transistor is about as relevant to electronics as the materials science of nuts and bolts is to motor engineering – and is about as complex. The transistor is fast becoming obsolescent as a discrete component, and an understanding of how transistor elements are employed in integrated circuits is far beyond this level of electronics. It might be added that the concept of 'holes' (much beloved of 'simple' explanations of the transistor) may be useful for those who have some understanding of electronics but it is just so much gobbledegook to the student meeting the transistor for the first time. Teach the physics of the transistor to a GCSE class and then test their understanding in the following lesson if you doubt this!

The transistor does provide two useful educational bridges in an elementary course. One is to supply the link between discrete components and integrated circuits, and the other is to provide a useful active device for a simple introduction to constructional work. Indeed, it is suggested that these two objectives should be combined. The steps in this stage in the development are as follows.

The transistor can be used as a current amplifier, and this is probably the best way to introduce it. It can be used as a driver for an output transducer. For example, the optical transmission system described in chapter 17 (page 162) could be enhanced if a more powerful light source could be used. An 0.5 watt bulb (preferably mounted in a reflector from a torch) can be driven from an operational amplifier, using a transistor such as 2N3053 as a current amplifier, and its behaviour in such an arrangement can be monitored using standard ammeters.

One emphasis arising from the systems approach is the importance of the transfer characteristic of the system, and there is no harm in spending a little time in establishing what the transfer characteristic is. Having done this, the effect of adding series resistance in the input circuit and load resistance in the output circuit can be investigated, **but without** referring to this as a voltage amplifier. The objective is to show the switching action of a transistor in series with a load resistor.

Once the switching action has been established, logic gate circuits can be considered and assembled. The assembly can provide a good exercise in soldering. A good way to do this is to use 'blob boards' (printed circuit boards with solder pads on them) and to solder the components on the copper side of the board.

Students are often expected to be able to do some basic calculations on the transistor switch circuit, and this is a good context in which to consider the effects of component tolerances. Using a robust transistor (such as 2N3053) and a 5 volt power supply, the risk of damage to components is small, so students can be given assignments containing an element of problem-solving (e.g. find the input resistor required to ensure that a 3.5 volt 0.3 amp bulb can be operated, without exceeding its rating, from an input signal of 5 volts).

Conclusion

It will be evident that the systems approach to electronics is more than the inclusion of a few ideas about 'black boxes'. It is an entire teaching approach, and requires an inversion of the approach typically used in science subjects. The starting point is not basic principles, but real applications of electronics. The direction of development is not from principles to their applications, but from real applications towards the principles necessary to understand these applications. The approach is from the outside working inwards, rather than from the central concepts working outwards. The students' text has been written with this teaching approach at its heart. Call it the 'onion' philosophy: you can peel an onion layer by layer; this is a far less messy way of cutting up an onion than starting in the middle, but the onion will taste the same either way. However, there will be far fewer tears if you start at the outside!

ANSWERS TO QUESTIONS

Chapter 1

1 Is this the text book? How do I open it? Is it the right way up? How do I find the index? Is this the index? Where is (say) J .. etc?

2 Cooker: power input is mains supply; signal input is turning on the switch; control input is setting of dials and also the thermostat; output is appropriate temperature in the oven. The food is nothing to do with the system, because the cooker will still work if there is no food there!

3 Signal to system to announce visitor's presence.

4 See text.

5 A system to provide a measured quantity of water, quickly, on demand.

Chapter 2

6 Aerial: from waves received from transmitter.
Loudspeaker: from power supply.

7 Start timing/stop timing is a switch; the timing mechanism is the clockwork cogs (the escapement); the indicator is the hands of the watch (and power = spring).

8 All this subsystem has to do is to send a signal to unlatch the latch and turn the system off.

9 The number display acts as an indicator.

10 The pulse generator must produce 100 pulses per second.

11 Back to front (e.g. 52 looks like 25).

Chapter 3

12 Your diagram should show the same four diagrams but with the second lamp 'on' and the other three lamps 'off'.

13 The meter needle would (try to) move off the scale to the left.

14 You need: a sensor to check when the car is fully in the garage; another to sense when it is fully out of the garage (beyond the magnetic sensor); a motor to close the door; suitable electronics and a relay to operate the motor.

15 If the power supply is not working, nothing else will work.

16 If there is no fault the voltmeter reads the same each time (5 V).

17 The voltmeter will read 0 V on the second and third test if the positive line is not connected between the power supply and the first block. If the fault is between the blocks, the third reading will be 0 V.

18 These tests will not show a fault in the negative power line connections.

19 The light transducer D.

20 Connect a voltmeter with + to the control input and − to the negative of the power supply. Varying the control gives voltmeter readings varying between 0 and 5 V.

21 See text following this question.

22 3 V.

Chapter 4

23 Stop when hand is near the cup.

24 Move to touch cup. Stop. Close fingers around cup. Stop. Raise cup vertically. Stop at correct height. Move cup towards mouth. Stop when rim touches lips. Open mouth. Tip cup until liquid just flows over the rim. Stop. Drink. If too much liquid tip back; if too little tip forward until right. Stop.

25 For NAND, both parents must be there to stop you going out but, for NOR, if either parent is there (or both) you cannot go out.

26 Sensor B gives 0 when the box is too full, so column B says the box is too full but column C tells you it is not filled.

27 Input connected to any one of NOR gate inputs.

28 OR: Inputs to NOR gate; output inverted (by another NOR gate as above).
AND: Each input inverted; inverted inputs to NOR gate.
NAND: Each input inverted; inverted inputs to NOR gate; NOR output to another inverter.

29 In line 4, Y = 1 when A = 0, B = 1, C = 1. Thus, NOT A = 1 AND B = 1 AND C = 1 gives Y = 1. Invert line A, then connect NOT A, B, and C, to an AND gate. The output is Y.

30 For Z = 1 you need line 2 or line 5 or line 6.
To get line 2 connect NOT A, NOT B and C to an AND gate.
To get line 5 connect A, NOT B and NOT C to an AND gate.
To get line 6 connect A, NOT B, and C to an AND gate.
The ouputs of the three AND gates go to an OR gate.

Chapter 5

31 To prevent too much current passing through the probe.

Chapter 6

32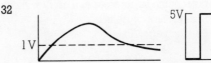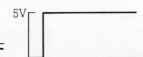

33 A TPP automatically resets itself after a set time.

34 A diode, either in parallel with the resistor 'pointing' upwards, or between the capacitor and the output, 'pointing' towards the output (see chapter 8).

35 The tuner on page 8, chapter 2. A filter allows through only the signal you want, but the two types of filter are different in the ways they operate.

36 Any alarm system; any control system where the system must carry on operating even if the button is released; any display system where the display must stay still long enough to be read, even if the system is changing rapidly; the alarm of an electronic alarm clock.

37 Insert an inverter on either side of the TPP.

38 See pages 45−46.

39 It triggers on a negative-edge trigger and produces an inverted output.

40 The trigger starts the trace at the same place on the wave every time.

41 See fig. 6.3.

42 Invert it: the mark-space ratio is 1/10 (0.1).

43 Peak-to-peak = 20 V; r.m.s. = 7 V approximately.

44

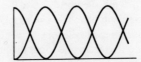

45 180° (see pages 40–41).

Chapter 7

46 Too expensive.

47 2.43 V.

48 Shallower (at 5 V, the current is 2.5 mA).

49 Lower (see page 65).

50 $R = \dfrac{1500 \times 3300}{1500 + 3300} = \dfrac{4\,950\,000}{4800} = 1030\ \Omega$

Chapter 8

51 Battery dud, lamp blown, diode burnt out, faulty connection.

52 Once voltage difference reaches 0.7 V and the diode conducts, it acts almost as a short circuit and bypasses any additional current around the meter.

53 The ouput waveform would give the negative part of the wave.

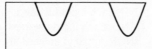

54 Using the labelling given on fig. 8.4, the diodes in fig. 8.9 are: D1 top left; D2 bottom left; D3 top right; D4 bottom right.

Chapter 9

55 The voltage varies between 0 V and (nearly) the peak voltage, as in fig. 8.8 and fig. 8.9, and so is not steady.

56 Lifting the handset opens the switch controlling the bell circuit, cutting off the bell.

57 The capacitor would be destroyed because it is an electrolytic type. The transistors would also probably be burnt out.

58 See fig. 9.8.

59 0.5 A is the maximum current the suppressor can carry without overheating. Larger currents may cause fire.

60 Because of its reactance (see page 79).

Chapter 10

61 See reference section B2.1, page 54.

62 Reverse the battery, reverse the meters.

63 200.

64 h_{FE} for BC108 may be anything between 110 and 800.

65 See the previous paragraph in the text.

66 V_{OUT} is positive. Current goes from V_{OUT} to virtual zero to V_{IN}.

Reference Section C

67 20% of 1000 is 200. The lowest possible value is therefore 800 Ω, which is less than 860 Ω

68 Using the lowest voltage gives the largest value of resistance, so protecting the diode under all conditions.

Chapter 11

69 No information is given about the output required.

70 The transistor **and** the load resistor together.

71 Zero.

72 Kirchhoff's voltage law (see Reference Section B1.12).

73 As the current increases the voltage across the transistor decreases. Voltage × current is maximum when the voltage across the transistor is equal to the voltage across the load resistor, i.e. 2.5 V in this case. The current at that voltage is half the maximum current, i.e. 5 mA. Power = 2.5 × 5 = 12.5 mW.

74 Collector current is zero so output voltage = supply voltage (no voltage difference across load resistor).

75 The diodes stop current going from one input to another.

76 Add 0.7 V voltage difference across the diode to 1.5 V.

77 Add an inverter to the output.

78 The bias resistor provides the base currrent when both inputs are high. When an input is low, the diode diverts that current.

79 To allow signals from the microphone to reach the base but prevent bias current passing through the microphone.

Chapter 12

80 If inputs are reversed, output will go **low** when signal input is greater than control input.

81 The inverting input is at the higher voltage, so the output is negative. The negative supply voltage is − 15 V.

82 (i) The voltmeter has a resistance of about 50 kΩ and acts as a voltage divider with the 33 kΩ resistor, giving 3 V at the junction; (ii) electrolytic capacitors have a 'leakage resistance' (about 100 kΩ in this case).

83 The op-amp is connected as an inverting amplifier.

Chapter 13

84 For portable equipment in constant use, or for back-up systems protecting against mains supply failure.

85 See chapter 5.

86 7.5 V.

87 Eight cells each giving 1.5 V (or six cells each giving 2 V, as in a car battery).

88 All the individual voltages in a series circuit are added together. Cells in a battery are in series.

89 Power is energy supplied **each second**. Any battery can supply high power for a short time or low power for a long time.

90 4 Ω: each cell has a resistance of 0.5 Ω

91 The five type AA cells each have 5 Ω resistance.

92 See fig. 6.11, page 49.

93 Period = 1/50 s = 0.02 s.

94 Period = 1/60 s = 0.0167 s.

95 Green and yellow.

96

97 Larger: the capacitor must provide current for twice as long in half-wave rectification.

Reference Section D

98 2.6 V.

99 They are in series, so the currents must be the same.

100 When a load is connected and current passes through it.

101 The signal goes to the inverting input, so the output is inverted.

102 Output starts at 0 V and ramps down towards the negative power-supply voltage.

Chapter 14

103 Thirty-two, sixty-four, one hundred and twenty-eight, two hundred and fifty-six.

104 It will detect anything crossing the beam, e.g. birds.

105 The front wheels and the back wheels both give pulses.

106 Divide the number of pulses by two.

107 Subtract the number of cars leaving the car park.

108 Zero is one of the four (or eight) numbers in the sequence.

109 Five pulses give 0101 on the counter. Q outputs from the first and third bistable must go to the AND gate to produce the reset pulse.

110 10 is a decimal number. The counter works in binary.

111 Binary 1001 is decimal 9. The counter must reset on the *next* pulse *after* 1001.

112 Refer to chapter 1.

.13 For safety. An automatic sequence might open the gates before the train has gone past.

.14 We need to detect 01 on the counter, but the AND gate needs logic 1 inputs. When Q on the second bistable is 0, the NOT Q output of the bistable is at logic 1.

.15 The red light signal goes through an AND gate. The second input of the gate comes from a pulse generator.

.16 The Q output of each bistable is connected to the AND gate.

.17 Best done by putting a microswitch on the gate. When the gate closes, the red signal changes to green.

.18 Must switch OFF when both bistables give logic 1.

.19 Safety interlocks, sensors to confirm that the required sequence is happening, control of time periods, etc.

.20 Start by finding out what the sequence is. You need a counter to step through the sequence and a pulse generator to produce the flashing signal.

.21 Both outputs go to logic 1.

.22 The input signals should be logic 0 instead of logic 1.

Chapter 15

.23 Poster, street name, newspaper boards, one-way street, Underground, roadworks markers, LV sign, menu, café name, car indicators, diversion arrow, white lines on road, etc.

.24 The information is stored as letter patterns. The carrier is paper, modulated with ink. The second carrier is light. The signal is demodulated in the eye.

.25 So that information can be transferred from one system to another.

Chapter 16

.26 Walking: ROM; learning: RAM; bus times: RAM.

Chapter 17

.27 See text.

.28 The switch is the input transducer and modulator. The lamp is the carrier producer and transmitter.

.29 The LDR is the receiver; the transistor switch is the demodulator; the indicator is the output transducer.

.30 Each station needs a power supply, a calling signal and a channel to transmit signals. Radio does not need lines or an exchange but needs a tuner to select the channel. Each radio needs a separate power supply and an amplifier because most of the signal energy is lost in broadcasting. Anyone can listen in to radio messages.

.31 Microphone and earpiece are on the same handset. With the earpiece to your ear the microphone is in the right position.

.32 Buying and installing equipment; maintenance costs; charges made for accessing some Prestel pages.

.33 There are only two wires.

Chapter 18

34 Ambulance, fire, police and taxi services, air-traffic control, CB radio, amateur radio, walkie-talkies, cordless telephones, cellular telephone, ship-to-shore radio, and many more.

35 Power supply.

36 Diode with a capacitor and load resistance.

37 Both stations need a transmitter and a receiver.

38 See fig. 18.3.

39 If stations were less than 60 miles apart you could be less than 30 miles from two stations and receive them both, jumbled together.

40 Would not go under bridges and into garages; the aerial would have to be heavy and strong or it would wave about dangerously; risk of damage; big drag on the car.

141 See table 18.1, page 168.

142 0.5 m.

143 Higher frequency bands can have more channels. Because the range is only 30 miles the same channels can be used in different areas.

144 Fire service uses VHF because distances are short; Navy uses low and medium frequencies for reliable long-distance communication; the frequencies used by the Army depend on the distances involved.

145 Capacitor reactance decreases at higher frequencies, so smaller capacitors can be used.

146 The higher the price, the harder it is to sell.

147 A complete picture but with half of it brighter than the rest. In 1/20th of a second the screen is scanned 2½ times (see fig. 18.13).

148 Banks, petrol stations, shopping precincts, prisons, etc.

149 The camera watches all the time so a thief is not aware of being seen; one person can watch several screens; fewer store detectives are needed.

150 Radio link to staff in the area being watched.

Chapter 19

151 The cash dispenser and all accounts are controlled by the bank's central computer.

152 Expensive; system would have to be easy to use and protected from damage; a good idea if there is a full-time librarian; etc.

153 Magnets destroy information stored on floppy discs and tapes.

154 Standard letters and notices, work sheets, students' projects, etc.

155 Read-only memory.

156 Word processors.

157 Advantages: reliability, no programming, reduced manufacturing and servicing costs; disadvantages: costly to modify design, extra development costs.

Chapter 20

158 Most computer systems work on 8 or 16 bit words. Each bit needs a wire in a parallel system, and there is also one wire acting as a 'common' (0 V) return wire for all eight (or sixteen) circuits.

159 Inside a computer the common return is usually separate from the buses.

160 In television, it is pixels (single bits) that are important. In computers it is the speed of dealing with single bits that matters.

161 Use a 3-input AND gate.

162 Eight, including the code 000.

163 By using the code 00.

164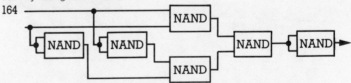

The same arrangement using NOR gates also gives EOR.

165 To stop signals from one input affecting the other input lines.

166 To collect the carry signal from either half-adder.

167 See chapter 15.

168 They do not operate fast enough.

Chapter 21

169 The transistor behaves as two diodes connected as: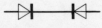

170 One will be labelled Y1, the other Y2.

SOLUTIONS TO EXERCISES

Reference Section A

1 NTC: 2000 Ω; PTC: 100 Ω
2 63°C
3 1000 Ω

Reference Section B

4 $12 \times 200 \times 5 = 12\,000$ J
5 $3 \times 0.3 \times 3600 = 3240$ J
6 2400 W; 0.9 W
7 3 V
8 $40 \times 40 = 1600$
9 40
10 Period = 200/8 = 25 μs
   frequency = 40 kHz
11 1/200 000 s (5 μs)

Reference Section C

12 200 Ω
13 2.5 mA
14 0.6 V
15 800 Ω
16 2.7 MΩ (2.67 MΩ)
17 4.7 kΩ and 15 kΩ in series gives
   19.7 kΩ
18 0.9 kΩ
19 95 Ω
20 0.34 kΩ (340 Ω)
21 1 W minimum
22 Load disconnected: 2 V
   Load connected: 1.62 V

23 1 kΩ
24 (i) 1N5406 (ii) 1N4007 or BY127
   (iii) the cheapest one
25 270 Ω
26 680 Ω
27 Primary = 1200 turns;
   secondary = 60 turns
28 12 000 turns
29 75 V
30 400
31 0.2 mA (200 μA)
32 30
33 $R_{IN} = 3.3$ kΩ, $R_F = 10$ kΩ
   (i.e. R_F is three times R_{IN})

Reference Section D

34 (i) 3 mA (ii) 20 μA (iii) 1.64 V
35 Collector current = 1 mA
   collector voltage = 6.8 V
36 52 μA
37 0 V (the transistor is saturated;
   voltage is 0.2 V in practice)
38 −5 V
39 −9 V
40 1.5 kΩ
41 2
42 7.5 V; 4.5 V
43 23.4 V
44 4 Ω

45 (i) 0.19 A (ii) 8 Ω
46 Peak = 16.8 V; peak-to-peak = 33.6 V
47 28 V [about 27 V because of voltage
   across the diode(s)]
48 80 V

Reference Section E

49 See question
50 See question
51 182; 31
52 See question
53 See question
54 1001101; 1100100

Reference Section F

55 200 kHz
56 42.9 m
57 300 m/s (30 000 cm/s)

Reference Section G

58 See question
59 4271
60 See question
61 24E
62 1010101111001101

INDEX

To find out a **fact** or to **check information** then use the reference numbers (e.g. C2.1). These sections are easy to find. Look at the side of the book where the pages appear to be shaded.

To find out more about an **idea** which you are not sure about, then use the page numbers (e.g. *71*). You should always read to the end of the section which contains the idea, even if this means reading the following pages too.

Index items in CAPITALS are chapter headings or reference section titles. You may need to read the following pages or sections as well, to find what you are looking for.

a.c.	*71, 119*	C2.1, D3.12
a.c. blocking	*79*	C4.1
a.c. voltage	*49, 123*	D3.12
accumulator	*204*	G2.4
active components	*82*	A2.1
actuators		A2.1
adder	*202*	
address	*151, 205*	
address bus	*206*	G2.1
aerial	*8, 169, 172*	F2.6
alternating current *see* a.c.		
ALU	*199, 200*	G2.1
ammeter	*215*	B1.2, B2.4
amp	*61*	B1.2
AMPLIFIERS	*39*	B4
current	*84*	C5.4
difference	*88, 113*	A1.4, C7.1, C7.2
inverting	*89, 112*	A1.4, C7.3, D1.3, D2.1
non-inverting	*113*	A1.4, D2.4, D2.5
operational *see* operational amplifier		
power	*42*	A1.4, B4.4, D1.4
summing *see* summer		
transistor	*109*	C5.4, D1.3, D1.4
VOLTAGE	*39*	B4
amplifying blocks	*8*	A1.4
amplitude	*49*	B5.2, B5.4
amplitude modulation	*169, 171*	F2.2, F2.3
analogue to digital	*147, 197*	G2.2
analogue meters	*213*	
analogue signals	*16, 146*	A1.2, B4.1, E2.3
analogue summer	*112*	A1.4, D2.2, D2.3
anode	*70*	A2.15, A2.16

'and' decision	*31*	
AND gate	*32, 34, 36, 141*	A1.4, B3.2
ASCII	*146, 149*	E2.5
assembler language		G1.3
astable *see* continuous pulse producer		
avalanche diode	*74*	
bandwidth	*171*	F2.4
base	*83*	C5.3, D1.1
base current	*84, 108*	C5.4, D1.6
batteries	*118*	B1.7, D3.1
baud rate	*198*	B5.2
BC108	*107*	C5.2, C5.6
BCD	*140, 148*	E1.5, E2.5, D1.6
bias resistor		
biassing	*83, 107, 110*	D1.1, D1.2, D1.3, D1.6
binary arithmetic	*193*	
binary counting	*138, 193*	E1.1–4, E2.5, G1.5
bipolar transistor	*82*	C5.2, C5.5
bistable	*10, 137, 139, 142, 204*	A1.4, B2.5, E1.4, E3.1
bit	*139, 148*	E1.1
Boolean algebra	*32*	B3.9
bottoming *see* saturation		
bounce (switches)	*46*	A2.4
bridge rectifier	*72, 122*	C2.3
broadcast systems	*160*	F1.3
BS1852		C1.8
BS3939		B2
buffer	*113*	G2.5
building blocks	*4, 8*	A1.4, A1.5
buses	*196, 206*	G2.5
byte *see* word		
cables (safety)	*121*	D3.8
calculator	*193*	
capacitance	*176*	B2.6, C3.3
CAPACITORS	*76*	C3
electrolytic	*76*	
parallel		C3.5
series		C3.5
timing	*44, 46, 77, 115*	B5.3, C3.1, C3.4
tuning	*78*	C3.1
types		C3.2
uses	*76, 122*	C3.1, D2.6
values		C3.4
carriers	*146*	E2.2, F2.2
cascading amplifiers	*112*	B4.2
cascading counters	*13, 140*	E1.4
casing (safety)	*121*	D3.11, D3.14
catalogue	*151*	

cathode	*70*	A2.15, A2.16
cathode ray tube	*177*	A2.17
CCTV	*178*	F2.16
cells	*118*	
central processing unit	*199*	
channel	*170*	F1.1, F1.2, D3.10
circuit breakers		B2.1–5
circuit symbols		
clock pulses	*140, 208*	G2.1
clocked bistable	*204*	E3.1
CMOS logic		C6.1, C6.3
codes	*145, 147*	E2.4, E2.5
coil *see* inductor		
coincidence gate		B3.9
collector	*83*	C5.3, D1.1, D1.7
collector characteristic	*111*	D1.7
collector current	*84, 108*	C5.4, D1.6
colours code	*64*	C1.7
common (line)	*88, 206*	B1.11
common emitter	*83*	D1.1
COMMUNICATIONS SYSTEMS	*159*	F1
comparator	*10, 114*	A1.4, C7.2
components	*61*	
COMPUTER ARCHITECTURE	*196*	G2.1
COMPUTER SYSTEMS	*189*	G2
computation	*192*	G1.1
control	*194*	G1.1
language	*193, 208*	E2.5, G1.3
memory	*199, 204*	G2.4
program	*189, 207*	
uses	*189–195*	G1.1
COMPUTING		G1
conductor	*61*	B1.3
control inputs	*5, 8, 107*	A1.1
control systems	*141, 194*	G1.1
continuity tester	*216*	
continuous pulse producer (CPP)	*46*	A1.4, B5.3, B1.7, C3.3
coulomb		
counter	*9, 137, 140*	A1.4, E1.4, E3.1
COUNTING	*137*	E1
CPU	*199*	G2.3
crystal set	*72, 174*	
CURRENT	*61, 215*	B1, B2.6
amplifier	*84*	C5.4
at junctions	*67*	B1.10
conventional		B1.2, B1.9
definition	*61*	B1.2
in circuits	*42, 63*	B1.7, B1.9
measurement	*215*	
current gain	*84*	C5.4
current limiter		C1.1, C1.15
cycle	*71*	B5.1

bistable 204 B2.5, E3.1
data 151, 189 G2.3
data bus 206 G2.1
data latch 204 E3.1
data file 191
database 151, 190
database field 151
d.c. 71, 122 C2.1–3
d.c. blocking 76 C3.1
debounced switch 46 A2.4
decimal numbers 138, 193 E1.2, E1.3, E1.5

DECISION MAKING 31
dedicated computer 193
demodulator 8, 69, 72, 146, 160, 174 A1.4, C2.1, E2.1, F2.14
difference amplifier 88, 113 A1.4, C7.1, C7.2
differentiator 46
digital meters 117, 213, 216
digital signals 16, 32, 146, 149, 197 A1.2, B3.1, E2.4
d.i.l. packages 86 C6.1, C6.5
DIODES 69 C2
  avalanche 74
  characteristics 73 C2.4
  choosing 73 C2.5
  light emitting 69, 73 A2.3, A2.15, A2.16, C2.6
  uses 69 C2.1
  zener 74 C2.7
direct current see d.c.
disc memory 153 E3.3
display 9, 179 A2.17
drain 83
driver 42, 195 A1.4
duplex system F1.1
DVM 117, 216

E12 resistor series C1.9
earth B1.11, D3.11
earthing D3.11
earth leakage circuit breaker D3.10
electric shock 62 D3.6, D3.7
electrolyte 62
electrolytic capacitor 76 C3.2
electromagnetic radiation 168, 173 F2.8
electromotive force (e.m.f.) B1.7
electrons 42, 61 B1.1
emitter 83 C5.3, D1.1
emitter follower see buffer
energy 5, 63 B1.7, B1.8, B2.6
energy supply 5 A1.1, B1.7
EPROM 152 E3.2
evaluation 213
exclusive OR (EOR) 33, 201 A1.4, B3.7

falling edge see negative-going edge
farad 76 C3.3

FAULT FINDING 14, 213 A1.6
feedback 47, 49, 88, 114, 195 A1.1, C7.1, C7.3
ferrite 78, 174 C4.3
FIBRES 159, 162 F1.4
field 191
field-effect transistor (FET) 82 C5.2
file 190
filter 46, 174 A1.4, C3.1, F2.13
flip flop see bistable
flyback F2.16
frame F2.16
frequency 48, 49, 173 B2.6, B5.1, F2.8
frequency bands 168
frequency modulation 169, 171 F2.2, F2.4
FSD 15, 213
full adder 202
full-wave rectification 72, 122 C2.3
fuses D3.5, D3.9
gain 39, 88 B4.2, C5.4, C7.3
gain formula, op-amp 89 C7.3, D2.1
gates see logic gates
graphical methods see load lines
ground B1.11
heatsink 73 B4.4, D1.4
half-adder 202
half-wave rectification 71, 122 C2.2
Hall probe 40 A2.2
henry 78 C4.2
hertz 48 B5.1
hexadecimal 193 A2.16, G1.4, G1.5
h_{FE} 84, 107 C5.4, D1.6

IC see integrated circuit
impedance 80
indicator 9
inductance 78 C4.2
INDUCTORS 78 C4
  uses 78 C4.1
INFORMATION 144 E2
  retrieval 190
  processing 192 E2.1
  STORAGE 150, 190 E3
  systems 146 E2.1
  telephone 165 F1.4
input/output port 197 G2.1, G2.2
input resistance A1.5, C7.1
input resistor D1.6
inputs to systems 4, 39 A1.1
INPUT TRANSDUCERS 9 A2, B2.3
  characteristics A2.8
instruction 151
insulator 62 B1.5
INTEGRATED CIRCUITS 85 C6

connection C6.5
types C6.1, C6.4
integrator 115 A1.4, D2.6
interface, computer 195, 197 G2.2
interfacing device 46 A1.4, A1.5
intermediate frequency 175 F2.12
internal resistance 119, 122 A1.5, D3.2, D3.3
interpreter 151 G1.3
inverting amplifier 89, 112 A1.4, C7.3, D1.3, D2.1
inverting input 87 C7.1
inversion, analogue 40 B4.3, D2.1
inverter, digital 36, 41, 107 B3.4, D1.2
ionosphere 171
ions B1.1
isolating transformer see power supply

JK-bistable B2.5, E3.1
joule B1.7, B1.8

keyboard A2.2, A2.4
Kirchhoff's laws 67 B1.10, B1.12

languages, computer 193, 207 E2.5, G1.3
laser 162
latch 10, 137 A1.4, A2.13, E3.1
least significant bit (LSB) 139 E1.1, E1.2
letter symbols B2.6
light dependent resistor (LDR) 66 A2.2, A2.6, A2.8
light emitting diode (LED) 69, 73 A2.3, A2.15, A2.16, C2.1, C2.6
light communication 161 F1.4
linear IC C6.1
load 18, 67, 107 C1.1, C1.14
load line, resistor 66
load line, transistor 111 D1.8
local oscillator see superheterodyne
LOGIC GATES 33 B3
  block functions 33 A1.4, B3.2–7
  combining 36 B3.8
  in use 12, 200
  symbols B2.5
LOGIC, SEQUENTIAL 137
logic signals see digital signals
logic systems 33, 200
loudspeaker 8, 80 A2.3, A2.11, C4.1
low-voltage power supply D3.15

machine code 193, 199 G1.3
magneto-dependent resistor (MDR) A2.2, C1.3
magnetic recording 153 E3.3, G2.4
mainframe computer G1.2
mains electricity 71, 119 D3.4, D3.12

234 INDEX

mains safety 121 D3.7, D3.14
mains 13A plug D3.5
matching device 46 A1.4, A1.5
mark 47, 137 B5.2
mark-space ratio 48 B5.2
mark-time 47 B5.2
maximum power transfer A1.5
MEASUREMENTS 213
mechanical outputs A2.9
MEMORY 31, 150 E3
 computer 152, 199, 204 G2.4
 electronic 152 E3.2
 in decisions 31, 137, 150
 peripheral 153 E3.3
 G1.2
microcomputer G1.2
microfarad 76 C3.3
microphone A2.2, A2.5, C4.1
microprocessor 189, 194, 199, 200 G1.2
microwave radio 166
milliammeter 63
Mil-spec B2.5
minicomputer G1.2
mixer see summer
modem 165 F1.4, G2.5
modulation 146, 169
modulator 146, 160 A1.4, E2.1, F2.2
monostable see triggered pulse producer
most significant bit (MSB) 139 E1.2
motor A2.3, A2.9, A2.10, C4.1
multimeter 213
multiplex systems F1.1
multiplier B2.6
multivibrators 44 A1.4
NAND gate 32, 35 A1.4, B3.5
NAND NAND systems 35 B3.8
negative feedback see feedback
negative-going edge 44, 137
nominal value C1.9
non-inverting amplifier 113 A1.4, D2.4, D2.5
non-inverting input 87 C7.1
non-volatile memory 152 E3.3, G2.4
NOR gate 33, 36 A1.4, B3.6
'not' decision 31
NOT gate 32, 36 A1.4, B3.4
n-p-n transistor 82 C5.2
NTC thermistor A2.7
offset null 116
ohm 64 C1.4
ohm-meter 69, 215 B2.4
Ohm's law 64, 71 C1.5
operation see process
OPERATIONAL AMPLIFIERS 85, 86, 112 C7

characteristics 87 C7.1
CIRCUITS 112 D2
 gain formula 89 C7.3
 uses 40, 112 C7.2
optical fibres 162 F1.4
opto-isolator 161 G2.5
'or' decision 31
OR gate 32, 34, 36 A1.4, B3.3
oscillator 9, 176 A1.4
oscilloscope 48, 49, 213, 217 B2.4, B5.1
output from systems 4 A1.1
output port 197 G2.1, G2.2
OUTPUT TRANSDUCERS 9 A2, B2.3
parallel circuits 67 B1.10, C1.11, C1.12, C3.5, D3.2
parallel signals 139, 198 G2.1, G2.5
parity 149
passive components 82 A2.1
peak inverse voltage (PIV) 73 C2.4
peak voltage 50, 123 D3.12
peak-to-peak voltage 50 D3.12
period 48 B5.1
peripherals 197 G2.2
peripheral memory 153 E3.3
person-to-person 160, 163 F1.2
phase 50
photodiode A2.2
phototransistor A2.2
pixels 177 F2.16
plug D3.5
p-n-p transistor 82 C5.2
polarised capacitor see electrolytic capacitor
positive-going edge 44, 137
potential difference see voltage difference
potential divider see voltage divider
potentiometer see resistor, variable
power 43 B1.8, B2.6
power amplifier 42 A1.4, B4.4
power equation 43 B1.8
power input 5 A1.1, B1.7
power rating 109 C1.13
POWER SUPPLY 5, 39, 118 D3
 components D3.15
 connections 17, 88
 protection D3.14
preferred values C1.9
prefixes B2.6
Prestel 165 F1.4
primary 120 C4.3
processor 4 A1.1
processing blocks A1.1, A1.3, A1.4
program 3, 31, 151
program (computer) 189, 207
program counter 208
PROM E3.2
protection diodes 70, 81 C2.1, C4.4
PTC thermistor A2.7

pulses 44 B5.2
pulse chains 47 B5.3
pulse code modulation 169 F2.2, F2.5
PULSE GENERATORS 44 A1.4, B5.3
 in use 9, 140
 transistor 111 C5.1
 op-amp C7.2
RADIO 168 F2
 construction 176
 developments 177
 receiver 8, 169, 174 F2.11, F2.12
 simple system 8
 superheterodyne 175 F2.12
 tuner A1.4, F2.13
 TRF 174 F2.11
 uses 168 F2.10
radio waves 168, 171 F2.6, F2.7
RAM 150, 152, 204 E3.2
ramp generator 115 A1.4, D2.6
ramp rate 115 D2.6
raster 116, 177 F2.16
RC circuits 46, 78, 116 B5.3, C3.1
reactance 77, 79 C3.4
read/write line 206 G2.1
receiver 159, 169
record 190
recording 153 E3.3, G2.4
rectification 71, 122 C2.1–3
reed switch A2.4
reference voltage 74
register 151, 199, 203 E3.1, G2.1, G2.4
regulator 74, 123 D3.13
relay 80 A2.3, A2.4, A2.12–14, B2.2, C4.1, C4.4
reset 45, 47, 140, 143 E3.1
residual-current circuit breaker D3.10
resistance 62, 215 B1.6, B2.6, C1.4
resistance colours code 64 C1.7
resistance equation 64 C1.5
resistance line 65
resistance measurement 215
RESISTORS 61 C1
 colours code 64 C1.7
 load line 66
 non-linear C1.3
 numbers code C1.8
 parallel 67 C1.11, C1.12
 preferred values C1.9
 power ratings C1.13
 range 64 C1.6
 series 64 C1.10, C1.12
 tolerance C1.9
 types C1.2, C1.3
 uses C1.1, C1.17
 variable C1.2

resonance 78, 172 F2.9, F2.13
reversing switch A2.14
rheostat C1.2
rising edge *see* positive-going edge
r.m.s. voltage 50, 123 D3.12
ROM 150, 152 E3.2
RS-bistable 143, 204 B2.5, E3.1

safety, mains 121 D3.7, D3.14
saturation, op-amp 42, 114 C7.1
saturation, transistor 85, 108 D1.2, D1.3
Schmitt trigger A1.4
screen displays 179 A2.17
secondary 120 C4.3
self-induction 81
semiconductor 62, 70 B1.4
sensitivity 214
sensors 9 A2.1, A2.2, B2.3

SEQUENTIAL
LOGIC 137
serial access 152
serial signal 177, 197 G2.5
series circuits 64, 118 B1.12, C1.10, C1.12, C3.5, D3.1
set 143 E3.1
seven-segment
display 73 A2.16
shunts 215
sidebands 171 F2.3
SIGNAL
GENERATORS 49, 111 A1.4, B5
sine-wave 49 B5.4
square wave 47 B5.3
test equipment 213
signal sensitive
switch A1.4, D1.2
signal input 5 A1.1
signal line 16-19 A1.2
silicon 62, 70, 85 A2.7, B1.4

sine (sinusoidal)
wave 49, 50 B5.4, D3.12
smoothing 76, 122 C3.1
solenoid A2.3, A2.9, C4.1
source (FET) 83
source resistance 119, 122 A1.5, D3.2, D3.3
space 47, 137 B5.2
space-time 47 B5.2
specification 107, 220
spike generator 45
square waves 47 B5.2
stabilisers *see* voltage regulators
steering diodes 70 C2.1
stepper motor A2.10
storage *see* information storage
sub-system 4, 12
summer 112 A1.4, C7.2, D2.2, D2.3
superheterodyne 175 F2.1, F2.12
suppressor 80 C3.1, C4.1
switch A2.2, A2.4, B2.2
switch debouncing 46 A2.4
switching blocks A1.4
SYMBOLS B2
batteries 118 B2.1

bistables B2.5
capacitors 76 B2.1
diodes 70 B2.1, B2.3
inductors 79 B2.1, B2.3
logic 33 B2.5
relays B2.2
switches A2.4, B2.2
test instruments B2.4
transducers B2.3
transistor 83 B2.1, C5.3
using letters B2.6
sync 178, 218 F2.16
SYSTEMS 1 A1
definition 2
EXAMPLES 8
MAKING WORK 14
structure 4 A1.1
system X 163

T-bistable 139 B2.5, E1.4, E3.1
telecommunication 160
telephone
equipment 77, 164 F1.4
telephone system 162, 165 F1.4
teletext 166 F2.15
TELEVISION 177 F2
CCTV 178 F2.16
raster 116, 177 F2.16
sync signal 178 F2.16
uses 178 F2.15
test instruments 213 B2.4
testing circuits 14-19 A1.6
thermistor 66 A2.2, A2.7
thermocouple A2.2
threshold voltage 45
time B2.6
time-base 218
time constant 116 D2.6
time delay 46 B5.3
timer 9, 77,
see also pulse
generators 140
timing capacitors 46, 77, 115 B5.3, C3.1, C3.4
tolerance C1.9
TRANSDUCERS 9 A2, B2.3
active/passive A2.1
characteristics A2.8
transfer function 4, 109 D1.5
transformers 79, 120 C4.1, C4.3
TRANSISTOR 82 C5
biassing 83, 107, 110 D1.2, D1.3, D1.6
characteristics 111 C5.5, D1.5
connections 83 C5.6
data 107
saturation 85, 107 D1.2, D1.3
signal generator 111
symbols 83 B2.1, C5.3
types C5.2
uses 107 C5.1
TRANSISTOR
CIRCUITS 107 D1
amplifier 109 C5.1, D1.3, D1.4
calculations 108 D1.6
load line 111
logic 109 C5.1
switch 107 D1.2

transmitter 159, 168 F1.2, F1.3
TRF 174 F2.11
trigger 44, 143, 219
triggered bistable 139 E3.1
triggered pulse
producer 44-46 A1.4, B5.3
tristate buffer 206 G2.5
truth tables 33 B3.2-7, C6.1, C6.2
TTL C6.1, C6.2
tuner 8, 169 F2.9, F2.13
tuning capacitor 78, 174 C3.1, C3.4, F2.13
two-way radio 170 F1.1, F1.2
two-way system 160

uniselectors 141 A2.12

virtual earth 89
VLSI 86
volatile memory 152 E3.2, G2.4
volt B1.7
VOLTAGE B1
amplifiers *see* amplifiers
comparator 10, 114 A1.4, C7.2
difference 14, 43, 63, 214 B1.7, B1.11, B1.12
dividers 64, 67 C1.1, C1.2, C1.14
dropper C1.1, C1.16
measurement 14, 214
regulator 74, 123 D3.13
signals 14, 15 A1.5, B3.1
sources 118 D3.1, D3.2
voltage sensitive
switch A1.4
voltmeter 14, 15, 214 B1.7, B2.4
voltmeter, digital 117

watt 43 B1.8
waves, reflection F2.7
waveshape 49, 220 B5.4
wavespeed
equation 173 F2.8
wavelength 173 F2.8
WIRES 159, 166
word 148, 205
word processor 192 E2.1

zener diode 74 C2.1, C2.7
zero line *see* common line

1-bit processor 200
7-segment display A2.16
8-bit processing 199
13 A plug D3.5
74 series ICs C6.2
741 40, 86 C6.4